The Ultimate Guide to SAT Grammar

And

Eight Multiple Choice SAT Writing Tests

Erica L. Meltzer

ISBN-13: 978-1480114739
ISBN-10: 1480114731

CONTENTS

INTRODUCTION

My first encounter with the SAT Writing section came in early 2006, when I answered an online advertisement for practice-SAT test writers. The exam had recently been overhauled to include the Writing section, and suddenly test-prep companies needed lots of new material fast. The first questions I wrote, I regret to say, were not particularly faithful to the actual test. I simply leafed through a College Board guide, generally noted the sorts of questions that appeared, and wrote approximations. No one complained, so I assumed I was doing fine.

As I began spending more time tutoring SAT Writing, however, I began to investigate the section more deeply. Most of my students had little to no familiarity with grammatical terminology, so rather than simply reviewing concepts and offering up a couple of tricks, I had to teach them virtually all of the fundamentals of grammar. And I had to do it fast; there simply wasn't time to teach them four years worth of grammar and then apply it all to the test. Moreover, even if students did have some knowledge of grammar, they simply couldn't figure out what the questions were asking. It seemed that anything could be wrong with those sentences.

So I went back to the College Board book and labeled the kind of error contained in every single multiple-choice grammar question. When I was done, I made a list of all the categories of questions, ranking them in order of frequency. And I began to notice things. I noticed that punctuation problems, for example, occurred only in certain places, as did dangling modifiers and certain kinds of parallelism problems.

More importantly, I noticed that certain key words or phrases included in a sentence often pointed to particular errors.

For example:

-An underlined pronoun often pointed to a pronoun error.

-An underlined verb in the present tense frequently pointed to a subject-verb agreement error.

-The presence of a comparison such as *more than/less than* at the end of the Error-Identification section almost always pointed to a faulty comparison.

-The mention of a profession – physicist, veterinarian, or, in one memorable College Board question, entomologist (someone who studies insects) – virtually always indicated a noun agreement question.

And I had a realization: the questions themselves revealed what they were testing.

Furthermore, I noticed that specific kinds of questions always showed up at specific points in the test. For example:

-Faulty comparisons almost always showed up in the last three Error-Identification questions, as did certain kinds of tricky subject-verb agreement questions.

-The final Fixing Sentences question (#11 in the first Writing section, #14 in the second) very frequently dealt with parallel structure.

And so on.

I had cracked the test.

When I started teaching my students to actually anticipate the errors they would find on the test, their scores skyrocketed. The first student I worked with this way raised her SAT Writing score a whopping 180 points to a 750; the next one raised his by 190 points to a 700. Both were admitted to top schools. Although their Writing scores were hardly the deciding factors – both were straight-A students – it is unlikely that either of their applications would have gotten nearly as close a look with Writing scores in the 500s.

When I was working with both of these students, however, I had a finite number of College Board tests to tutor from. Afraid that I would run out of material, I went to the bookstore and looked through the standard commercially-produced test-prep books for additional exercises. When I looked closely at the practice questions they provided, I realized that not only did they frequently omit a number of major kinds of errors that regularly occurred on the exam, but they also covered rules that were never even tested! Furthermore, the level of the language contained in the sentences was often significantly easier than that found on the actual test. And the correct answer choices often seemed thoroughly arbitrary, a situation that is not true of the SAT. Even if there are "trick" answers, the right answer is the right answer because it conforms to a particular grammatical rule (not, incidentally, invented by the College Board). So I started writing my own questions. What started as ten or fifteen sentences jotted down on a piece of scrap paper gradually multiplied and multiplied and eventually became this book.

This guide is designed to systematically cover every major concept and type of question that can be reasonably expected to occur on the multiple-choice component of the SAT Writing section. Through a series of cumulative exercises, it also aims to continually reinforce concepts so that material covered early on will not be forgotten. While it contains information that applies to situations well beyond the SAT, its primary focus is that test, and my aim throughout is to make clear the application of particular grammatical rules to the precise ways in which the College Board handles them. I have therefore deliberately simplified explanations of some grammatical principles in order to make certain concepts easier to grasp, and I have also avoided including information that does not directly relate to the exam. The SAT will usually include a few unpredictable questions, but in general, 95% or so of the material tested can be safely anticipated. The goal of this book is to teach you how to anticipate it.

Erica Meltzer
New York City
July 2011

Multiple-Choice Grammar: Overview

The SAT contains 49 multiple-choice grammar and style questions divided between two Writing sections. Those two sections are always arranged as follows:

First Section: 35 questions

    -11 Fixing Sentences
    -18 Error-Identification
    -6 Fixing Paragraphs

Second Section: 14 questions

    -14 Fixing Sentences
    -Always Section 10

The three kinds of multiple-choice Writing questions are as follows:

1)   Fixing Sentences: 25 questions

    Test-takers are presented with a sentence, a portion of which is underlined, and are asked to choose the best version.

2)   Error-Identification: 18 questions

    Test-takers are presented with a sentence that has four underlined words or phrases, along with a "No error" option (always choice E), and must identify which part, if any, contains an error.

3)   Fixing Paragraphs: 6 questions

    Test-takers are presented with a short paragraph and are asked questions covering organization, grammar, and logical arrangement of information. Since it is necessary to identify the main idea of the paragraph and decide which evidence best supports it, this section combines both reading and writing skills.

In principle, Error-Identification and Fixing Sentences questions are intended to run from least to most difficult. So, for example, in the first Writing section, #11 is the most difficult Fixing Sentences question, but #12, the first Error-Identification question, starts over at the easiest level. Fixing Paragraphs questions are distributed in no particular order of difficulty.

In addition, a given letter is frequently used as the correct answer three times consecutively, so test-takers' attempts to outsmart the test by avoiding the letter they chose for the previous question are almost always unsuccessful.

Because the multiple-choice Writing section contains fewer questions than either Math or Critical Reading, students often wonder what all the fuss is about. After all, why memorize dozens of error-identification rules when there are only 18 questions on the entire test? The answer is that because there are fewer questions, each one counts a lot more. Consider this: the difference between a 700 and an 800 on the multiple-choice is about four questions. In contrast, it's possible to miss up to three Critical Reading questions on some tests and still get an 800. But if you want a 750+ – or even a 700 – on Writing, you basically have to get everything right.

A Note About Content

SAT Writing questions cover standard concepts of grammar and usage that high school juniors can reasonably be expected to have encountered. There is a heavy emphasis on subject-verb and pronoun agreement issues, as well as on parallel structure. Test-takers are expected to be able to differentiate between sentences and fragments and to select the version of a sentence that is clearest and most logical – all skills that are necessary for good analytical (not creative!) writing.

One of the most important features of SAT grammar questions, however, is the utter predictability of both their content and their structure. Specific concepts are *always* tested in specific ways, with some concepts appearing only in Fixing Sentences and others only in Error-Identification. Furthermore, although the sentences may seem random, their structures as well as the underlined words and phrases they contain frequently indicate the rules they are testing. That is, if you know what to look for.

Let me reiterate: the sentences that you will encounter on the SAT are not random assortments of confusing words. They are deliberate constructions, carefully arranged to test specific skills. All of things you can get away with when you write papers – the unnecessary commas, the semicolons that you're not 100% certain about, the arbitrary use of *which* and *that* – are fair game on the SAT. In fact, the test specifically targets those concepts, and if you don't know a rule, there's absolutely no way to fudge it and hope the Scantron scoring your test just doesn't notice.

So if you look at a sentence and think, "That sounds funny," you're probably thinking exactly what the College Board wants you to think. The sentence has been designed to sound that way precisely because most other high school students will think so as well. Keep in mind that the College Board tests all of its questions before it includes them on actual exams. That's what the experimental section is for.

Now, your ear could be right – and if you've read non-stop for the last ten years and have been exposed to a wide variety of English prose, it very well might be – but for most test-takers, it could just as well be wrong. Assuming that most people answer the questions by ear, the College Board has arranged the exam so that the average high school junior or senior will get most of the easy questions right, some of the medium questions right, and most of the hard questions wrong. So if you want a really high score, you're better off knowing the actual rules being tested. Cold.

When I first started picking apart exams and grouping their questions by category, I did not quite understand why the College Board chose to focus so heavily on certain types of errors (subject-verb agreement, pronoun agreement, parallel structure) and virtually ignore others. Contrary to what most guides say, "who vs. whom" is not actually tested on the SAT, even though *who*, and very occasionally *whom*, are underlined on various questions. Then, as a tutor, I read the writing of high school students – lots of them. And I started to notice that most of their writing was full of the exact errors tested on the SAT. Here it seems that the College Board does actually know what it's doing.

In my experience, most high school students will often pick wordier and more awkward constructions ("Being as it rained, I decided to stay home.") rather than simple and clear ones ("Because it rained, I decided to stay home.") if given the opportunity to do so because they mistakenly believe that the wordier ones sound more sophisticated. (Hint: they don't). The SAT favors clarity and simplicity, good goals for most high school students to aim for in their analytical writing.

From what I have observed, students who devote a reasonable amount of time to studying SAT grammar will often begin to notice and spontaneously correct errors both in their own and in other people's writing. I have had students email me, genuinely thrilled to have spotted a dangling modifier in a magazine or on a website.

I often tell my students that if they learn the rules and then decide to ignore them, it's their right; but that if they are going to break the rules, they should do so deliberately and in order to create a particular stylistic effect, not because they don't know how to write correctly. It's the difference between being in control of your writing – being able to express your thoughts clearly and coherently – and being at its mercy. And it's a big difference.

Parts of Speech

There are eight parts of speech in the English language, seven of which are tested on the SAT. If you are not comfortable identifying them, it is suggested that you begin by reviewing this section. Although portions of these definitions are repeated throughout the guide, familiarizing yourself with these terms before you begin will help you move through the explanations and exercises more easily. Even if you are already comfortable identifying parts of speech, it is strongly suggested that you complete the exercise beginning on page 8.

The seven major parts of speech tested on the SAT are as follows:

1. <u>Verb</u>

Verbs indicate **actions** or **states of being**.

Examples: To be
To have
To seem
To go
To speak
To believe

The "to" form of a verb is known as the **infinitive**. All of the verbs listed above are infinitives. If you are uncertain whether a word can be used as a verb, try placing *to* in front of it to form an infinitive.

Verbs are not always used as infinitives, however. In order to indicate who is performing an action, we must **conjugate** the verb and provide its **subject**.

To be and *to have* are the most frequently tested verbs on the SAT. Because they are **irregular**, their conjugated forms are different from their infinitives; you must therefore make sure that you are comfortable distinguishing between their singular and plural forms.

Conjugation of the verb *to be:*

<u>Singular</u>	<u>Plural</u>
I am	We are
You are	You (pl.) are
He, She, It, One is	They are

Conjugation of the verb *to have:*

<u>Singular</u>	<u>Plural</u>
I have	We have
You have	You (pl.) have
He, She, It, One has	They have

The **number** of a verb tells us whether it is singular or plural.

I, you, he, she, it, one speaks = Singular

We, you, they speak = Plural

The **tense** of a verb tells us when an action occurred.

She speaks = Present	She would speak = Conditional 假定
She has spoken = Present Perfect	She would have spoken = Past Conditional
She spoke = Simple Past	She will speak = Future
She had spoken = Past Perfect	She will have spoken = Future Perfect

2. Noun

Nouns indicate people, places, objects, and ideas, and can always be preceded by *a(n)* or *the*.
Proper nouns indicate specific people and places.

> **Examples:** house, bicycle, supervisor, notion, Mark Twain, Chicago
>
> The **girl** rode her **bicycle** down the **street** to her **house**.
>
> The **politician** walked out of the **press conference** in **Washington** with his **head** in his **hands**.

3. Pronoun

Pronouns replace nouns.

> **Examples:** she, you, one, we, him, it(s), their, this, that, which, both, some, few, many, (n)either
>
> Samantha loves basketball. **She** plays **it** every day after school.
>
> Marco walks to school with Sherri and Ann. **He** meets **them** at the corner.

Personal Pronouns are often referred to in the following manner:

1st Person Singular = I	1st Person Plural = We
2nd Person Singular = You	2nd Person Plural = You
3rd Person Singular = He, She, It, One	3rd Person Plural = They

4. Preposition

Prepositions indicate where someone/something is, or when something happened.

> **Example:** The dog ran **under** the fence and jumped **into** the neighboring yard
> **in** only a matter **of** seconds.

Common prepositions include:

Of	To	Within/out	Over	Beside	Next to	Against
From	At	Above	Above	About	Toward(s)	Upon
In	For	Under	Along	Among	Before	Around
On	By	Beneath	Beyond	Near	After	Outside
Off	With	Below	Behind	Across	During	Opposite

5. <u>Adjective</u>

Adjectives modify nouns and pronouns.

> **Examples:** large, pretty, interesting, solid, wide, exceptional, smart, dull, caring, simple

> The class was so **boring** that I thought I would fall asleep.

> The **stunning** view left him at a loss for words.

> It was so **exciting** I could hardly contain myself.

6. <u>Adverb</u>

Adverbs modify verbs, adjectives, and other adverbs. They frequently end in –ly

> **Examples:** rapidly, calmly, serenely, shockingly, mildly, boldly, sharply, well, fast, very

> She smiled **warmly** at him when he entered the room.

> He received an **exceedingly** good grade on the test.

7. <u>Conjunction</u>

Conjunctions indicate relationships between words, phrases, and clauses.

> **Examples:** and, but, however, therefore, so, although, yet, when

> Alice went to the dentist, **but** first she went to the candy store.

> **Although** it has been raining all week, it should be sunny tomorrow.

Preliminary Exercise: Identifying Parts of Speech

For the following sentences, identify the part of speech contained in each underlined word or phrase. (Answers p. 146)

1. A large stash of books that once belonged to Thomas Jefferson was recently
     A   B   C   D   E

   discovered.

2. Although the center of Los Angeles has long been famous for its traffic jams,
     A   B   C

   the city's center is becoming increasingly accessible to pedestrians.
                                    D   E

3. The presence of the Olympic stadium has transformed the formerly run-down
       A   B   C

   area of the city.
       D   E

4. The author's first novel has received generally favorable reviews, but it has thus
                                 A   B C

   far failed to become an overwhelming success.
             D   E

5. The increasing emphasis on test scores has some education experts concerned
      A   B   C

   that young children's ability to learn through play is being compromised.
                      D   E

6. The discovery that both Lewis Carroll and Chopin had epilepsy is threatening to
      A   B   C

   redefine the concept of genius.
            D   E

7. Drum languages, once common throughout Africa as a means of sending
                    A   B

   messages, began to disappear almost as soon as they were documented.
          C   D   E

8. <u>British</u> scientist J.D. Bernal <u>believed</u> that people would <u>eventually</u> be replaced
   A   B   C

<u>by</u> creatures that <u>were</u> half-human and half-machine.
D   E

9. New research <u>shows</u> that <u>those</u> <u>who</u> live on islands are far more likely to
                   A   B   C

suffer <u>from</u> obesity than those who live in other <u>environments</u>.
       D   E

10. The <u>book</u> *Cane*, written <u>by</u> poet and author Jean Toomer, <u>contains</u> a mix <u>of</u>
     A   B   C   D

fiction, poetry, and <u>drama</u>.
                 E

11. Protests <u>against</u> the country's government <u>have</u> been growing in
         A   B

<u>recent</u> days, and observers <u>fear</u> that they may <u>explode</u> into utter chaos.
C   D   E

12. Painted by Paul Cézanne, *The Card Players* <u>depicts</u> three men seated <u>around</u>
                                             A   B

a table, <u>with</u> a fourth gazing <u>watchfully</u> <u>in</u> the background.
         C   D   E

13. <u>It</u> is arguable whether Mark Augustus Landis, responsible <u>for</u> perpetrating
   A   B

one <u>of</u> the <u>largest</u> art-forgery sprees ever, ever actually <u>broke</u> the law.
    C   D   E

14. <u>Activities</u> such as bird-watching <u>evolved</u> from people's desire to observe the
    A   B

<u>natural</u> world without <u>actively</u> participating in <u>it</u>.
C   D   E

15. <u>Australian</u> geography is <u>remarkably</u> varied; although Australia <u>is</u> the world's
    A   B   C

<u>smallest</u> continent, <u>it</u> is the sixth largest country.
   D   E

Error-Identification: Introduction

Error-Identification questions fall into 16 major categories, listed below in approximate descending order of frequency. Please note that errors involving verbs and pronouns appear far more often than any other kind of error and comprise approximately one-third of the multiple choice grammar questions.

Verbs:

    1. Subject-Verb Agreement
    2. Verb Tense/Form

Pronouns:

    3. Pronoun-Antecedent
    4. Pronoun Case

Additional Errors:

    5. Adjectives vs. Adverbs
    6. Parallel Structure: Lists
    7. Prepositions/Idioms
    8. Faulty Comparisons
    9. Word Pairs
    10. Noun Agreement
    11. Comparatives vs. Superlatives
    12. Relative Pronouns
    13. Double Negatives/Double Positives
    14. Conjunctions
    15. Redundancy
    16. Diction

While other kinds of errors such as misplaced modifiers or conjunctions do appear (see the Fixing Sentences section for explanations), they are very comparatively rare, and I have thus chosen to discuss them in the section devoted to Fixing Sentences.

The format of Error-Identification questions is deceptively simple: a sentence is presented with four options underlined (corresponding to choices A, B, C, and D), along with a "No error" option (E), and the test-taker is asked to identify which choice, if any, contains an error. There are, however, two potential difficulties:

1) Several of the underlined words or phrases often sound as if they could be wrong.

    Typically, the more test-takers contemplate the choices, the more they start to think that, well, it could be just about any of the answers.

    That's why I've nicknamed this section, "Is it weird, or is it wrong?" Sometimes it can just be very hard to tell.

2) Option E

    Option E (aka the dreaded "No error" option) is the bane of most students' existence on this section. They want there to be an error so badly.... It just seems wrong for there not to be one – the section is called Error-Identification, after all! – and the sentence sounds so awkward. Besides, ETS wouldn't ever be cruel enough to do it twice in a row.

In fact, it isn't that cruel. It's crueler. ETS has actually been known to make the answer E three times in a row. Hey, get over it. The test-writers can do whatever they want.

The most important thing to keep in mind is that finding the right answer often has nothing to do with figuring how you would say the sentence. Again, this does work sometimes, but unless your ear is always spot on, you're likely to end up with a score somewhere in the 500s. Remember, the test is designed that way. It isn't uncommon for test-takers to get hung up on a tiny little unfamiliar turn of phrase while missing a massive grammatical error staring them right in the face. If, on the other hand, you train yourself to know exactly – and I mean exactly – what to look for, the errors will virtually pop out at you. But that takes practice.

So let's go.

1. VERBS

Two types of verb questions appear on the SAT:

1) Subject-Verb Agreement

2) Verb Tense and Form

Subject-Verb Agreement

All verbs must agree with their subject in number:

-Singular subjects take singular verbs.
-Plural subjects take plural verbs.

Virtually all SAT questions that deal with number ask about verbs in the 3rd person singular (*he*/*she*/*it*/*one*) and 3rd person plural (*they*) forms.

3rd person singular verbs always end with an –s; 3rd person plural verbs do not. Note that this is the opposite of nouns, which take an –s in the plural rather than the singular.

	Correct	Incorrect
Singular Subject:	The politician speaks	The politician speak
Plural Subject:	The politicians speak	The politicians speaks
	The politician and his aide are holding a press conference.	The politician and his aide is holding a press conference.

Unfortunately, most subject-verb agreement questions that appear on the SAT are not nearly this straightforward. Subjects rarely appear next to the their verbs, making it difficult to spot disagreements.

The ways in which the SAT separates subjects from their verbs are, however, highly predictable. It is important that you practice recognizing the following structures because they will appear over and over again.

A. Subject – Non-Essential Clause – Verb

Identifying Non-Essential Clauses

A **non-essential clause** describes a noun, often (but not always) the noun that is the subject of a sentence. It is known as a non-essential clause because the description or information it provides is not essential to the meaning of the sentence – it's more like an interruption, which means it can be removed without causing any major grammatical problem or change in meaning. Non-essential clauses have two main identifying features:

1) They are surrounded by commas.

2) If they are removed from a sentence, the sentence will still make perfect grammatical sense.

In addition:

-They often begin with a "w-word" (or **relative pronoun**), such as *which, who, whose,* and *where,* that refers to the noun immediately preceding it.

-They are usually followed by verbs.

Let us examine the following sentence:

> Moroccan green tea**, which is prepared with a healthy dose of sugar and mint leaves,** is one of the most popular drinks across North Africa.

When we examine the sentence's structure, we see it contains a **relative clause** that begins with *which* and that is surrounded by commas. If we remove that clause, we are left with:

> Moroccan green tea […] is one of the most popular drinks across North Africa.

The sentence that remains makes complete sense on its own.

Appositives

It is not absolutely necessary to begin a non-essential clause with a "w-word," however. A non-essential clause that does not begin with one of those words is known as an **appositive**. You do not have to remember the term, but you do have to be able to recognize that the structure is correct, even though it may sound odd to you. The following sentence contains an example of an appositive:

> Moroccan green tea**, a drink prepared with a healthy amount of sugar and mint leaves,** is one of the most popular drinks across North Africa.

Non-Essential Clauses on the SAT

On the SAT, non-essential clauses are typically inserted between subjects and verbs in order to distract the test-taker from the fact that the subject is singular and the verb is plural or vice-versa.

Incorrect:	Moroccan green tea, which is prepared with a healthy amount of sugar and mint leaves, **are** one of the most popular drinks across North Africa.
Correct:	Moroccan green tea, which is prepared with a healthy amount of sugar and mint leaves, **is** one of the most popular drinks across North Africa.

Whenever you encounter a non-essential clause, you should immediately cross it out. Most often it is used to distract you from spotting subject-verb agreement errors, but it can be used to distract from other types of errors as well (described later). Do not forget to do this! Otherwise, you risk overlooking errors that can be easily spotted.

Sometimes, however, the error will appear *within* the non-essential clause, so if you've crossed one out and can't find another problem in the sentence, go back and check. For example:

Incorrect: <u>Moroccan green tea</u>, which **are** prepared with a healthy amount of sugar and mint leaves, is one of the most popular drinks across North Africa.

Correct: <u>Moroccan green tea</u>, which **is** prepared with a healthy amount of sugar and mint leaves, is one of the most popular drinks across North Africa.

Occasionally, you will encounter a non-essential clause followed by the word *and*. This construction is always wrong because if you cross out the non-essential clause, you are left with nonsense:

Incorrect: <u>Moroccan green tea</u>, which is prepared with a healthy amount of sugar and mint leaves, **and it is** one of the most popular drinks across North Africa.

Incorrect: Moroccan green tea and it is one of the most popular drinks across North Africa.

Essential Clauses with "That"

Occasionally, you will see subject-verb agreement questions based on **essential clauses** beginning with *that*. Such clauses are not set off by commas, but the verbs they contain must still agree with their subjects.

Incorrect: Green tea is a beverage <u>that</u> **have** long been used as a form of medicine in many countries.

Correct: Green tea is a beverage <u>that</u> **has** long been used as a form of medicine in many countries.

B. Subject – Prepositional Phrase – Verb

A prepositional phrase is, quite simply, a phrase that begins with a preposition (e.g. *in the box*, *under the table*, *over the hill*). These are often inserted between subjects and verbs to distract from disagreements.

In the sentences below, the subject is underlined, the prepositional phrase is italicized, and the verb is in bold.

Incorrect: <u>Changes</u> *in the balance of trade* **seems** remote from everyday concerns, but they can drastically affect how we spend our money.

Correct: <u>Changes</u> *in the balance of trade* **seem** remote from everyday concerns, but they can drastically affect how we spend our money.

The above sentence contains a classic trick: the subject (*changes*) is plural and thus requires a plural verb (*seem*). However, the prepositional phrase inserted between the subject and the verb has as its last word a singular noun (*trade*), which, if you are not paying close attention, can easily appear to be the subject of the verb that follows. If you don't see an error the first time you read a sentence, cross out all prepositional phrases and check for subject-verb agreement.

The last word of a prepositional phrase will always be the last word right before the verb, so be careful not to cross out verbs when getting rid of prepositional phrases.

Hint: If you see an underlined verb close to the beginning of a sentence, the subject will usually be the first word or couple of words of the sentence.

C. Prepositional Phrase – Verb – Subject

In this structure, the normal word order (or **syntax**) of a sentence is reversed so that the prepositional phrase appears at the beginning of a sentence, followed by the verb and then subject, always in that order.

In the sentences below, the subject is underlined, the prepositional phrase is italicized, and the verb is in bold.

Incorrect: *Along the Loup Canal in Nebraska* **extends** <u>parks, lakes, and trails</u> owned and operated by the Loup power district.

Correct: *Along the Loup Canal in Nebraska* **extend** <u>parks, lakes, and trails</u> owned and operated by the Loup power district.

Prepositional Phrase–Verb–Subject errors almost always appear as questions #27-29 and are signaled by a preposition at the beginning of the sentence. Most often, the preposition will be the first word of the sentence, but sometimes it will be the second.

Incorrect: Running *along the Loup Canal in Nebraska* **is** <u>parks, lakes, and trails</u> owned and operated by the Loup power district.

Correct: Running *along the Loup Canal in Nebraska* **are** <u>parks, lakes, and trails</u> owned and operated by the Loup power district.

It is common for test-takers to become confused because the reversed syntax makes the sentence sound odd. It is important to understand, however, that the unusual syntax is not what makes the sentence incorrect. It is simply a distraction to keep you from hearing the disagreement between the subject and the verb.

Sometimes a sentence in this form will not contain an agreement error; in those cases, the answer is very likely to be "No error."

Important: the SAT will often incorrectly pair two singular nouns connected by *and* (a structure known as a **compound subject**) with a singular verb, especially in Prepositional Phrase–Verb–Subject sentences, so always make sure you determine the *entire* subject before deciding whether the verb is right or wrong.

Usual Syntax: <u>A park and a lake</u> **runs** *along the Loup Canal*, a hydroelectric and irrigation canal located in eastern Nebraska.

Unusual Syntax: *Along the Loup Canal* **runs** <u>a park and a lake</u>, both of which are owned and operated by the Loup Power District.

Note that in the second version, the error is much more difficult to hear.

It is also important that you determine the entire subject because errors will very occasionally appear in which the verb comes before the subject but is not preceded by a prepositional phrase:

Incorrect: Radioactivity is generally not considered harmful when people are exposed to it at low levels for brief periods, but less clear **is** <u>its long-term effects</u>.

Correct: Radioactivity is generally not considered harmful when people are exposed to it at low levels for brief periods, but less clear **are** <u>its long-term effects</u>.

D. There is/There are, etc.

There is
There was   } go with **singular** nouns
There has been

There are
There were   } go with **plural** nouns
There have been

    Incorrect: In recent months, there **has been** <u>many questions</u> raised about the handling of the company's finances.

    Correct: In recent months, there **have been** <u>many questions</u> raised about the handling of the company's finances.

E. Neither...Nor + Verb

When *neither* and *nor* are used with two singular nouns, the verb should be singular.

Neither (Singular Noun) + Nor (Singular Noun) = Singular Verb

    Incorrect: Neither the <u>senator</u> nor her <u>aide</u> **are** expected to speak to the press today.

    Correct: Neither the <u>senator</u> nor her <u>aide</u> **is** expected to speak to the press today.

Although rule is the same for *either...or*, that word pair is not generally tested in regard to subject-verb agreement.

In general, the SAT only incorrectly pairs singular nouns connected by *neither...nor* with plural verbs. Errors involving plural nouns or combined singular and plural nouns do not appear.

The rule, however, is that the verb takes the number of the noun that follows *nor* (e.g. *Neither the senator nor her aide <u>is</u> expected to speak to the press today*, BUT *Neither the senator nor her aides <u>are</u> expected to speak to the press today*).

When *(n)either* is not paired with *(n)or* and is used with two singular nouns, a singular verb should also be used:

    Incorrect: Both the senator and her aide were present at the conference, but neither **were** willing to speak to the press.

    Correct: Both the senator and her aide were present at the conference, but neither **was** willing to speak to the press.

Very Important:

Collective Nouns = Singular

Collective Nouns are **singular nouns** that refer to groups of people. Common examples include *agency, institution, school, committee, jury, city, country, company, university,* and *team*. While many people consider it perfectly acceptable to use such nouns with plural verbs, the SAT only considers singular verbs to be correct.

Incorrect:	After many days of deliberation, the jury **have** finally returned with a verdict.
Correct:	After many days of deliberation, the jury **has** finally returned with a verdict.

Watch out for collective nouns. They appear often, and their presence in a sentence often indicates an agreement error.

A number of = Plural

The number = Singular

Correct:	A number of people **are** expected to attend the party tonight.
BUT	
Correct:	The number of people at the party last night **was** quite large.

Each = Singular

Incorrect:	Each of the students in Ms. Chang's class **are** expected to give a presentation next week.
Correct:	Each of the students in Ms. Chang's class **is** expected to give a presentation next week.

(Every) One = Singular

Incorrect:	(Every) one of the students in Ms. Chang's class **are** expected to give a presentation next week.
Correct:	(Every) one of the students in Ms. Chang's class **is** expected to give a presentation next week.

Gerunds when used as subjects = Singular

Incorrect:	Going to the movies **are** a common way for people to relax.
Correct:	Going to the movies **is** a common way for people to relax.

Subject-Verb Agreement Exercises

In the following sentences, fix any subject-verb agreement error that appears. Label all subjects, verbs, and prepositional phrases, and make sure to cross out any non-essential clauses. Some of the sentences may not contain an error. (Answers p. 146, Official Guide question list p. 128)

1. The process of living vicariously through a fictional character in order to purge one's emotions are [is] known as catharsis.

2. Along the border between China and Tibet lies the Himalaya Mountains, which includes some of the highest peaks in the world.

3. Recognized for formulating unorthodox social theories, Lev Gumilev and D.S. Mirsky was [were] partly responsible for founding the neo-eurasianist political and cultural movement.

4. The works of artist Alan Chin draws inspiration from both the California gold rush and the construction of the transcontinental railroad.

5. The maps of historian and cartographer John Speed depict some of the first visual representations of many towns and cities throughout England, Ireland, and Scotland.

6. Playboating, a discipline of whitewater rafting or canoeing in which players stay in one spot while performing certain maneuvers, involves specialized canoes designed for the sport.

7. Often found in plastic drinking bottles is [are] substantial amounts of a potentially toxic chemical called Bisphenol A.

8. The African violet, which is known for its striking pink and purple leaves, belongs to the Saintpaulia family of flowering plants rather than to the violet family.

9. Among the finds from a recent archaeological dig in London was [were] earthenware knobs originally used for "pay walls," boxes into which Elizabethan theater-goers deposited their admission fees.

10. One of the animal kingdom's best jumpers is the flea, whose ability to leap up to 200 times its own body length is nearly unsurpassed.

11. Stiles, structures that provide people with a passage through or over a fence, are often built in rural areas or along footpaths.

12. The patent for the first mechanical pencils were [was] granted to Sampson Morgan and John Hawkins in England during the early nineteenth century.

13. Each of the Taino's five chiefdoms, which inhabited the Bahamas before the arrival of Europeans, were [was] ruled by a leader known as a cacique.

14. If there is [are] sufficient funds remaining, the teacher's request for new classroom supplies will most likely be approved by the school board.

15. Possible explanations for the suspicion surrounding Shakespeare's *Macbeth* includes the superstition that the witches' song is an actual incantation and the belief that theaters only mount the play when they are in need of money.

16. In the galleries of the Louvre museum hang Leonardo da Vinci's *Mona Lisa* and Eugene Delacroix's *Liberty Leading the People*, two of the best-known paintings in the world.

17. Galaxies, far from being randomly scattered throughout the universe, appears to be distributed in bubble-shaped patterns.

18. For the past several years, the theater company have ~~has~~ traveled to various schools throughout the city in order to expose students to classic works.

19. Over the past several days, a number of disturbing reports has ~~have~~ filtered in to the news agency, suggesting that the country's government is on the verge of collapse.

20. According to the law of diminution, the pitches of notes sounded by an orchestra remains the same even as the amount of sound diminishes.

21. There are a number of prominent economists who consider changes in the demand for goods to be one of the fundamental causes of inflation.

22. Although the criminal protested his innocence vehemently, neither he nor his lawyer were ~~was~~ ultimately able to offer a convincing alibi.

23. Sebastian Díaz Morales, like the other members of his generation of artists, know ~~knows~~ how to draw on the social experiences of his country to produce works that entirely escape any simple interpretation.

24. Historians describe the chariot as a simple type of horse carriage that were ~~was~~ used by ancient civilizations for peacetime travel and military combat.

25. Along the deepest part of the ocean floor sits ~~sit~~ the Mariana Trench and the HMRG Deep, the two lowest spots that researchers have ever identified on earth.

Verb Tense and Form

Like subject-verb agreement errors, verb tense and form errors regularly appear on the SAT in specific formats and in highly predictable ways.

Important: The inclusion of a date or time period in a sentence is usually a tip-off that the question is testing verb tense. When you see one of these clues, make sure to check the tenses of all verbs first.

A. Consistency

Verbs should remain consistent (or **parallel)** in tense or form throughout a sentence.

Unless the information in the sentence clearly indicates otherwise, sentences that start in the past should stay in the past, and sentences that start in the present should stay in the present.

Incorrect:	Since serious drama unaccompanied by music **was** forbidden in all but two London theatres during the eighteenth century, the renowned Queen's Theatre **becomes** an opera house.
Correct:	Since serious drama unaccompanied by music **was** forbidden in all but two London theatres during the eighteenth century, the renowned Queen's Theatre **became** an opera house.

The sentence begins in the past tense, as indicated by the verb *was*, and must continue in the past tense since there is nothing to suggest otherwise.

B. Date in the Past = Simple Past

Any sentence that includes a date or time period in the past and that describes a completed action should contain a verb in the **simple past (**e.g. *he went, she drank*) only. Often, the **present perfect** (e.g. *he has gone, she has drunk*) will be incorrectly used instead.

Incorrect:	During the <u>nineteenth century</u>, Charles Dickens **has been renowned** as one of the most famous British novelists.
Correct:	During the <u>nineteenth century</u>, Charles Dickens **was renowned** as one of the most famous British novelists.

In the above sentence, the time period "nineteenth century" indicates that the verb must be in the simple past.

C. Would vs. Will

Would and *Will* are switched almost exclusively with one another.

Whenever you see *would* or *will* underlined in a sentence, replace it with the other one and see if it works better.

If you are not sure when to use *would* and *will*, the rule is that you should not mix past and future in the same sentence.

-Sentences that contain verbs in the past tense should not contain the word *will*.

-Sentences that contain verbs in the present tense should not also contain the word *would*.

Incorrect:	William Shakespeare, who **will** become the greatest English dramatist, **was** born in Stratford-upon-Avon in 1564.
Correct:	William Shakespeare, who **would** become the greatest English dramatist, **was** born in Stratford-upon-Avon in 1564.

In the incorrect version of the above sentence, for example, the verb *was* appears. Since *was* is a verb in the past tense, *will become*, a verb in the future tense, should not also appear. And since *will* and *would* are switched with one another, *would become* must be the correct answer.

Likewise, a sentence containing a verb in the present tense should not contain *would*.

Incorrect:	If it rains today, I **would** go to the movies instead of the park.
Correct:	If it rains today, I **will** go to the movies instead of the park.

Since the verb *rains* is in the present tense, *would go* cannot be correct. *Will go* is the only other option.

Important: although a sentence can contain both *would have* and *if*, the two should not appear together in the same clause. *Had* should be used in place of *would have*. (For more information, see p. 114.)

Incorrect:	If company officials and union leaders **would have compromised** on several important issues, the labor crisis would have been averted.
Correct:	If company officials and union leaders **had compromised** on several important issues, the labor crisis would have been averted.

D. Gerunds vs. Infinitives

Infinitive = TO form of a verb

Gerund = -ING form of a verb*

Infinitive	**Gerund**
To be	Being
To run	Running
To have	Having
To fly	Flying

On the SAT, gerunds and infinitives are nearly always switched with one another. If you see a gerund underlined, plug in the infinitive and vice-versa.

Incorrect:	Though she was one of the few women of her time **gaining** international prominence, Clara Barton would not have described herself as a proponent of women's rights.
Correct:	Though she was one of the few women of her time **to gain** international prominence, Clara Barton would not have described herself as a proponent of women's rights.

---

* A gerund is a verb that acts as a noun (e.g. *I was annoyed by his <u>singing</u>*). When a verb acts as an adjective (e.g. *a <u>singing</u> bird*), it is a **participle**. Although both end in "–ing," they have different functions. For more information, see p. 101.

Important: Often, when switching a gerund with an infinitive, you must place a preposition before the gerund in order for a sentence to make sense. Inserting only the gerund will not usually fix the sentence.

Incorrect: Deactivated viruses form the basis of many vaccines known for their effectiveness **to prevent** disease.

Incorrect: Deactivated viruses form the basis of many vaccines known for their effectiveness **preventing** disease.

Correct: Deactivated viruses form the basis of many vaccines known for their effectiveness **in preventing** disease.

Sometimes, both a gerund and an infinitive are acceptable. In such cases, neither will be considered incorrect.

Correct: Today, the members of Ms. Moreno's physics class will begin **to review** for the final exam.

Correct: Today, the members of Ms. Moreno's physics class will begin **reviewing** for the final exam.

In general, it is necessary to rely on your ear in order to determine whether the gerund or the infinitive is correct. There is no rule that governs which one is used, and the gerunds and infinitives tested are fairly random. So while I do not advocate trying to memorize all the expressions that require gerunds vs. infinitives (expressions that in all likelihood will not appear on the test), it may be helpful to know the following expressions, some which have appeared on past exams:

Idioms with Gerund	Idioms with Infinitive
Regarded as (being)	Consider to be
Viewed as (being)	Require to be
Seen as (being)	Deserve to be
Praised/celebrated as (being)	Agree to be
In the hope(s) of being	Promise to be
Effective in/at being	Refuse to be
Accustomed/used to being	Threaten to be
Enjoy being	Inclined to be
Admired for being	Decline to be
Capable of being	Seek/strive to be
Succeed in/at being	Encourage to be
Stop being	Choose/decide to be
Insist on being	Intend to be
Accused of being	Inspire to be
Deny being	Shown to be
Report being	Claim to be
Consider being	Arrange to be
Postpone being	Prepare to be
Avoid being	Neglect to be
Admit to being	Offer to be
Resent being	Attempt to be
Imagine being	Fail to be
Describe being	Struggle to be
Prevent from being	Want/wish to be
Without being	Reluctant to be
Mind being	Tend to be
Discuss being	Allow to be
Before being	Manage to be
After being	Appear/seem to be
Risk being	Expect to be

E. Past Participle vs. Simple Past

The **past participle** is used after any form of the verb *to have* (e.g. *to have, had, has, having*).

Examples: **Having sung** for hours, the bird fell silent.

Since a number of unexpected issues **had arisen** during the meeting, we were forced to remain an extra hour.

Since it first opened in 1857, New York City residents **have chosen** to spend their free time relaxing in Central Park.

The verb tense that is formed by combining *have* or *has* + past participle (e.g. *has been, has gone, has chosen*) is the **present perfect**.

The present perfect is used for an action that started in the past and that is continuing into the present. When the words *for* or *since*, or a phrase such as *over the past several years*, appear, the present perfect is usually required.

Incorrect: Many groundbreaking scientific discoveries **were** made <u>since</u> the start of the twentieth century.

Correct: Many groundbreaking scientific discoveries **have been** made <u>since</u> the start of the twentieth century.

Correct: Groundbreaking scientific discoveries **have been** continually made <u>for</u> the last hundred years.

However, the **simple past** is used for actions that began and ended in the past.

The bird **sang** for hours and then fell silent.

A number of unexpected issues **arose** during the meeting, so we **were** forced to remain an extra hour.

Between 1858 and 1873, New York City's Central Park **was** improved and expanded according to a plan designed by Frederick Law Olmsted and Calvert Vaux.

On the SAT, the simple past rather than the past participle will always incorrectly follow a form of the verb *to have* or *to be*; the past participle is never used to replace the simple past (e.g. *he done the work*).

Incorrect: Having **saw** the thief sneak into her neighbor's home, the woman promptly called the police.

Correct: Having **seen** the thief sneak into her neighbor's home, the woman promptly called the police.

Many common verbs take different past participle and simple past forms, and often, if you're not paying attention, you can easily overlook errors involving them. The verb *to go*, for example, has two different forms in the past: *gone* (past participle) and *went* (simple past). Here is a list of some common verbs that have different forms for their simple past and past participle.

Infinitive	Simple Past	Past Participle
To (a)rise	(A)rose	(A)risen
To (a)waken	(A)woke	(A)woken
To be	Was	Been
To become	Became	Become
To begin	Began	Begun
To blow	Blew	Blown
To break	Broke	Broken
To choose	Chose	Chosen
To do	Did	Done
To draw	Drew	Drawn
To drink	Drank	Drunk
To drive	Drove	Driven
To fly	Flew	Flown
To freeze	Froze	Frozen
To get	Got	Gotten*
To go	Went	Gone
To hide	Hid	Hidden
To give	Gave	Given
To grow	Grew	Grown
To know	Knew	Known
To ride	Rode	Ridden
To ring	Rang	Rung
To run	Ran	Run
To see	Saw	Seen
To sew	Sewed	Sewn
To shrink	Shrank	Shrunk/Shrunken
To sink	Sank	Sunk/Sunken
To sing	Sang	Sung
To speak	Spoke	Spoken
To spring	Sprang	Sprung
To steal	Stole	Stolen
To stink	Stank	Stunk
To swim	Swam	Swum
To take	Took	Taken
To tear	Tore	Torn
To throw	Threw	Thrown
To wear	Wore	Worn
To write	Wrote	Written

---

*Although *got* is used as the past participle of *get* in British English, *gotten* is considered standard in American English.

F. The Past Perfect

Past Perfect = *Had* + Past Participle

Examples: had done, had gone, had been, had seen

Sometimes a sentence will describe two events or actions that occurred in the past. The **past perfect** is used to indicate that one of those actions occurred before the other.

Incorrect: By the time it adjourned, the committee **made** several important decisions.

Correct: By the time it adjourned, the committee **had made** several important decisions.

Logically, the committee must have made several important decisions (action #1) before it adjourned (action #2); therefore, the past perfect is required.

Whenever a verb in the past perfect appears, ask yourself whether the sentence makes it clear that the event or action the verb describes clearly occurred before a second event or action. If it does not, the sentence is incorrect.

Important: the phrase "by the time" is usually a tip-off that the past perfect is required.

There are, however, instances when either the past perfect or the simple past is perfectly acceptable. For example:

Correct: Before a complete version of Louisa May Alcott's novel *Little Women* appeared in 1880, the book **had been published** in two separate volumes.

Correct: Before a complete version of Louisa May Alcott's novel *Little Women* appeared in 1880, the book **was published** in two separate volumes.

In the first sentence, the past perfect is used to emphasize the appearance of the book in two volumes before its appearance in one; however, the simple past in the second sentence is also correct because it describes two actions that took place in the past and keeps the tense of the sentence consistent.

In the Error-Identification sentence, you may encounter sentences that contain only the simple past but that could also be written with the past perfect, as in the first example above. (For a College Board example, see question 26, p. 957 in the *Official Guide*, 2nd Edition.) Since both versions are acceptable, an underlined simple past verb that falls into this category will not be the error. In general you will only be required to recognize whether the past perfect – rather than the simple past – is being used incorrectly (see question 21, p. 777; question 17, p. 894; and question 24, p. 957).

Verb Tense and Form Exercises

In the following exercises, underline the date or words that indicate a tense question, and fix any verb not in the correct tense or form. Some of the sentences may not contain an error. (Answers p. 147, Official Guide question list p. 129)

1. Built in Newcastle upon Tyne, England and launched in 1873, the *SS Dunraven* was powered by both steam and sail and was intended to travel between Britain and India.

2. In 1498, Dutch scholar Erasmus of Rotterdam has moved from Paris to England, where he became a professor of ancient languages at Cambridge.

3. M.J. Hyland, who authored the acclaimed 2003 novel *How the Light Gets In*, is often praised to [as] be a subtle and complex portrayer of human psychology.

4. Composer Georgi Tutev, who will [would] become one of the principal figures of Bulgarian modernism, was born of a German mother and a Bulgarian father.

5. According to researchers, the Antarctic ice shelf has shrank [shrank] by approximately 50 gigatons of ice each year since 1992.

6. By 1900, McKim, Mead and White had become New York's largest architectural firm; today it remains among the most famous in the city's history.

7. The nearly 200-ton Mayflower was chartered by a group of British merchants and setting [set] sail from Plymouth, England in 1620.

8. Mahatma Gandhi, who was born in India, studied law in London and in 1893 went to South Africa, where he spends [spent] twenty years opposing discriminatory legislation against Indians.

9. Accidentally discovered by Procter and Gamble researchers in 1968, the fat substitute Olestra has been shown in causing [to cause] stomach upset in those who consume excessive amounts of it.

10. The country's economists speculated that thousands more jobs would have been lost if consumer demand for domestically manufactured products would have [had] continued to decline.

11. In the sixteenth century, writer and jurist Noël du Fail has written [wrote] many stories documenting rural life in France during the Renaissance.

12. Defying predictions that he will [would] fade from the public eye, former Czech president Vaclav Havel became a film director after his retirement from office.

13. Descended from a long line of university professors, Marie Goeppert-Mayer received the majority of her training in Germany and eventually teaching [taught] at a number of universities in the United States.

14. After a 1991 attempt to overthrow Mikhail Gorbechav failed, power had shifted to Russian president Boris Yeltsin.

15. New facts, especially when they replace beliefs already in one's mind, commonly take as long as several weeks being [to be] fully accepted as true.

16. During the Renaissance, glass products made on the island of Murano could only be crafted according to traditional techniques, and local artisans were forbidden to leave and sell their creations elsewhere.

17. The illustrator often photographed multiple models for each drawing and has made his selection only when the final prints arrived in his hands.

18. Toward the end of the sixteenth century, the Iroquois League, a confederation of six Native American nations, has formed in the northeastern United States.

19. NASA scientists have decided to delay the space shuttle's launch in order to determine whether recently repaired parts would cause damage if they break off in orbit.

        broke

20. After weeks of careful scrutiny, the consumer protection agency informed the public that a number of products will *would* be recalled because of safety concerns.

21. Even before the beginning of the twentieth century, when the electronic age was still in its infancy, the first attempts to generate sound from electricity had already begun.

22. Far from being a recluse, Goethe corresponded with the leading literary, political, and scientific figures of his day with an energy that few of his readers could ever hope to match.

23. Several dozen boats are known to have *sunk* sank off of the French Frigate Shoals, part of an enormous protected zone that covers nearly 150,000 square miles in the Pacific Ocean.

24. Emperor Frederick the Great of Prussia believed that to fight a successful war was creating minimal intrusion into the lives of civilians.

        to creat

25. According to cognitive scientist Daniel Willingham, one major reason more students do not enjoy school is that abstract thought is not something people's brains are designed to be good at or enjoying.

        to enjoy

26. The Empire of Mali on the west coast of Africa was founded by King Sundiata Kesa, a hero of the Mandinka people, during the Middle Ages.

27. Hardly a stranger to self-censorship, Mark Twain never hesitated to change his prose if he believed that the alterations will improve the sales of his books.

        would

28. Some critics have argued that Dostoevsky was unique among nineteenth-century authors in that he surrendered fully to his characters and has allowed himself to write in voices other than his own.

2. PRONOUNS

Next to verbs, pronouns are the most commonly tested part of speech on the SAT. There are two kinds of pronoun questions that appear on the SAT:

1) Pronoun-Antecedent

2) Pronoun Case

Pronoun-Antecedent

A **pronoun** is a word such as *he, she, it, them, their,* or *us* that is used to replace a noun.

> In the sentence, *The ball is on the table,* the noun *ball* can be replaced by the pronoun *it.*

> Likewise, in the sentence, *Mary threw the ball,* the name *Mary* can be replaced by the pronoun *she.*

An **antecedent** is simply the word (noun, pronoun, or gerund) to which a pronoun refers. Although the prefix –*ante* means "before," an antecedent can appear either before or after the noun to which it refers. (If you find the term "antecedent" too confusing, however, you can use **referent** instead.)

All pronouns must **agree** with their antecedents. Just as singular verbs must agree with singular subjects and plural verbs must agree with plural subjects, so must singular pronouns agree with singular nouns and plural pronouns with plural nouns.

> For example, in the sentence, *Katie dribbled the ball, and then **she** shot it at the basket,* the word *ball* is the antecedent referred to by the pronoun *it.* The word *Katie* is the antecedent of the pronoun *she.*

> If we said, *Katie dribbled the ball, and then she shot them at the basket,* there would be a disagreement between the antecedent and the pronoun because the antecedent *ball* is singular and the pronoun *them* is plural.

> Likewise, if we said, *Katie dribbled the ball, and then they shot it at the basket,* there would also be an pronoun-antecedent disagreement because the antecedent *Katie* is singular, while the pronoun *they* is plural.

Whenever you see a pronoun underlined, you should immediately try to figure out what noun that pronoun is referring to. If the noun and the pronoun do not agree, whichever one is underlined will be incorrect. You will never find both the noun and the pronoun underlined.

A. One vs. You

One and *You* are frequently switched with one another (although they are also occasionally switched with other pronouns). They cannot be mixed and matched within a sentence but must remain consistent throughout.

You → You
One → One

> Incorrect: If **one** wants to avoid insect invasions, **you** should refrain from leaving crumbs lying on the floor.

> Correct: If **one** wants to avoid insect invasions, **one** should refrain from leaving crumbs lying on the floor.

> Correct: If **you** want to avoid insect invasions, **you** should refrain from leaving crumbs lying on the floor.

B. Singular vs. Plural

Singular nouns are referred to by singular pronouns.

Plural nouns are referred to by plural pronouns.

Sometimes different pronouns are used to refer to people and to things.

For people (e.g. actors, judges, athletes):

For Singular Nouns		For Plural Nouns
He, She	→	They
His, Her	→	Their

> Incorrect: <u>A person</u> who wishes to become an Olympic-caliber athlete must devote virtually all of **their** time to training.

> Correct: <u>A person</u> who wishes to become an Olympic-caliber athlete must devote virtually all of **his or her** time to training.

> Incorrect: <u>People</u> who wish to become Olympic-caliber athletes must devote virtually all of **his or her** time to training.

> Correct: <u>People</u> who wish to become Olympic-caliber athletes must devote virtually all of **their** time to training.

Important: the singular of "they" will always be given as the phrase "he or she" when gender is not specified.

For things (e.g. cities, books, ideas):

For Singular Nouns		For Plural Nouns
It	→	They/Them
Its	→	Their
This	→	These
That	→	Those

Incorrect: When <u>the economy</u> does poorly, **their** performance is of all-abiding interest to the public.

Correct: When <u>the economy</u> does poorly, **its** performance is of all-abiding interest to the public.

Incorrect: <u>The lights</u> began to flicker wildly, and only moments later **it** went out altogether.

Correct: <u>The lights</u> began to flicker wildly, and only moments later **they** went out altogether.

Important: When you see *it(s)* or *they/their* underlined in a sentence, check it first because there's a very good chance that it's wrong. If the antecedent does not agree with the pronoun, you've found your error.

In addition, remember to look out for collective nouns (e.g *country, jury, university, agency*). They are tested frequently in regard to pronoun agreement, and because they are singular, they should always be referred to by singular pronouns (*it* or *its*).

C. Ambiguous Antecedent

Sometimes it is unclear which antecedent a pronoun refers to.

Incorrect: Afraid that they would be late to the party, <u>Rosa and Caroline</u> decided to take **her** car rather than walk.

Whose car did Rosa and Caroline take? We don't know. Since we have two female names, "her" could refer to either one of them. In order to fix this sentence, we must make it clear whose car they took. We can therefore say:

Correct: <u>Rosa and Caroline</u> decided to take **Rosa's** car to the party.

Correct: <u>Rosa and Caroline</u> decided to take **Caroline's** car to the party.

(When these questions appear in Fixing Sentences, you will *not* be given the option of saying, "Rosa and Caroline took **their** car to the party.")

D. Missing Antecedent

Any pronoun that appears in a sentence must have a **clear antecedent** that is a noun, pronoun, or gerund. If a sentence includes a pronoun without an antecedent, that sentence cannot be correct, no matter how obvious its meaning may be.

Incorrect: In some countries, extreme weather conditions have led to shortages of food, and consequently **they** must struggle to receive adequate nutrients.

Correct: In some countries, extreme weather conditions have led to shortages of food, and consequently **their inhabitants** must struggle to receive adequate nutrients.

In the incorrect version, it is understood that the word *they* refers to the inhabitants of countries with extreme weather conditions; however, there is no noun anywhere in the sentence that explicitly says who *they* are.

Incorrect: In the report released by the committee, **it** stated that significant budget cuts would be necessary for the following year.

In the above sentence, we do not know who or what the word *it* refers to. The writers of the report? The report itself? The sentence never tells us. There are several ways to fix this issue in order to make the antecedent clear. We can either eliminate the pronoun completely:

Correct: The report released by the treasury committee **stated** that significant budget cuts would be necessary for the following year.

Or, we can make it clear what *it* refers to:

Correct: The treasury committee stated in **its** report that significant budget cuts would be necessary for the following year.

Antecedents ≠ Verbs or Adjectives

Only nouns, pronouns, and gerunds can be antecedents. Any sentence that attempts to use another part of speech, such as a **verb** or an **adjective**, as an antecedent cannot be correct.

Do so = Right
Do it = Wrong

Incorrect: Activists who defend endangered species from poaching **do it** on the grounds that such animals, once gone, are irreplaceable.

What does *it* refer to in this sentence? *Defending* endangered species. But since the gerund *defending* doesn't actually appear in the sentence (only the verb *defend*) there is no real antecedent. When no real antecedent is present, the correct phrase is *do so*:

Correct: Activists who defend endangered species from poaching **do so** on the grounds that such animals, once gone, are irreplaceable.

Important: when "do it" is underlined, it is virtually always wrong.

*The following errors usually appear in Fixing Sentences but are discussed here for the sake of consistency.

Adjective as "Trick" Antecedent

One of the trickiest ways that antecedents are presented in incorrect form is as follows:

Incorrect: The canine <u>penchant</u> for hierarchy has its roots in wolf society, which always designated **its** specific role within the pack.

What does *its* refer to? A canine. But *canine* isn't acting as a noun – it's actually an adjective that modifies *penchant*. And since antecedents can only be nouns or gerunds, *its* has no antecedent. What makes this so incredibly tricky is that the word *canine* is usually used as a noun – except that here it isn't. In order to make the sentence correct, we must repeat the word *canine*, this time using it as a noun.

Correct: The canine <u>penchant</u> for hierarchy has its roots in wolf society, which always designated **a canine's** specific role within the pack.

This, Which, and That

The same rule that applies to *it* applies to *this*, *which*, and *that*: each of these pronouns must refer to an antecedent (specific noun, pronoun, or gerund) that appears within the sentence. If the antecedent does not appear, the sentence cannot be correct.

Occasionally, the pronoun *this* will be used without an antecedent.

Incorrect: Australian Jessica Watson became the youngest person ever to sail around the world, completing **this** in March of 2010.

Correct: Australian Jessica Watson became the youngest person ever to sail around the world, completing **her journey** in March of 2010.

Although it is clear in the incorrect version that the word *this* refers to Jessica Watson's journey, the sentence cannot be correct because the noun *journey* does not actually appear in the sentence.

Which is made incorrect in the same way:

Incorrect: Australian Jessica Watson became the youngest person ever to sail around the world, **which** she achieved in March of 2010.

Here again, it is clear from the information provided in the sentence that *which* refers to the feat of sailing around the world. But the noun *sailing* never actually appears – only *to sail*, which is a verb and therefore unable to be an antecedent. In order for the sentence to be correct, we must either provide a noun that states exactly what Jessica Watson achieved:

Correct: Australian Jessica Watson became the youngest person ever to sail around the world, **a feat** that she achieved in March of 2010.

Correct: Australian Jessica Watson became the youngest person ever to sail around the world, achieving **that feat** in March of 2010.

Note that it is perfectly acceptable to replace *which* with a present participle (in this case *achieving*) in order to eliminate a pronoun that lacks an antecedent. (For an explanation of present participles, please see p. 101.)

Same thing for *that*

Incorrect: Australian Jessica Watson became the youngest person ever to sail around the world, and she achieved **that** in March of 2010.

Correct: Australian Jessica Watson became the youngest person ever to sail around the world, and she achieved **that feat** in March of 2010.

In the incorrect version of the sentence, the pronoun *that* does not refer to a specific noun. Only when we supply the noun that it refers to (*feat*) does it become correct.

Pronoun-Antecedent Exercises

In the following sentences, label all pronouns and their antecedents. Some of the sentences may not contain an error. (Answers p. 148, Official Guide question list p. 130)

1. Not until the early twentieth century did the city become capable of maintaining their [*its*] population and cease to be dependent on rural areas for a constant stream of new inhabitants.

2. Cleota Davis, the mother of jazz legend Miles Davis, was an accomplished pianist in her own right, but she hid that fact from her son until he was an adult.

3. Pain doesn't show up on a body scan and can't be measured in a test, and as a result, many chronic pain sufferers turn to art in an effort to depict that. [*it*]

4. The nitrogen cycle describes its [*nitrogen*] movement from the air into organic compounds and then back into the atmosphere.

5. If you [*You*] exercise to prevent diabetes, one may also want to avoid vitamins C and E since these antioxidants have been shown to correlate with it.

6. With the price of art lower, collectors for the most part don't want to part with a prized painting or sculpture unless they are forced to do it. [*so*]

7. Once common across southwest Asia, the Indian cheetah was driven nearly to extinction during the late twentieth century and now resides in the fragmented pieces of their [*its*] remaining suitable habitat.

8. Although Alice Sebold does not write her books with any particular age group in mind, it has [*they have*] proven popular with middle and high school students.

9. Some critics of the Internet have argued that it is a danger to people because its vastness, often heralded as a benefit, threatens our [*their*] intellectual health.

10. The woolly mammoth and the saber-toothed tiger might have survived as late as 10,000 B.C., although it [*they*] went extinct fairly abruptly right around that time.

11. When the auditorium closes next year for renovations, the theater company will probably hold their [*its*] productions at another location.

12. While most editors are concerned with how accurate a biography is, others are more interested in how rapidly it can be published.

13. One measure of a society's openness to newcomers is the quality of the space they [*it*] create for people of unfamiliar cultural and linguistic backgrounds.

14. Though recipes for yeast-free muffins were commonly found in nineteenth-century cookbooks, by the twentieth century most muffin recipes were calling for it. [*yeast*]

15. Although the jury spent many hours arguing over the details of the trial, it was ultimately unable to reach a consensus.

16. The Egyptian temple complex at Karnak, situated on the eastern bank of the Nile, was their [*Egyptian*] sacred place of worship.

17. The city's economy has weakened significantly over the past decade, and ~~this has~~ *leading* led to an overwhelming loss of manufacturing jobs.

18. In the announcement, the school committee states that ~~they~~ *it* will substantially overhaul the eleventh grade curriculum at some point during the next year.

19. The world's population could climb to 10.5 billion by 2050, which ~~raises~~ *raising* questions about how many people the Earth can support.

20. Paul and Julio had just returned from a long and exhausting hike along the Appalachian Trail when ~~he~~ *Paul* stumbled and hit his head.

21. In order to become truly great at a sport, players must spend most of ~~his or her~~ *their* free time practicing.

22. Japan's status as an island country means that ~~they~~ *it* must rely heavily on other countries for the supply of natural resources that are indispensable to national existence.

23. The Marquesa islands were among the first South Pacific islands to be settled, and from ~~its~~ *their* shores departed some of the greatest navigators of all time.

24. Google's dominance as an Internet search function has allowed the company to expand ~~their~~ *its* ambitions to include virtually all aspects of the online world.

25. Autobiographies are often structured differently from memoirs, which follow the development of an author's personality rather than the writing of his or her works.

Pronoun Case

Case refers to whether a pronoun is being used as a **subject** or an **object**.

A subject is:

1. the person or thing that is the main focus of the sentence, OR

2. the person or thing performing the action described in the sentence.

In the following sentences, the subject is in bold:

1. **Jonah** read the book.
   (Who read the book? Jonah)

2. **The coat** is more attractive than warm.
   (What is more attractive than it is warm? The coat)

3. Unable to find a place to plug in their computers, **Sarah and Ansel** decided to read instead.
   (Who was unable to find a place to plug in their computers? Sarah and Ansel)

All subjects can be replaced by **subject pronouns**:

I	**We**
You	**You**
She/ He/ It/ One	**They**

If we replace our subjects in the above sentences with pronouns, they become:

1. **Jonah** read the book.
   → **He** read the book.

2. **The coat** is more attractive than warm.
   → **It** is more attractive than warm.

3. Unable to find a place to plug in their computers, **Sarah and Ansel** decided to read instead.
   → Unable to find a place to plug in their computers, **they** decided to read instead.

An **object** is the person or thing that receives an action. In the following sentences, the object is in bold.

1. Jonah read **the book**.
   (What was being read? The book)

2. Akil threw **the basketballs** across the court.
   (What did Akil throw? The basketballs)

3. Serena waved to **Sam and me** from the parking lot.
   (To whom did Serena wave? Sam and me)

All objects can be replaced by **object pronouns**:

Me	**Us**
You	**You**
Her/ Him/ It/ One	**Them**

If we replace the objects in the above sentences with object pronouns, they become:

1. Jonah read **the book**.
   → Jonah read **it**.

2. Akil threw the basketballs across the court.
   → Akil threw **them** across the basketball court.

3. Serena waved to **Sam and me** from the parking lot.
   → Serena waved to **us** from the other side of the parking lot.

Note that proper names (*Serena, Sam, Akil, Sarah*) can be either subjects or objects, but that most pronouns (*I, she, they, them*) can be only one or the other.

Pronoun case errors on the SAT involve only the following subject/object pairs:

**I / Me
She, He / Her, Him
We / Us
They / Them**

For example, in the sentence *Mary threw the ball to Alisha*, *Mary* is the subject and *Alisha* is the object. Both are proper names. We can rewrite the sentence several ways to include pronouns:

She threw the ball to Alisha. (*Mary* replaced with object pronoun)

Mary threw the ball to **her**. (*Alisha* replaced with subject pronoun)

She threw the ball to **her**. (*Alisha* replaced with subject pronoun and *Mary* with object pronoun)

What we cannot do, however, is the following:

Her threw the ball to Alisha.

Mary threw the ball to **she**.

Her threw the ball to **she**.

When pronouns are used incorrectly with singular subjects or objects, as in the above sentences, the error is usually pretty easy to spot. Most people clearly would not say, "*My little brother always wants to play with I*," or "*Him went to the store for some milk*." But when the subject or object is plural, people tend to get confused. And pronoun case questions will nearly always contain a compound subject or object, usually one with a proper name, that includes the word *and*. For example:

Incorrect: Roosevelt High School's annual prize for citizenship was presented to **Annabel and he** by the vice-principal at the spring awards banquet.

The only thing to remember is that what goes for singular goes for plural. When you see an underlined subject or object pronoun paired with another noun, cross out *and + noun*, and see if the pronoun can stand on its own.

Roosevelt High School's annual prize for citizenship was presented to ~~**Annabel and**~~ **he** by the vice-principal at the spring awards banquet.

Since you would say, *The prize was presented to him* rather than, *The prize was presented to he*, the sentence must be rewritten as follows:

Correct: Roosevelt High School's annual prize for citizenship was presented to **Annabel and him** by the vice-principal at the spring awards banquet.

To reiterate:

Incorrect: After giving a stern lecture on the necessity of checking the validity of our sources, the teacher gave **Jonah and I** back the report we had turned in at the beginning of the week.

In the above sentence, we notice that there is a pronoun paired with a proper name. When we cross out *proper name + and,* we are left with:

Incorrect: After giving a stern lecture on the necessity of checking the validity of our sources, the teacher gave ~~Jonah and~~ I back the report we had turned in at the beginning of the week.

Would you say, *The teacher gave I back the report?* Obviously not. So you wouldn't say, *The teacher gave my friend and I back our report* either. But since you would say, *The teacher gave me back the report*, the sentence should read:

Correct: After giving a stern lecture on the necessity of checking the validity of our sources, the teacher gave **Jonah and me** back the report we had turned in at the beginning of the week.

Occasionally, however, an underlined subject or object pronoun will appear without the word *and.*

Incorrect: <u>To</u> **we** students, it seems awfully unfair that school should start at 7:30 a.m.

Correct: <u>To</u> **us** students, it seems awfully unfair that school should start at 7:30 a.m.

When this is the case, there are several ways to determine whether a pronoun is correct.

First, you can use the following rule: **any pronoun that follows a preposition must be an object pronoun.** *We* cannot be correct because it is a subject pronoun, and it follows *to*, which is a preposition.

You can also simply cross out the noun after the pronoun (in this case, *students*). Would you ever say, *To we it seems awfully unfair?* Probably not. So you wouldn't say, *To we students it seems awfully unfair* either.

Important: *Between* is always paired with *me*, NOT with *I.*

Incorrect: Although the start of the movie was delayed, I still missed the first few scenes because the meeting between **my boss and I** ran much later than expected.

Correct: Although the start of the movie was delayed, I still missed the first few scenes because the meeting between **my boss and me** ran much later than expected.

This error is tested frequently on the SAT, and quick recognition of it can save you a lot of time. There are no exceptions to it.

Pronoun Case Exercises

In the following sentences, fix any pronoun case error that appears. Some of the sentences may not contain an error. (Answers p. 149, Official Guide question list p. 132)

1. Although our parents have little difficulty distinguishing between my twin sister and I [*me*], our teachers are much more easily fooled.

2. For we [*us, our*] voters, it is exceedingly difficult to choose between the two candidates because their positions on so many issues are so similar that they are virtually indistinguishable.

3. After listening patiently to our admittedly flimsy excuses, the principal decided to sentence Akiko and I [*me*] to a week of detention.

4. Along with our project, the professor handed Shalini and I [*me*] a note requesting that we remain after class in order to discuss our research methods with her.

5. Evidently moved by the strength of their testimony, the jury awarded Tom and him a two million dollar settlement for the injuries they had sustained in the accident.

6. The conversation between my supervisor and me went surprisingly well despite the numerous disputes we had engaged in over the past several weeks.

7. When the gubernatorial candidate arrived at the auditorium to give a speech, we found it [*him*] nearly impossible to distinguish between she and her assistant, so similar were they in height and appearance.

8. My lab partner and myself [*I, me*] were awarded first prize in the science fair for our work on the breakdown of insulin production in people who suffer from diabetes.

9. Walking through Yellowstone National Park, Jordan, Sam, and me [*I*] were so astonished by our surroundings that we found ourselves at a loss for words.

10. An unfamiliar subject when the class began, Roman history became increasingly fascinating to he [*him*] and Alexis over the course of the semester.

CUMULATIVE REVIEW #1

The following exercises cover all of the categories discussed thus far. For each sentence, fix the error and label its category. Some sentences may not contain an error. (Answers p. 149)

1. The works of Paulus Barbus has [*have*] largely been lost, although many editions of his works were both published and esteemed during the Renaissance.

2. Among the writings of linguist Margaret Landon was [*were*] a dictionary of the Native American Degueño dialect and a comparative study of Central American languages.

3. Many runners, even those who train regularly, do not have a clear sense of their potential since one tends [*they tend*] to stick to an established distance.

4. For centuries, Norwegians hang [*have*] dolls dressed as witches in their kitchens because they believe that such figures have the power to keep pots from burning over.

5. When the fossil of an enormous ancient penguin was unearthed in Peru, archaeologists discovered that their [*its*] feathers were brown and gray rather than black and white.

6. Although the waiter offered to bring Ramon and I [*me*] a list of desserts, we had already eaten too much and found the prospect of more food unappetizing.

7. At the meeting point of the Alaskan and the Aleutian mountains rises [*rise*] an immense alpine tundra and sparkling lakes, which give way to thundering waterfalls.

8. Since 1896, the Kentucky Derby – arguably the best-known horse race in America – has took [*taken*] place on a track measuring one-and-a-quarter miles.

9. Sultan Suleyman I, known as Suleyman the Magnificent, has been [*was*] responsible for the expansion of the Ottoman Empire from Asia Minor to North Africa before his death in 1566.

10. Long Island was the setting for F. Scott Fitzgerald's novel *The Great Gatsby*, but finding traces of them there [*it*] is as much a job for the imagination as it is for a map and a guidebook.

11. The country's government is so worried about alienating voters that it is proceeding very cautiously in limiting benefits such as unemployment insurance.

12. People who seek out extreme sports such as skydiving and mountain climbing often do so because he or she [*they*] feels compelled to explore the limits of their endurance.

13. While one is [*You are*] cooking a recipe that involves large quantities of hot chili peppers, you should generally try to avoid touching your eyes.

14. Chicago's Sears Tower was the tallest office building in the world for nearly thirty years, a distinction it has lost only upon the completion of the Taipei 101 Tower in 2004.

15. Born in Spain in 1881, Pablo Picasso ~~will~~ *would* become one of the most celebrated and revolutionary painters of the twentieth century because of his invention of the cubist style.

16. The Sherlock Holmes form of mystery novel, which ~~revolve~~ *revolves* around a baffling crime solved by a master detective and his assistant, contrasts the scientific method with prevailing superstitions.

17. In the early years of the fourteenth century, Pope Clement V moved the papacy to the French city of Avignon and ~~leaving~~ *left* Rome prey to the ambitions of local overlords.

18. Along the side of the winding country road stretch a long line of pine trees and a low, crumbling stone wall covered with both moss and snow.

19. Although the two books recount the same series of events, they do ~~it~~ *so* from different perspectives and are not intended to be read in any particular order.

20. Roberta and her supervisor, Ms. Altschuler, were commended at the company's dinner for ~~her~~ *Ms. Altschuler* exceptional performance during the previous year.

21. Some of the book's passages wonderfully describe the physical realities of the Middle Ages, while others reflect the dazzling debates that would later lead to the Renaissance.

22. South Africa experienced a series of massive and devastating blackouts in 2008, and consequently ~~they~~ *it has* have been rationing electricity ever since that time.

23. Though extremely long, the meeting between my advisor and ~~I~~ *me* was unusually productive because it provided me with many new ways of thinking about a familiar subject.

24. Although prairie dogs were once on the verge of extinction, their numbers have ~~rose~~ *risen* to pre-twentieth century levels because of the work of the environmentalists who lobbied for their salvation.

25. In response to ~~be~~ *being* criticized for the poor nutritional value of its food, the restaurant chain has altered its menu to include more healthful options.

3. ADJECTIVES VS. ADVERBS

Adjectives modify nouns or pronouns.

> The dog is **wild**.

> The wave became **calm**.

> It is not **difficult** to accomplish.

Adverbs modify verbs, adjectives, or other adverbs.

> He speaks **slowly**.

> She runs **very quickly**.

> Mr. Samson is a **highly** interesting conversationalist.

Adverbs are usually formed by adding –ly to the adjective.

For adjectives that already end in –y, the adverb is formed by adding –ily.

Adjective	**Adverb**
Slow	Slowly
Calm	Calmly
Quiet	Quietly
Hasty	Hastily
Noisy	Noisily

Irregularly formed adjectives such as *good* (adj.) → *well* (adv.) are not tested on the SAT.

If there are two consecutive adjectives not separated by a comma, one of the adjectives must often be changed to an adverb.

Incorrect:	That book is only **mild** engaging.
Correct:	That book is only **mildly** engaging.

Important: on the SAT, adverbs and adjectives are switched only with one another.

If an adjective is underlined, replace it with the adverb; if an adverb is underlined, replace it with the adjective. If the original version is correct, there cannot be an error. Most often, adverbs will be replaced with adjectives, although the reverse does appear occasionally.

Adverb Replaced by Adjective

Incorrect: The patient recovered **quick**, although he had been very ill earlier in the week.

Correct: The patient recovered **quickly**, although he had been very ill earlier in the week.

Adjective Replaced by Adverb

Incorrect: Because the man looked somewhat **oddly**, he received a number of suspicious glances from people who passed him on the street.

Correct: Because the man looked somewhat **odd**, he received a number of suspicious glances from people who passed him on the street.

The incorrect version of the above sentence means that the manner in which the man was performing the act of looking was odd, not that other people perceived his appearance to be odd. While it is grammatically acceptable, its meaning is also highly illogical under normal circumstances.

Adjective vs. Adverb Exercises

For the following exercises, fix any error in adjective or adverb usage. Some of the sentences may not contain an error. (Answers p. 150, Official Guide question list p. 132)

1. In many countries that lack medical workers, citizens with little or no professional preparation have been successfully trained to substitute for doctors and nurses.

2. Explorers who arrived at the central stretch of the Nile River ~~excited~~ *excitedly* reported the discovery of elegant temples and pyramids, ruins of the ancient Kushite civilization.

3. By looking ~~close~~ *closely* at DNA markers, scientists may have found traces of the first African hunter-gatherers to migrate to other continents.

4. Although the room appeared tidy at first glance, we saw upon closer inspection that books, pens, and pieces of paper had been scattered haphazardly beneath a desk.

5. When examined under a microscope, the beaker of water revealed a hodgepodge of microscopic drifters that looked quite differently from other sea creatures.

6. When Mt. Vesuvius first began to show signs of eruption, many of the people living at the base of the volcano ~~hasty~~ *hastily* abandoned their villages to seek cover in nearby forests.

7. The archaeologists were lauded for their discovery of the ancient city, once a ~~dense~~ *densely* populated urban area that profited from the trade of precious metals.

8. During an era noted for its barbarity, the ancient city of Persepolis, located in modern-day southern Iran, was a relatively cosmopolitan place.

   副词 + 形容词 ✓

9. Italian nobleman Cesare Borgia was ruthless and vain, but he was also a brilliant Renaissance figure who was ~~exceeding~~ *exceedingly* well-educated in the classics.

10. Though few people believe that human beings are entirely rational, a world governed by anti-Enlightenment principles would surely be ~~infinite~~ *infinitely* worse than one governed by Voltaire and Locke.

11. Lake Pergusa, the only naturally occurring lake in Sicily, is surrounded by a well-known racing circuit that was created in the 1960's and that has hosted many international sporting events since that time.

12. Even when his theme is the struggle to find a place in a seemingly irrational cosmos, Oscar Wilde writes with lively sympathy and hopefulness.

44

4. PARALLEL STRUCTURE I: LISTS

In any given list or **series** of three or more items, each item should appear in the exact same format: noun, noun, and noun; verb, verb, and verb; or gerund, gerund, and gerund. Any inconsistency is incorrect.

"List" parallelism questions appear primarily in the Error-Identification section, although they do sometimes appear in Fixing Sentences as well.

List with nouns

Incorrect: Changes in wind circulation patterns, runoff from sewage, and **using** chemical fertilizers can lead to the creation of ocean waters low in oxygen and inhospitable to marine life.

Correct: Changes in wind circulation patterns, runoff from sewage, and **use** of chemical fertilizers can lead to the creation of ocean waters low in oxygen and inhospitable to marine life.

List with verbs

Incorrect: When Yukio arrives home from soccer practice, he makes himself a snack, sits down at his desk, and **then he will start** his homework.

Correct: When Yukio arrives home from soccer practice, he makes himself a snack, sits down at his desk, and **starts** his homework.

List with gerunds

Incorrect: Because they have a highly developed sense of vision, most lizards communicate by gesturing with their limbs, changing their colors, or **to display** their athletic abilities.

Correct: Because they have a highly developed sense of vision, most lizards communicate by gesturing with their limbs, changing their colors, or **displaying** their athletic abilities.

Parallel Structure I: List Exercises

In the following sentences, identify and correct any error in parallel structure that appears. Some of the sentences may not contain an error. (Answers p. 151, Official Guide question list p. 133)

1. Lady Jane Grey, known as the nine-day queen, was renowned for her sweetness, her beauty, and being subjected [*her ...ion*] to the whims of her mother.

2. Mediterranean cooking is best known for its reliance on fresh produce, whole grains, and it uses significant amounts of olive oil as well.

3. The biggest beneficiaries of the Grateful Dead archive may prove to be business scholars who are discovering that the Dead were visionaries in the way they created customer value, promoted networking, and implemented strategic business planning.

4. Knife injuries acquired while cooking should be washed thoroughly with a disinfectant, covered completely, and then you should apply pressure to them. [*have pressure applied*]

5. Seeing the Grand Canyon, standing in front of a beautiful piece of art, and to listen [*listening*] to a beautiful symphony are all experiences that may inspire awe.

6. Neighbors of the proposed park argue that an amphitheater would draw more traffic, disrupt their neighborhood, and their only patch of open space would diminish.

7. Evidence suggests that the aging brain retains and even increases its capacity for resilience, growth, and having a sense of well-being.

8. Antiques are typically objects that show some degree of craftsmanship or attention to design, and they are considered desirable because of their beauty, rarity, or being useful*ness*

9. Spiders use a wide range of strategies to capture prey, including trapping it in sticky webs, lassoing it with sticky bolas, and to mimic [*mimicing*] other insects in order to avoid detection.

10. According to medical authorities at the Mayo Clinic, building muscle can boost metabolism, aiding in weight loss, and increase stamina and focus.

5. PREPOSITIONS AND IDIOMS

Prepositions indicate position, either in terms of **location** or **time**. They are always followed by nouns or pronouns.

> **After** the party
> **On** the table
> **For** me and you

Certain verbs and nouns must be followed by specific prepositions.

> Incorrect: A familiarity **in** Latin is useful for anyone who wishes to pursue serious study of a modern romance language.
>
> Correct: A familiarity **with** Latin is useful for anyone who wishes to pursue serious study of a modern romance language.

In the above sentence, the phrase *a familiarity* always requires the preposition *with*; any other preposition is incorrect.

A fixed phrase such as *a familiarity with* is known as an **idiom**. Idioms are not correct or incorrect for any logical reason; they simply reflect the fact that certain phrases have evolved to be considered standard usage.

On the SAT, a preposition may also appear where none is necessary.

> Incorrect: The students have been **criticizing about** the administration's decision to begin classes half an hour earlier on most days.
>
> Correct: The students have been **criticizing** the administration's decision to begin classes half an hour earlier on most days.

In addition, when a sentence contains two verbs that require different prepositions, a separate preposition must follow each verb. Very occasionally, the SAT will omit one of the prepositions.

> Incorrect: After her lecture, the author announced that she would **accept questions** and **respond to** audience members.
>
> Correct: After her lecture, the author announced that she would **accept questions from** and **respond to** audience members.

Unfortunately, preposition/idiom questions are among the most difficult to study for because there are thousands of possible errors and no real pattern to the prepositions tested. It is therefore not terribly constructive to spend your time memorizing long lists of phrases. In general, though, if a given preposition sounds somewhat odd, it's probably wrong. This is one case that requires you to trust your ear. That said, I am including a list of common idioms, including a number that have appeared on previous tests.

(Pre)occupation with
Consistent/inconsistent with
Sympathize with
Correlate with
Identify with
Familiar/unfamiliar with
In contrast to (BUT: contrast with)
Be native to (BUT: be a native of)
Have a tendency toward
Biased toward
Recommend to
Listen to
Try to (NOT: try and)
Prefer x to y
Devoted to
A threat to/threaten to
Central to
Unique to
Similar to
Parallel to
An alternative to
Enter into
Have insight into
Interested in
Succeed in/at
Adept in/at
Have confidence in
Engage in/with
Take pride in
Insist on
Focus on
Rely on
Reflect on
Dwell on
Draw (up)on
Based on
Suspicious of
Devoid of
A proponent of
A command of
A source of
An offer of
An understanding/knowledge of
Approve/disapprove of
Take advantage of
In awe of
A variety/plethora of

In the hope(s) of
Characteristic/typical of
Convinced of
Consist of
Composed/comprised of
In recognition of
Capable/incapable of
A mastery of
Have an appreciation of/for
Criticize for
Necessary for
Prized for
Endure/last for
Wait for
Watch/look (out) for
Responsible for
Compensate for
Strive for
Have a tolerance for
Famous/Celebrated for
Recognized/known for
Named for/after
Worry about
Complain about
Wonder about
Curious about
Think about
Bring about
Be particular about
Protect from/against
Defend from/against
Apparent from
Predate by
Followed by
Confused/puzzled/perplexed by
Accompanied by
Encouraged by
Outraged by
Surprised/stunned/shocked by
Amazed/awed by
Impressed by
Known as/to be
Far from
Differ(ent) from
Refrain from
Have power/control over
Mull over

Preposition and Idiom Exercises

In the following sentences, identify and correct any preposition error that appears. Some of the sentences may not contain an error. (Answers p. 151, Official Guide question list p. 132)

1. The Wave, a sandstone rock formation located near the Utah-Arizona border, is famous on *[for]* its colorful forms and rugged, unpaved trails.

2. Frank Lloyd Wright was a proponent for *[of]* organic architecture, a philosophy that he incorporated into structures such as the Fallingwater residence.

3. Although the author's diaries provide a wealth of information about her daily interests and concerns, they fail to present a comprehensive picture of her life.

4. As an old man, Rousseau acknowledged that it was arrogant of him to promote virtues that he was unable to embody into *[in]* his own life.

5. In contrast against *[to]* his contemporaries, whose work he viewed as conventional and uninspiring, Le Corbusier insisted on using modern industrial techniques to construct buildings.

6. Beethoven, who strongly sympathized to *[with]* the ideals of the French Revolution, originally planned to name the *Eroica* symphony after Napoleon.

7. Choreographer Alvin Ailey Jr. is credited to *[with]* popularizing modern dance and integrating traditional African movements into his works.

8. As a result of its new program, which consists in *[of]* three world premiers, the ballet troupe has become one of the few eminent companies to promote choreographic innovation.

9. The Industrial Revolution, which began toward the end of the eighteenth century, marked the start of the modern era in both Europe and the United States.

10. Created in Jamaica during the late 1960's, reggae music emerged out of a number of sources that ranged from traditional African songs and chants to contemporary jazz and blues.

11. Since reports given by the various witnesses at the crime scene were highly inconsistent to *[with]* one another, the detective was thoroughly perplexed.

12. Teachers have begun to note with alarm that the amount of time their students spend playing video games and surfing the Internet has severely impacted their ability to focus at *[on]* a single task for an extended period of time.

13. During the early decades of the Heian Empire, a person who lacked a thorough knowledge in *[of]* Chinese could never be considered fully educated.

14. Both bizarre and familiar, fairy tales are intended to be told rather than read, and they possess a truly inexhaustible power on *[over]* children and adults alike.

49

6. FAULTY COMPARISONS

Faulty Comparison questions appear primarily in the Error-Identification section, typically in the last three questions and often as question #27. They do, however, also appear in Fixing Sentences, usually at in the last three questions as well. The general rule for forming comparisons is as follows:

Compare things to things and people to people.

Faulty comparisons can often be anticipated by the presence of a comparison such as *more than*, *less than*, or *(un)like*.

Singular faulty comparison

Incorrect:	In twentieth century America, Norman Rockwell's art was better known than Russian painter Wassily Kandinsky.

In the above sentence, art (a thing) is being compared to Wassily Kandinsky (a person). In order to make the sentence correct, art must be compared to art. Most people will instinctively correct the sentence as follows:

> In twentieth century America, Norman Rockwell's **art** was better known than Russian painter **Wassily Kandinsky's art.**

The SAT, however, will ask you to fix such errors with the phrase *that of* when they appear in Fixing Sentences.

Correct:	In twentieth century America, Norman Rockwell's **art** was better known than **that of** Russian painter Wassily Kandinsky.
BUT NOT:	In twentieth century America, Norman Rockwell's **art** was better known than **that of** Russian painter **Wassily Kandinsky's**. (= the art of Wassily Kandinsky's *art*)

Plural faulty comparison

A plural faulty comparison should be corrected with the phrase *those of*.

Incorrect:	In Victorian England, Charles Dickens' **novels** were more widely read than **Victor Hugo.**
Correct:	In Victorian England, Charles Dickens' **novels** were more widely read than **those of** Victor Hugo.
BUT NOT:	In Victorian England, Charles Dickens' **novels** were more widely read than **those of** **Victor Hugo's**. (= the novels of Victor Hugo's *novels*)

Important: the inclusion of an author or artist's name in a sentence often indicates a faulty comparison.

Exception to the Person vs. Thing Rule

Occasionally, the SAT will throw in a faulty comparison that does not involve comparing things and people but rather two things. In such cases, you must make sure that the two things being compared are truly equivalent.

Incorrect: Unlike a train, the length of a tram is usually limited to one or two cars, which may run either on train tracks or directly on the street.

What is being compared here?

1) A train

2) The length of a tram

Even though both *train* and *length* are nouns, they are not equivalent. We must either compare a train to a train or a length to a length.

Correct: Unlike **the length of/that of** a train, the length of a tram is usually limited to one or two cars, which may run either on train tracks or directly on the street.

Faulty Comparison Exercises

In the following sentences, identify and correct any faulty comparison that appears. Some of the sentences may not contain an error. (Answers p. 152, Official Guide question list p. 134)

1. The writings of John Locke, unlike Thomas Hobbes, emphasize the idea that people are by nature both reasonable and tolerant. *those of*

2. Company officials announced that there would be no major changes made to the eligibility requirements for its benefits package, an offering that makes its plan more generous than other major retailers. *those of*

3. As part of its application, the university asks students to compose a short essay in which they compare their educational interests and goals to that of other students. *those*

4. David Cerny, the daring Czech sculptor who shook the eastern European art world during the 1990's, has been accused of pursuing an artistic and political rebellion that is bolder and louder than his predecessors. *those of*

5. Unlike dyslexia, people with dysgraphia often suffer from fine motor-skills problems that leave them unable to write clearly. *People*

6. Today's neuroscientists, unlike thirty years ago, have access to sophisticated instrumentation that has only been developed over the past decade. *those of*

7. Norwegian doctors prescribe fewer antibiotics than any other country, so people do not have a chance to develop resistance to many kinds of drug-resistant infections. *those of*

8. Archaeologists have long been far more puzzled by members of the Saqqaq culture, the oldest known inhabitants of Greenland, than by those of other prehistoric North American cultures. *that*

9. The reproduction of ciliates, unlike other organisms, occurs when a specimen splits in half and grows a completely new individual ~~from each piece.~~ *that of other organisms*

10. The hands and feet of Ardi, the recently discovered human ancestor who lived 4.4 million years ago, are much like *those of* other primitive extinct apes.

11. At the age of twenty-four, playwright Thornton Wilder was balding and bespectacled, and his clothes were like a *those of* much older man.

12. In ancient Greece, women were not allowed to vote or hold property, their status differing from slaves only in name. *that of*

7. WORD PAIRS

On the SAT, the following pairs of words (or **correlative conjunctions**) must appear together; any deviation is considered incorrect. While the following list is fairly extensive, *(n)either...(n)or*, *not only...but also*, and *as...as* are the most commonly tested pairs, and you should therefore focus on learning them first.

A. Either...or

Either the company's president **or** her assistant will be present at the meeting later on this afternoon.

B. Neither...nor

According to the politician, **neither** the recent crisis **nor** any other period of economic turmoil had been caused by environmental protection policies.

C. Not only...but also

Apples **not only** taste very good, **but** they **also** contain numerous essential vitamins and minerals.

D. Both...and

The news station, while successful, trails its competitor in **both** the morning **and** the evening news broadcast.

E. As...as

Although she began training later than many other gymnasts, Jessica is just **as** good an athlete **as** many of her competitors.

F. Between...and

When purchasing a computer, many people find it difficult to decide **between** buying a Macintosh **and** buying a different brand.

G. So/such...that

Roberto's birthday cake was **so** large **that** the guests at his party found they were unable to finish all of it.

Roberto had **such** a large birthday cake **that** the guests at his party found they were unable able to finish all of it.

H. More/less...than

Although Jane Austen's novels are **more** widely read **than** those of her contemporaries, Austen was hardly the only female author in nineteenth-century England.

I. Just as...so

Just as Thomas Edison is known for inventing the electric light bulb, **so** is Albert Einstein is known for developing a theory of general relativity.

J. From...to

The shift **from** monarchy **to** totalitarianism occurred in Russia over a remarkably short period of time in the early twentieth century.

K. At once...and

The politician is **at once** controversial because of his refusal to compromise **and** beloved because of his personal charisma.

L. No sooner...than

No sooner had the senator announced her intention not run for re-election **than** the media began to speculate about the next stage of her political career.

M. Not so much...as

Although her plays have garnered praise from many critics, Toni Morrison is known **not so much** for her theatrical works **as** she is for her novels.

Word Pair Exercises

In the following sentences, identify and correct any word pair error that appears. Some of the sentences may not contain an error. (Answers p. 152, Official Guide question list p. 134)

1. Across the United States, companies are taking advantage not only of retirees' expertise and in addition [*but also*] their desire to stay involved and engaged with the world through work.

2. After weeks of protests, the workers have finally agreed to discuss the overtime dispute with both outside mediators in addition to [*and*] company officials.

3. Often stereotyped as savants because of their depictions in movies such as *Rain Man*, people on the autistic spectrum are typically neither superhuman memory machines or [*nor*] incapable of performing everyday tasks.

4. Obedience to authority is not only a way for rulers to keep order in totalitarian states, and it is [*but also*] the foundation on which such states exist.

5. Finding himself cornered, the thief was forced to choose between leaping ten stories to the ground or [*and*] surrendering to the police.

6. Audiences find the play at once amusing because of the comedic skills of its leading actors, but it is [*and*] also tedious because of its excessive length.

7. It is almost as difficult to find consistent information about the Fort Pillow incident during the American Civil War than [*as*] it is to determine the moral significance of its outcome.

8. So great was the surplus of food created by the ancient Mesopotamians that it led to the establishment of the first complex civilization in human history.

9. Because the Articles of Confederation did not provide for the creation of either executive agencies and [*nor*] judiciary institutions, they were rejected in favor of the Constitution.

10. Just as moral intelligence, an innate sense of right and wrong, allowed human societies to flourish, so did a strong sense of hierarchy allow canine societies to thrive.

11. One of the main effects of industrialization was the shift from a society in which women worked at home with [*to*] one in which women worked in factories and brought home wages to their families.

12. Over the past decade, Internet usage has become so pervasive and [*that*] many psychologists are beginning to study its effect on the lives of young people.

CUMULATIVE REVIEW #2

The following exercises cover all of the categories discussed thus far. For each sentence, fix the error and label its category. Some sentences may not contain an error. (Answers p. 153)

1. Three million years ago, the creation of the Panama Isthmus wreaked ecological havoc by triggering extinctions, diverting ocean currents, and it also transformed the climate.
   transforming

2. The professor's appearance was very striking to everyone in the room, for not only was he extremely thin, but his height ~~also~~ surpassed a normal man. *also*
   that of

3. Although many children want to read digitized books and would read for fun more frequently if they could obtain them, most do not want to give up traditional print books completely.

4. Before Staughton Lynd vanished from intellectual society, he was one of the most recognizable and controversial thinkers that the United States had ever produced.

5. Although clarinetist Artie Shaw spent far more of his long life writing prose than making music, a careful look at his compositions reveals that he was a musician of genius.

6. At the bottom of the staircase stands an umbrella rack, a large mirror, and a table containing a lacquered vase and a bowl of goldfish.

7. Although the movie has alternately been described as a social satire, a comedy of manners, and being a Greek tragedy, it contains elements of all three.

8. In the early nineteenth century, a number of adventurous artists and writers flocked to Lake Geneva to savor about its inspiring mountain scenery and serene atmosphere.

9. The Mayflower pilgrims who landed in the New World in 1620 were poorly equipped to navigate their new environment and struggled ~~in surviving~~ during the winter.
   to survive

10. *The Europeans*, a short novel by Henry James, contrasts the behavior and attitudes of two visitors from Italy with ~~their~~ cousins from New England.
    those of

11. Thomas Jefferson believed that prisoners of war should be treated humane and, during the Revolutionary War, requested that British and Hessian generals be held in mansions rather than behind bars.
    humanely

12. Ten years after Native American chief Squanto had been kidnapped and brought to Spain, he returned home and befriended some of the first English colonists.

13. The company's board voted in favor of conducting an inquiry into the conduct of several employees suspected of embezzling funds.
    into

14. Although the best-selling author had ~~grew~~ comfortable with her role as a public figure, when given the choice, she preferred to be alone.
    grown

15. While reactions to the exhibition were mixed, neither the artist's exceptional showmanship nor his astonishing technique were questioned by the spectators. *was*

16. Unlike *those of* Nathaniel Hawthorne and F. Scott Fitzgerald, Jonathan Franzen's novels have not yet received unanimous acceptance as classic works of literature.

17. Supporters of bilingual education often imply that students miss a great deal by not *being* to be taught in the language spoken by their parents and siblings at home.

18. A small frontier town in the 1830's, Chicago had grown to more than two million residents by 1909, and some demographers predicted that it will soon be the largest city on earth. *would*

19. John Breckinridge, who came closest *to* to defeating Abraham Lincoln in the 1860 election, held strong personal convictions that made it difficult for him to navigate a moderate course in an era of extremes.

20. According to many urban planners, the most efficient way of building prosperous cities is to make it *them* not only attractive but also healthy.

21. The origin of the senators' proposal dates to the mid-twentieth century, making it one of the most eagerly anticipated pieces of legislation this year.

22. Societies located at river deltas tend to foster innovation because of their flexibility to deal *in dealing* with potentially shifting landscapes.

23. In general, the design and management of highways and parking lots are handed over to traffic engineers, whose decisions heavily influence people's behavior within those spaces.

24. The City Beautiful movement, which swept America during the late nineteenth century, was embodied in the stately lines, formal balance, and grand scale of the buildings constructed during that period.

25. When the Cooper Union for the Advancement of Science and Art opened its doors in 1859, it represented for Peter Cooper the realization of an idea that had occupied his imagination for nearly thirty years.

8. NOUN AGREEMENT

Nouns must agree in number when they are connected by a **linking verb** such as *to be* or *to become*: singular subjects must go with singular nouns, and plural subjects must go with plural nouns.

Singular noun agreement

Incorrect: After visiting the physics laboratory with their class, <u>Michael and Lakeisha</u> were inspired to become **a scientific researcher** when they grew up.

Correct: After visiting the physics laboratory with their class, <u>Michael and Lakeisha</u> were inspired to become **scientific researchers** when they grew up.

Plural noun agreement

Usually, the SAT will pair a plural subject with a singular noun, as in the above sentence. Occasionally, however, it will pair a singular subject with a plural noun.

Incorrect: <u>Mozart</u>, along with Haydn and Beethoven, were **members** of the First Viennese School of classical music.

Correct: <u>Mozart</u>, along with Haydn and Beethoven, was **a member** of the First Viennese School of classical music.

You can identify and correct such sentences by treating them as simple subject-verb agreement questions. Since the sentences contains a non-essential clause, simply cross out the clause and the error will reveal itself:

> Mozart…were members of the First Viennese School of classical music.

Since Mozart is one person, he must have been *a member* rather than *members* of the First Viennese School.

Important: Sentences testing noun agreement will often include phrase "as a + profession" (e.g. writer, scientist, photographer). Any time a profession is mentioned, check the noun agreement first.

Noun agreement and faulty comparison errors are the only two common errors that involve underlined nouns. In virtually all other cases, underlined nouns can be automatically eliminated as error options.

Noun Agreement Exercises

In the following sentences, identify and correct any noun agreement error that appears. Some of the sentences may not contain an error. (Answers p. 154, Official Guide question list p. 134)

1. Both Wilfrid Daniels and Leonard Chuene, now powerful figures in South African sports, grew up as ~~a~~ promising athlete*s* who could never compete internationally because of apartheid.

2. Because they evolved in the warm climate of Africa before spreading into Europe, modern humans had ~~a~~ bod*ies* adapted to tracking prey over great distances.

3. Many of the great classical composers, including Mozart, Bach, and Mendelssohn, were born into musical families and began studying ~~an~~ instrument*s* seriously when they were ~~a child~~ *children*

4. Thomas Abercrombie, along with his older brother, became a photographer after building a camera out of mirrors, discarded lenses, and scraps of plastic.

5. Known for creating a unique sound and style through the use of non-traditional instruments such as the French horn, Miles Davis joined Louis Armstrong and Ella Fitzgerald as *one of* the greatest jazz musicians of the twentieth century.

6. Inscribed ostrich eggs and pieces of shell jewelry are ~~an~~ example*s* of early human attempts to record thoughts symbolically rather than literally.

7. Joseph Charles Jones and George Bundy Smith, who fought for African-Americans as ~~a~~ civil rights activist*s* during the early 1960's, were separated for nearly forty years after being arrested in Alabama in 1961.

8. The Opium Wars, which introduced the power of western armies and technologies to China, marked the end of Shanghai and Ningpo as ~~an~~ independent port-cit*ies*

9. Although neither came from a literary family, novelists Amy Tan and Maxine Hong Kingston became ~~an~~ avid reader*s* while growing up near San Francisco.

10. The military and the orchestra are examples of distinct entities that must interact with their own subsystems or units in order to survive.

9. COMPARATIVES VS. SUPERLATIVES

Comparative

Comparative = -ER form of adjective or *MORE + ADJECTIVE*

Examples: smaller, larger, faster, brighter, more interesting, more exciting

Comparatives are used only when comparing **two** things:

Incorrect: Between the rhino and the hippo, the rhino is the **heavier** creature, while the hippo is the **most** ferocious.

Correct: Between the rhino and the hippo, the rhino is the **heavier** creature, while the hippo is the **more** ferocious.

Superlative

Superlative = -EST form of adjective or *MOST + ADJECTIVE*

Examples: smallest, largest, fastest, brightest, most interesting, most exciting

Superlative are used only when comparing **three or more** things:

Incorrect: The executive interviewed <u>five</u> candidates for the position and ultimately decided that Sergei was the **more** qualified.

Correct: The executive interviewed <u>five</u> candidates for the position and ultimately decided that Sergei was the **most** qualified.

Important: Whenever you see a comparative underlined, replace it with the superlative and vice-versa. Comparatives and superlatives are switched only with one another.

Comparative vs. Superlative Exercises

In the following sentences, identify and correct any error in the use of comparatives or superlatives. Some of the sentences may not contain an error. (Answers p. 154, Official Guide question list p. 135)

1. Between the black leopard and the snow leopard, the black leopard possesses the more effective camouflage while the snow leopard has the most striking tail.

2. Of the two top-ranked players on the university's tennis team, Ken is seen as the more likely candidate for a national championship.

3. Asked to choose between Gary Kasparov and Bobby Fischer, most chess experts would declare Fischer to be the better player.

4. While triathlons, competitions that consist of swimming, biking, and running, are drawing increasing numbers of participants, athletic events devoted to a single sport remain most popular.

5. Although many viewers find his work on color and geometric shapes to be excessively abstract and inaccessible, Paul Klee is nonetheless regarded as one of the most innovative artists of the early twentieth century.

6. Confronted with two equally qualified finalists, the awards committee is struggling to determine which one is most deserving of the top prize.

7. When the influenza virus, one of the most commonly diagnosed diseases in the United States, was formally recognized in 1933, many doctors believed that a cure would be found shortly.

8. Though London has a longstanding reputation as a city whose weather is defined by rain and fog, in reality Paris receives the highest amount of rainfall each year.

9. Both poodles and pugs are known for making excellent pets, but between the two breeds, pugs have the sweetest disposition while poodles are smarter.

10. Although mental puzzles such as Sudoku can help people keep their minds nimble as they age, physical exercise such as biking or running is most effective.

10. RELATIVE PRONOUNS:
Who, Which, When, Where & That

Who(m) vs. Which

Use *who* or *whom*, not *which*, when referring to people.*

Incorrect: King Henry VIII was a British <u>monarch</u> **which** ruled England during the Tudor period and was known for his many wives.

Correct: King Henry VIII was a British <u>monarch</u> **who** ruled England during the Tudor period and was known for his many wives.

Very Important: *who vs. whom* is not tested on the SAT. If *whom* is underlined, ignore it. That said, *which* will very occasionally be used incorrectly to replace *whom* rather than *who*. You will not, however, be responsible for supplying the correction, only for recognizing that *which* is being incorrectly used to refer to a person.

Incorrect: The members of the youth orchestra, **many of which** have been studying music since a very young age, are frequently praised for the exceptional quality of their playing.

Correct: The members of the youth orchestra, **many of whom** have been studying music since a very young age, are frequently praised for the exceptional quality of their playing.

Whom is used to refer to an object, and in the above sentence, it is the object of the preposition *of*.

Which vs. That

Which = Comma

That = No comma

Which is always preceded by a comma and is used to set off a non-essential clause.

Incorrect: The movie, **that** opened last Friday, has earned rave reviews from critics and fans alike.

Correct: The movie, **which** opened last Friday, has earned rave reviews from critics and fans alike.

That is never preceded by a comma and is used to set off an essential clause.

Incorrect: The movie **which** opened last Friday has earned rave reviews from critics and fans alike.

Correct: The movie **that** opened last Friday has earned rave reviews from critics and fans alike.

*Although *that* can also be used to refer to people, the SAT generally prefers *who*.

Where

Where is for places (physical locations) only. To refer to books, use *in which*.

Incorrect: The novel *Life of Pi*, written by Yann Martel, is a story **where** the protagonist survives on a raft in the ocean for nearly a year, accompanied only by a tiger.

Correct: The novel *Life of Pi*, written by Yann Martel, is a story **in which** the protagonist survives on a raft in the ocean for nearly a year, accompanied only by a tiger.

When a place is being referred to, however, *where* and *in which* are equally acceptable. *In which* is simply a bit more formal.

Correct: Although Einstein predicted the presence of black holes, regions of space **where** gravity is so intense that not even light can escape, he had difficulty believing that they could actually exist.

Correct: Although Einstein predicted the presence of black holes, regions of space **in which** gravity is so intense that not even light can escape, he had difficulty believing that they could actually exist.

When

When is for times/time periods.

Incorrect: The Middle Ages was a period **where** many farmers were bound to the lands they worked.

Correct: The Middle Ages was a period **when** many farmers were bound to the lands they worked.

Preposition + which is also acceptable.

Correct: The Middle Ages was a period **in/during which** many farmers were bound to the lands they worked.

Important: although the word *which* will often be wrong when it appears by itself, the construction *preposition + which* will virtually always be correct when it is underlined in the Error-Identification section.

Relative Pronoun Exercises

In the following sentences, identify and correct any relative pronoun error that appears. Some of the sentences may not contain an error. (Answers p. 155, Official Guide question list p. 135)

1. For delicate patients which *[who]* cannot handle the rigors of modern medicine, some doctors are now rejecting the assembly line of modern medical care for older, gentler options.

2. In its later years, the Bauhaus architectural movement became a kind of religion in which heretics had to be excommunicated by those who held the true light.

3. When readers which *[who]* get their news from electronic rather than printed sources send articles to their friends, they tend to choose ones that contain intellectually challenging topics.

4. In 1623, Galileo published a work where *[in which]* he championed the controversial theory of heliocentrism, thus provoking one of the greatest scientific controversies of his day.

5. In classical Athenian democracy, citizens which *[who]* failed to pay their debts were barred from attending assembly meetings and appearing in court in virtually any capacity.

6. Carol Bove, an artist who is known for her drawings and installations concerning the social and political movements of the 1960's, often found inspiration for her work in vintage books and magazines.

7. Researchers have claimed that subjects which *[who]* stood on a rapidly vibrating platform during an experiment were able to slightly improve their athletic performance for a short time afterward.

8. In his utopian novel *Walden Two*, B.F. Skinner invents a world in which emotions such as envy have become obsolete because people are conditioned as children to reject them.

9. One of the least popular of all the Romance languages, Romansch is traditionally spoken by people which *[who]* inhabit the southern regions of Switzerland.

10. The wave of fascination greeting the film's release is a phenomenon that seems worthy of attention, regardless of the movie's artistic merit.

11. DOUBLE NEGATIVES AND DOUBLE POSITIVES

Double Negative

Always use *any* with the words *scarcely* and *hardly*. On the SAT, *any* will usually be incorrectly replaced with *no*.

Incorrect: When I looked in the refrigerator, I realized that there was **scarcely/hardly no** milk left.

Correct: When I looked in the refrigerator, I realized that there was **scarcely/hardly any** milk left.

Double Positive

Never use *more* or *most* in addition to the comparative or superlative form of an adjective.

Comparative

Incorrect: When traveling over large distances, most people choose to go by airplane rather than by train because the airplane is the **more faster** option.

Correct: When traveling over large distances, most people choose to go by airplane rather than by train because the airplane is the **faster** option.

Superlative

Incorrect: Imitation, long considered the **most sincerest** form of flattery, may carry evolutionary benefits for both model and mimic alike.

Correct: Imitation, long considered the **sincerest** form of flattery, may carry evolutionary benefits for both model and mimic alike.

Double Negative and Double Positive Exercises

In the following sentences, identify and correct any double negative or double positive error that appears. Some of the sentences may not contain an error. (Answers p. 155, Official Guide question list p. 135)

1. When selecting a host city from among dozens of contenders, Olympic officials must take into consideration which one is most likeliest to benefit from the legacy of the games.

2. Although the plays of Lillian Hellman and Bertolt Brecht were met with great popularity during the 1920's, they are scarcely never performed anymore in the United States.

3. Since the advent of commercial flight and high-speed rail in the twentieth century, hardly no significant technological change has affected the traveling public.

4. An evolutionary adaptation that might have promised survival during prehistoric times is more likelier nowadays to produce diseases in modern humans.

5. Though the Panama Canal is hardly new, having opened nearly a hundred years ago, the idea of a waterway connecting the Atlantic and Pacific Oceans is significantly older than the canal itself.

6. The Indian sub-continent was home to some of the most earliest civilizations, ranging from urban society of the Indus Valley to the classical age of the Gupta Dynasty.

7. During the early days of cable television, many viewers were only able to access four channels, with reception being weakest in rural areas and most clearest in large cities.

8. The Industrial Revolution, which began in the late 1700's and lasted more than fifty years, was the period when machine power became more stronger than hand power.

9. Although many people have attempted to solve the mystery of Stonehenge, its purpose is hardly any clearer than it was centuries ago.

10. To thoroughly understand historical figures, we must study them not only in the bright light of the present but also in the more cloudier light of the circumstances they encountered in their own lifetimes.

12. CONJUNCTIONS

Conjunction questions test your ability to recognize logical connections between ideas.

There are three main types of conjunctions:

Continuers

Continuers are words such as *and*, *in addition*, *furthermore*, and *moreover*, which indicate that a sentence is continuing in the direction it began. The main continuer that appears in the Error-Identification section is *and*.

> Continuer: The sun streamed through the window into the living room, **and** its brightness was so great that it lit up the hall as well.

Contradictors

Contradictors are words such as *but*, *yet*, *although*, and *however* that indicate a sentence is shifting directions or introducing contradictory information.

> Contradictor: To remove about a quarter of a long, complicated book was close to an impossible task, **but** over the course of several months, the author accomplished it.

> Contradictor: To remove about a quarter of a long, complicated book was close to an impossible task; **however,** over the course of several months, the author accomplished it.

Cause and Effect

Common examples are *so*, *for*, *therefore*, *because*, and *since*. They indicate that an action or occurrence is causing a particular result, or that a particular result is occurring because of an action or occurrence.

> Cause/Effect: The first astronauts were required to undergo mental evaluation before their flight **because** the psychological danger inherent in space travel was judged to be as important as the physiological one.

There are two main kinds of conjunction errors:

1) Incorrect Conjunction Type

2) Double Conjunction

Incorrect Conjunction Type

In this error, a contradictor is most often replaced with a continuer:

Incorrect: Many runners attempt to complete a marathon, **and** many fail to do so because they lack the necessary stamina.

Correct: Many runners attempt to complete a marathon, **but** many fail to do so because they lack the necessary stamina.

An underlined conjunction in the Error-Identification section can signal a conjunction error. To figure out the relationship between the clauses and thus the correct conjunction, cross out the existing conjunction in order to avoid being prejudiced by it, then ask yourself whether the clauses express the same idea or opposing ideas.

Clause 1:   Many runners attempt to complete a marathon.

Clause 2:   Many fail to do so because they lack the necessary stamina.

Clearly, the second clause presents an opposing idea (*they fail to do so*), and therefore a transition that indicates opposition (*but*) is required.

Watch out for "when"

Sometimes, however, the relationship between the two clauses will be made less obvious, a trick that is often accomplished by replacing a clear-cut continuer or contradictor such as *and* or *but* with *when*. I call *when* a "dummy" conjunction because it sounds just odd enough that most test-takers can sense that something isn't quite right but not so obviously wrong that they can necessarily put their finger on the problem. For example:

Incorrect: Santiago's failure to complete the marathon surprised no one, least of all his training partners, **when** he had not spent enough time building the necessary stamina.

At first reading, the sentence may sound somewhat strange, but it is difficult to identify precisely why. At this point, the goal is to simplify the sentence into a more manageable form. If we consider the structure of the sentence, we notice that there are two commas in the interior of the sentence, indicating a non-essential clause. If we remove the non-essential clause, we are left with the following:

> Santiago's failure to complete the marathon surprised no one, **when** he had not spent enough time building the necessary stamina.

Clearly, the fact that Santiago didn't complete the marathon is a <u>result</u> of his failure to build the necessary stamina, so a transition such as *for* or *because* is required.

Correct: Santiago's failure to complete the marathon surprised no one, least of all his training partners, **for** he had not spent enough time building the necessary stamina.

Correct: Santiago's failure to complete the marathon surprised no one, least of all his training partners **because** he had not spent enough time building the necessary stamina.

Double Conjunction

Only one conjunction is typically necessary to connect two clauses. The SAT will occasionally make a sentence incorrect by adding an extra conjunction where it is not needed.

Incorrect:	**Although** Santiago had trained hard for the marathon, **but** he was unable to finish the entire course.
Correct:	**Although** Santiago had trained hard for the marathon, he was unable to finish the entire course.
Correct:	Santiago had trained hard for the marathon, **but** he was unable to finish the entire course.

The SAT will only give you the option of removing one of the conjunctions; you will never have to choose between them.

Conjunction Exercises

In the following sentences, identify and correct any conjunction error that appears. Some of the sentences may not contain an error. (Answers p. 155, Official Guide question list p. 135)

1. In the past, coffees were blended and branded to suit a homogenous popular taste, ~~and~~ *but* that has recently changed in response to a growing awareness of regional differences.

2. Since Frederic Chopin's charming and sociable personality drew loyal groups of friends and admirers, including George Sand, but his private life was often painful and difficult.

3. The Taj Mahal is regarded as one of the eight wonders of the world, ~~although~~ *and* some historians have noted that its architectural beauty has never been surpassed.

4. Music serves no obvious evolutionary purpose when it has been, ~~and~~ *but* remains, part of every known civilization on earth.

5. There is no escaping the fact that most of the world's big cats are in serious trouble because of poaching, and tigers are no exception to this situation.

6. Although saving an endangered species requires preservationists to study it in detail, but unfortunately scientific information about some animals is scarce.

7. Pyramids are most commonly associated with ancient Egypt, so it comes as a surprise to many people that Nubian civilization, located in modern-day Sudan, produced far more pyramids than Egyptian civilization ever did.

8. Modern chemistry keeps insects from ravaging crops, lifts stains from carpets, and saves lives, ~~and~~ *but* the constant exposure to chemicals is taking a toll on many people's health.

9. If people were truly at home under the light of the moon and stars, they would live happily in darkness, ~~and~~ *but* their eyes are adapted to living in the sun's light.

10. No one truly knows where the pirate known as Blackbeard called home, but author Daniel Defoe, a self-appointed piracy expert, claimed that he came from the English city of Bristol.

11. Roman women could only exercise political power through men, the only people considered true citizens, ~~when~~ *because* they were not allowed to participate directly in politics.

CUMULATIVE REVIEW #3

The following exercises cover all of the categories discussed thus far. For each sentence, fix the error and label its category. Some sentences may not contain an error. (Answers p. 156)

1. In their stories, originally published in the eighteenth century, the Brothers Grimm have embraced a number of themes that have never vanished from life, despite modern advances in science and technology.

2. The flexible scales around the side of the shortfin mako shark allow it to swiftly change direction while maintaining a high speed.

3. An experiment in which scientists threw paradise tree snakes from a 50-foot tower suggests that the snakes are ~~is~~ active fliers, manipulating their bodies to aerodynamic effect.

4. Although historians spend much time judging one another, he ~~or~~ *they* she rarely asks what qualities make a particular scholar worthy of attention.

5. A recently undertaken survey of drivers and cyclists has revealed that, compared to drivers, cyclists are *more* ~~most~~ likely to use hand signals.

6. Lan Samantha Chang is a critically acclaimed novelist ~~which~~ *who* counts among her influences authors as varied as Charlotte Brontë and Edgar Allan Poe.

7. In response to their critics, advocates of genetically modified foods typically insist that such crops grow faster, require fewer pesticides, and they ~~are reducing~~ *reduce* stress on natural resources.

8. Much like human beings, wolves are capable of exerting a profound influence on the environments that ~~it~~ *they* inhabits.

9. Giant galaxies like the Milky Way and the nearby Andromeda galaxy, which is even ~~more~~ larger, possess the power to create and retain a wide variety of elements.

10. Many scientists are baffled from the appearance of Yersinia pestis, a fungus that has been destroying bat populations throughout the United States in recent years.

11. Migrating animals maintain a fervid attentiveness that allows them to be neither distracted by temptations or *either* deterred by challenges that would turn other animals aside.

12. For all the fear and loathing Aztec rulers instilled in the inhabitants of the regions that they conquered, their power was ultimately short-lived.

13. Dumping pollution in oceans not only adds to the unsightliness of the formerly pristine waters, and it *but also* destroys the marine life that inhabits them.

14. Between 1903 and 1913, the British suffragettes, a group devoted to helping women win the right to vote, resorted to increasingly extreme measures to make their voices heard.

15. When it was first built, the Spanish Armada was said to be invincible, a designation that quickly became ironic since it was destroyed by the British in hardly ~~no~~ any time.

16. A desire to be published at all costs can lead to the erosion of a writer's sense of responsibility for ~~one's~~ his or her own work.

17. Construction on the Great Wall of China began many thousands of years ago and initially ~~involving~~ involved the construction of hundreds of miles of fortresses to defend against foreign invaders.

18. The earliest surviving guitars date from the sixteenth century, ~~and~~ but images of guitar-like instruments were depicted in Egyptian paintings and murals as early as 1900 B.C.

19. The company has been criticized ~~on~~ for its improper disposal of harmful chemicals and has drawn strict warnings from both environmental and political leaders.

20. A new generation of powerful digital tools and databases ~~are~~ is transforming the study of literature, philosophy, and other humanistic fields.

21. Under the feudal system, which prevailed in Europe during the Middle Ages, the status of an individual and his or her interactions with members of different social classes were rigidly specified.

22. Well into the twentieth century, to defend the notion of full social and political equality for all members of society was ~~being~~ to be considered a fool.

23. Although George Washington and General Lafayette were great friends, they came from widely disparate backgrounds and had little in common.

24. The great ancient city of Tenochtitlan was in many ways a repository of customs, images, and practices borrowed from previous civilizations.

25. Although birds are not generally known for their intelligence, recent findings have established that parrots often possess skills similar to ~~human~~ those of human toddlers.

*The following two categories appear far less frequently than the ones discussed previously, so you should only focus on them once you are fully comfortable identifying more common errors. I have not provided exercises for Redundancy and Diction because these errors occur so rarely.

13. REDUNDANCY

Redundancy errors occur rarely, but they can appear in both the Error-Identification and Fixing Sentences sections.

Incorrect: The upper basin of Utah's Lake Powell provides a minimum **annual** flow of eight million tons of water **per year** to states across the Southwest.

Correct: The upper basin of Utah's Lake Powell provides a minimum **annual** flow of eight million tons of water to states across the Southwest.

Correct: The upper basin of Utah's Lake Powell provides a minimum flow of eight million tons of water **per year** to states across the Southwest.

Since annual and per year mean exactly the same thing, it is unnecessary to include both in the sentence. Either one by itself is correct.

14. DICTION

Diction errors (also known as usage or "wrong word" errors) generally appear at most once per test, and often they do not appear at all. They are created by switching two similar or identical-sounding but differently spelled words.

Incorrect:	The work of Portuguese Renaissance painter Gregorio Lopes **insists** mostly of frescoes for monasteries across the Iberian Peninsula.
Correct:	The work of Portuguese Renaissance painter Gregorio Lopes **consists** mostly of frescoes for monasteries across the Iberian Peninsula.

Below is a list of word pairs of the sort that may appear on the SAT. Please be aware, however, that like preposition errors, diction errors are often extremely random and cannot be predicted with any degree of confidence.

Accept vs. Except	Comprehensive vs. Comprehensible	Incur vs. Occur
Access vs. Excess	Conscious vs. Conscience	Indeterminate vs. Interminable
Addition vs. Edition	Contribute vs. Attribute	Influence vs. Affluence
Adopt vs. Adapt	Contemptuous vs. Contemptible	Ingenious vs. Ingenuous
Advice vs. Advise	(In)credible vs. (In)credulous	Laid vs. Lain
Affect vs. Effect	Desirous vs. Desirable	Lead vs. Led
Afflict vs. Inflict	Devise vs. Device	Lie vs. Lay
Allusion vs. Illusion	Elicit vs. Illicit	Lose vs. Loose
Ambivalent vs. Ambiguous	Elude vs. Allude	Manner vs. Manor
Anecdote vs. Antidote	Emit vs. Omit	Precede vs. Proceed
Appraise vs. Apprise	Ensure vs. Assure	Precedent vs. President
Assent vs. Ascent	Exhaustive vs. Exhausting	Perpetrate vs. Perpetuate
Auditory vs. Audible	Expandable vs. Expendable	Persecute vs. Prosecute
Averse vs. Adverse	Explicit vs. Implicit	Principal vs. Principle
Capital vs. Capitol	Flaunt vs. Flout	Respectively vs. Respectfully
Censor vs. Censure	Foreboding vs. Forbidding	Supposed to, NOT suppose to
Cite vs. Site vs. Sight	Formally vs. Formerly	Than vs. Then
Collaborate vs. Corroborate	Imminent vs. Eminent	Visual vs. Visible
Command vs. Commend	Imply vs. Infer	Would/Could/Should have, NOT of

15. MISCELLANEOUS: ERROR-IDENTIFICATION

The following are common "trick" words and phrases that often sound wrong but that are actually correct.

A means of

There is nothing wrong with this phrase. A lot of test-takers think that it is incorrect because the words *means* seems plural, and of course you can't have the construction *a + plural noun*. In this case, the word *means* is singular, and it's fine.

Long since

This is another construction that the SAT is fond of. Test-takers tend to get tricked because they think it sounds odd, but it's perfectly acceptable. If the following sentence were an SAT question, the answer would be "No error."

Correct: The ruins of the Roman arena had a desolate atmosphere, abandoned as they were by spectators **long since** gone.

"That" as part of a subject

When used to begin a sentence, the phrase *the fact that* is often simply reduced to *that*. Although you may not be familiar with the construction, it is correct.

Correct: <u>**That** Mark Twain made substantial contributions to nineteenth century literary theory</u> should come as no surprise given his importance in the world of letters.

"What" as part of a subject

There is absolutely nothing wrong with starting a sentence with *what*, even if it's not a question. Note that *what*, when used a subject, always takes a singular verb.

Correct: <u>**What** has been criticized</u> **is** the author's refusal to discuss her work publicly, not the content of her novels.

"Whether" as part of a subject

This is yet another construction that many test-takers are unfamiliar with and incorrectly believe is wrong. Again, it's perfectly acceptable, regardless of how odd you may think it sounds. As is true for *what*, *whether* takes a singular verb.

Correct: <u>**Whether** *The Tale of Genji* was actually written entirely by Murasaki Shikibu</u> **is** unlikely to ever be determined unless a major archival discovery is made.

Herself/Himself/Itself

All of these words are correct when used for emphasis. Just make sure that they agree with the noun they emphasize.

Incorrect:	What has been criticized is the author's refusal to discuss her work publicly, not the quality of <u>the writing</u> **herself**.
Correct:	What has been criticized is the author's refusal to discuss her work publicly, not the quality of <u>the writing</u> **itself**.

Alike

The word *alike* tends to throw people off because it sounds like it could be wrong. It's not. It's fine, so ignore it.

Correct:	The media's criticism has been directed at both the company's executives and its shareholders **alike**.

(Al)though + Adjective or Past Participle

Correct:	**Though known** to audiences primarily for his appearances in films such as *Glory*, André Braugher has also appeared in numerous theatrical productions.

People tend to get fooled by this construction because they think it should read, *Though <u>he is known</u> to audiences primarily for his appearances in films such as Glory....* In reality, the sentence is correct either way. The pronoun and verb are optional.

In that

> In that = because

Although the phrase may sound somewhat awkward, there's nothing inherently wrong with it. If it's underlined in the Error-Identification section and creates the correct logical relationship, it's fine.

One of a kind vs. One of its kind

Incorrect:	In 2008, engineers in Geneva completed the Large Hadron Collider, an immense high-energy particle accelerator that is the only **one of a kind** in Europe.
Correct:	In 2008, engineers in Geneva completed the Large Hadron Collider, an immense high-energy particle accelerator that is the only **one of its kind** in Europe.

Since the Large Hadron Collider is not the only particle accelerator in the world, *one of its kind* should be used instead.

Any vs. Any other

Incorrect:	A source of intense fascination for both art historians and museum patrons, Leonardo da Vinci's *Mona Lisa* is perhaps more famous than **any** painting in the world.
Correct:	A source of intense fascination for both art historians and museum patrons, Leonardo da Vinci's *Mona Lisa* is perhaps more famous than **any other** painting in the world.

By saying the *Mona Lisa* is more famous than *any* painting, the first version implies that the *Mona Lisa* is not a painting.

16. ERROR-IDENTIFICATON STRATEGIES

So now that you know pretty much everything there is to know about Error-Identification questions, let's look at how you can use that knowledge to attack the test.

If, after reading a sentence closely several times, you still cannot find an obvious error, don't panic! Instead of simply trying to hear something that sounds wrong, you are now going to work from the information you've been given – the underlined words and phrases – and use it, along with your knowledge of the errors and clues, to very systematically determine whether there is in fact a problem. And if there isn't, you're going to shut your eyes, hope for the best, and just pick option E (although you should probably open your eyes before you fill in the little bubble).

As a general rule, you want to check for the most common errors first: if *its* or *there is* underlined, you should start with that answer choice because there's a very good chance that it's the problem. Otherwise, check the verbs first: *is/are*, *was/were*, and *has/have*, along with any other verbs in the present tense, should be very high on your list – no matter how complicated the sentence might appear. While there are theoretically many possibilities for errors, the reality is that only a handful of errors show up very frequently, and you need to make sure to look out for them. If there isn't a problem with subject-verb agreement, verb tense, or pronoun agreement, there's *already* a reasonable chance that the answer is "No error." One of the things that the SAT tests is the ability to sort through lots of information and figure out which parts of it are actually relevant to the task at hand. It is not in the least unusual to encounter a complex, awkward-sounding, multi-clause sentence, only to have the error turn out to be something as simple as *is*.

Remember: if a particular error is indicated by the structure and/or wording of a sentence, and that error does not appear, the answer is likely to be "No error." So, for example, if a sentence includes a date or time period but no verb error, there's a good chance that nothing is wrong.

While it can be tempting is to skip steps and just assume you'll hear the error if there is one, that's usually wishful thinking. SAT sentences are constructed very deliberately to make things that are right sound wrong, and things that are wrong sound right. If you're truly the exception and happen to have a fabulous ear, you can stop right here, but if you're not – a category that includes 99% of test-takers – keep reading.

Example #1

Writing about scientific matters poses a problem because one
      A   B

must choose imprecise metaphors that allow you to put new
                 C   D

findings in perspective for non-scientists. No error
                                            E

If you can spot the clue (or the error) in the sentence right away, great. But regardless, you can still use this process as a model – or a **paradigm**, to use a favorite SAT word – for what to do when you can't spot the error easily. Choice by choice, we're going to consider the error possibilities by category.

Choice B:

poses = singular verb, present tense

This is our top error candidate, so we start with it. We have two options: subject-verb agreement or verb tense.

Since subject-verb agreement is the most common error, we start by looking for the subject: *writing*. It's singular, so that's fine. It is, however, separated from the verb by a prepositional phrase that ends with a plural noun (*about scientific matters*), so careful not to get tricked into thinking that *matters* is the subject of *poses*.

Now we move to tense. There's no date or time period, which suggests that this is not a tense question, but just to be sure, we check the other verbs in the sentence: *must* and *allow*. Both are in the present tense, so *poses* is ok.

Choice A:

writing = gerund

about = preposition

We'll start with the gerund: gerunds get switched with infinitives, so we plug in the infinitive:

> **To write** about scientific matters poses a problem because one must choose imprecise metaphors that allow you to put new findings in perspective for non-scientists.

An infinitive can work as the subject of a sentence, but here, there's no grammatical or stylistic reason (e.g. preserving parallel structure) to use one in place of the gerund. So *writing* is fine.

Now the preposition: *write about* is standard usage, so that's not the problem either.

Choice C:

imprecise = adjective

Adjectives get switched with adverbs, so we plug in the adverb:

> Writing about science poses a problem because one must choose **imprecisely** metaphors that allow you to put new findings in perspective for non-scientists.

Ick.

Choice D:

you = pronoun

you gets switched with *one*, so we plug in *one*:

> Writing about science poses a problem because **one** must choose imprecise metaphors that allow **one** to put new findings in perspective for non-scientists.

Bingo! How do we know this is the answer? Because *one* already appears in the sentence, and the pronoun must stay consistent.

Choice E:

No longer an option.

In case you were wondering, here's the **shortcut:** the pronouns *one* and *you* typically appear in sentences only when one of them is incorrect. So right from the start, D is actually the most likely candidate.

Of course you won't have time to pore over every question on the test this way. But training yourself to look systematically at the error options gives you a means of getting out of trouble when you don't spot a problem immediately. Even if you have to slow down a little for one or two questions, you're a whole lot more likely to answer them correctly than you would be if you just guessed. Besides, once you get used to working through sentences like this, the process goes much, much faster. The payoff can also be massive: well over 100 points, and sometimes close to 200.

So let's try another one.

Example #2

Sumerian cuneiform <u>script</u>, one of the first writing systems,

                       A

<u>was</u> <u>comprised in</u> symbols carved into soft clay and grew out

 B   C

of merchants' schemes <u>for keeping</u> accounts. <u>No error</u>

                    D   E

Choice B:

Again, we're going to start with the underlined verb.

was = singular verb, simple past

Subject-Verb Agreement: What's the subject? *Script*, which is singular. So we're ok.

Tense: even if you don't know who the Sumerians were, you have a clue (*one of the <u>first</u> writing systems*) that suggests we're talking about something that happened a pretty long time ago. So simple past is fine.

Choice A:

script = noun

Nouns are usually right, so we're going to ignore it for the time being.

Choice C:

in = preposition

This is tricky. Is the phrase *comprised in*, or is there some other preposition that should be used?

If you don't know, leave it.

Choice D:

for keeping = preposition + gerund

Gerunds get switched with infinitives, so plug in the infinitive:

> Sumerian cuneiform script, one of the first writing systems, was comprised in symbols carved into soft clay and grew out of merchants' schemes **to keep** accounts.

It's ok, but *for keeping* sounds better. Which leaves us with C and E. Is it weird, or is it wrong?

In this case, it's wrong (the phrase is *comprised of*), but even if you didn't know that, you could get it down to two choices. And whenever you're left with a preposition option and E, you should in fact think about how you'd say the phrase. If what you would say doesn't match, chances are the preposition is incorrect.

One more.

Example #3

Let's pretend that this is question #27 of the first Writing section (third to last Error-Identification question). Right away, that gives us some clues as to what kind of error, if any, is likely to appear. Our likeliest categories are:

- Faulty comparison
- Subject-verb agreement (involving a prepositional phrase)
- Pronoun-antecedent
- Preposition/idiom
- No error

Like Aesop's fables, <u>the Brothers Grimm</u> used talking animals to
                     A

expose human vices and in <u>doing so</u> challenged <u>rigid</u>
                 B   C

boundaries between humans <u>and</u> other species. <u>No error</u>
               D   E

We're going to approach this question a little differently from how we approached the previous one. First, there are three options we can eliminate almost immediately:

Choice B:

The phrase *doing so* is generally correct. The problem usually is with the phrase *doing it.* So for the moment, we're going to assume that it's ok.

Choice C:

> *rigid* = adjective

The only other option is the adverb, *rigidly,* which clearly doesn't work when we plug it in.

Choice D:

and is correctly paired with *between,* so that can't be the answer.

Choice A:

We know that a faulty comparison is likely, and the word *like* provides a big clue because it tells us right away that two things are being compared. What's being compared to what?

> *Aesop's fables* = things   vs.   *The Brothers Grimm* = people

So the sentence should correctly read:

> Like Aesop's fables, **those of** the Brothers Grimm used talking animals to expose human vices and in doing so challenged rigid boundaries between humans and other species.

So now you try it. **(Answers are on p. 157)**

Practice #1

Blessed <u>with</u> an <u>exceptional</u> rugged natural landscape,
        A   B
New Zealand <u>has drawn</u> thrill-seeking athletes in search
              C
<u>of</u> adventure for decades. <u>No error</u>
D   E

Clues (if any):

And if you're still not sure:

Choice A

Category: _____

Choice B

Category: _____

Choice C

Category: _____

Choice D

Category: _____

Answer: exceptionally B

Practice #2

Franz Kafka's novel *The Trial* <u>opens with</u> the unexplained
                                        A

arrest <u>of</u> Josef K. by <u>a</u> <u>mysterious</u> organization that runs
      B   C

<u>their</u> courts outside the normal criminal-justice system.
  D

<u>No error</u>
    E

Clues (if any):

And if you're still not sure:

Choice A

Category: _____

Choice B

Category: _____

Choice C

Category: _____

Choice D

Category: _____

Answer: its D

Practice #3

Hidden in a trunk for nearly seventy years <u>were</u> a
A   B
camera and <u>nearly</u> a thousand photographic negatives
         B
<u>given to</u> former Mexican ambassador Francisco Aguilar
    C
Gonzalez <u>for</u> safekeeping. <u>No error</u>
              D   E

Clues (if any):

And if you're still not sure:

Choice A

Category: _____

Choice B

Category: _____

Choice C

Category: _____

Choice D

Category: _____

Answer:

Error-Identification Test

1. *The Last Five years*, a musical <u>written by</u> Jason
   A
   Robert Brown, premiered <u>in</u> Chicago in 2001 and
   B
   was
   <u>being produced</u> numerous times <u>both</u> in the
   C   D
   United States and internationally. <u>No error</u>
   E

2. <u>Among</u> the many reasons healthcare
   A
   professionals <u>choose</u> jobs that require travel <u>are</u>
   B   C
   higher pay, professional growth and development,
   opportunity for
   and <u>to have</u> personal adventures. <u>No error</u>
   D   E

3. The tower of London, which <u>lies</u> within the
   A
   is
   Borough of Tower Hamlets, <u>are</u> separated from
   B
   the city <u>itself</u> by a stretch of <u>open</u> space. <u>No error</u>
   C   D   E

4. Originally a common breakfast eaten by farmers
   Who
   <u>which</u> lived in the canton of Bern, rösti <u>is</u> today
   A   B
   <u>considered</u> the unofficial national dish <u>of</u>
   C   D
   Switzerland. <u>No error</u>
   E

5. The Australian frilled lizard <u>responds to</u> attacks
   A
   <u>by</u> unfurling the colorful skin flap that encircles
   B
   nimbly
   <u>its</u> head, but if all else fails it will scoot <u>nimble</u> up
   C   D
   the nearest tree. <u>No error</u>
   E

6. Sofia Tolstoy, <u>the wife of</u> Russian author
   A
   Leo Tolstoy, was a woman <u>of strength</u> and
   B
   would
   spirit <u>who understood</u> the high price she <u>will pay</u>
   C   D
   to live next to one of the greatest writers in
   history. <u>No error</u>
   E

7. James Watson and Francis Crick <u>were</u> renowned
   A
   scientists
   as <u>a scientist</u> because <u>they</u> discovered the DNA
   B   C
   triple helix and in 1962 were <u>awarded</u> the Nobel
   D
   Prize in Medicine. <u>No error</u>
   E

8. Among nations known <u>for producing</u>
   A
   nor
   exceptional chess players, neither China <u>or</u> Russia
   B
   can compete with Armenia for the <u>sheer number</u> of
   C
   grandmasters <u>it has produced</u>. <u>No error</u>
   D   E

9. Humor is a far <u>more subtler</u> process <u>than</u> a
   A   B
   primeval pleasure such as <u>eating</u>, but it is just as
   C
   much <u>tied to</u> the inner complexity of the brain.
   D
   <u>No error</u>
   E

10. Frequently <u>dismissed as</u> a vice, gossip is in fact
    A
    <u>a means of</u> creating alliances <u>and</u> friendships
    B   C
    among <u>members of</u> groups. <u>No error</u>
    D   E

11. The secret of the Mona Lisa's enigmatic smile

is a matter of which cells in the retina pick up the
A   B   C

image and how it channels the information to the
                D

brain. No error   *they channel*
       E

12. Located on the outskirts of Lincoln National
    A
Forest in New Mexico, White Oaks had become a
                                      B
boomtown after silver and gold were discovered
                                    C
in the nearby Jicarilla Mountains in 1879. No error
        D   E

13. The Ethiopian wolf, the only species of wolf

          to
native in Africa, can be identified by its distinctive
       A   B   C
red coat and black-and-white tail. No error
         D   E

14. Far from eliminating war, the new diplomatic
    A
system instituted in Europe during the early
       B
nineteenth century simply changed the reasons

to fight and the methods of combat. No error
   C   D   E
for fighting

15. With genes that are virtually identical to *those of*

humans, Neanderthals can offer many insights into
A   B   C
the evolution and development of the modern
                 D
brain. No error
       E

16. The popularity of games such as cricket and

                                          is
squash in former English colonies are often
                                   A
attributed to the lingering influence of British
B   C   D
culture. No error
       E

17. Central to the emergence of women as a major
    A
force in American political life was the rise of the
B   C
female career politician determined to devote her
                                    D
life to public service. No error
                         (E)

Answers to this test can be found on p. 157

17. FIXING SENTENCES: INTRODUCTION AND RULES FOR CHOOSING ANSWERS

Although most of the errors that appear in the Error-Identification section appear in Fixing Sentences as well, there are also some important differences. While the former often contains errors that revolve around misuse of individual words and parts of speech (e.g. verbs, pronouns, adjectives, prepositions), the latter is more concerned with errors in the structure of the sentences themselves. Fixing Sentences tests your ability to distinguish full sentences from sentence fragments and to distinguish clear and concise phrasings from long and awkward ones. The major concepts that are covered primarily in Fixing Sentence are as follows:

1) Sentences and Fragments

2) Commas and Semicolons

3) Gerunds and Wordiness

4) Dangling Modifiers

5) Active vs. Passive Voice

6) "Phrase" Parallel Structure

Subject-Verb Agreement, Pronoun-Antecedent, Verb Tense and Form, "List" Parallel Structure, Noun Agreement, Faulty Comparisons, Conjunctions, and Word Pairs are also tested, but to a somewhat lesser extent than in the Error-Identification section.

Relative Pronoun, Redundancy, and Preposition errors appear as well, but rarely.

The following errors do not generally appear in Fixing Sentences:

  -Pronoun Case
  -Double Negatives/Double Positives
  -Comparatives vs. Superlatives
  -Adjectives vs. Adverbs
  -Diction

Rules for Choosing Answers

While it is always most effective to identify and correct errors before looking at the answers, working this way can be an exercise in frustration if you do not know quite what you are looking for or are unsure of how to fix it. If you do choose to look at the answers, there are three general rules that should dictate your approach to eliminating choices.

1) Shorter is Better

Always check answers in order of length, starting with the shortest one. Since you are being tested on your ability to eliminate wordiness, it is logical that more concise answers are more likely to be correct.

When you are faced with two grammatically correct answers that express the same essential information, the shorter one will virtually always be right.

2) Gerunds (-ING words), especially "Being" = BAD

Gerunds create sentence fragments and awkwardness. In the vast majority of cases that require you to choose between a conjugated verb and a gerund, the conjugated verb will be correct.

In general, you should only choose a gerund in the following cases:

-It is necessary to preserve parallel structure.

-It is required by standard usage.

-It is required to create the cleanest, clearest, and most concise version of a sentence.

Furthermore, you should automatically eliminate any answer that contains the word *being*, unless it is absolutely, incontrovertibly necessary (not the case 98% of the time).

3) Passive Voice = BAD

Active = The politician **gave** a speech.

Passive = A speech **was given** by the politician.

The passive version is unnecessarily wordy. You should automatically eliminate any answer containing this construction unless the sentence does not make sense without it.

18. SENTENCES AND FRAGMENTS

Every sentence must contain two elements: a subject and a verb that corresponds to it. A sentence can consist of only one word (*Go!* is a sentence because the subject, *you*, is implied), or of many complex clauses, but provided that it contains a subject and a verb, it is considered to be grammatically complete – *regardless of whether it makes logical sense outside of any context.*

Any phrase that lacks a subject (noun or pronoun) and a main verb that corresponds to it cannot be a sentence. Instead, it is a fragment.

Important: Fixing Sentences answer choices that contain fragments are always incorrect.

In Fixing Sentences, there are two general types of fragments:

   1) Gerunds replace verbs

   2) Relative clause errors

Gerunds Replace Verbs

As described on page 21, gerunds are formed by adding –ING to verbs (e.g. to run → running; to go → going).

Gerunds are sneaky: they look like verbs but act like nouns. What this means, practically speaking, is that a clause containing only a gerund cannot be a sentence. Instead, it is a fragment.

   Fragment: George C. Williams **being** one of the most important recent thinkers in the field of evolutionary biology.

To turn a fragment containing a gerund into a sentence, simply replace the gerund with a conjugated verb:

   Sentence: George C. Williams **was** one of the most important recent thinkers in the field of evolutionary biology.

Important: "being" is the most frequently used gerund on the SAT.

The conjugated forms of it are as follows:

   Present: is/are

   Past: was/were

Relative Clause Errors

A sentence that contains a relative clause must always contain a main verb that corresponds to the subject. Relative clauses can be either essential or non-essential.

Non-essential relative clauses with "which" or "who(se)"

Fragment: George C. Williams, who was one of the most important thinkers in the field of evolutionary biology.

In the above fragment, the construction *comma + who* suggests that a non-essential clause is beginning, but there is never a second comma – the sentence ends without a resolution.

The only verb (*was*) that appears in the sentence is part of the relative clause begun by the relative pronoun *who*, not part of the main clause begun by the subject (*George C. Williams*).

The fastest and easiest way to turn this fragment into a sentence is to remove the comma and the relative pronoun, thereby eliminating the relative clause and making the entire sentence into a single main clause.

Sentence: George C. Williams was one of the most important thinkers in the field of evolutionary biology.

Now the verb *was* clearly belongs to the subject.

Many of the fragments that appear in Fixing Sentences will be slightly longer, however:

Fragment: George C. Williams, who was one of the most important thinkers in evolutionary biology, and who made a number of lasting contributions to his field.

In the above sentence, we can identify what appears to be a non-essential clause (*who was…biology*) because it begins with *who* and is surrounded by commas. If we cross it out, however, we are left with:

Fragment: George C. Williams…**and who made** a number of lasting contributions to his field.

Clearly this is not a sentence. Making it into a sentence, however, is relatively simple: since the first word after the end of a non-essential clause is typically a verb, we can cross out all the excess words before the verb. This leaves us with:

Sentence: George C. Williams…~~and who~~ made a number of lasting contributions to his field.

With the elimination of those two words, the fragment suddenly becomes a sentence. When we plug the non-essential clause back in, we get something much clearer:

Sentence: George C. Williams, who was one of the most important thinkers in evolutionary biology, **made** a number of lasting contributions to his field.

Another possible solution is to remove the non-essential clause entirely.

Sentence: George C. Williams **was** one of the most important thinkers in the field of evolutionary biology and made a number of lasting contributions to his field.

This is one of the most common Fixing Sentences errors. A version of it nearly always appears at least once per section, often in the first three or four questions.

To sum up:

The easiest way to attack sentences like this is to see if there is a verb immediately following a non-essential clause. If there is not, the sentence is virtually always incorrect. (The only exception would be something along the lines of: *George C. Williams, who was one of the most important recent American thinkers in evolutionary biology, also made a number of lasting contributions to his field*, because the sentence still makes sense if the non-essential clause is eliminated.)

Cross out everything after the second comma and before the verb, and the sentence that remains will nearly always match the correct answer choice.

Again:

Fragment:	Mobile robot technology, which has historically been used by both the military and the police, and it is now becoming widespread at businesses and hotels.
Reduce:	Mobile robot technology, ~~which has historically been used by both the military and the police,~~ and it is now becoming widespread at businesses and hotels.
Cross Out:	Mobile robot technology…~~and it~~ is now becoming widespread at businesses and hotels.
Sentence:	Mobile robot technology, which has historically been used by both the military and the police, is now becoming widespread at businesses and hotels.

Important: occasionally you will be asked to fix the beginning of a non-essential clause rather than the end.

Fragment:	Mobile robot technology has historically been used by both the military and the police, is now becoming widespread at businesses and hotels.

Sentences like these can be tricky because the beginning looks fine; it's the end that appears to need fixing. In cases such as these, however, the second comma followed by a verb is your clue that a non-essential clause needs to be created in order to correct the sentence.

Sentence:	Mobile robot technology, **which has** historically been used by both the military and the police, is now becoming widespread at businesses and hotels.

Essential relative clauses with "that"

Clauses beginning with the relative pronoun *that* function exactly like those beginning with *which* or *who(se)*, even though they are essential (or **restrictive**) and do not require commas to be placed around them.

Fragment:	The mobile robot technology that has historically been used by both the military and the police and that is now becoming widespread at businesses and hotels.
Cross out:	The mobile robot technology that has historically been used by both the military and the police ~~and that~~ is now becoming widespread at businesses and hotels.
Sentence:	The mobile robot technology that has historically been used by both the military and the police is now becoming widespread at businesses and hotels.

Important: an answer choice that contains a properly used non-essential clause is virtually always correct.

The College Board will frequently include correct sentences with short non-essential clauses or phrases in unexpected places because they know that many test-takers are unaccustomed to such constructions. For example:

> Correct: A planet capable of harboring life, astronomers think, may be identified sometime within the next decade.

> Correct: St. Petersburg is a charming, if frigid, city to visit during the wintertime.

Do not be fooled by the unexpected syntax. Both of these sentences are perfectly fine as is. And yes, people do actually write this way sometimes!

Sentence and Fragment Exercises

Label each of the following phrases as either a sentence or a fragment. Rewrite all fragments as sentences. (Answers p. 158, Official Guide question list p. 136)

1. Shirley Jackson, best known for her shocking short story "The Lottery," ~~and who~~ was born in San Francisco in 1916.

2. The tenth legion, among the oldest in the imperial Roman army, originally fought on horseback under Caesar's command.

3. The pyramids of ancient Egypt, intended to be monuments to the Pharaohs' greatness and were built with the help of great armies of slaves.

4. The Red Belt ~~was~~ *which is* one of several colored belts used in some martial arts to denote a practitioner's skill level and rank, originated in Japan and Korea.

5. The plan to overhaul the country's higher education system ~~being~~ *is* a model for moving other desperately needed projects forward.

6. Patients who receive anesthesia during surgery are put into a semi-comatose state, not, as many people assume, a deep state of sleep.

7. Recent findings from research on moose, which have suggested that arthritis in human beings may be linked in part to nutritional deficits.

8. A new study ~~reporting~~ *reports* that the physical differences among dog breeds are determined by variations in only about seven genetic regions.

9. George Barr McCutcheon, a popular novelist and playwright, and he is best known for the series of novels set in Graustark, a fictional Eastern European country.

10. Forensic biology *which* is the application of biology to law enforcement, has been used to identify illegal products from endangered species and investigate bird collisions with wind turbines.

11. Human computers, who once performed basic numerical analysis for laboratories, and ~~they~~ were behind the calculations for everything from the first accurate prediction of the return of Halley's Comet to the success of the Manhattan Project.

12. Nicollet Island, an island in the Mississippi River just north of Minneapolis, and ~~which~~ was named after cartographer Joseph Nicollet.

13. Malba Tahan, who was a fictitious Persian scholar ~~and who~~ was the pen name created by Brazilian author Júlio César de Mello e Souza.

14. The Rochester International Jazz Festival ~~taking~~ *takes* place in June of each year and typically attracts more than 100,000 fans from towns across upstate New York.

15. Although Rodin purposely omitted crucial elements such as arms from his sculptures, his consistent use of the human figure attesting to his respect for artistic tradition.

16. Brick nog *is* ~~a~~ *arrested* commonly used construction technique in which one width of bricks is used to fill the vacancies in a wooden frame.

17. The unusually large size of the komodo dragon, the largest species of lizard, w~~h~~ich has been attributed to its ancient ancestor, the immense varanid lizard.

18. One of the most popular ballets, *Swan Lake*, which was fashioned from Russian folk tales, tell~~i~~s the story of Odette, a princess turned into a swan by an evil sorcerer's curse.

19. Simone Fortini, a postmodern choreographer who was born in Italy but moved to the United States at a young age, rapidly became known for a style of dancing based on improvisation and everyday movements.

20. Pheidon, a king of the Greek city Argos during the seventh century B.C., ~~and~~ he ruled during a time when monarchs were figureheads with little genuine power.

21. Batsford Arboretum, a 55-acre garden that contains Great Britain's largest collection of Japanese cherry trees ~~and it~~ is open daily to the public for most of the year.

19. COMMAS AND SEMICOLONS

Comma and semicolon usage are two of the most commonly tested concepts in Fixing Sentences. They are tested only in relation to combining full sentences (or **independent clauses**) with one another.

There are three principal ways in which two independent clauses can be joined:

1) Comma + Coordinating (FANBOYS) Conjunction

2) Semicolon Only

3) Semicolon + Conjunctive Adverb

A. Comma + Coordinating Conjunction

There are seven coordinating conjunctions, known by the acronym FANBOYS:

For
And
Nor
But
Or
Yet
So

FANBOYS conjunctions are used to join independent clauses to one another. These conjunctions must always be preceded by a comma. Without a comma, a sentence that uses a FANBOYS conjunction to join two independent clauses is technically a run-on sentence, regardless of how short it is.

Incorrect: London is a very old **city but** it also has some extremely modern buildings.

Correct: London is a very old **city, but** it also has some extremely modern buildings.

Identifying Comma Splices

A comma must also never be used to separate two independent clauses without a conjunction. Otherwise, a **comma splice** is formed. Comma splices are always wrong – no exceptions – and they are *everywhere* in Fixing Sentences. A substantial number of questions in any given section will contain one or more answer choices that include them.

In order to recognize comma splices, you must know when a clause can stand on its own as a sentence – and when it cannot. While that distinction may in principle seem obvious, it is not always as straightforward as you might imagine.

    Comma Splice: London is a very old **city, it** also contains some extremely modern buildings.

Most people wouldn't have much trouble identifying the first clause as a sentence. But what about the second? It doesn't make much sense out of context: we don't know *what* has some extremely modern buildings. It does, however, have a subject (the pronoun *it*) and a main verb that corresponds to it (*has*), so it **can** actually stand on its own as a sentence. The fact that it doesn't make sense is *entirely* irrelevant.

Very Important: When it comes to defining what is and is not a sentence, grammar is more important than meaning. It is perfectly acceptable to make a pronoun such as *it*, *she*, *some*, or *many*, rather than a specific noun (*author*, *island*, *music*), the subject of a sentence – even if it is unclear just what or whom that pronoun refers to when the sentence is read on its own.

Shortcut: The construction *comma + pronoun* often signals a comma splice. When you see an answer containing that construction, you should be very suspicious, regardless of how correct it may sound to you.

Fixing Comma Splices

The simplest way to fix a comma splice is to add a FANBOYS conjunction after the comma, but sometimes you will not have the option of adding one. In such cases, you must make one of the independent clauses a **dependent clause**.

One option is to add a **subordinating conjunction** such as *(al)though*, *when*, or *because* to the start of one of the clauses.

    Incorrect: London is a very old city, some of its buildings are extremely modern.

    Correct: **Although** London is a very old city, some of its buildings are extremely modern.

    Correct: London is a very old city, **although** some of its buildings are extremely modern.

Another option is to rewrite the second clause so that it contains the construction *preposition + which*

    Incorrect: London is a very old city with many neighborhoods, some **of them** are very modern.

    Correct: London is a very old city with many neighborhoods, some **of which** are very modern.

In some cases, it is also possible to correct a comma splice by changing the first clause into a **participial phrase**.

    Incorrect: **We finally arrived** at our destination after a long and difficult journey, we promptly fell asleep.

    Correct: **Having finally arrived** at our destination after a long and difficult journey, we promptly fell asleep.

Note: In the correct version of the sentence, the word *having* is a participle rather than a gerund and thus does not violate the "no gerund" rule. (See pp. 101-102 for more information.)

B. Semicolon

A semicolon functions almost exactly like a period: it is used to separate two independent clauses. A semicolon should not, however, be used before a FANBOYS conjunction:

Incorrect: London is a very old **city; but it** also contains some very modern buildings.

Correct: London is a very old **city; it** also contains some very modern buildings.

Important: a properly used semicolon very often – but not always – indicates a correct answer.

C. Semicolon + Conjunctive Adverb

Place a semicolon before the following five **conjunctive adverbs** when they are used to begin a clause:

However
Therefore
Moreover
Consequently
Nevertheless

Incorrect: London is a very old **city, however,** some of its buildings are very modern.

Correct: London is a very old **city; however,** some of its buildings are very modern.

But: when these transitions appear alone in the middle of a clause, they should be surrounded by commas.

Correct: London is a very old city; some of its **buildings, however,** are very modern.

Important Additional Information

When using a FANBOYS conjunction to join two independent clauses with the same subject, do not use a comma if the subject is not repeated in the second clause.

Incorrect: London is a very old **city, but** also contains some very modern buildings.

Correct: London is a very old **city but** also contains some very modern buildings.

Also: contrary to what you may have learned, you can begin a sentence with *because*, as long as it contains a main clause.

Incorrect: Because London is a very old city.

Correct: Because London is a very old city, it contains buildings from many eras.

But: any answer choice that contains the construction *comma + because* is incorrect.

Incorrect: London contains buildings from many **eras, because** it is a very old city.

Correct: London contains buildings from many **eras because** it is a very old city.

Comma and Semicolon Exercises

In the following sentences, identify and correct any comma or semicolon error that appears. Some of the sentences may not contain an error. (Answers p. 159, Official Guide question list p. 137)

1. In large doses, many common substances found in household items have horrific effects; however, many toxicologists insist that in minuscule amounts they are completely innocuous.

2. César Chávez became an iconic figure as the leader of the Farm Workers' movement, but it was as a martyr who embodied the contrast between Mexico and the United States that he commanded the most attention.

3. The Atlantic bluefin tuna is considered a delicacy from Osaka to Omaha, but its sheer popularity among consumers has caused its population to plummet over the past several decades.

4. Vitamin D has been long known for its critical role in the body's processing of calcium, yet increasing amounts of evidence suggest that it also protects the body by significantly cutting the risk for most forms of cancer.

5. Universities typically offer a wide variety of continuing education classes, many of these are offered over the ~~which~~ Internet.

6. When the Mayan city of Palenque was first discovered, it was completely overwhelmed by the plant life of the rainforest; today it is a massive archaeological site that attracts thousands of tourists each year.

7. International sports competitions are symbolic showdowns that are more about winning than about universal friendship; however, they are a far more civilized alternative to actual warfare.

8. The Roman emperor Hadrian commissioned the building of the Pantheon; its administration was managed by Marcus Agrippa.

9. The First World War began in August of 1914; it was directly caused by the assassination of Archduke Franz Ferdinand of Austria by Bosnian revolutionary Gavrilo Princeps.

10. In 43 A.D., Britain was already a territory of the Roman Empire; it remained a part of Rome until more than four centuries later.

11. Over the past several years, the country's food prices have increased dramatically; they are now at their highest rate in two decades.

12. In medieval Europe, proficiency in the arts was the goal of an educated person; only in the nineteenth century did the concept come to denote painting, drawing, and sculpting.

13. An ethnocentric approach stems from judging an unfamiliar culture in relation to pre-conceived values; it indicates the inability to escape one's own biases and prevents objective analysis.

14. Culture has become a force that may accelerate human evolution because people have no choice but to adapt to pressures and technologies of their own creation.

15. Both the Parthenon and the Pantheon are temples to the deities of the people who built them, the Parthenon was ~~but~~ built by the ancient Greeks while the Pantheon was constructed by the Romans.

16. The eyes of many predatory animals are designed to enhance depth perception; however, in other organisms, they are designed to maximize the visual field.

17. Paris is the world capital of cinephilia; moreover, it has played a central role in films of every imaginable genre.

18. Sugar and cavities go hand in hand; dentists therefore recommend that the amount of sugar people consume be kept to a minimum.

19. Despite strains, fractures and tears, many athletes continue to work out; consequently, at least one expert would say they are addicted to exercise.

20. The Mid-Autumn Festival, a popular harvest festival celebrated in Asia, dates back 3,000 years to China's Shang Dynasty and is traditionally held on the fifteenth day of the eighth month.

21. Carl Bohm was one of the most prolific German pianists and composers during the nineteenth century; few people would, however, recognize his name today.

22. The photo booth debuted in 1925 and quickly became a popular form of entertainment; it also served as a practical and inexpensive way for people to make images of themselves.

20. GERUNDS AND WORDINESS

To reiterate: the correct answer in Fixing Sentences will always be the most concise grammatically correct option. This cannot be stated strongly enough.

Very often, conjunctions such as *so, because* and *in order to* will be unnecessarily re-written in an excessively wordy and awkward manner. Other times, extra words will simply be added onto an otherwise straightforward sentence.

Wordy: Every year, hundreds of wild stallions are hunted down by modern cowboys in the southwestern United States, **with the reducing of the horse population to more sustainable levels being their goal**.

Concise: Every year, hundreds of wild horses are hunted down by modern cowboys in the southwestern United States **(in order) to reduce** the population to more sustainable levels.

Unnecessarily wordy versions of sentences, as in the above case, will often be signaled by an excessive use of gerunds. Note that the first version of the sentence contains two gerunds while the second version contains none.

Below are some common SAT Fixing Sentences phrases in both their wordy and concise versions:

<u>Wordy</u>	<u>Concise</u>
Being that	Because
Because of (her/him) being	Because she/he was
Despite (her/him) being In spite of (her/him) being	Although she/he was
For the purpose of going	To go In order to go

Whenever possible, replace a gerund with a noun or pronoun + conjugated verb.

Incorrect: The renowned physicist's book has been praised **because of making** difficult concepts accessible to an audience with little mathematical knowledge.

Correct: The renowned physicist's book has been praised **because it makes** difficult concepts accessible to an audience with little mathematical knowledge.

So when is it ok to use a gerund...?

When standard usage requires one

Incorrect: The Spanish city of Cádiz held the distinction **to be** the only city in continental Europe to survive a siege by Napoleon.

Correct: The Spanish city of Cádiz held the distinction **of being** the only city in continental Europe to survive a siege by Napoleon.

To preserve parallel structure

Incorrect: The panelists at the conference are responsible both for presenting original research and **they respond** to questions about its potential applications.

Correct: The panelists at the conference are responsible both for presenting original research and **for responding** to questions about its potential applications.

To indicate method or means

No Gerund: Flaubert attempted to achieve stylistic perfection in his novels, **and he rewrote** each sentence ten times.

Gerund: Flaubert attempted to achieve stylistic perfection in his novels **by rewriting** each sentence ten times.

Gerunds vs. Present Participles

Every verb has two participles: a **past participle** (discussed on p. 23) and a **present participle**.

Although present participles end in "–ing" and are identical in appearance to gerunds, the two forms have different functions. **While gerunds are verbs that act as nouns, participles are verbs that act as adjectives.** Participles are used to modify nouns and pronouns.

It is important that you be able to distinguish between them because unlike gerunds, present participles do not usually affect whether a particular Fixing Sentences answer is right or wrong.

On the SAT, present participles are typically used in two ways:

1) Immediately before a noun

2) To begin a participial phrase

Immediately before a noun

Participle: Although it lacks traditional circus elements such as animals and clowns, Cirque du Soleil is regarded by both audiences and critics as an **exciting** spectacle.

In the above sentence, the participle "exciting" simply modifies "spectacle." It does nothing to make the sentence unnecessarily wordy. Compare the version with the participle to this version, which contains a gerund and is considerably more awkward:

Gerund: **In spite of its lacking** traditional circus elements such as animals and clowns, Cirque du Soleil is regarded by both audience and critics as an exciting spectacle.

To begin a participial phrase

Participial phrases can appear in the beginning, middle, or end of a sentence. In Fixing Sentences, they appear primarily at the beginning (as introductory clauses describing the subject), although they do sometimes appear at the end as well.

Introductory Clause

Correct: **Rejecting** a quiet life in Norway, Roald Amundsen chose to seek his fortune at sea and became the first person to reach both the North and South Poles.

At the end of a sentence, a participial phrase is often used to replace a pronoun that lacks an antecedent (see also p. 32) or to replace a passive and awkward construction. In Fixing Sentences, this usage is virtually always correct.

Missing Antecedent

Incorrect: Artists are not frequently associated with domestic serenity, **which** makes literary families cells of both inspiration and psychological investigation.

Correct: Artists are not frequently associated with domestic serenity, **making** literary families cells of both inspiration and psychological investigation.

Passive Construction

Incorrect: The notion that Shakespeare did not revise his works is extremely logical, **and an explanation is therefore provided** for his ability to direct, write, and perform in multiple plays each year.

Correct: The notion that Shakespeare did not revise his works is extremely logical, **providing** an explanation for his ability to direct, write, and perform in multiple plays each year.

In this case, you might ask why it isn't possible to just eliminate the "-ing" word entirely?

Shorter: The notion that Shakespeare did not revise his works is extremely logical **because it provides** an explanation for his ability to direct, write, and perform in multiple plays each year.

Well, sometimes you won't have that option. The participle will be the best answer available because all of the other options will contain a serious error such as a missing verb, extreme awkwardness, or a comma splice.

To Sum Up: Although it may seem as if there are a lot of exceptions to the "no -ing" rule, these exceptions are rare. The bottom line is that if you stick to the clearest and most concise version of a given sentence, you'll probably be fine.

Gerund and Wordiness Exercises

Rewrite the following sentences to eliminate wordiness and incorrectly used gerunds. Some of the sentences may not contain an error. (Answers p. 160, Official Guide question list p. 136)

1. It can hardly be considered a surprise that Incan emperors covered themselves in gold because ~~of~~ holding [*they held*] themselves to be the sun's human incarnation.

2. The museum's artistic director has arranged the exhibition thematically, with the purpose b~~e~~ing [*in order*] to provide a new understanding of the multifaceted complexity of Native American life.

3. In the early 1920's, the music industry was already well on its way to becoming a major business, producing millions of dollars worth of goods and exerting a strong influence on popular culture.

4. ~~Despite the fact of being~~ [*Although it is*] a smaller city than either London or New York, Dublin possesses a thriving theater scene whose productions regularly achieve international renown.

5. Heralds were the predecessors of modern diplomats, traveling under the orders of kings or noblemen in order to convey messages or proclamations.

6. Bongoyo Island, located off the coast of Tanzania, has become a popular vacation spot for both tourists and Tanzanians because of it ~~having~~ [*has*] such close proximity to the mainland.

7. The Province House, home to royal governors in seventeenth-century Massachusetts, was considered one of the grandest examples of colonial architecture because ~~of possessing~~ [*it possess*] beautiful Tudor-style chimneystacks.

8. Contrary to popular belief, people should alternate rooms while studying because ~~of retaining~~ [*they retain*] more information that way.

9. Some excellent teachers prance in front of the classroom like Shakespearean actors, while others are notable because of ~~their being~~ [*they are*] aloof or timid.

10. Having trained as a dancer for much of her life, Mae Jemison rejected a career in ballet in order to study engineering and in 1987 became a member of NASA's astronaut-training program.

11. *Prince Jellyfish*, an unpublished novel by author and journalist Hunter S. Thompson, was rejected by a number of literary agents because ~~of lacking~~ [*it lack*] popular appeal.

12. Large sections of the Great Lakes often freeze in winter, thereby forcing manufacturers to find other methods of shipping their goods. [*Although*]

13. ~~In spite of~~ [*Although*] traffic often blocking[s] its main arteries, East London contains side streets that can, on occasion, be as tranquil and pleasant as country lanes.

14. In scientific fields, scale models known as homunculi are often used ~~for the purpose of~~ [*to*] illustrating physiological characteristics of the human body.

21. PASSIVE VOICE

In an **active** construction, the subject of a sentence typically precedes the object:

<u>William Shakespeare</u>   <u>wrote</u>   <u>*Hamlet*</u>.
    Subject   **verb**   **object**

In a **passive** construction, on the other hand, the subject and the object are flipped. The passive voice also includes a form of the verb *to be* + past participle and the preposition *by*.

<u>*Hamlet*</u>   <u>was written</u>   <u>by</u>   <u>William Shakespeare</u>.
subject   **verb**   **prep**   **object**

Because passive constructions are always wordier than active ones, answers that include them are generally incorrect.

<u>Active</u>	<u>Passive</u>
Elena **drinks** the water.	The water **is drunk by** Elena.
The students in Professor Garcia's Chemistry class **conducted** an experiment yesterday.	An experiment **was conducted by** the students in Professor Garcia's Chemistry class yesterday.
A lack of concern for workers' environments **causes** some tensions between bosses and their employees.	Some tensions between bosses and their employees **are caused by** a lack of concern for workers' environments.

Passive Required

You will, however, sometimes have to choose a passive option in order to correct a more serious error such as a dangling modifier.

Incorrect: With its steep hills and stunning views of the surrounding harbor, visitors to San Francisco are unlikely to forget it.

Correct: With its steep hills and stunning views of the surrounding harbor, San Francisco **is** unlikely to be forgotten **by** visitors.

In addition, SAT will occasionally test this rule in reverse: a verb that requires the passive voice will be made active. In such cases, you must choose the passive option in order for the sentence to make sense.

Incorrect: The musician **admired** by his fans for his ability to make instruments out of everyday objects.

Correct: The musician **is admired** by his fans for his ability to make instruments out of everyday objects.

Passive Voice Exercises

In the following sentences, rewrite passive constructions to make them active. Some sentences may require the passive voice. (Answers p. 160, Official Guide question list p. 138)

1. In the later works of Nikola Stoyanov, also known by the pseudonym Emiliyan Stanev, nature is often described in great detail by the author.

2. Michael J. Rosen has written works ranging from picture books to poetry, and several anthologies varying almost as broadly in content have also been edited by him.

3. In the movie *The Killing Fields*, Cambodian photojournalist Dith Pran was portrayed by first-time actor Haing S. Ngor, a role for which Ngor won an Academy Award.

4. Although desserts typically characterized by their sweetness, bakers are now creating ones that feature intriguing blends of sweet and savory.

5. *The Nereus*, a remotely operated underwater hybrid vehicle, was designed by scientists at the Woods Hole Oceanographic Institute to function at depths of up to 36,000 feet.

6. Michael Balls, a British zoologist and biology professor, is known by many pharmaceutical company executives as an outspoken opponent of animal laboratory testing.

7. Between the late 1970's and 1980's, nine albums were recorded by Jamaican reggae musician Lone Ranger, born Anthony Alphonso Waldron.

8. Time Lapse Dance, a New York-based dance company whose mission is to provide modern reinterpretations of classic works, was founded by performance artist Jody Sperling in 2000.

9. Murtabak, a dish composed of mutton, garlic, egg, onion, and curry sauce, is frequently eaten by people throughout the Middle East, Singapore, and Indonesia.

10. Over the last thirty years, many forms of meditation have been examined by researchers, and a number of them have been deemed ineffective.

22. MODIFICATION ERRORS

In any given sentence, modifiers should be placed as close as possible to the nouns, pronouns, or phrases they modify; sentences that separate modifiers from the things they modify are often unclear and sometimes completely absurd.

Two kinds of modification errors are tested on the SAT:

1) Dangling Modifiers

2) Misplaced Modifiers

Dangling Modifiers

Dangling modifiers are one of the most frequent errors that appear exclusively in Fixing Sentences. Virtually every section will have at least one and as many as four questions that test your knowledge of them. It is therefore important that you be able to recognize this error quickly and easily.

Sentences that include dangling modifiers are characterized by an introductory clause that describes the subject but does not name it. This clause is always set off from the rest of the sentence by a comma.

Whenever a sentence contains such an introductory clause, the subject must appear immediately after the comma. If the subject does not appear there, the modifier is said to be dangling, and the sentence is incorrect.

> Incorrect: An elementary school teacher from Arkansas, increased funding and support for public libraries were what Bessie Boehm Moore advocated for.

The first thing we can note about the above sentence is that it contains an introductory clause (*An elementary school teacher from Arkansas*) that does not name the subject – it does not tell us who the elementary school teacher from Arkansas *is*.

We must therefore ask ourselves whom or what it is referring to. When we look at the rest of the sentence, it is clear that this description can only refer to Bessie Boehm Moore.

The words *Bessie Boehm Moore* do not appear immediately after the comma, so the modifier is dangling.

In order to fix the sentence, we must place Bessie Boehm Moore's name after the comma.

> Correct: An elementary school teacher from Arkansas, **Bessie Boehm Moore** advocated for increased funding and support for public libraries.

One very common SAT trick is to put a possessive version of the subject immediately after the introductory clause. In general, any possessive noun placed immediately after an introductory clause will be incorrect.

Incorrect:	An elementary school teacher from Arkansas, **Bessie Boehm Moore's goal** was to achieve increased funding and support for public libraries.

At first glance, this sentence looks and sounds correct. But who is the elementary school teacher from Arkansas? *Bessie Boehm Moore*, not her *goal*. And here, the *goal* is the subject – not *Bessie Boehm Moore*. The modifier is therefore dangling.

Correct:	An elementary school teacher from Arkansas, **Bessie Boehm Moore** had the goal of achieving increased funding and support for public libraries.

When fixing dangling modifiers, it is most important that you identify the subject – the rest of the sentence is not nearly as important – because when you look at the answer choices, you are looking for an option that places the subject immediately after the introductory clause. If the subject is not there, you can immediately eliminate the option.

Important: it is acceptable to begin the main clause with an adjective or adjectives describing the subject because that description is considered part of the complete subject.

In addition, the presence of a participle, particularly a present participle, at the beginning of a sentence often signals a dangling modifier.

In the sentences below, the participles are in bold and the complete subject is underlined.

Present Participle

Incorrect:	**Stretching** from one end of the city to the other, the efficiency of <u>the new tram system</u> often surprises both tourists and city residents.
Correct:	**Stretching** from one end of the city to the other, <u>the new tram system</u> often surprises both tourists and city residents with its efficiency.

Past Participle

Incorrect:	**Born** in a small town in Missouri, the majority of <u>singer and actress Josephine Baker</u>'s career was spent performing throughout Europe.
Correct:	**Born** in a small town in Missouri, <u>singer and actress Josephine Baker</u> spent the majority of her career performing throughout Europe.

In general, dangling modifier answer choices follow a highly predictable pattern. Of five choices, only two will successfully place the subject after the introductory clause and correct the dangling modification; the other three can be eliminated immediately. Of the two that remain, one will be wordy and awkward, and the other will be correct. While it is always a good idea to read both answers, the shorter one will usually be right.

Occasionally, however, you will have no choice but to rearrange the entire sentence. For example:

Correct:	The train system stretches from one end of the city to the other and often surprises tourists and city residents with its efficiency.
Correct:	The train system, which stretches from one end of the city to the other, often surprises tourists and city residents with its efficiency.

Dangling Modifier Exercises

In the following exercises, identify the subject of each sentence, and rewrite as necessary to eliminate any dangling modifier that appears. Some of the sentences may not contain an error. (Answers p. 161, Official Guide question list p. 138)

1. Characterized by scenes that are shot quickly and in real time, low budgets and simple props are both typical elements of guerilla filmmaking.

2. One of the greatest musicians of her time, Clara Wieck's piano studies began when she was five years old; by the age of twelve she was renowned as both a performer and a composer.

3. Born in St. Lucia in the West Indies, author Derek Walcott's work includes a number of plays and poems, most notably *Omeros*.

4. One of hundreds of islands that form the Indonesian archipelago, the width of Bali is less than 100 miles, yet it holds within its borders a rich and dramatic history.

5. Historically based on the carving of walrus ivory, which was once found in abundance, since the mid-twentieth century Inuit art has also included prints and figures made from soft stone.

6. Located in the southern Andes and covered by glaciers, the most recent eruption of the volcano known as Tronador occurred many centuries ago.

7. An inspiration to European artists such as Gauguin, van Gogh, and Toulouse-Lautrec, the eighteenth century was when Japanese painter Katsushika Hokusai lived.

8. Projecting an image of pain and brutality that has few parallels among advanced paintings of the twentieth century, *Guernica* was painted by Pablo Picasso in the aftermath of a World War II bombing.

9. Though educated and well mannered, the status of Jane Eyre remains low throughout the majority of the novel that bears her name.

10. Born at Dromland Castle in County Clare, Ireland in 1821, artist and engineer George O'Brien's aristocratic background seemed at odds with his life in the Australian outback.

11. A member of the ruralism movement, Czech writer Josef Holocek made life in Bohemia one of the principal subjects of his work.

12. Despite winning several architectural awards, the impractical layout of the university's new dormitory has been criticized by students.

13. One of the earliest authorities to take a stand against pollution, it was proclaimed by King Edward I in 1306 that sea coal could not be burned because the smoke it created was hazardous to people's health.

14. Predicting renewed interest in their country's natural resources, a plan has been established by political leaders to create mines in the most underdeveloped regions.

15. Having remained under Moorish rule until the twelfth century, Arabic was still spoken by many Spaniards when their cities first came under the control of European monarchs.

Misplaced Modifiers

Although misplaced modifiers are far less common than dangling modifiers, they do appear from time to time. They may also, in very rare instances, appear in the Error-Identification section.

Unlike dangling modifiers, misplaced modifiers do not necessarily involve introductory clauses and can occur anywhere in a sentence. They do, however, also involve modifiers separated from the words or phrases they are intended to modify and often result in sentences whose meanings are unintentionally ridiculous.

Incorrect: Alexander Fleming discovered the first antibiotic accidentally introducing contamination into a laboratory experiment.

In the above sentence, it sounds as if the first antibiotic was responsible for accidentally introducing contamination into a laboratory experiment, when it was clearly *Fleming* who introduced the contamination.

In order to correct the sentence, we need to make it clear that Fleming was responsible for the contamination.

Correct: Alexander Fleming discovered the first antibiotic when he accidentally introduced contamination into a laboratory experiment.

Misplaced Modifier Exercises

In the following sentences, correct any misplaced modification error that occurs. Some of the sentences may not contain an error. (Answers p. 161, Official Guide question list p. 138)

1. The Spanish city of Valencia is the birthplace of horchata, a drink said to date from the eighth century made from the juice of tiger nuts.

2. Claude McKay was one of the most important poets of the Harlem Renaissance that moved to New York after studying agronomy in Kansas.

3. The California Street Cable Railroad is an established public transit company in San Francisco, which was founded by Leland Stanford.

4. Many police officers have switched from patrolling city streets on horseback to patrolling them in cars, which have become the most popular form of urban transportation.

5. Praised by consumer magazines for being both versatile and affordable, the food processor performs a wide range of functions, including chopping, dicing, and pureeing, when flipping a switch.

6. Many ancient cities were protected from bands of invaders by fortresses roaming in search of settlements to plunder.

7. Some of the world's fastest trains run between the cities of Tokyo and Kyoto, which can reach speeds of up to 200 miles per hour.

8. Originally constructed during the Roman Republic, the House of Livia contains brightly colored frescoes dating back to the first decades B.C. that depict bucolic landscapes and mythological scenes.

9. The Georgian port of Batumi fell into decline in the mid-twentieth century, which once housed some of the world's first oil pipelines.

10. The bass viol has experienced a resurgence in popularity over the past several decades resembling the cello.

23. PARALLEL STRUCTURE II: PHRASES

Unlike the "list" form of parallel structure described in Chapter Seven, this kind of parallel structure requires you to work with phrases rather than single words. And also unlike list parallel structure, it usually – though not always – involves only two items.

The most difficult "phrase" parallel structure questions typically appear at the end of Fixing Sentences – usually as one of the last three questions, most often as the final question. In their simpler form (see the first example below), they may also occasionally appear in the Error-Identification Section or at the beginning of Fixing Sentences.

Since you will most likely encounter these questions after sitting through more than four hours of test-taking, the point at which you are most likely to be fatigued, it is important that you be able to recognize them without too much effort. These questions can be identified by the presence of certain conjunctions or comparisons:

-And
-But
-Not only…but also
-So…that
-At once…and
-Both…and
-Any other word pair (for the complete list, see p. 53)

If one of these conjunctions appears on the final sentence of a Fixing Sentences section, it is virtually guaranteed to be a parallel structure question. The rule is as follows:

> **The construction on one side of any given conjunction or comparison must match the construction on the other side of the conjunction or comparison as closely as possible.**

If one side contains the construction *noun + preposition + noun*, the other must contain *noun + preposition + noun*; if one side contains a preposition, the other must contain a preposition, etc.

If the two sides do not match in their constructions, the result is an error in parallel structure.

Let us consider the following sentence:

Incorrect: More than simply providing badly needed space in cramped cities, skyscrapers **connect** people, <u>and</u> **creativity is fostered** in them.

The presence of the word *and* tells us that the constructions on either side of it must match. But since one side is active and the other passive, the construction is not parallel. To correct it, we must make both sides active:

Correct: More than simply providing badly needed space in cramped cities, skyscrapers **connect** people <u>and</u> **foster** creativity.

Now we're going to try something a little harder:

Incorrect: The researchers called for enforcement of existing cigarette sale regulations as well as investigating teenagers' motivations for smoking.

In the above sentence, the construction on either side of the conjunction *as well as* must be the same.

So next we want to look at the specific construction of those two pieces of information.

What did the researchers call for?

1) enforcement of existing cigarette sale regulations

2) investigating teenagers' motivations for smoking

When we examine the two sides, we see that their constructions do not match.

-The first one contains the classic *noun + of + noun* structure (*enforcement of… regulations*).

-The second contains a *gerund + noun* structure (*investigating…motivations*).

To make the two sides parallel, we must replace the gerund *investigating* with its noun form, *investigation*, and add *of*.

Correct: The researchers called for **enforcement <u>of</u> existing cigarette sale regulations** <u>as well as</u> **an investigation <u>of</u> teenagers' motivations for smoking**.

Occasionally, this type of parallel structure question will include a third item. In such cases, the principle is exactly the same: each item must contain *noun + of + noun*.

Incorrect: A remarkable self-publicist, Margaret Cavendish was a composer <u>of</u> poetry, a writer <u>of</u> philosophy, **plus she invented romances**.

Correct: A remarkable self-publicist, Margaret Cavendish was a composer <u>of</u> poetry, a writer <u>of</u> philosophy, and **an inventor <u>of</u> romances**.

Important: parallel structure questions frequently double as word-pair questions. If you can spot the word pair, you can often eliminate several answers immediately.

For example:

In order to be an effective driver, one must have **both** an understanding of how to handle a vehicle <u>as well as being willing to obey traffic laws strictly</u>.

(A) as well as being willing to obey
(B) and having a willingness in obeying
(C) with a willingness for obeying
(D) plus being willing to obey
(E) and a willingness to obey

Since *both* must go with *and*, we can immediately eliminate choices A, C, and D. Choice B is long and contains a gerund, so that gives us E, which is the answer.

Parallel Structure II: Phrase Exercises

In the following sentences, identify the conjunction or comparison indicating that parallel structure is required, and rewrite the sentence to include a parallel construction. Some of the sentences may not contain an error. (Answers p. 162, Official Guide question list p. 133)

1. Hans Holbein was one of the most exquisite draftsmen of all time, renowned for the precise rendering of his drawings and the compelling realism of his portraits.

2. The figure skater was praised not only for her mastery of difficult technical skills, but also her performance was elegant and graceful.

3. While the novel has many detractors, it also has many admirers who argue that its popularity is based on its gripping storyline and its characters' motives are believable.

4. Known for her musical compositions as well as for her poems and letters, Hildegard of Bingen was just as renowned in the twelfth century as the twentieth.

5. The university is installing an electronic course-evaluation system so that students can decide whether they should register for certain classes or should they avoid them altogether.

6. For fans of the legendary food writer Charles H. Baker, the contents of a dish are less compelling than what the story is behind it.

7. During the sixteenth century, an outbreak of fighting in Europe led to the invention of new weapons and to old weapons growing and evolving.

8. In contemporary education, there is a disturbing contrast between the enormous popularity of certain approaches and the lack of credible evidence for their effectiveness.

9. It is believed that many animals are capable of drawing a connection between the odor of a harmful substance and how toxic it is.

10. The bass clarinet, although similar to the more common soprano clarinet, is distinguished both by the greater length of its body plus several additional keys are present.

11. At its peak, the Roman army was nearly unconquerable because of the discipline of its soldiers, the hard and effective training of its commanders, and its troops were exceptionally well-organized.

12. The development of identity was one of psychologist Erik Erikson's greatest concerns, both in his own life and his theory.

24. THE SUBJUNCTIVE

The subjunctive is a **mood** that is used to express necessity, requests, and suggestions, and to describe hypothetical situations. It is tested relatively infrequently, and you should therefore look at this section only after you feel comfortable recognizing all of the other errors discussed in this guide.

Although the subjunctive appears in both the Error-Identification and Fixing Sentences sections, it appears more frequently in the latter, and thus I have listed it here. **When it is underlined in an Error-Identification sentence, however, it will generally be used correctly; only in Fixing Sentences will you regularly be responsible for actually correcting errors that involve it.**

Present Subjunctive

The major distinction between **subjunctive** and **indicative** (regular) verbs occurs in the third person singular (*he/she/it/one*). While an –*s* is added in the indicative (e.g. *she goes*, *talks*, *works*), no –*s* is added in the subjunctive.

The easiest way to think of it is that subjunctive = infinitive minus the word *to*. Thus, the subjunctive form of *to be* = *be*; the subjunctive form of *to have* = *have*; and the subjunctive form of *to do* = *do*.

Indicative	Subjunctive
Marcus **speaks** to me.	I <u>demand</u> that Marcus **speak** to me.
Sunita **finishes** her work.	The teacher <u>recommends</u> that Sunita **finish** her work.
Cole **arrives** home at six o'clock.	Cole's parents <u>insist</u> that he **arrive** home at six o'clock.

Past Subjunctive

The past subjunctive is used for hypothetical situations – ones that have not actually occurred. Clauses that include the past subjunctive thus often begin with *if*. In the past subjunctive, the verb *to be* is always conjugated as *were*, never *was*.

Indicative	Subjunctive
Marcus **spoke** to me.	If Marcus **were to speak** to me **Were** Marcus to **speak** to me
Sunita **finished** her work early.	If Sunita **had finished** her work early **Had** Sunita **finished** her work early (NOT: If Sunita **would have finished** her work early)
Cole **arrived** home at six o'clock.	If Cole **were to have arrived** home at six o'clock **Were** Cole **to have arrived** home at six o'clock

25. MISCELLANEOUS: FIXING SENTENCES

Errors with "because"

The SAT likes to test your knowledge of the word *because*, and there are several predictable ways in which it does so.

A noun cannot "be because"

An event can only *take place* or *occur*; it cannot *be because*.

Incorrect:	**The beginning** of the American Civil War **was because** of a skirmish that broke out at Fort Sumter in South Carolina.
Correct:	**The beginning** of the American Civil War **occurred** when a skirmish broke out at Fort Sumter in South Carolina.
Even Better:	**The American Civil War began** when a skirmish broke out at Fort Sumter in South Carolina.

Redundancy

- The reason is because
- Because…is the reason that
- Because…is why

All of these phrases are redundant and thus **incorrect**. Use either *the reason is that* or simply *because*.

Note: The SAT rarely tests *the reason is because* in isolation – it is usually accompanied by another problem such as an unnecessary gerund or extreme wordiness. Knowing *the reason is that* is the correct phrase can, however, help you spot the right answer more quickly when this error does appear.

Incorrect:	In the 1970's, Quito, the capital of Ecuador, was named a World Heritage Site, and **the reason is because** of its historic center being exceptionally well preserved.
Incorrect:	**Because** its historic center was exceptionally well preserved **is the reason that** Quito, the capital of Ecuador, was named a World Heritage Site in the 1970's.
Correct:	In the 1970's, Quito, the capital of Ecuador, was named a World Heritage Site **because** its historic center was exceptionally well preserved.

The question is whether, NOT the question is if

Incorrect: After the closing arguments of the trial, the members of the jury faced the question of **if** they should convict the defendant or, on the contrary, set him free.

Correct: After the closing arguments of the trial, the members of the jury faced the question of **whether** they should convict the defendant or, on the contrary, set him free.

The rule is the same for words like *debate, challenge, decide, choose,* and *argue*:

Incorrect: After the closing arguments of the trial, the members of the jury argued about **if** they should convict the defendant or, on the contrary, set him free.

Correct: After the closing arguments of the trial, the members of the jury argued about **whether** they should convict the defendant or, on the contrary, set him free.

Whereby and Thereby

Whereby means "by which," and although it may sound awkward, its appearance does not necessarily indicate an incorrect answer.

Correct: Desalination is a process **whereby** salt and other minerals are removed from water in order to produce a liquid that is suitable for human consumption.

Thereby is a synonym for "thus" and "therefore" and can be used interchangeably with those words. Like *whereby*, it may seem awkward but does not by itself indicate an incorrect answer.

Correct: The Scientific Revolution was an era in which new ideas in astronomy, biology, and medicine transformed medieval and ancient views of nature, **thereby** laying the foundation for most modern discoveries.

For all

This is a fairly common "trick" phrase in Fixing Sentences. It means *despite*, and don't get fooled because you think it sounds funny. It's correct.

Correct: **For all** his interest in abstract forms, Picasso remained devoted to painting the human figure for much of his career.

Plus

The word *plus*, especially when it is followed by a gerund, is virtually always wrong.

Incorrect: Jonas Salk, the creator of the first polio vaccine, was seen by many as a savior **plus achieving** rapid fame.

Correct: Jonas Salk, the creator of the first polio vaccine, was seen by many as a savior **and achieved** rapid fame.

26. FIXING SENTENCES STRATEGIES

So now that you know what to look for, let's consider some strategies for identifying answers in Fixing Sentences.

Example #1

The landscapes of the Caribbean islands are famous for their jewel-like <u>beauty, and some of their most amazing scenery lies hidden underwater</u>.

(A) beauty, and some of their most amazing scenery lies
(B) beauty, and some of its most amazing scenery lies
(C) beauty, but some of their most amazing scenery lying
(D) beauty, some of their most amazing scenery lies
(E) beauty; however, some of their most amazing scenery lies

Shortcut: spot the conjunction error

An underlined conjunction in Fixing Sentences frequently indicates that the conjunction itself is being tested. So let's look at the relationship between the clauses:

Clause 1: The landscapes of the Caribbean islands are famous for their jewel-like beauty.

Clause 2: Some of their most amazing scenery lies underwater.

-The two clauses contradict one another, so we need a contradictor such as *but*. That eliminates A and B.

-C contains a gerund, and D contains a comma splice, so we can eliminate them as well.

-So that leaves us with **E**.

You could also figure out the answer this way:

-Start by eliminating C because it contains a gerund and D because it contains a comma splice.

-B contains the singular pronoun *its*, while A and E contains the plural pronoun *their*. What's the antecedent? *landscapes*, which is plural, so that eliminates B.

-E contains a correctly-used semicolon. When an answer choice contains a correctly-used semicolon, that answer is usually right.

Example #2

Frequently dismissed as a buffoonish entertainer during his lifetime, <u>some now recognize jazz musician Cab Calloway as a creative genius</u>.

(A) some now recognize jazz musician Cab Calloway
    as a creative genius
(B) a creative genius is what some now recognize jazz
    musician Cab Calloway to be
(C) jazz musician Cab Calloway is now recognized by
    some as a creative genius
(D) jazz musician Cab Calloway now being recognized
    by some people as a creative genius
(E) jazz musician Cab Calloway's music is now recognized
    by some as the product of a creative genius

Shortcut: The first thing we can notice about this sentence is that it contains an introductory clause that describes but does not name the subject; we don't know *who* was frequently dismissed as a buffoonish entertainer during his lifetime. The presence of that introductory clause suggests that we're probably dealing with a dangling modifier, so the first thing we need to do is identify the subject.

So *who* was frequently dismissed as a buffoonish entertainer during his lifetime?

Jazz musician Cab Calloway. So the correct answer must start with those words.

    -That eliminates A and B.

    -E contains the classic trick of making the subject possessive (*Cab Calloway's*), so that's out too.

    -That leaves us with C and D.

    -D contains the gerund *being*, so the answer is **C**.

Example #3

Throughout his career, George Washington was criticized for his clumsy military <u>tactics, but he earned praise because his politics were insightful</u>.

(A) tactics, but he earned praise because his politics were insightful

(B) tactics, and he earned praise for having insightful politics

(C) tactics, although showing insight in his politics

(D) tactics, and he was insightful politically

(E) tactics but praised for his insightful politics

Shortcut: The presence of the conjunction *but* suggests that we are dealing with a parallel structure question. Furthermore, the phrase *for his weak military tactics* in the non-underlined portion of the sentence is key because it tells us that the correct answer must contain the basic construction *for his + adjective + noun*.

The only answer that fulfills those requirements is **E**.

Fixing Sentences Test

1. Benjamin Franklin demonstrated his enthusiasm for inoculation against smallpox, he collaborated on many studies that demonstrated the procedure's effectiveness.

   (A) smallpox, he collaborated
   (B) smallpox, and he collaborated
   (C) smallpox by collaborating
   (D) smallpox and collaborating
   (E) smallpox, he was collaborating

2. Although once being found in abundance on the North American continent, many species of Amazon parrot have now become nearly extinct.

   (A) Although once being found in abundance
   (B) Although they were once found in abundance
   (C) Despite their being found once in abundance
   (D) Once they were found in abundance
   (E) Even though it was once found in abundance

3. Because they did not want to miss a second of the comet's collision with Jupiter, the astronomers have kept their telescopes fixed on the sky until the consequences of the impact became clear.

   (A) have kept
   (B) having kept
   (C) keep
   (D) kept
   (E) keeping

4. Amelia Griffiths, one of the most prominent amateur scientists of the early nineteenth century, and she was a beachcomber and phycologist who made many important collections of algae specimens.

   (A) nineteenth century, and she was a beachcomber and phycologist who made
   (B) nineteenth century, being a beachcomber and phycologist making
   (C) nineteenth century, was a beachcomber and phycologist who made
   (D) nineteenth century, a beachcomber and phycologist who made
   (E) nineteenth century, she was a beachcomber and phycologist who had made

5. Although most people do not realize it, skiing on fresh snow, skating on reflective ice, and hikes at high altitudes can expose people to more harmful ultraviolet rays than a day at the beach.

   (A) skiing on fresh snow, skating on reflective ice, and hikes at high altitudes
   (B) skiing on fresh snow, to skate on reflective ice, and to hike at high altitudes
   (C) to ski on fresh snow, to skate on reflective ice, and hiking
   (D) skiing on fresh snow, skating on reflective ice, and hiking at high altitudes
   (E) skiing on fresh snow and skating on reflective ice, hiking at high altitudes

6. Despite negotiations that were threatening to collapse, the senators were able to salvage the bill that they had worked so long to prepare.

   (A) negotiations that were threatening to collapse
   (B) negotiations whose collapse was threatening
   (C) negotiations, threatening to collapse
   (D) negotiations, for which collapse was a threat
   (E) negotiations where collapse was threatened

7. Most often associated with medieval Europe, Japanese society was based on feudalism during the same period.

   (A) Most often associated with medieval Europe, Japanese society was based on feudalism
   (B) Most often associated with medieval Europe, feudalism formed the basis of Japanese society
   (C) Most often associated with medieval Europe, Japanese society based on feudalism
   (D) Its association with medieval Europe occurring most often, Japanese society was based on feudalism
   (E) Being most often associated with medieval Europe, feudalism had also been the basis for Japanese society

8. The mineral azurite has an exceptionally deep blue hue, and for that reason they have tended to be associated since antiquity with the color of winter skies.

(A) The mineral azurite has an exceptionally deep blue hue, and for that reason they have tended to be
(B) The mineral azurite has an exceptionally deep blue hue, and this is why it has tended to be
(C) The mineral azurite has an exceptionally deep blue hue, it has
(D) The mineral azurite has an exceptionally deep blue hue, so they have
(E) The mineral azurite has an exceptionally deep blue hue; therefore, it has often been

9. Responding to pressure from business leaders and politicians alike, the labor union has announced that they will begin to hold discussions about the proposed contract early next week.

(A) the labor union has announced that they will begin
(B) the labor union have announced that they would begin
(C) the labor union announcing that they would begin
(D) the labor union having announced that it would begin
(E) the labor union has announced that it will begin

10. Cajun cuisine is predominantly rustic, relying on locally available ingredients and preparation of it is simple.

(A) and preparation of it is simple
(B) plus preparation being simple
(C) and simple preparation
(D) and preparation as simple
(E) with simplicity in its preparation

11. Born in 1917, dozens of Chinese-American architect I.M. Pei's buildings have become landmarks, and he is often called a master of modern architecture.

(A) dozens of Chinese-American architect I.M. Pei's buildings have become landmarks,
(B) Chinese-American architect I.M. Pei's buildings, of which dozens have become landmarks,
(C) dozens of landmark buildings being among Chinese-American architect I.M. Pei's designs,
(D) Chinese-American architect I.M. Pei has designed dozens of landmark buildings,
(E) Chinese-American architect I.M. Pei having designed dozens of landmark buildings,

12. Every chess game contains millions of potential moves, which makes it impossible to predict a player's strategy more than a few minutes into the future.

(A) which makes it impossible to predict
(B) making it impossible to predict
(C) making it impossible in predicting
(D) so predicting is not possible
(E) it is therefore impossible to predict

13. The roundscale spearfish and the white marlin are two separate, if closely related, aquatic species.

(A) separate, if closely related, aquatic species
(B) separate aquatic species, although being closely related
(C) separate aquatic species, but also closely related
(D) separate aquatic species, whereas they are related closely
(E) separate aquatic species, although their relationship is a close one

14. Patrons of the restaurant find it at once impressive because of its superior quality, but its poor service makes eating there unpleasant.

(A) quality, but its poor service makes eating there unpleasant
(B) quality, although its poor service makes it unpleasant for them to eat there
(C) quality, and its poor service makes eating there unpleasant also
(D) quality while having poor service that makes eating there unpleasant
(E) and unpleasant because of its poor service

Answers to this test can be found on p. 162

27. FIXING PARAGRAPHS

The Fixing Paragraphs section always contains six questions divided into two types:

1) Grammar and Style

2) Paragraph Organization

The order of the questions follows the order of the paragraph (usually about 15 sentences long), and grammar/style and paragraph organization questions are distributed randomly. Some sections are divided evenly between the two kinds of questions, while others include mostly one kind or the other, and there's no way to predict which way a particular test might skew.

The major difference between Fixing Paragraphs and the other two multiple-choice Writing sections is that Fixing Paragraphs questions are not isolated sentences that can be considered individually; rather, they must be considered in context. A sentence that does not contain any major grammatical errors will therefore not be the correct answer if it does not make sense within the larger scope of the paragraph.

In addition, Fixing Paragraphs questions have a somewhat heavier emphasis on transitions than do either Error-Identification or Fixing Sentences questions.

Grammar and Style

Grammar and style issues are further broken down into two main types of questions:

- **Sentence Revision** questions require you to identify the best revision of a sentence or portion of a sentence.

- **Combining Sentences** questions require you to identify the best way to combine two sentences into a single sentence.

The most important thing to remember about grammar and style questions is that the rules they test are identical those tested in Fixing Sentences. This means that all of the same grammar and style rules apply. To reiterate:

1) Shorter = Better

2) Gerunds = Bad

3) Passive = Bad

4) Comma Splices = Bad

So if a sentence seems to fit the context of a paragraph but violates one of the above rules, look again. There's probably a better answer.

Paragraph Organization

Paragraph organization and rhetoric questions typically appear in the following forms:

- **Sentence Insertion** questions require you to identify which new sentence should be inserted at a specific point in the paragraph.

- **Sentence Order** questions require you to identify where in the paragraph an existing sentence would best belong.

- **Information Insertion** questions require you to identify specific words or information that would strengthen a sentence or paragraph.

- **Transition** questions require you to identify which transition should be placed at the beginning of a given sentence.

- **Rhetorical Strategy** questions require you to identify a particular rhetorical strategy (e.g. personification, anecdote, analogy) used in a portion of the paragraph.

- **Paragraph Division** questions require you to identify where a paragraph break would most logically be inserted in a passage.

Since it's really not possible to closely examine how to handle these kinds of questions without an actual passage, let's look at one:

When Merriwether Lewis and William Clark set out in 1803 to explore the lands west of the Mississippi River, they couldn't make the journey alone. (1) The wilderness was dense, and Native American attacks were common. (2) Luckily, when Lewis and Clark arrived in what is now North Dakota, they met Sacagawea. (3) A member of the Shoshone tribe, her marriage to a French trader named Charbonneau had made Sacagawea accustomed to interacting with settlers. (4) She would go down in history for leading Lewis and Clark thousands of miles, from present-day North Dakota all the way to the Pacific Ocean. (5)

Although Sacagawea is famous for being Lewis and Clark's guide, she didn't just give them directions. (6) She did much more than that. (7) She served as an interpreter between the explorers and the Shoshone people. (8) So that they could interact peacefully. (9) Also, since women did not accompany war parties, her being there showed Native Americans that the explorers did not have hostile intentions and prevented conflicts between the two groups – with only one exception. (10) However, for most of the nineteenth century, Sacagawea was forgotten. (11) That changed in 1902, when suffragist Eva Emery Dye published *The Conquest: The True Story of Lewis and Clark*. (12) Since then, Sacagawea has been honored with countless memorials and statues. (13) Almost as soon as the book appeared, Sacagawea was quickly claimed as a hero by women's rights groups, and many books and essays were written about her. (14) Her face has even appeared on her own specially issued dollar coin. (15)

Rhetorical Strategy

An important strategy used in the first paragraph is to:

(A) present a difficult problem and describe its successful resolution
(B) explain the cultural advantages of bilingualism for members of the Shoshone tribe
(C) provide an explicit critique of early American policy toward Native Americans
(D) convey a detailed impression of the wilderness west of the Mississippi River
(E) compare the kinds of travel common in nineteenth century America to the kinds of travel common today

Strategy:

Although they appear on the Writing sections, questions like these are fundamentally about reading. The main thing to remember is that you should go back to the passage and sum up the focus of the first paragraph for yourself.

What does the first paragraph discuss? Why Lewis and Clark needed a guide (dense wilderness, Native American attacks) and how they found an excellent one (Sacagawea). In other words, a problem and its solution.

So the answer must be A.

Don't be fooled by the fact that A doesn't explicitly include people or places mentioned in the passage. Just like Critical Reading questions, these kinds of writing questions will ask you to translate concrete information into a more abstract form.

Sentence Revision:

Which of the following is the best version of the underlined portion of sentence 3 (reproduced below)?

A member of the Shoshone tribe, her marriage to a French trader named Charbonneau had made Sacagawea accustomed to interacting with settlers.

(A) Sacagawea had become accustomed to interacting with settlers because of her marriage to a French trapper named Charbonneau.

(B) Sacagawea's familiarity with how to interact with settlers was because of her husband Charbonneau, a trapper.

(C) a trapper named Charbonneau, to whom Sacagawea was married, is why Sacagawea was accustomed to interacting with settlers.

(D) it was because of her marriage to a trapper named Charbonneau that Sacagawea was accustomed to interacting with settlers.

(E) her being married to a trapper named Charbonneau had led to her being accustomed to interacting with settlers.

Strategy:

Let's go back to our Fixing Sentences rules and examine the construction of the original sentence. We notice that it begins with an introductory clause that describes but does not name the subject:

A member of the Shoshone tribe,

That tells us right away that we're probably dealing with a dangling modifier.

-Who was a member of the Shoshone tribe? Sacagawea.

So we know that the first word after the introductory clause must be the word *Sacagawea*.

That is only true of A, so it must be the answer.

Information Insertion:

Paragraph two would best be improved by the addition of:

(A) the inclusion of specific words translated by Sacagawea

(B) an example of the kind of directions Sacagawea gave Lewis and Clark

(C) the name of a woman who was known for leading a war party

(D) more information about how Sacagawea's first encounter with settlers

(E) a description of a confrontation between Lewis and Clark and hostile Native Americans.

Strategy:

When faced with a question like this, you have two choices: you can either plug in the answer choices one by one, or you can start by going back to the passage and figuring out what's missing. While the former might feel safer, the latter is far more effective.

When we read through paragraph two, we notice that it ends rather abruptly. The majority of the passage focuses on Sacagawea's success in helping Lewis and Clark navigate their relations with Native Americans, but at the end, a new idea is suddenly introduced: we are told that there was a conflict, but that conflict is never explained. The most effective way to improve the paragraph would therefore be to provide more details about the conflict.

So the answer is E.

Combining Sentences

In context, which is the best way to combine sentences 6 and 7 (reproduced below?)

She served as an interpreter between the explorers and the Shoshone people. So that they could interact peacefully.

(A) She served as an interpreter between the explorers and the Shoshone people, they could interact peacefully that way.
(B) She served as an interpreter between the explorers and the Shoshone people, whereas she allowed them to interact peacefully.
(C) She served as an interpreter between the explorers and the Shoshone people and allowing them interact peacefully.
(D) She served as an interpreter between the explorers and the Shoshone people, whereby their peaceful interaction was allowed.
(E) She served as an interpreter between the explorers and the Shoshone people, allowing them to interact peacefully.

Strategy:

We're going to treat this exactly like a Fixing Sentences question.

Choice A contains a comma splice and can therefore be eliminated immediately.

The transition *whereas* in choice B incorrectly indicates a contradiction between the two ideas.

Choice C contains verbs whose tenses are not parallel and can be eliminated as well.

Choice D contains a passive construction, so that's gone too.

Which leaves us with E.

Sentence Order

Where is the best place for sentence 14?

(A) where it is now
(B) after sentence 10
(C) after sentence 11
(D) after sentence 12
(E) after sentence 15

Strategy:

Instead of plugging sentence 12 into each of the answer choices (and wasting a lot of time in the process), we're going to figure the answer out logically.

Sentence 14 describes what happened *almost as soon as the book was published*. What book? Well, the only book that is mentioned is Eva Emery Dye's book in sentence 11. And if we're talking about what happened right after the book's publication, then that information should appear right after sentence 11.

So the answer is C.

Transitions

Which of the following would most appropriately be inserted at the beginning of sentence 6 (reproduced below)?

She did much more than that.

(A) However,
(B) Essentially,
(C) Meanwhile,
(D) In fact,
(E) On the other hand,

Strategy:

This question requires us to determine the relationship between this sentence and the previous sentence. To do so, we must examine them separately and see if they are talking about the same idea or different ideas.

Sentence 1: Although Sacagawea is famous for being Lewis and Clark's guide, she didn't just give them directions.

Sentence 2: She did much more than that.

Both sentences contain the same idea. That eliminates A, C, and E because they would be used to connect two contradicting thoughts.

So that leaves us with B and D.

Now we look more closely at the relationship between the sentences: the second sentence is emphasizing the information presented in the first, which means that D, *In fact*, works.

Choice B, *Essentially*, would be used to clarify an idea, which is not quite what's going on here.

So the answer is D.

Paragraph Division

Where is the most logical place to begin a new paragraph?

(A) After sentence 9
(B) After sentence 10
(C) After sentence 12
(D) After sentence 13
(E) After sentence 14

Strategy:

This question requires us to determine where in the passage the idea shifts. When we look back at the second paragraph, we see that sentences 6 through 10 describe events that occurred in Sacagawea's time, while sentences 11 through 15 describe how Sacagawea was viewed in later times. The logical break therefore occurs after sentence 10, when we move from a discussion of Sacagawea's ability to mediate between Lewis and Clark and the Shoshone people to the statement that Sacagawea was forgotten for most of the nineteenth century.

So the answer is B.

Appendix A

Note: The following lists are based on the questions in the Official SAT Study Guide, Second Edition[1] (©
2009 by The College Board). In general, I have attempted to categorize each question according the *primary*
concept it tests, even though there may be secondary errors contained in the answer choices (e.g. a question
designed primarily to test pronoun-antecedent usage is listed as a pronoun-antecedent question, despite the
fact that several of the answer choices contain improperly used gerunds). Whenever possible, I have also
listed the sub-category into which each question falls. For cases in which a question truly does test multiple
concepts simultaneously, however, I have listed it in multiple categories. "No error" questions are indicated as
such and are also listed according to the primary concepts they test. Errors discussed in the book but not
listed below are based on questions from officially administered exams that have been released but that were
not included in the Official Guide.

Key:

s-nec-v = subject – non-essential clause – verb

s-pp-v = subject – prepositional phrase – verb

pp-v-s = prepositional phrase – verb – subject

NE = No error

Subject-Verb Agreement (p. 12)

Test: 1	Section: 6	Question: 20	(NE, the number)	p: 410
Test: 1	Section: 6	Question: 23	(s-nec-v, s-pp-v)	p: 410
Test: 1	Section: 6	Question: 24	(NE)	p: 410
Test: 1	Section: 6	Question: 28	(s-pp-v)	p: 410
Test: 1	Section: 10	Question: 1	(there is/ are)	p: 429
Test: 1	Section: 10	Question: 13	(s-pp-v)	p: 431
Test: 2	Section: 6	Question: 20	(simple disagreement)	p: 472
Test: 2	Section: 6	Question: 22	(s-pp-v)	p: 472
Test: 2	Section: 6	Question: 25	(s-nec-v)	p. 472
Test: 3	Section: 6	Question: 15	(relative clause)	p: 533
Test: 3	Section: 6	Question: 19	(s-nec-v)	p: 534
Test: 3	Section: 6	Question: 23	(compound subject)	p: 534
Test: 4	Section: 7	Question: 6	(NE, s-nec-v)	p: 600
Test: 4	Section: 7	Question: 27	(pp-v-s)	p: 602
Test: 5	Section: 6	Question: 3	(s-pp-v)	p: 656
Test: 5	Section: 6	Question: 7	(compound subject)	p: 657

---

[1] There are seven tests in the second edition that overlap with the tests in the first (2005) edition. Test #4 in the second edition
corresponds to Test #2 in the first edition; Test #5 in the second edition corresponds to Test #3 in the first edition, and so on.

Verb Tense and Form (p. 20)

Test: 3	Section: 10	Question: 5	(consistency)	p: 554
Test: 4	Section: 7	Question: 12	(consistency)	p: 601
Test: 4	Section: 7	Question: 13	(consistency)	p: 601
Test: 4	Section: 7	Question: 18	(consistency)	p: 601
Test: 4	Section: 7	Question: 22	(consistency, gerund vs. infinitive)	p: 602
Test: 4	Section: 10	Question: 1	(gerund vs. infinitive)	p: 614
Test: 4	Section: 10	Question: 4	(consistency)	p: 614
Test: 5	Section: 6	Question: 9	(consistency)	p: 657
Test: 5	Section: 6	Question: 15	(consistency)	p: 658
Test: 5	Section: 6	Question: 16	(gerund vs. infinitive)	p: 658
Test: 5	Section: 6	Question: 21	(gerund vs. infinitive)	p: 659
Test: 5	Section: 6	Question: 22	(gerund vs. infinitive)	p: 659
Test: 5	Section: 10	Question: 1	(would)	p: 676
Test: 5	Section: 10	Question: 11	(NE, present perfect)	p: 677
Test: 6	Section: 6	Question: 3	(consistency)	p: 718
Test: 6	Section: 6	Question: 9	(NE, past perfect)	p: 719
Test: 6	Section: 6	Question: 13	(NE, would vs. will)	p: 720
Test: 6	Section: 6	Question: 18	(consistency, gerund vs. infinitive)	p: 720
Test: 6	Section: 6	Question: 19	(past participle vs. simple past)	p: 720
Test: 6	Section: 6	Question: 23	(NE, present perfect)	p: 721
Test: 6	Section: 6	Question: 21	(past perfect)	p: 777
Test: 7	Section: 4	Question: 26	(gerund vs. infinitive)	p: 777
Test: 7	Section: 10	Question: 10	(gerund vs. infinitive)	p: 802
Test: 8	Section: 4	Question: 9	(consistency)	p: 837
Test: 8	Section: 4	Question: 13	(would vs. will)	p: 838
Test: 8	Section: 4	Question: 14	(NE, gerund vs. infinitive)	p: 838
Test: 8	Section: 4	Question: 16	(would)	p: 838
Test: 8	Section: 4	Question: 21	(would vs. will)	p. 839
Test: 8	Section: 4	Question: 22	(NE, would)	p: 839
Test: 8	Section: 10	Question: 1	(consistency)	p: 862
Test: 8	Section: 10	Question: 8	(gerund vs. infinitive)	p: 863
Test: 9	Section: 3	Questions: 3	(gerund vs. infinitive)	p: 892
Test: 9	Section: 3	Question: 12	(past perfect)	p: 894
Test: 9	Section: 3	Question: 20	(consistency)	p: 895
Test: 9	Section: 3	Question: 25	(for = present perfect)	p: 895
Test: 9	Section: 3	Question: 29	(NE, past perfect)	p: 896
Test: 9	Section: 10	Question: 7	(would vs. will)	p: 925
Test: 10	Section: 3	Question: 13	(gerund vs. infinitive)	p: 956
Test: 10	Section: 3	Question: 17	(consistency)	p: 956
Test: 10	Section: 3	Question: 20	(consistency)	p: 957
Test: 10	Section: 3	Question: 24	(past tense required)	p: 957
Test: 10	Section: 10	Question: 13	(consistency)	p: 988

Pronoun-Antecedent (p. 28)

Test: 1	Section: 6	Question: 19	(singular vs. plural:)	p: 409
Test: 1	Section: 6	Question: 26	(collective noun = singular)	p: 410
Test: 1	Section: 10	Question: 2	(missing antecedent)	p: 429
Test: 1	Section: 10	Question: 4	(ambiguous antecedent)	p: 429

Test: 2	Section: 6	Question: 28	(ambiguous antecedent)	p: 472
Test: 3	Section: 6	Question: 1	(missing antecedent)	p: 531
Test: 3	Section: 6	Question: 10	(collective noun= singular)	p: 532
Test: 3	Section: 6	Question: 17	(NE, singular vs. plural)	p: 533
Test: 3	Section: 6	Question: 20	(singular vs. plural)	p: 533
Test: 3	Section: 6	Question: 22	(singular vs. plural)	p: 534
Test: 4	Section: 6	Question: 27	(collective noun = sing.)	p: 535
Test: 4	Section: 7	Question: 15	(singular vs. plural)	p: 601
Test: 4	Section: 7	Question: 28	(singular vs. plural)	p: 602
Test: 4	Section: 10	Question: 9	(missing antecedent: this)	p: 615
Test: 5	Section: 6	Question: 5	(missing antecedent: it)	p: 657
Test: 5	Section: 6	Question: 6	(missing antecedent: this)	p: 657
Test: 5	Section: 6	Question: 10	(missing antecedent: which)	p: 657
Test: 5	Section: 6	Question: 11	(singular vs. plural)	p: 657
Test: 5	Section: 6	Question: 20	(singular vs. plural)	p: 659
Test: 5	Section: 10	Question: 23	(NE)	p: 659
Test: 5	Section: 6	Question: 28	(singular vs. plural)	p: 660
Test: 5	Section: 10	Question: 6	(missing antecedent: they)	p: 677
Test: 5	Section: 10	Question: 8	(NE, "which" used correctly)	p: 677
Test: 6	Section: 7	Question: 8	(collective noun = singular)	p: 719
Test: 6	Section: 6	Question: 15	(singular vs. plural)	p: 720
Test: 6	Section: 6	Question: 16	(NE, each = singular)	p: 720
Test: 6	Section: 6	Question: 20	(collective noun = singular)	p: 721
Test: 6	Section: 6	Question: 23	(NE)	p: 721
Test: 6	Section: 10	Question: 4	("which" used correctly)	p: 738
Test: 6	Section: 10	Question: 6	(NE, "there" is missing an antecedent in C, D, and E)	p: 739
Test: 6	Section: 10	Question: 7	(antecedent of "our" = "we")	p: 739
Test: 6	Section: 10	Question: 8	(missing antecedent: their)	p: 739
Test: 6	Section: 10	Question: 10	(singular vs. plural)	p: 739
Test: 7	Section: 4	Question: 5	(singular vs. plural)	p: 775
Test: 7	Section: 4	Question: 15	(verb consistency)	p: 776
Test: 7	Section: 4	Question: 23	(one vs. you)	p: 777
Test: 7	Section: 4	Question: 25	(one vs. he or she)	p: 777
Test: 7	Section: 10	Question: 4	("this" and "which")	p: 801
Test: 7	Section: 10	Question: 5	(collective noun: it/they)	p: 802
Test: 8	Section: 4	Question: 5	(every = singular: her/their)	p: 837
Test: 8	Section: 4	Question: 7	(NE, singular vs. plural)	p: 837
Test: 8	Section: 4	Question: 10	(NE, "which" used correctly)	p: 837
Test: 8	Section: 4	Question: 19	(singular vs. plural)	p: 838
Test: 8	Section: 4	Question: 25	(missing antecedent: it)	p: 839
Test: 8	Section: 4	Question: 26	("do it" vs. "do so")	p: 839
Test: 8	Section: 10	Question: 14	(missing antecedent: this)	p: 864
Test: 9	Section: 3	Question: 17	(NE, "those" used correctly)	p: 894
Test: 9	Section: 3	Question: 19	(singular vs. plural)	p: 895
Test: 9	Section: 10	Question: 9	(someone = he or she)	p: 925
Test: 9	Section: 10	Question: 11	(she = ambiguous antecedent)	p: 925
Test: 10	Section: 3	Question: 4	(missing antecedent = they)	p: 954
Test: 10	Section: 3	Question: 10	(singular vs. plural)	p: 955
Test: 10	Section: 3	Question: 26	(she = ambiguous antecedent)	p: 957
Test: 10	Section: 10	Question: 8	(NE, "which" used correctly)	p: 987

Pronoun Case (p. 36)

Test: 2	Section: 6	Question: 12		p: 471
Test: 4	Section: 7	Question: 21		p: 602
Test: 4	Section: 7	Question: 26		p: 602
Test: 6	Section: 6	Question: 27		p: 721
Test: 7	Section: 4	Question: 14		p: 776
Test: 8	Section: 4	Question: 23		p: 839
Test: 9	Section: 3	Question: 28		p: 896
Test: 10	Section: 3	Question: 22		p: 957

Adjectives vs. Adverbs (p. 42)

Test: 1	Section: 6	Question: 14		p: 409
Test: 1	Section: 6	Question: 17		p: 409
Test: 4	Section: 7	Question: 29		p: 602
Test: 5	Section: 10	Question: 23	(NE)	p: 659
Test: 6	Section: 6	Question: 22		p: 721
Test: 7	Section: 4	Question: 13		p: 776
Test: 7	Section: 4	Question: 16	(NE)	p: 776
Test: 8	Section: 4	Question: 12		p: 838
Test: 8	Section: 4	Question: 15		p: 838
Test: 8	Section: 4	Question: 28	(NE)	p: 839
Test: 10	Section: 3	Question: 15		p: 956

Prepositions and Idioms (p. 47)

Test: 2	Section: 6	Question: 10	(NE, for all = ok)	p: 470
Test: 2	Section: 6	Question: 23	(arrived in)	p: 472
Test: 2	Section: 6	Question: 26	(offers of)	p: 472
Test: 4	Section: 7	Question: 25	(preoccupation with)	p: 602
Test: 4	Section: 10	Question: 6	(assert that)	p: 615
Test: 5	Section: 10	Question: 23	(NE)	p: 659
Test: 6	Section: 6	Question: 5	(determine whether)	p: 718
Test: 6	Section: 6	Question: 17	(condition for)	p: 720
Test: 6	Section: 6	Question: 21	(threat to)	p: 721
Test: 6	Section: 6	Question: 23	(NE)	p: 721
Test: 7	Section: 4	Question: 26	(regarded as/as being)	p: 777
Test: 8	Section: 4	Question: 18	(prefer to)	p: 838
Test: 8	Section: 4	Question: 23	(protest against, or no preposition)	p: 839
Test: 8	Section: 4	Question: 28	(NE)	p: 839
Test: 8	Section: 10	Question: 8	(adopted by)	p: 863
Test: 9	Section: 3	Question: 24	(far from)	p: 895
Test: 9	Section: 3	Question: 25	(inconsistent with)	p: 896
Test: 9	Section: 3	Question: 29	(NE, intolerable to)	p: 896
Test: 10	Section: 3	Question: 23	(idiom, something of = ok)	p: 957
Test: 10	Section: 3	Question: 25	(listen to)	p: 957
Test: 10	Section: 10	Question: 1	(to think of something as)	p: 986

Parallel Structure (p. 45 & p. 111)

Test: 1	Section: 6	Question: 9		p: 408
Test: 1	Section: 10	Question: 12	(list)	p: 431
Test: 1	Section: 10	Question: 14		p: 431
Test: 2	Section: 6	Question: 1		p: 469
Test: 2	Section: 6	Question: 11	(NE)	p: 470
Test: 2	Section: 6	Question: 21		p: 472
Test: 2	Section: 10	Question: 8		p: 492
Test: 2	Section: 10	Question: 9		p: 492
Test: 3	Section: 6	Question: 7	(list)	p: 532
Test: 3	Section: 6	Question: 11		p: 532
Test: 3	Section: 6	Question: 12	(list)	p: 533
Test: 3	Section: 10	Question: 14	(NE)	p: 555
Test: 4	Section: 7	Question: 1		p: 599
Test: 4	Section: 7	Question: 6		p: 600
Test: 4	Section: 7	Question: 9	(list)	p: 600
Test: 4	Section: 7	Question: 10		p: 600
Test: 4	Section: 7	Question: 11		p: 600
Test: 4	Section: 7	Question: 20		p: 602
Test: 4	Section: 10	Question: 3		p: 614
Test: 4	Section: 10	Question: 4		p: 614
Test: 4	Section: 10	Question: 7		p: 615
Test: 4	Section: 10	Question: 13		p: 616
Test: 5	Section: 6	Question: 13		p: 658
Test: 5	Section: 10	Question: 6		p: 677
Test: 5	Section: 10	Question: 13	(NE)	p: 678
Test: 5	Section: 10	Question: 14	(NE)	p: 678
Test: 6	Section: 6	Question: 2	(list)	p: 718
Test: 6	Section: 10	Question: 5		p: 739
Test: 7	Section: 4	Question: 6		p: 775
Test: 7	Section: 4	Question: 11		p: 775
Test: 7	Section: 4	Question: 15		p: 776
Test: 7	Section: 4	Question: 17	(NE)	p: 776
Test: 7	Section: 10	Question: 10		p: 802
Test: 7	Section: 10	Question: 11		p: 803
Test: 7	Section: 10	Question: 12		p: 803
Test: 8	Section: 4	Question: 6	(list)	p: 837
Test: 8	Section: 4	Question: 9		p: 837
Test: 8	Section: 10	Question: 4	(list)	p: 862
Test: 9	Section: 3	Question: 8		p: 893
Test: 9	Section: 3	Question: 22	(list)	p: 895
Test: 9	Section: 10	Question: 5	(list)	p: 924
Test: 9	Section: 10	Question: 13		p: 926
Test: 10	Section: 3	Question: 9		p: 955
Test: 10	Section: 10	Question: 12		p: 987
Test: 10	Section: 10	Question: 13		p: 988

Faulty Comparisons (p. 50)

Test: 1	Section: 6	Question: 21		p: 410
Test: 1	Section: 6	Question: 29		p: 410
Test: 2	Section: 10	Question: 11		p: 492
Test: 3	Section: 6	Question: 13		p: 533
Test: 3	Section: 6	Question: 25		p: 534
Test: 4	Section: 7	Question: 1		p: 599
Test: 4	Section: 7	Question: 3		p: 599
Test: 5	Section: 6	Question: 27		p: 660
Test: 6	Section: 6	Question: 14		p: 720
Test: 6	Section: 10	Question: 2		p: 738
Test: 7	Section: 4	Question: 28		p: 777
Test: 7	Section: 10	Question: 13		p: 802
Test: 9	Section: 3	Question: 6		p: 893
Test: 9	Section: 3	Question: 7	(NE)	p: 893
Test: 9	Section: 10	Question: 14		p: 926
Test: 10	Section: 10	Question: 4	(NE)	p: 986

Word Pairs (p. 53)

Test: 1	Section: 6	Question: 18	(neither...nor)	p: 409
Test: 1	Section: 10	Question: 6	(so...that)	p: 430
Test: 2	Section: 6	Question: 15	(neither...nor)	p: 471
Test: 3	Section: 6	Question: 19	(both...and)	p: 534
Test: 3	Section: 10	Question: 9	(either...or)	p: 554
Test: 4	Section: 7	Question: 14	(either...or)	p: 601
Test: 4	Section: 10	Question: 11	(so...that)	p: 616
Test: 5	Section: 10	Question: 4	(no sooner...than)	p: 676
Test: 6	Section: 6	Question: 12	(as...as)	p: 720
Test: 6	Section: 6	Question: 28	(neither...nor)	p: 721
Test: 6	Section: 10	Question: 13	(so...that)	p: 740
Test: 7	Section: 4	Question: 10	(just as...so)	p: 775
Test: 8	Section: 4	Question: 29	(between...and)	p: 839
Test: 10	Section: 3	Question: 18	(neither...nor)	p: 956
Test: 10	Section: 10	Question: 12	(as...as)	p: 987

Noun Agreement (p. 58)

Test: 1	Section: 6	Question: 12		p: 409
Test: 1	Section: 10	Question: 3		p: 429
Test: 2	Section: 6	Question: 17		p: 471
Test: 3	Section: 6	Question: 4		p: 531
Test: 3	Section: 6	Question: 18	(NE)	p: 534
Test: 7	Section: 4	Question: 12		p: 776
Test: 10	Section: 3	Question: 19		p: 957
Test: 10	Section: 3	Question: 28		p: 957

Comparatives vs. Superlatives (p. 60)

Test: 5	Section: 6	Question: 24		p: 659
Test: 5	Section: 6	Question: 29	(NE)	p: 660
Test: 9	Section: 3	Question: 16	(NE)	p: 894
Test: 9	Section: 3	Question: 27		p: 896
Test: 10	Section: 3	Question: 27	(NE)	p: 957
Test: 10	Section: 3	Question: 29	(NE)	p: 957

Relative Pronouns (p. 62)

Test: 4	Section: 7	Question: 19	(NE)	p: 601
Test: 5	Section: 6	Question: 14		p: 658
Test: 7	Section: 4	Question: 7		p: 775
Test: 8	Section: 4	Question: 17		p: 838
Test: 8	Section: 4	Question: 17	(NE)	p: 839
Test: 9	Section: 3	Question: 15		p: 894
Test: 10	Section: 3	Question: 21		p: 957

Double Negatives and Double Positives (p. 65)

Test: 5	Section: 6	Question: 18	p: 659
Test: 6	Section: 6	Question: 4	p: 718
Test: 9	Section: 3	Question: 13	p: 894

Conjunctions/Logical Relationship (p. 67)

Test: 1	Section: 6	Question: 5		p: 407
Test: 4	Section: 7	Question: 24		p: 602
Test: 5	Section: 6	Question: 17		p: 658
Test: 5	Section: 6	Question: 25		p: 659
Test: 6	Section: 6	Question: 25		p: 721
Test: 7	Section: 4	Question: 2		p: 774
Test: 7	Section: 4	Question: 18		p: 776
Test: 7	Section: 10	Question: 8		p: 802
Test: 8	Section: 10	Question: 5		p: 862
Test: 8	Section: 10	Question: 6		p: 863
Test: 8	Section: 10	Question: 9		p: 863
Test: 8	Section: 10	Question: 13	(NE)	p: 864
Test: 9	Section: 10	Question: 1		p: 924
Test: 9	Section: 10	Question: 8		p: 925
Test: 9	Section: 10	Question: 12		p: 925

Redundancy (p. 73)

Test: 3	Section: 6	Question: 10	p: 554
Test: 3	Section: 6	Question: 29	p: 535
Test: 6	Section: 10	Question: 1	p: 738
Test: 9	Section: 3	Question: 9	p: 893

Fragments/Non-Essential Clause Errors (p. 89)

Commas and Semicolons (p. 95)

Unnecessary/Incorrect Use of Gerund (p. 100)

Gerund or Present Participle Required (p. 101)

Test: 5	Section: 10	Question: 7	p: 677
Test: 10	Section: 10	Question: 5	p: 987
Test: 10	Section: 10	Question: 11	p: 987

Dangling Modifiers (p. 106)

Test: 1	Section: 6	Question: 7	p: 408
Test: 1	Section: 6	Question: 10	p: 408
Test: 1	Section: 10	Question: 5	p: 430
Test: 1	Section: 10	Question: 8	p: 430
Test: 1	Section: 10	Question: 9	p: 430
Test: 2	Section: 6	Question: 3	p: 469
Test: 2	Section: 6	Question: 7	p: 470
Test: 2	Section: 6	Question: 9	p: 470
Test: 2	Section: 10	Question: 6	p: 492
Test: 2	Section: 10	Question: 13 (NE)	p: 493
Test: 3	Section: 6	Question: 8	p: 532
Test: 4	Section: 7	Question: 5	p: 599
Test: 4	Section: 7	Question: 8	p: 600
Test: 4	Section: 7	Question: 11	p: 600
Test: 4	Section: 10	Question: 10	p: 616
Test: 4	Section: 10	Question: 12	p: 616
Test: 5	Section: 10	Question: 12	p: 677
Test: 6	Section: 6	Question: 6	p: 719
Test: 6	Section: 6	Question: 10	p: 719
Test: 6	Section: 10	Question: 14	p: 740
Test: 7	Section: 4	Question: 3	p: 774
Test: 7	Section: 10	Question: 1	p: 801
Test: 9	Section: 3	Question: 1	p: 892
Test: 9	Section: 10	Question: 7	p: 925
Test: 9	Section: 10	Question: 10	p: 925
Test: 10	Section: 3	Question: 5	p: 955
Test: 10	Section: 3	Question: 11	p: 955
Test: 10	Section: 10	Question: 6	p: 987

Misplaced Modifiers (p. 109)

Test: 3	Section: 6	Question: 16	p: 533
Test: 3	Section: 6	Question: 21	p: 534
Test: 3	Section: 10	Question: 2	p: 553
Test: 5	Section: 10	Question: 3	p: 676
Test: 7	Section: 10	Question: 14	p: 803

Active vs. Passive Voice (p. 104)

Test: 2	Section: 10	Question: 14	p: 493
Test: 3	Section: 10	Question: 7	p: 554
Test: 3	Section: 10	Question: 8	p: 554
Test: 5	Section: 10	Question: 4	p: 676
Test: 5	Section: 10	Question: 13	p: 678
Test: 7	Section: 4	Question: 1	p: 774

Appendix B: Questions by Test

Test 1

Section: 6 (p. 407)

1. Comma splice; gerund required to indicate means
2. Gerund
3. Fragment
4. Verb consistency
5. Conjunction
6. NE; main concept tested = tense consistency
7. Pronoun-antecedent: missing antecedent (it)
8. NE; main concept tested = non-essential clause
9. Parallel Structure; word pair
10. Dangling Modifier
11. Non-essential clause
12. Noun Agreement
13. NE; concepts tested = tense; adjective vs. adverb
14. Adjective vs. adverb
15. Verb consistency
16. Gerund vs. infinitive
17. Adjective vs. adverb
18. Word pair (neither…nor)
19. Pronoun-antecedent: (passengers = their, not "his or her")
20. NE; main concept tested = subject-verb agreement: the number of
21. Faulty comparison
22. Preposition; gerund vs. infinitive
23. Subject-verb agreement: s-nec-v
24. NE; main concept tested = subject-verb agreement: compound subject
25. Gerund vs. infinitive
26. Pronoun-antecedent: collective noun = singular
27. NE; main concepts tested: idiomatic usage (all more than, long since)
28. Subject-verb agreement: s-pp-v; between you and me
29. Faulty comparison

Section: 10 (p. 429)

1. Subject-verb agreement: there is/are
2. Antecedent-pronoun: missing antecedent (it)
3. Noun agreement
4. Antecedent pronoun: ambiguous antecedent
5. Dangling modifier
6. Word pair (so…that)
7. Miscellaneous: a noun cannot "be because"
8. Dangling modifier
9. Gerund/fragment
10. NE; main concept tested = non-essential clause
11. Gerund: being that = bad, because = good
12. Parallel Structure
13. Subject-verb agreement: s-pp-v
14. Parallel Structure

Test 2

Section: 6 (p. 469)

1. Parallel Structure
2. Non-essential clause/fragment
3. Dangling modifier
4. Gerund/wordy
5. Comma splice
6. Non-essential clause; passive
7. Dangling modifier
8. NE; main concept tested = gerund (required for idiomatic phrasing)
9. Dangling modifier
10. NE; main concept tested = idiom (for all their = correct)
11. NE; main concept tested = parallel structure
12. Pronoun Case (I vs. me)
13. Verb consistency (present vs. simple past)
14. Verb consistency; gerund
15. Word pair (either…or)
16. Tense: present perfect vs. simple past
17. Noun agreement
18. Pronoun-antecedent: tax = singular vs. plural (tax = singular, it)
19. NE; concepts tested = tense: present perfect ("has shown" = ok), long been = ok
20. Subject-verb agreement (managers = plural, holds = singular)
21. Parallel structure
22. Subject-verb agreement: s-pp-v
23. Preposition: arrived in

24. NE; concepts tested = tense: past perfect, negation (hardly anyone)
25. Subject-verb agreement: s-nec-v
26. Preposition: offers of
27. NE; main concept tested = "what" as subject
28. Pronoun-Antecedent: ambiguous antecedent
29. NE; concepts tested = gerund vs. infinitive, "herself" used for emphasis, idiomatic structure: "complicated as they were"

Section: 10 (p. 491)

1. Tense: would; gerund
2. Non-essential clause; gerund
3. Gerund
4. Comma splice; gerund required (idiom)
5. Miscellaneous: it took + infinitive
6. Dangling modifier
7. NE; main concept tested = tense: would vs. will
8. Parallel structure
9. NE; concepts tested = parallel structure, word pair (both…and)
10. Conjunction; gerund (being that = bad, because = good)
11. Faulty comparison
12. Gerund; modification
13. NE; main concept tested = dangling modifier
14. Passive

Test 3

Section: 6 (p. 531)

1. Pronoun-antecedent (missing antecedent: it)
2. Gerund
3. NE; main concept tested = semicolon
4. Noun agreement
5. Non-essential clause
6. Verb consistency
7. Parallel structure
8. Dangling modifier
9. Non-essential clause
10. NE; main concept tested = pronoun-antecedent: collective noun = singular
11. Parallel structure
12. Parallel structure
13. Faulty comparison
14. Gerund/fragment
15. Subject-verb agreement
16. Misplaced modifier
17. Word pair (either…or)
18. NE; main concept tested = tense (present perfect, gerund vs. infinitive); noun agreement
19. Subject-verb agreement: s-nec-v

20. Pronoun-antecedent: singular/plural (other types = plural)
21. Misplaced modifier
22. Pronoun-antecedent: singular/plural (the gecko = singular)
23. Subject-verb agreement: compound subject = plural
24. Tense: present perfect vs. simple past
25. Faulty Comparison
26. Tense: past perfect (we had waited)
27. Pronoun-antecedent: collective noun = singular
28. NE; miscellaneous: although + adjective = ok
29. Redundancy

Section: 10 (p. 553)

1. NE; main concept tested = tense (would)
2. Misplaced modifier
3. Gerund/fragment
4. Verb consistency
5. Verb consistency
6. Comma splice, semicolon
7. Passive
8. Passive; present participle
9. Word pair (either…or)
10. Redundancy
11. NE; main concept tested = Semicolon
12. Non-essential clause
13. Miscellaneous: awkward phrasing
14. NE; concepts tested = comma splice, semicolon verb consistency, gerunds

Test 4

Section: 7 (599)

1. Faulty Comparison/parallel structure: missing preposition
2. Comma splice; pronoun-antecedent
3. Faulty comparison
4. Passive
5. Dangling modifier
6. Subject-verb agreement; "the reason is that"
7. NE; main concept tested = non-essential clause
8. Dangling modifier
9. Parallel structure
10. Verb consistency
11. Parallel structure
12. Verb consistency
13. Verb consistency
14. Word pair (either…or)
15. Pronoun-antecedent: singular vs. plural (shards = singular, its)
16. NE; subject-verb agreement: pp-v-s

17. NE; concepts tested = subject-verb agreement; tense (present perfect); adjective vs. adverb
18. Verb consistency
19. NE; main concept tested = relative pronoun (in which = ok)
20. Parallel structure
21. Pronoun case
22. Verb consistency; gerund vs. infinitive
23. NE; concepts tested = preposition, gerund vs. infinitive
24. Conjunction: double conjunction
25. Preposition: preoccupation with
26. Pronoun case (I vs. me)
27. Subject-verb agreement: pp-v-s
28. Pronoun-antecedent: singular vs. plural (tablets = plural, their)
29. Adjective vs. adverb

Section: 10 (p. 614)

1. Gerund vs. infinitive
2. Non-essential clause
3. NE; main concept tested = parallel structure
4. Parallel structure
5. Gerund required to indicate means
6. Preposition: "asserted" does not require a preposition
7. Parallel structure
8. NE; main concept tested = non-essential clause
9. Pronoun-antecedent: missing antecedent (this)
10. Dangling modifier
11. Word pair (so…that)
12. Dangling modifier
13. Parallel structure
14. Non-essential clause

Test 5

Section: 6 (p. 656)

1. Gerund
2. Gerund; no "would" in the same clause as "if" (choice E)
3. Subject-verb agreement: s-pp-v
4. Fragment
5. Non-essential clause; gerund; "do so" not "do it"
6. Pronoun-antecedent: missing antecedent (this)
7. NE; main concept tested = subject-verb agreement: compound subject
8. Gerund
9. Gerund
10. Comma + FANBOYS
11. Pronoun-antecedent: singular plural
12. Gerund/fragment

13. Parallel structure
14. Who vs. which
15. Tense; gerund
16. Gerund vs. infinitive
17. Conjunction
18. Double positive
19. Subject-verb agreement: s-pp-v
20. Pronoun-antecedent: singular vs. plural (crabs = plural, they)
21. Gerund vs. infinitive
22. Gerund vs. infinitive
23. NE; concepts tested = preposition, pronoun-antecedent, adjective vs. adverb
24. Comparative vs. superlative
25. Conjunction
26. Subject-verb agreement (the number of = singular)
27. Faulty comparison
28. Pronoun-antecedent: singular vs. plural (trucks = plural, they)
29. NE; main concept tested = comparative vs. superlative

Section: 10 (p. 676)

1. Tense: verb in simple past tense ("believed") requires "would," not "would have"
2. Non-essential clause
3. Misplaced modifier
4. Word pair (no sooner…than)
5. The reason that
6. Parallel structure
7. Gerund required to indicate means
8. NE; main concept tested = pronoun-antecedent, "which" used correctly to modify "programs"
9. Non-essential clause; gerund
10. Gerund; pronoun-antecedent: singular vs. plural (walruses = plural, they)
11. NE; main concept tested = tense: present perfect, used correctly with "since"
12. Dangling modifier
13. NE; main concept tested = parallel structure
14. Parallel structure: active vs. passive

Test 6

Section: 6 (p. 718)

1. Subject-verb agreement (s-pp-v)
2. Parallel structure: active vs. passive
3. Verb consistency
4. Double positive
5. Preposition: "determine" does not require a preposition
6. Dangling modifier

7. Miscellaneous: that = ok as subject
8. Pronoun-antecedent: collective noun (school) = singular
9. NE; main concept tested = tense: past perfect
10. Dangling modifier
11. NE: shortest and clearest
12. Word pair (as…as)
13. NE; main concept tested = would vs. will
14. Faulty comparison
15. Pronoun-antecedent: singular vs. plural (that/those)
16. NE: main concept tested = antecedent-pronoun: each = singular, its
17. Preposition: a condition for
18. Verb consistency: gerund vs. infinitive
19. Verb form: past participle vs. simple past (swam vs. swum)
20. Pronoun-antecedent: collective noun (agency) = singular
21. Preposition: a threat to
22. Adjective vs. adverb
23. NE; concepts tested = tense (present perfect) and preposition
24. Subject-verb agreement (s-nec-v)
25. Conjunction
26. Subject-verb agreement
27. Pronoun case
28. Word pair (neither…nor)
29. Subject-verb agreement (pp-v-s)

Section: 10 (p. 738)

1. Miscellaneous: wordiness
2. Faulty comparison
3. Non-essential clause; gerund
4. Antecedent-Pronoun: *which* ok, modifies *Kaissa*
5. Parallel structure
6. NE: main concept tested = antecedent-pronoun ("there" lacks an antecedent in C, D, and E)
7. Antecedent-pronoun: we…our
8. Parallel structure
9. Gerund
10. Antecedent-pronoun: singular vs. plural (programs = plural, they)
11. Miscellaneous: wordiness
12. Comma splice; wordiness
13. Word pair; wordiness
14. Faulty comparison

Test 7

Section: 4 (p. 774)

1. Passive
2. Conjunction; wordiness
3. Dangling modifier
4. Non-essential clause
5. Gerund
6. Parallel structure
7. Gerund; relative pronoun ("when" modifies nineteenth century)
8. Fragment
9. Semicolon
10. NE; main concept tested = word pair (just as…so)
11. Parallel structure
12. Noun agreement
13. Adjective vs. adverb
14. Pronoun case
15. Parallel structure
16. NE; main concept tested = tense, present perfect
17. NE; main concept tested = parallel structure
18. Conjunction
19. Subject-verb agreement (pp-v-s)
20. Gerund; tense: verb in simple past ("discovered") requires conditional: "a pass that *would* soon become"
21. Tense: past perfect
22. Gerund; "plus"
23. Pronoun-antecedent: you vs. one
24. NE; main concept tested: subject-verb agreement: s-pp-v
25. Pronoun-antecedent: a student = he or she
26. Gerund vs. infinitive OR idiom: regarded as (being)
27. Subject-verb agreement: s-pp-v
28. Faulty comparison
29. NE: main concept tested = long since

Section: 10 (p. 801)

1. Dangling modifier
2. Gerund
3. Miscellaneous: wordiness
4. Semicolon; pronoun-antecedent
5. Pronoun-antecedent: collective noun (fire department) = singular
6. Miscellaneous: modification. One does not watch "of television."
7. Parallel structure
8. Conjunction; logical relationship
9. Non-essential clause
10. Verb consistency; parallel structure
11. Parallel structure
12. Parallel structure: active vs. passive
13. Faulty comparison
14. Misplaced modifier

Test 8

Section: 4 (p. 836)

1. Fragment
2. Gerund
3. Run-on sentence
4. Gerund required to indicate means
5. Pronoun-antecedent: singular vs. plural (every = singular, her)
6. Parallel structure
7. NE; main concept tested = pronoun-antecedent, it = ok because antecedent is a gerund (finding)
8. Subject-verb agreement (s-nec-v)
9. Parallel structure
10. NE; main concept tested = pronoun-antecedent, "which" modifies "serious interest in drama"
11. Pronoun Antecedent: collective noun (empire) = singular
12. Adjective vs. adverb
13. Tense: would vs. will ("will" should not appear with a verb in the past)
14. NE; main concepts tested =
15. Adjective vs. adverb
16. Tense: past conditional vs. past ("would" indicates a recurring action in the past; "would have" is hypothetical indicates an action that did not actually occur)
17. Relative pronoun: who vs. which
18. Idiom: prefer x to y, not x more than y
19. Pronoun-antecedent: people = they, not "your"
20. Subject-verb agreement: s-pp-v
21. Tense: would vs. will
22. NE: main concept tested: would vs. will ("would" = ok because the sentence contains a verb in the past tense)
23. Preposition: protest against or no preposition
24. Pronoun case: between + me
25. Noun agreement
26. Pronoun-antecedent: "do so" not "do it"
27. Subect-verb agreement: s-pp-v
28. NE; main concepts tested = preposition, adjective vs. adverb
29. Word pair (between…and)

Section: 10 (p. 862)

1. Verb consistency/gerund
2. Miscellaneous: no comma between subject and verb
3. Gerund
4. Parallel structure
5. NE: main concept tested: although = ok without subject and verb after it
6. Conjunction
7. Non-essential clause; gerund

8. Preposition: adopted by
9. Conjunction
10. Non-essential clause
11. Non-essential clause
12. Pronoun-antecedent; semicolon
13. NE; concepts tested = gerund, wordiness, tense, conjunction
14. gerund; semicolon

Test 9

Section: 3 (p. 892)

1. Pronoun-antecedent: missing antecedent (that)
2. Verb consistency
3. Gerund
4. Subject-verb agreement: s-pp-v
5. Miscellaneous: wordiness
6. Faulty comparison
7. NE; main concept tested = faulty comparison
8. Parallel structure: missing preposition
9. Redundancy
10. NE; concepts tested = gerund, comma splice
11. Comma splice
12. Verb form: past participle vs. simple past (had written)
13. Double positive
14. Subject-verb agreement: there is/are
15. Relative pronoun: who vs. which
16. NE: main concept tested = comparative vs. superlative (two things compared so "more" is correct)
17. NE: concepts tested = pronoun-antecedent, gerund vs. infinitive, preposition
18. Subject-verb agreement = there is/are
19. Pronoun-antecedent: singular vs. plural (signs = plural, these or them)
20. Verb consistency
21. Subject-verb agreement: compound subject ("itself" = trick answer)
22. Parallel structure
23. Subject-verb agreement: s-pp-v
24. Preposition/idiom: far from
25. Tense: for = present perfect
26. Preposition: inconsistent with
27. Comparative vs. superlative
28. Pronoun case: between + me
29. NE; concepts tested = preposition, past perfect, "long since"

Section: 10 (p. 924)

1. Conjunction/logical relationship
2. Gerund; idiom: stated that
3. Gerund

4. Miscellaneous: wordiness
5. Parallel structure
6. Comma splice
7. Tense: would vs. will (sentence contains a verb in past tense, so "would" is required)
8. Non-essential clause; conjunction/logical relationship
9. Pronoun-antecedent: someone = he or she
10. Dangling modifier
11. Pronoun-antecedent: ambiguous antecedent (she)
12. NE; concepts tested = gerund, conjunction
13. Parallel structure: active vs. passive
14. Faulty comparison

Test 10

Section: 3 (p. 954)

1. Gerund
2. Fragment
3. NE; main concept tested = gerund, dangling modifier
4. Pronoun-antecedent: missing antecedent (they)
5. Dangling modifier
6. Comma splice; wordiness
7. Gerund
8. Miscellaneous: wordiness
9. Parallel structure
10. Pronoun-antecedent: singular vs. plural (it/their)
11. Dangling modifier
12. Subject-verb agreement (s-nec-v, verb before subject)
13. Gerund vs. infinitive
14. NE; main concept tested = gerund ok as subject
15. Adjective vs. adverb
16. Subject-verb agreement: s-pp-v
17. Verb consistency

18. Word pair (neither...nor)
19. Noun agreement
20. Tense
21. Relative pronoun (in which vs. that)
22. Pronoun case
23. NE; concepts tested: idiom (something of), "alike"
24. Subject-verb agreement (s-nec-v)
25. Preposition (listen to)
26. Pronoun-antecedent: ambiguous antecedent (she)
27. NE; main concept tested = comparative vs. superlative
28. Noun agreement
29. NE; concepts tested = subject-verb agreement (s-pp-v, "which" = singular) comparative vs. superlative

Section: 10 (p. 986)

1. Miscellaneous/idiom: to think of something "as if," not "that"
2. NE; main concept tested = subject-verb agreement (s-pp-v)
3. Comma splice; semicolon
4. NE: main concept tested = Faulty comparison
5. Gerund required to indicate means
6. Dangling modifier
7. Subject-verb agreement (s-pp-v)
8. NE; main concept tested = pronoun-antecedent ("which" is correctly used to modify "cost")
9. Passive
10. Semicolon; verb consistency
11. Participle required; wordiness
12. NE; concepts tested = parallel structure, word pair (as...as)
13. Parallel structure: verb form
14. NE; concepts tested = subject-verb agreement: compound subject; pronoun-antecedent: singular vs. plural (paint = singular, its)

ANSWER KEY

Identifying Parts of Speech (p. 8)

1. A: Adjective, B: Noun, C: Verb, D: Verb, E: Adverb

2. A: Conjunction, B: Adjective, C: Pronoun, D: Adverb, E: Preposition

3. A: Noun, B: Verb, C: Adverb, D: Preposition, E: Noun

4. A: Adverb, B: Conjunction, C: Pronoun, D: Verb (Infinitive), E: Adjective

5. A: Adjective, B: Preposition, C: Verb, D: Verb (Infinitive), E: Verb

6. A: Noun, B: Verb, C: Verb, D: Noun, E: Preposition

7. A: Adjective, B: Noun (Singular), C: Verb, D: Pronoun, E: Verb

8. A: Adjective, B: Verb, C: Adverb, D: Preposition, E: Verb

9. A: Verb, B: Pronoun, C: Pronoun, D: Preposition, E: Noun

10. A: Noun, B: Preposition, C: Verb, D: Preposition, E: Noun

11. A: Preposition, B: Verb, C: Adjective, D: Verb, E: Verb

12. A: Verb, B: Preposition, C: Preposition D: Adverb, E: Preposition

13. A: Pronoun, B: Preposition, C: Preposition, D: Adjective, E: Verb

14. A: Noun, B: Verb, C: Adjective, D: Adverb, E: Pronoun

15. A: Adjective, B: Adverb, C: Verb, D: Adjective, E: Pronoun

Subject-Verb Agreement (p. 18)

1. The process of living vicariously through a fictional character in order to purge one's emotions **is** known as catharsis.

2. Along the border between China and Tibet **lie** the Himalaya Mountains, which include some of the highest peaks in the world.

3. Recognized for formulating unorthodox social theories, Lev Gumilev and D.S. Mirsky **were** partly responsible for founding the neo-eurasianist political and cultural movement.

4. The works of artist Alan Chin **draw** inspiration from both the California gold rush and the construction of the transcontinental railroad

5. Correct

6. Playboating, a discipline of whitewater rafting or canoeing in which players stay in one spot while performing certain maneuvers, **involves** specialized canoes designed for the sport.

7. Often found in plastic drinking bottles **are** substantial amounts of a potentially toxic chemical called Bisphenol A.

8. The African violet, which is known for its striking pink and purple leaves, **belongs** to the Saintpaulia family of flowering plants rather than to the violet family.

9. Among the finds from a recent archaeological dig in London **were** earthenware knobs originally used for "pay walls," boxes into which Elizabethan theater-goers deposited their admission fees.

10. Correct

11. Stiles, structures that **provide** people with a passage through or over a fence, are often built in rural areas or along footpaths.

12. The patent for the first mechanical pencils **was** granted to Sampson Morgan and John Hawkins in England during the early nineteenth century.

13. Each of the Taino's five chiefdoms, which inhabited the Bahamas before the arrival of Europeans, **was** ruled by a leader known as a cacique.

14. If there **are** sufficient funds remaining, the teacher's request for new classroom supplies will most likely be approved by the school board.

15. Possible explanations for the suspicion surrounding Shakespeare's *Macbeth* **include** the superstition that the witches' song is an actual incantation and the belief that theaters only mount the play when they are in need of money.

16. Correct

17. Galaxies, far from being randomly scattered throughout the universe, **appear** to be distributed in bubble-shaped patterns.

18. For the past several years, the theater company **has** traveled to various schools throughout the city in order to expose students to classic works.

19. Over the past several days, a number of disturbing reports **have** filtered in to the news agency, suggesting that the country's government is on the verge of collapse.

20. According to the law of diminution, the pitches of notes sounded by an orchestra **remain** the same even as the amount of sound diminishes.

21. Correct

22. Although the criminal protested his innocence vehemently, neither he nor his lawyer **was** ultimately able to offer a convincing alibi.

23. Sebastian Díaz Morales, like the other members of his generation of artists, **knows** how to draw on the social experiences of his country to produce works that entirely escape any simple interpretation.

24. Historians describe the chariot as a simple type of horse carriage that **was** used by ancient civilizations for peacetime travel and military combat.

25. Along the deepest part of the ocean floor **sit** the Mariana Trench and the HMRG Deep, the two lowest spots that researchers have ever identified on earth.

Verb Tense and Form (p. 26)

1. Correct

2. In 1498, Dutch scholar Erasmus of Rotterdam **moved** from Paris to England, where he became a professor of ancient languages at Cambridge.

3. M.J. Hyland, who authored the acclaimed 2003 novel *How the Light Gets In*, is often praised **as (being)** a subtle and complex portrayer of human psychology.

4. Composer Georgi Tutev, who **would** become one of the principal figures of Bulgarian modernism, was born of a German mother and a Bulgarian father.

5. According to researchers, the Antarctic ice shelf has **shrunk** by approximately 50 gigatons of ice each year since 1992.

6. Correct

7. The nearly 200-ton Mayflower was chartered by a group of British merchants and **set** sail from Plymouth, England in 1620.

8. Mahatma Gandhi, who was born in India, studied law in London and in 1893 went to South Africa, where he **spent** twenty years opposing discriminatory legislation against Indians.

9. Accidentally discovered by Procter and Gamble researchers in 1968, the fat substitute Olestra has been shown **to cause** stomach upset in those who consume excessive amounts of it.

10. The country's economists speculated that thousands more jobs would have been lost if consumer demand for domestically manufactured products **had continued** to decline.

11. In the sixteenth century, writer and jurist Noël du Fail **wrote** many stories documenting rural life in France during the Renaissance.

12. Defying predictions that he **would** fade from the public eye, former Czech president Vaclav Havel became a film director after his retirement from office.

13. Descended from a long line of university professors, Marie Goeppert-Mayer received the majority of her training in Germany and eventually **taught** at a number of universities in the United States.

14. After a 1991 attempt to overthrow Mikhail Gorbechav failed, power **shifted** to Russian president Boris Yeltsin.

15. New facts, especially when they replace beliefs already in one's mind, commonly take as long as several weeks **to be** fully accepted as true.

16. Correct

17. The illustrator often photographed multiple models for each drawing and **made** his selection only when the final prints arrived in his hands.

18. Toward the end of the sixteenth century, the Iroquois League, a confederation of six Native American nations, **formed** in the northeastern United States.

19. NASA scientists have decided to delay the space shuttle's launch in order to determine whether recently repaired parts **will** cause damage if they **break** off in orbit. (or: whether repaired parts **would** cause damage if they **broke** off in orbit.)

20. After weeks of careful scrutiny, the consumer protection agency informed the public that a number of products **would** be recalled because of safety concerns.

21. Correct

22. Correct

23. Several dozen boats are known to have **sunk** off of the French Frigate Shoals, part of an enormous protected zone that covers nearly 150,000 square miles in the Pacific Ocean.

24. Emperor Frederick the Great of Prussia believed that to fight a successful war was **to create** minimal intrusion into the lives of civilians.

25. According to cognitive scientist Daniel Willingham, one major reason more students do not enjoy school is that abstract thought is not something our brains are designed to be good at or **to enjoy**.

26. Correct

27. Hardly a stranger to self-censorship, Mark Twain never hesitated to change his prose if he believed that the alterations **would** improve the sales of his books.

28. Some critics have argued that Dostoevsky was unique among nineteenth-century authors in that he surrendered fully to his characters and **allowed** himself to write in voices other than his own.

Pronoun-Antecedent (p. 34)

1. Not until the early twentieth century did the city become capable of maintaining **its** population and cease to be dependent on rural areas for a constant stream of new inhabitants.

2. Correct

3. Pain doesn't show up on a body scan and can't be measured in a test, and as a result, many chronic pain sufferers turn to art in an effort to depict **that sensation/it**.

4. The nitrogen cycle describes **nitrogen's** movement from the air into organic compounds and then back into the atmosphere.

5. If you exercise to prevent diabetes, **you** may want to avoid vitamins C and E since these antioxidants have also been shown to correlate with it.

6. With the price of art lower, collectors for the most part don't want to part with a prized painting or sculpture unless they are forced to do **so**.

7. Once common across southwest Asia, the Indian cheetah was driven nearly to extinction during the late twentieth century and now resides in the fragmented pieces of **its** remaining suitable habitat.

8. Although Alice Sebold does not write her books with any particular age group in mind, **they have** proven popular with middle and high school students.

9. Some critics of the Internet have argued that it is a danger to people because its vastness, often heralded as a benefit, threatens **their** intellectual health.

10. The woolly mammoth and the saber-toothed tiger might have survived as late as 10,000 B.C., although **they** went extinct fairly abruptly right around that time.

11. When the auditorium closes next year for renovations, the theater company will probably hold **its** productions at another location.

12. Correct

13. One measure of a society's openness to newcomers is the quality of the space **it** creates for people of unfamiliar cultural and linguistic backgrounds.

14. Though recipes for yeast-free muffins were commonly found in nineteenth-century cookbooks, by the twentieth century most muffin recipes were calling for **yeast**.

15. Correct

16. The Egyptian temple complex at Karnak, situated on the eastern bank of the Nile, was the **Egyptian's** sacred place of worship.

17. The city's economy has weakened significantly over the past decade, **leading/a situation that has led** to an overwhelming loss of manufacturing jobs.

18. In the announcement, the school committee states that **it** will substantially overhaul the eleventh grade curriculum at some point during the next year.

19. The world's population could climb to 10.5 billion by 2050, **raising/a statistic that raises** questions about how many people the Earth can support.

20. Paul and Julio had just returned from a long and exhausting hike along the Appalachian Trail when **Paul/Julio** stumbled and hit his head.

21. In order to become truly great at a sport, players must spend most of **their** free time practicing.

22. Japan's status as an island country means that **the Japanese** must rely heavily on other countries for the supply of natural resources that are indispensable to national existence.

23. The Marquesa islands were among the first South Pacific islands to be settled, and from **their** shores departed some of the greatest navigators of all time.

24. Google's dominance as an Internet search function has allowed the company to expand **its** ambitions to include virtually all aspects of the online world.

25. Correct

Pronoun Case (p. 39)

1. Although our parents have little difficulty distinguishing between my twin sister and **me**, our teachers are much more easily fooled.

2. For **us** voters, it is exceedingly difficult to choose between the two candidates because their positions on so many issues are so similar that they are virtually indistinguishable.

3. After listening patiently to our admittedly flimsy excuses, the principal decided to sentence Akiko and **me** to a week of detention.

4. Along with our project, the professor handed Shalini and **me** a note requesting that we remain after class in order to discuss our research methods with her.

5. Correct

6. Correct

7. When the gubernatorial candidate arrived at the auditorium to give a speech, we found it nearly impossible to distinguish between **her** and her assistant, so similar were they in height and appearance.

8. My lab partner and **I** were awarded first prize in the science fair for our work on the breakdown of insulin production in people who suffer from diabetes.

9. Walking through Yellowstone National Park, Jordan, Sam, and **I** were so astonished by our surroundings that we found ourselves at a loss for words.

10. An unfamiliar subject when the class began, Roman history became increasingly fascinating to **him** and Alexis over the course of the semester.

Cumulative Review #1 (p. 40)

1. The works of Paulus Barbus **have** largely been lost, although many editions of his works were both published and esteemed during the Renaissance.

2. Among the writings of linguist Margaret Landon **were** a dictionary of the Native American Degueño dialect and a comparative study of Central American languages.

3. Many runners, even those who train regularly, do not have a clear sense of their potential since **they tend** to stick to an established distance.

4. For centuries, Norwegians **have hung** dolls dressed as witches in their kitchens because they believe that such figures have the power to keep pots from burning over.

5. When the fossil of an enormous ancient penguin was unearthed in Peru, archaeologists discovered that **its** feathers were brown and gray rather than black and white.

6. Although the waiter offered to bring Ramon and **me** a list of desserts, we had already eaten too much and found the prospect of more food unappetizing.

7. At the meeting point of the Alaskan and the Aleutian mountains **rise** an immense alpine tundra and sparkling lakes, which give way to thundering waterfalls.

8. Since 1896, the Kentucky Derby – arguably the best-known horse race in America – has **taken** place on a track measuring one-and-a-quarter miles.

9. Sultan Suleyman I, known as Suleyman the Magnificent, **was** responsible for the expansion of the Ottoman Empire from Asia Minor to North Africa before his death in 1566.

10. Long Island was the setting for F. Scott Fitzgerald's novel *The Great Gatsby*, but finding traces of **it/the book/the characters** there is as much a job for the imagination as it is for a map and a guidebook.

11. Correct

12. People who seek out extreme sports such as skydiving and mountain climbing often do so because **they** feel compelled to explore the limits of their endurance.

13. While **you are** cooking a recipe that involves large quantities of hot chili peppers, you should generally try to avoid touching your eyes.

14. Chicago's Sears Tower was the tallest office building in the world for nearly thirty years, a distinction it **lost** only upon the completion of the Taipei 101 Tower in 2004.

15. Born in Spain in 1881, Pablo Picasso **would** become one of the most celebrated and revolutionary painters of the twentieth century because of his invention of the cubist style.

16. The Sherlock Holmes form of mystery novel, which **revolves** around a baffling crime solved by a master detective and his assistant, contrasts the scientific method with prevailing superstitions.

17. In the early years of the fourteenth century, Pope Clement V moved the papacy to the French city of Avignon and **left** Rome prey to the ambitions of local overlords.

18. Correct

19. Although the two books recount the same series of events, they do **so** from different perspectives and are not intended to be read in any particular order.

20. Roberta and her supervisor, Ms. Altschuler, were commended at the company's dinner for **Roberta's (or: Ms. Alschuler's)** exceptional performance during the previous year.

21. Correct

22. South Africa experienced a series of massive and devastating blackouts in 2008, and consequently **it has** been rationing electricity ever since that time.

23. Though extremely long, the meeting between my advisor and **me** was unusually productive because it provided me with many new ways of thinking about a familiar subject.

24. Although prairie dogs were once on the verge of extinction, their numbers have **risen** to pre-twentieth century levels because of the work of the environmentalists who lobbied for their salvation.

25. In response **to being** criticized for the poor nutritional value of its food, the restaurant chain has altered its menu to include more healthful options.

Adjectives vs. Adverbs (p. 44)

1. Correct

2. Explorers who arrived at the central stretch of the Nile River **excitedly** reported the discovery of elegant temples and pyramids, ruins of the ancient Kushite civilization.

3. By looking **closely** at DNA markers, scientists may have found traces of the first African hunter-gatherers to migrate to other continents.

4. Although the room appeared tidy at first glance, I saw upon closer inspection that books, pens, and pieces of paper had been scattered **haphazardly** beneath a desk.

5. When examined under a microscope, the beaker of water revealed a hodgepodge of microscopic drifters that looked quite **different** from other sea creatures.

6. When Mt. Vesuvius first began to show signs of eruption, many of the people living at the base of the volcano **hastily** abandoned their villages to seek cover in nearby forests.

7. The archaeologists were lauded for their discovery of the ancient city, once a **densely** populated urban area that profited from the trade of precious metals.

8. Correct

9. Italian nobleman Cesare Borgia was ruthless and vain, but he was also a brilliant Renaissance man who was **exceedingly** well-educated in the classics.

10. Though few people believe that human beings are entirely rational, a world governed by anti-Enlightenment principles would surely be **infinitely** worse than one governed by Voltaire and Locke.

11. Lake Pergusa, the only **naturally** occurring lake in Sicily, is surrounded by a well-known racing circuit that was created in the 1960's and that has hosted many international sporting events since that time.

12. Even when his theme is the struggle to find a place in a **seemingly** irrational cosmos, Oscar Wilde writes with lively sympathy and hopefulness.

Parallel Structure I: Lists (p. 46)

1. Lady Jane Grey, known as the nine-day queen, was renowned for her sweetness, her beauty, and **her subjection to** the whims of her mother.

2. Mediterranean cooking is best known for its reliance on fresh produce, whole grains, **and significant amounts** of olive oil.

3. Correct

4. Knife injuries acquired while cooking should be washed thoroughly with a disinfectant, covered completely, and **have pressure applied** to them.

5. Seeing the Grand Canyon, standing in front of a beautiful piece of art, and **listening** to a beautiful symphony are all experiences that may inspire awe.

6. Neighbors of the proposed park argue that an amphitheater would draw more traffic, disrupt their neighborhood, and **diminish** their only patch of open space.

7. Evidence suggests that the aging brain retains and even increases its capacity for resilience, growth, and **well-being**.

8. Antiques are typically objects that show some degree of craftsmanship or attention to design, and they are considered desirable because of their beauty, rarity, or **usefulness**.

9. Spiders use a wide range of strategies to capture prey, including trapping it in sticky webs, lassoing it with sticky bolas, and **mimicking** other insects in order to avoid detection.

10. According to medical authorities at the Mayo Clinic, building muscle can boost metabolism, **aid** in weight loss, and increase stamina and focus.

Prepositions and Idioms (p. 49)

1. The Wave, a sandstone rock formation located near the Utah-Arizona border, is famous **for** its colorful forms and rugged, unpaved trails.

2. Frank Lloyd Wright was a proponent **of** organic architecture, a philosophy that he incorporated into structures such as the Fallingwater residence.

3. Correct

4. As an old man, Rousseau acknowledged that it was arrogant of him to promote virtues that he was unable to embody **in** his own life.

5. In contrast **to** his contemporaries, whose work he viewed as conventional and uninspiring, Le Corbusier insisted on using modern industrial techniques to construct buildings.

6. Beethoven, who strongly sympathized **with** the ideals of the French Revolution, originally planned to name the *Eroica* symphony after Napoleon.

7. Choreographer Alvin Ailey Jr. is credited **with** popularizing modern dance and integrating traditional African movements into his works.

8. As a result of its new program, which consists **of** three world premiers, the ballet troupe has become one of the few eminent companies to promote choreographic innovation.

9. Correct

10. Correct

11. Since reports given by the various witnesses at the crime scene were highly inconsistent **with** one another, the detective was thoroughly perplexed.

12. Teachers have begun to note with alarm that the amount of time their students spend playing video games and surfing the Internet has severely impacted their ability to focus **on** a single task for an extended period of time.

13. During the early decades of the Heian Empire, a person who lacked a thorough knowledge **of** Chinese could never be considered fully educated.

14. Both bizarre and familiar, fairy tales are intended to be told rather than read, and they truly possess an inexhaustible power **over** children and adults alike.

Faulty Comparisons (p. 52)

1. The writings of John Locke, unlike **those of** Thomas Hobbes, emphasize the idea that people are by nature both reasonable and tolerant.

2. Company officials announced that there would be no major changes made to the eligibility requirements for its benefits package, an offering that makes its plan more generous than **those of** other major retailers.

3. As part of its application, the university asks students to compose a short essay in which they compare their educational interests and goals to **those of** other students.

4. David Cerny, the daring Czech sculptor who shook the eastern European art world during the 1990's, has been accused of pursuing an artistic and political rebellion that is bolder and louder than **that of (or: those of)** his predecessors.

5. Unlike **people/those with** dyslexia, people with dysgraphia often suffer from fine motor-skills problems that leave them unable to write clearly.

6. Today's neuroscientists, unlike **those of** thirty years ago, have access to sophisticated instrumentation that has only been developed over the past decade.

7. Norwegian doctors prescribe fewer antibiotics than **those of** any other country, so people do not have a chance to develop resistance to many kinds of drug-resistant infections.

8. Correct

9. The reproduction of ciliates, unlike **that of other organisms**, occurs when a specimen splits in half and grows a completely new individual from each piece.

10. The hands and feet of Ardi, the recently discovered human ancestor who lived 4.4 million years ago, are much like **those of** other primitive extinct apes.

11. At the age of twenty-four, playwright Thornton Wilder was balding and bespectacled, and his clothes were like **those of** a much older man.

12. In ancient Greece, women were not allowed to vote or hold property, their status differing from **that of** slaves only in name.

Word Pairs (p. 55)

1. Across the United States, companies are taking advantage **not only** of retirees' expertise **but also** their desire to stay involved and engaged with the world through work.

2. After weeks of protests, the workers have finally agreed to discuss the overtime dispute with both outside mediators **and** company officials.

3. Often stereotyped as savants because of depictions such as the movie *Rain Man*, people on the autistic spectrum are typically **neither** superhuman memory machines **nor** incapable of performing everyday tasks.

4. Obedience to authority is **not only** a way for rulers to keep order in totalitarian states **but also** the foundation on which such states exist.

5. Finding himself cornered, the thief was forced to choose **between** leaping ten stories to the ground **and** surrendering to the police.

6. Audiences find the play **at once** amusing because of the comedic skills of its leading actors **and** tedious because of its excessive length.

7. It is almost **as** difficult to find consistent information about the Fort Pillow incident during the American Civil War **as** it is to determine the moral significance of its outcome.

8. Correct

9. Because the Articles of Confederation did not provide for the creation of either executive agencies **or** judiciary institutions, they were rejected in favor of the Constitution.

10. Correct

11. One of the main effects of industrialization was the shift **from** a society in which women worked at home **to** one in which women worked in factories and brought home wages to their families.

12. Over the past decade, Internet usage has become **so** pervasive **that** many psychologists are beginning to study its effect on the lives of young people.

Cumulative Review #2 (p. 56)

1. Three million years ago, the creation of the Panama Isthmus wreaked ecological havoc by triggering extinctions, diverting ocean currents, and **transforming** the climate. (Parallel Structure)

2. The professor's appearance was very striking to everyone in the room, for not only was he extremely thin, but his height also surpassed **that of** a normal man. (Faulty Comparison)

3. Although many children want to read digitized books and would read for fun more **frequently** if they could obtain them, most do not want to give up traditional print books completely. (Adjective vs. Adverb)

4. Correct

5. Although clarinetist Artie Shaw spent far more of his long life writing prose than making music, a careful look at his compositions **reveals** that he was a musician of genius. (Subject–Verb Agreement: Subject–Prepositional Phrase–Verb)

6. At the bottom of the staircase **stand** an umbrella rack, a large mirror, and a table containing a lacquered vase and a bowl of goldfish. (Subject–Verb Agreement: Prepositional Phrase–Verb–Subject)

7. Although the movie has alternately been described as a social satire, a comedy of manners, and **a Greek tragedy**, it contains elements of all three. (Parallel Structure)

8. In the early nineteenth century, a number of adventurous artists and writers flocked to Lake Geneva to **savor its** inspiring mountain scenery and serene atmosphere. (Preposition)

9. The Mayflower pilgrims who landed in the New World in 1620 were poorly equipped to navigate their new environment and struggled **to survive** during the winter. (Gerund vs. Infinitive)

10. *The Europeans*, a short novel by Henry James, contrasts the behavior and attitudes of two visitors from Italy with **those of** their cousins from New England. (Faulty Comparison)

11. Thomas Jefferson believed that prisoners of war should be treated **humanely** and, during the Revolutionary War, requested that British and Hessian generals be held in mansions rather than behind bars. (Adjective vs. Adverb)

12. Correct

13. The company's board voted in favor of conducting an inquiry **into** the conduct of several employees suspected of embezzling funds. (Preposition)

14. Although the best-selling author had **grown** comfortable with her role as a public figure, when given the choice, she preferred to be alone. (Tense: Past Participle vs. Simple Past)

15. While reactions to the exhibition were mixed, neither the artist's exceptional showmanship nor his astonishing technique **was** questioned by the spectators. (Subject-Verb Agreement: Neither…Nor)

16. Unlike **those of (or: the novels of)** Nathaniel Hawthorne and F. Scott Fitzgerald, Jonathan Franzen's novels have not yet received unanimous acceptance as classic works of literature. (Faulty Comparison)

17. Supporters of bilingual education often imply that students miss a great deal by not **being** taught in the language spoken by their parents and siblings at home. (Gerund vs. Infinitive)

18. A small frontier town in the 1830's, Chicago had grown to more than two million residents by 1909, and some demographers predicted that it **would** soon be the largest city on earth. (Tense: Would vs. Will)

19. John Breckinridge, who came closest **to** defeating Abraham Lincoln in the 1860 election, held strong personal convictions that made it difficult for him to navigate a moderate course in an era of extremes. (Preposition)

20. According to many urban planners, the most efficient way of building prosperous cities is to make **them** not only attractive but also healthy. (Pronoun-Antecedent)

21. The origin of the senators' proposal dates to the mid-twentieth century, making it one of the most **eagerly** anticipated pieces of legislation this year. (Adjective vs. Adverb)

22. Societies located at river deltas tend to foster innovation because of their flexibility **in dealing** with potentially shifting landscapes. (Gerund vs. Infinitive)

23. Correct

24. Correct

25. Correct

Noun Agreement (p. 59)

1. Both Wilfrid Daniels and Leonard Chuene, now powerful figures in South African sports, grew up as promising **athletes** who could never compete internationally because of apartheid.

2. Because they evolved in the warm climate of Africa before spreading into Europe, modern humans had **bodies** adapted to tracking prey over great distances.

3. Many of the great classical composers, including Mozart, Bach, and Mendelssohn, were born into musical families and began studying music seriously when they were **children**.

4. Correct

5. Known for creating a unique sound and style through the use of non-traditional instruments such as the French horn, Miles Davis joined Louis Armstrong and Ella Fitzgerald **as one of** the greatest jazz musicians of the twentieth century.

6. Inscribed ostrich eggs and pieces of shell jewelry are **examples** of early human attempts to record thoughts symbolically rather than literally.

7. Joseph Charles Jones and George Bundy Smith, who fought for African-Americans as **civil rights activists** during the early 1960's, were separated for nearly forty years after being arrested in Alabama in 1961.

8. The Opium Wars, which introduced the power of western armies and technologies to China, marked the end of Shanghai and Ningpo as independent **port cities**.

9. Although neither came from a literary family, Amy Tan and Maxine Hong Kingston became **avid readers** while growing up near San Francisco.

10. Correct

Comparatives vs. Superlatives (p. 61)

1. Between the black leopard and the snow leopard, the black leopard possesses the more effective camouflage while the snow leopard has the **more** striking tail.

2. Correct

3. Correct

4. While triathlons, competitions that consist of swimming, biking, and running, are drawing increasing numbers of participants, athletic events devoted to a single sport remain **more** popular.

5. Correct

6. Confronted with two equally qualified finalists, the awards committee is struggling to determine which one is **more** deserving of the top prize.

7. Correct

8. Though London has a longstanding reputation as a city's whose weather is defined by rain and fog, in reality Paris receives the **higher** amount of rainfall each year.

9. Both poodles and pugs are known for making excellent pets, but between the two breeds, pugs have the **sweeter** disposition while poodles are smarter.

10. Although mental puzzles such as Sudoku can help people keep their minds nimble as they age, physical exercise such as biking or running is **more** effective.

Relative Pronouns (p. 64)

1. For delicate patients **who** cannot handle the rigors of modern medicine, some doctors are now rejecting the assembly line of modern medical care for older, gentler options.

2. Correct

3. When readers **who** get their news from electronic rather than printed sources send articles to their friends, they tend to choose ones that contain intellectually challenging topics.

4. In 1623, Galileo published a work **in which** he championed the controversial theory of heliocentrism, thus provoking one of the greatest scientific controversies of his day.

5. In classical Athenian democracy, citizens **who** failed to pay their debts were barred from attending assembly meetings and appearing in court in virtually any capacity.

6. Correct

7. Researchers have claimed that subjects **who** stood on a rapidly vibrating platform during an experiment were able to slightly improve their athletic performance for a short time afterward.

8. Correct.

9. One of the least popular of all the Romance languages, Romansch is traditionally spoken by people **who** inhabit the southern regions of Switzerland.

10. Correct

Double Negatives and Double Positives (p. 66)

1. When selecting a host city from among dozens of contenders, Olympic officials must take into consideration which one is **likeliest** to benefit from the legacy of the games.

2. Although the plays of Lillian Hellman and Bertolt Brecht were met with great popularity during the 1920's, they are scarcely **ever** performed anymore in the United States.

3. Since the advent of commercial flight and high-speed rail in the twentieth century, hardly **any** significant technological change has affected the traveling public.

4. An evolutionary adaptation that might have promised survival during prehistoric times is **likelier** nowadays to produce diseases in modern humans.

5. Correct

6. The Indian sub-continent was home to some of the **earliest** civilizations, ranging from urban society of the Indus Valley to the classical age of the Gupta Dynasty.

7. During the early days of cable television, many viewers were only able to access four channels, with reception being weakest in rural areas and **clearest** in large cities.

8. The Industrial Revolution, which began in the late 1700's and lasted more than fifty years, was the period when machine power became **stronger** than hand power.

9. Correct

10. To thoroughly understand historical figures, we must study them not only in the bright light of the present but also in the **cloudier** light of the circumstances they encountered in their own lifetimes.

Conjunctions (p. 70)

1. In the past, coffees were blended and branded to suit a homogenous popular taste, **but** that has recently changed in response to a growing awareness of regional differences.

2. Frederic Chopin's charming and sociable personality drew loyal groups of friends and admirers, including George Sand, **but** his private life was often painful and difficult.

3. The Taj Mahal is regarded as one of the eight wonders of the world, **and** some historians have noted that its architectural beauty has never been surpassed.

4. Music serves no obvious evolutionary purpose, **but** it has been, and remains, part of every known civilization on earth.

5. Correct

6. Saving an endangered species requires preservationists to study it in detail, **but** unfortunately scientific information about some animals is scarce. (Or: **Although** saving an endangered species requires preservationists to study it in detail, unfortunately scientific information about some animals is scarce.)

7. Correct

8. Modern chemistry keeps insects from ravaging crops, lifts stains from carpets, and saves lives, **but** the constant exposure to chemicals is taking a toll on many people's health.

9. If people were truly at home under the light of the moon and stars, they would go in darkness happily, **but** their eyes are adapted to the sun's light.

10. Correct

11. Roman women could only exercise political power through men, the only people considered true citizens, **for/because** they were not allowed to participate directly in politics.

Cumulative Review #3 (p. 71)

1. In their stories, originally published in the eighteenth century, the Brothers Grimm **embraced** a number of themes that have never vanished from life, despite modern advances in science and technology. (Tense Consistency: Present Perfect vs. Simple Past)

2. Correct

3. An experiment in which scientists threw paradise tree snakes from a 50-foot tower suggests that the snakes are active **fliers**, manipulating their bodies to aerodynamic effect. (Noun Agreement)

4. Although historians spend much time judging one another, **they** rarely ask what qualities make a particular scholar worthy of attention. (Pronoun-Antecedent)

5. A recently undertaken survey of drivers and cyclists has revealed that, compared to drivers, cyclists are **more** likely to use hand signals. (Comparative vs. Superlative)

6. Lan Samantha Chang is a critically acclaimed novelist **who** counts among her influences authors as varied as Charlotte Brontë and Edgar Allan Poe. (Who vs. Which)

7. In response to their critics, advocates of genetically modified foods typically insist that such crops grow faster, require fewer pesticides, and **reduce** stress on natural resources. (Parallel Structure)

8. Much like human beings, wolves are capable of exerting a profound influence on the environments that **they** inhabit. (Pronoun-Antecedent)

9. Giant galaxies like the Milky Way and the nearby Andromeda galaxy, which is even **larger**, possess the power to create and retain a wide variety of elements. (Double Positive)

10. Many scientists are baffled **by** the appearance of Yersinia pestis, a fungus that has been destroying bat populations throughout the United States in recent years. (Preposition)

11. Migrating animals maintain a fervid attentiveness that allows them to be **neither** distracted by temptations **nor** deterred by challenges that would turn other animals aside. (Word Pair)

12. Correct

13. Dumping pollution in oceans **not only** adds to the unsightliness of the formerly pristine waters **but it also** destroys the marine life that inhabits them. (Word Pair)

14. Correct

15. When it was first built, the Spanish Armada was said to be invincible, a designation that quickly became ironic since it was destroyed by the British in **hardly any** time. (Double Negative)

16. A desire to be published at all costs can lead to the erosion of a writer's sense of responsibility for **his or her** own work. (Pronoun-antecedent)

17. Construction on the Great Wall of China began many thousands of years ago and initially **involved** the construction of hundreds of miles of fortresses to defend against foreign invaders. (Tense Consistency)

18. The earliest surviving guitars date from the sixteenth century, **but** images of guitar-like instruments were depicted in Egyptian paintings and murals as early as 1900 B.C. (Conjunction)

19. The company has been criticized **for** its improper disposal of harmful chemicals and has drawn strict warnings from both environmental and political leaders. (Preposition)

20. A new generation of powerful digital tools and databases **is** transforming the study of literature, philosophy and other humanistic fields. (Subject-Verb Agreement: Subject-Prepositional Phrase-Verb)

21. Correct

22. Well into the twentieth century, to defend the notion of full social and political equality for all members of society was **to be** considered a fool. (Verb Consistency; Gerund vs. Infinitive)

23. Although George Washington and General Lafayette were great friends, they came from **widely** disparate backgrounds and had little in common. (Adjective vs. Adverb)

24. Correct

25. Although birds are not generally known for their intelligence, recent findings have established that parrots often possess skills similar to **those of** human toddlers. (Faulty Comparison)

Practice Error-Identifications (p. 82)

1. B: Adjective vs. Adverb

Blessed with an **exceptionally** rugged natural landscape, New Zealand has drawn thrill-seeking athletes in search of adventure for decades.

2. D: Pronoun-Antecedent

Franz Kafka's novel *The Trial* opens with the unexplained arrest of Josef K. by a mysterious organization that runs **its** courts outside the normal criminal-justice system.

Clue: The word "organization" is a collective noun, which points to either a subject-verb agreement or a pronoun-antecedent error

3. E: Correct

Clue: The prepositional phrase ("in a trunk") that appears at the beginning of the sentence suggests that this is a Prepositional Phrase–Verb–Subject error. The fact that this error does not then appear indicates that the correct answer is likely to be E.

Error-Identification Test

1. C: Tense Consistency

The Last Five years, a musical written by Jason Robert Brown, premiered in Chicago in 2001 and **was** produced numerous times both in the United States and internationally.

2. D: Parallel Structure

Among the many reasons healthcare professionals choose jobs that require travel are higher pay, professional growth and development, and **opportunity for** personal adventures. (suggested)

3. B: Subject-Verb Agreement: Subject–Non-Essential Clause–Verb

The tower of London, which lies within the Borough of Tower Hamlets, **is** separated from the city itself by a stretch of open space.

4. A: Who vs. Which

Originally a common breakfast eaten by farmers **who** lived in the canton of Bern, rösti is today considered the unofficial national dish of Switzerland.

5. D: Adjective vs. Adverb

The Australian frilled lizard responds to attacks by unfurling the colorful skin flap that encircles its head, but if all else fails it will scoot **nimbly** up the nearest tree.

6. D: Would vs. Will

Sofia Tolstoy, the wife of Russian author Leo Tolstoy, was a woman of strength and spirit who understood the high price she **would** pay to live next to one of the greatest writers in history.

7. B: Noun Agreement

James Watson and Francis Crick were renowned as **scientists** because they discovered the DNA triple helix and in 1962 were awarded the Nobel Prize in Medicine.

8. B: Word Pair

Among nations known for producing exceptional chess players, **neither** China **nor** Russia can compete with Armenia for the sheer number of grandmasters it has produced.

9. A: Double Positive

Humor is a far **subtler** process than a primeval pleasure such as eating, but it is just as much tied to the inner complexity of the brain.

10. E: No Error

11. D: Pronoun-Antecedent

The secret of the Mona Lisa's enigmatic smile is a matter of which cells in the retina pick up the image and how **they channel** the information to the brain.

12. B: Tense Consistency/Past Perfect

Located on the outskirts of Lincoln National Forest in New Mexico, White Oaks **became** a boomtown after silver and gold were discovered in the nearby Jicarilla Mountains in 1879.

13. A: Preposition

The Ethiopian wolf, the only species of wolf native **to** Africa, can be identified by its distinctive red coat and black-and-white tail.

14. C: Gerund vs. Infinitive

Far from eliminating war, the new diplomatic system instituted in Europe during the early nineteenth century simply changed the reasons **for fighting** and the means of combat.

15. A: Faulty Comparison

With genes that are virtually identical to **those of** humans, Neanderthals can offer many insights into the evolution and development of the modern brain.

16. A: Subject-Verb Agreement (Subject–Prepositional Phrase–Verb)

The popularity of games such as cricket and squash in former English colonies **is** often attributed to the lingering influence of British culture.

17. E: No Error

Sentences and Fragments (p. 93)

1. Shirley Jackson, best known for her shocking short story **"The Lottery," was** born in San Francisco in 1916.

2. Correct

3. The pyramids of ancient Egypt, intended to be monuments to the Pharaohs' **greatness, were** built with the help of great armies of slaves.

4. The Red **Belt, (which was) one of** several colored belts used in some martial arts to denote a practitioner's skill level and rank, originated in Japan and Korea.

5. The plan to overhaul the country's higher education system **is** a model for moving other desperately needed projects forward.

6. Correct

7. Recent findings from research on moose **have suggested** that arthritis in human beings may be linked in part to nutritional deficits.

8. A new study **reports** that the physical differences among dog breeds are determined by variations in only about seven genetic regions.

9. George Barr McCutcheon, a popular novelist and **playwright, is** best known for the series of novels set in Graustark, a fictional Eastern European country.

10. Forensic biology, **(which is) the application** of biology to law enforcement, has been used to identify illegal products from endangered species and investigate bird collisions with wind turbines.

11. Human computers, who once performed basic numerical analysis for **laboratories, were** behind the calculations for everything from the first accurate prediction of the return of Halley's Comet to the success of the Manhattan Project.

12. Nicollet Island, an island in the Mississippi River just north of **Minneapolis, was** named after cartographer Joseph Nicollet.

13. Malba Tahan, (who was) a fictitious Persian **scholar, was** the pen name created by Brazilian author Julio Cesar de Mello e Souza.

14. The Rochester International Jazz Festival **takes** place in June of each year and typically attracts more than 100,000 fans from towns across upstate New York.

15. Although Rodin purposely omitted crucial elements such as arms from his sculptures, his consistent use of the human figure **attested** to his respect for artistic tradition.

16. Brick nog **is** a commonly used construction technique in which one width of bricks is used to fill the vacancies in a wooden frame.

17. The unusually large size of the komodo dragon, the largest species of **lizard, has** been attributed to its ancient ancestor, the immense varanid lizard.

18. One of the most popular ballets, *Swan Lake*, which was fashioned from Russian folk tales, **tells** the story of Odette, a princess turned into a swan by an evil sorcerer's curse.

19. Correct

20. Pheidon, a king of the Greek city Argos during the seventh century **B.C., ruled** during a time when monarchs were figureheads with little genuine power.

21. Batsford Arboretum, a 55-acre garden that contains Great Britain's largest collection of Japanese cherry **trees, is** open daily to the public for most of the year.

Commas and Semicolons (p. 98)

1. Correct

2. César Chávez became an iconic figure as the leader of the Farm Workers' **movement, but** it was as a martyr who embodied the contrast between Mexico and the United States that he commanded the most attention.

3. Correct

4. Vitamin D has been long known for its critical role in the body's processing of **calcium, yet** increasing amounts of evidence suggest that it also protects the body by significantly cutting the risk for most forms of cancer.

5. Universities typically offer a wide variety of continuing education classes, **many of which** are offered over the Internet.

6. When the Mayan city of Palenque was first discovered, it was completely overwhelmed by the plant life of the **rainforest; today** it is a massive archaeological site that attracts thousands of tourists each year.

7. International sports competitions are symbolic showdowns that are more about winning than about universal **friendship; however,** they are a far more civilized alternative to actual warfare.

8. The Roman emperor Hadrian commissioned the building of the **Pantheon; its** administration was managed by Marcus Agrippa.

9. The First World War began in August of **1914; it** was directly caused by the assassination of Archduke Franz Ferdinand of Austria by Bosnian revolutionary Gavrilo Princeps.

10. In 43 A.D., Britain was already a territory of the Roman **Empire; it** remained a part of Rome until more than four centuries later.

11. Over the past several years, the country's food prices have increased **dramatically; they** are now at their highest rate in two decades.

12. Correct

13. An ethnocentric approach stems from judging an unfamiliar culture in relation to pre-conceived **values; it** indicates the inability to escape one's own biases and prevents objective analysis.

14. Culture has become a force that may accelerate human **evolution because** people have no choice but to adapt to pressures and technologies of their own creation.

15. Both the Parthenon and the Pantheon are temples to the deities of the people who built **them, but** the Parthenon was built by the ancient Greeks while the Pantheon was constructed by the Romans.

16. The eyes of many predatory animals are designed to enhance depth **perception; however,** in other organisms, they are designed to maximize the visual field.

17. Paris is the world capital of **cinephilia; moreover,** it has played a central role in films of every imaginable.

18. Sugar and cavities go hand in **hand; dentists therefore** recommend that the amount of sugar people consume be kept to a minimum.

19. Despite strains, fractures and tears, many athletes continue to **work out; consequently,** at least one expert would say they are addicted to exercise.

20. The Mid-Autumn Festival, a popular harvest festival celebrated in Asia, dates back 3,000 years to China's Shang **Dynasty and** is traditionally held on the fifteenth day of the eighth month.

21. Carl Bohm was one of the most prolific German pianists and composers during the nineteenth **century; few** people would, however, recognize his name today.

22. Correct

Gerunds and Wordiness (p. 103)

1. It can hardly be considered a surprise that Incan emperors covered themselves in gold **because they held** themselves to be the sun's human incarnation.

2. The museum's artistic director has arranged the exhibition thematically **in order to provide** a new understanding of the multifaceted complexity of Native American life.

3. Correct

4. **Although it is** a smaller city than either London or New York, Dublin possesses a thriving theater scene whose productions regularly achieve international renown.

5. Correct

6. Bongoyo Island, located off the coast of Tanzania, has become a popular vacation spot for both tourists and Tanzanians **because it has** such close proximity to the mainland.

7. The Province House, home to royal governors in seventeenth-century Massachusetts, was considered one of the grandest examples of colonial architecture **because it possessed** beautiful Tudor-style chimneystacks.

8. Contrary to popular belief, people should alternate rooms while studying **because they retain** more information that way.

9. Some excellent teachers prance in front of the classroom like Shakespearean actors, while others are notable **because they are** aloof or timid.

10. Correct

11. *Prince Jellyfish*, an unpublished novel by author and journalist Hunter S. Thompson, was rejected by a number of literary agents **because it lacked** popular appeal.

12. Correct

13. **Although traffic often blocks** its main arteries, East London contains side streets that can, on occasion, be as tranquil and pleasant as country lanes.

14. In scientific fields, scale models known as homunculi are often used **to illustrate** physiological characteristics of the human body.

Passive Voice (p. 105)

1. In the later works of Nikola Stoyanov, also known by the pseudonym Emiliyan Stanev, the author often describes nature in great detail.

2. Michael J. Rosen has written works ranging from picture books to poetry, and he has also edited several anthologies varying almost as broadly in content.

3. In the movie *The Killing Fields*, first-time actor Haing S. Ngor portrayed Cambodian photojournalist Dith Pran, a role for which Ngor won an Academy Award.

4. Although desserts **are** typically characterized by their sweetness, bakers are now creating ones that feature intriguing blends of sweet and savory.

5. Scientists at the Woods Hole Oceanographic Institute designed *The Nereus*, a remotely operated underwater hybrid vehicle, to function at depths of up to 36,000 feet.

6. Many pharmaceutical company executives know Michael Balls, a British zoologist and biology professor, as an outspoken opponent of animal laboratory testing.

7. Between the late 1970's and 1980's, Jamaican reggae musician Lone Ranger, born Anthony Alphonso Waldron, recorded nine albums.

8. In 2000, performance artist Jody Sperling founded Time Lapse Dance, a New York-based dance company whose mission is to provide modern reinterpretations of classic works.

9. People throughout the Middle East, Singapore, and Indonesia frequently eat Murtabak, a dish composed of mutton, garlic, egg, onion, and curry sauce.

10. Over the last thirty years, researchers have examined many forms of meditation and deemed a number of them ineffective.

Dangling Modifiers (p. 108)

Suggested Answers

1. Characterized by scenes that are shot quickly and in real time, **guerilla filmmaking** is typically characterized by low budgets and simple props.

2. One of the greatest musicians of her time, **Clara Wieck** began piano studies when she was five years old; by the age of twelve she was renowned as both a performer and a composer.

3. Born in St. Lucia in the West Indies, **author Derek Walcott** work includes a number of plays and poems, most notably *Omeros*.

4. One of hundreds of islands that form the Indonesian archipelago, **Bali** is less than 100 miles wide, yet it holds within its borders a rich and dramatic history.

5. Historically based on the carving of walrus ivory, which was once found in abundance, **Inuit art** has, since the mid-twentieth century, also included prints and figures made from soft stone.

6. Located in the southern Andes and covered by glaciers, **Tronador** is an extinct volcano whose last eruption occurred many centuries ago.

7. An inspiration to European artists such as Gauguin, van Gogh, and Toulouse-Lautrec, **Japanese painter Katsushika Hokusai** lived during the eighteenth century.

8. Correct

9. Though educated and well mannered, **Jane Eyre** remains of low status throughout the majority of the novel that bears her name.

10. Born at Dromland Castle in County Clare, Ireland in 1821, **artist and engineer George O'Brien** had an aristocratic background that seemed to be at odds with his life in the Australian outback.

11. Correct

12. Despite winning several architectural awards, **the university's new dormitory** has been criticized by students for its impractical layout.

13. One of the earliest authorities to take a stand against pollution, **King Edward I** proclaimed in 1306 that sea coal could not be burned because the smoke it created was hazardous to people's health.

14. Predicting renewed interest in their country's natural resources, **political leaders** have established a plan to create mines in the most underdeveloped regions.

15. Having remained under Moorish rule until the twelfth century, **many Spaniards** still spoke Arabic when their cities first came under the control of European monarchs.

Misplaced Modifiers (p. 110)

1. The Spanish city of Valencia is the birthplace of horchata, a drink made from the juice of tiger nuts and said to date from the eighth century.

2. One of the most important poets of the Harlem Renaissance, Claude McKay moved to New York after studying agronomy in Kansas.

3. Founded by Leland Stanford, the California Street Cable Railroad is an established public transit company in San Francisco.

4. Correct

5. Praised by consumer magazines for being both versatile and affordable, the food processor performs a wide range of functions, including chopping, dicing, and pureeing, when a switch is flipped.

6. Fortresses protected many ancient cities from bands of invaders roaming in search of settlements to plunder.

7. Some of the world's fastest trains, which can reach speeds of up to 200 miles per hour, run between the cities of Tokyo and Kyoto.

8. Originally constructed during the Roman Republic, the House of Livia contains brightly colored frescoes that depict bucolic landscapes and mythological scenes and that date back to the first decades B.C.

9. The Georgian port of Batumi, which once housed some of the world's first oil pipelines, fell into decline in the mid-twentieth century.

10. The bass viol, which resembles the cello, has experienced a resurgence in popularity over the past several decades.

Parallel Structure II: Phrases (p. 113)

1. Correct

2. The figure skater was praised not only for her mastery of difficult technical skills **but also for the elegance and grace of her performance**.

3. While the novel has many detractors, it also has many admirers who argue that its popularity is based on its gripping storyline **and the believability of its characters' motives**.

4. Known for her musical compositions as well as for her poems and letters, Hildegard of Bingen was just as renowned in the twelfth century **as (she was) in** the twentieth.

5. The university is installing an electronic course-evaluation system so that students can decide whether they should register for certain classes **or avoid them altogether.**

6. For fans of the legendary food writer Charles H. Baker, the contents of a dish are **less compelling than the story behind it**.

7. During the sixteenth century, an outbreak of fighting in Europe led to the invention of new weapons **and to the growth and evolutions of old ones.**

8. Correct

9. It is believed that many animals are capable of drawing a connection between the odor of a harmful substance **and its toxicity.**

10. The bass clarinet, although similar to the more common soprano clarinet, is distinguished both by the greater length of its body **and by the presence of several additional keys.**

11. At its peak, the Roman army was nearly unconquerable because of the discipline of its soldiers, the hard and effective training of its commanders, **and the exceptional organization of its troops.**

12. The development of identity was one of psychologist Erik Erikson's greatest concerns, both in his own life **and in his theory**.

Fixing Sentences Test (p. 120)

1. C: Gerund Required

2. B: Improper Gerund Use

3. D: Tense Consistency

4. C: Fragment/Non-Essential Clause

5. D: Parallel Structure

6. A: No Error

7. B: Dangling Modifier

8. E: Semicolon; Pronoun-Antecedent

9. E: Pronoun-Antecedent; Would vs. Will

10. C: Parallel Structure

11. D: Dangling Modifier

12. B: Missing Antecedent/Participle Required

13. A: No Error

14. E: Parallel Structure

Eight Multiple Choice SAT Writing Tests

Test 1

Section 1

1. Ⓐ Ⓑ Ⓒ Ⓓ Ⓔ
2. Ⓐ Ⓑ Ⓒ Ⓓ Ⓔ
3. Ⓐ Ⓑ Ⓒ Ⓓ Ⓔ
4. Ⓐ Ⓑ Ⓒ Ⓓ Ⓔ
5. Ⓐ Ⓑ Ⓒ Ⓓ Ⓔ
6. Ⓐ Ⓑ Ⓒ Ⓓ Ⓔ
7. Ⓐ Ⓑ Ⓒ Ⓓ Ⓔ
8. Ⓐ Ⓑ Ⓒ Ⓓ Ⓔ
9. Ⓐ Ⓑ Ⓒ Ⓓ Ⓔ
10. Ⓐ Ⓑ Ⓒ Ⓓ Ⓔ
11. Ⓐ Ⓑ Ⓒ Ⓓ Ⓔ
12. Ⓐ Ⓑ Ⓒ Ⓓ Ⓔ
13. Ⓐ Ⓑ Ⓒ Ⓓ Ⓔ
14. Ⓐ Ⓑ Ⓒ Ⓓ Ⓔ
15. Ⓐ Ⓑ Ⓒ Ⓓ Ⓔ
16. Ⓐ Ⓑ Ⓒ Ⓓ Ⓔ
17. Ⓐ Ⓑ Ⓒ Ⓓ Ⓔ
18. Ⓐ Ⓑ Ⓒ Ⓓ Ⓔ
19. Ⓐ Ⓑ Ⓒ Ⓓ Ⓔ
20. Ⓐ Ⓑ Ⓒ Ⓓ Ⓔ
21. Ⓐ Ⓑ Ⓒ Ⓓ Ⓔ
22. Ⓐ Ⓑ Ⓒ Ⓓ Ⓔ
23. Ⓐ Ⓑ Ⓒ Ⓓ Ⓔ
24. Ⓐ Ⓑ Ⓒ Ⓓ Ⓔ
25. Ⓐ Ⓑ Ⓒ Ⓓ Ⓔ
26. Ⓐ Ⓑ Ⓒ Ⓓ Ⓔ
27. Ⓐ Ⓑ Ⓒ Ⓓ Ⓔ
28. Ⓐ Ⓑ Ⓒ Ⓓ Ⓔ
29. Ⓐ Ⓑ Ⓒ Ⓓ Ⓔ
30. Ⓐ Ⓑ Ⓒ Ⓓ Ⓔ
31. Ⓐ Ⓑ Ⓒ Ⓓ Ⓔ
32. Ⓐ Ⓑ Ⓒ Ⓓ Ⓔ
33. Ⓐ Ⓑ Ⓒ Ⓓ Ⓔ
34. Ⓐ Ⓑ Ⓒ Ⓓ Ⓔ
35. Ⓐ Ⓑ Ⓒ Ⓓ Ⓔ

Section 2

1. Ⓐ Ⓑ Ⓒ Ⓓ Ⓔ
2. Ⓐ Ⓑ Ⓒ Ⓓ Ⓔ
3. Ⓐ Ⓑ Ⓒ Ⓓ Ⓔ
4. Ⓐ Ⓑ Ⓒ Ⓓ Ⓔ
5. Ⓐ Ⓑ Ⓒ Ⓓ Ⓔ
6. Ⓐ Ⓑ Ⓒ Ⓓ Ⓔ
7. Ⓐ Ⓑ Ⓒ Ⓓ Ⓔ
8. Ⓐ Ⓑ Ⓒ Ⓓ Ⓔ
9. Ⓐ Ⓑ Ⓒ Ⓓ Ⓔ
10. Ⓐ Ⓑ Ⓒ Ⓓ Ⓔ
11. Ⓐ Ⓑ Ⓒ Ⓓ Ⓔ
12. Ⓐ Ⓑ Ⓒ Ⓓ Ⓔ
13. Ⓐ Ⓑ Ⓒ Ⓓ Ⓔ
14. Ⓐ Ⓑ Ⓒ Ⓓ Ⓔ

SECTION 1

Time – 25 Minutes
35 Questions

Directions: For each question in this section, select the best answer from among the choices given and fill in the corresponding circle on the answer sheet.

The following sentences test correctness and effectiveness of expression. Part of each sentence or the entire sentence is underlined; beneath each sentence are five ways of phrasing the underlined material. Choice A repeats the original phrasing; the other four choices are different. If you think the original phrasing produces a better sentence than any of the alternatives, select choice A; if not, select one of the other choices.

In making your selection, follow the requirements of standard written English; that is, pay attention to grammar, choice of words, sentence construction, and punctuation. Your selection should result in the most effective sentence—clear and precise, without awkwardness or ambiguity.

EXAMPLE:

Anna Robertson Moses completed her first painting <u>and she was seventy-six years old then</u>.

(A) and she was seventy-six years old then
(B) when she was seventy-six years old
(C) at age seventy-six years old
(D) upon arriving at the age of seventy-six
(E) at the time when she was seventy-six years old

1. Bats can perceive and stalk their prey in complete <u>darkness, and they use</u> a system of ultrasonic sounds to produce echoes that identify its location.

   (A) darkness, and they use
   (B) darkness, they use
   (C) darkness by using
   (D) darkness and using
   (E) darkness, they are using

2. As they were studying the lamp shell, a primitive form of marine <u>life, researchers were being surprised to discover</u> that it contained an eye.

   (A) life, researchers were being surprised to discover
   (B) life; researchers were surprised in discovering
   (C) life, researchers being surprised in their discovery
   (D) life, researchers having been surprised to discover
   (E) life, researchers were surprised to discover

3. Munich's altitude and proximity to the northern edge of the Alps <u>means that precipitation is high there</u>.

   (A) means that precipitation is high there
   (B) being the causes of high precipitation
   (C) which create a high level of precipitation
   (D) create a high level of precipitation
   (E) creating a high level of precipitation

4. After her acclaimed novel *The God of Small Things* was published, Arundhati Roy <u>has turned</u> her attention to writing works of non-fiction and to working as a political activist.

   (A) has turned
   (B) having turned
   (C) turned
   (D) turns
   (E) turning

5. In his lifetime, Michel de Montaigne was a bestselling author, almost a <u>celebrity, and his enduring appeal rests</u> on his remarkable ordinariness.

   (A) celebrity, and his enduring appeal rests
   (B) celebrity, and it so happens that his enduring appeal rests
   (C) celebrity, but his enduring appeal resting
   (D) celebrity, whereas his enduring appeal is resting
   (E) celebrity; however, his enduring appeal rests

6. The senatorial <u>candidate, previously known for his open and candid manner but who has become</u> increasingly evasive about his beliefs in recent weeks.

   (A) candidate, previously known for his open and candid manner but who has become
   (B) candidate, previously known for his open and candid manner, has become
   (C) candidate, previously known for his open and candid manner but who had become
   (D) candidate, previously known for his open and candid manner, he has become
   (E) candidate, previously known for his open and candid manner but having become

7. <u>Unsure that he was prepared for the championship boxing match, Carlos's day off was spent practicing and refining his strategies.</u>

   (A) Unsure that he was prepared for the championship boxing match, Carlos's day off was spent practicing and refining his strategies.
   (B) Carlos was unsure that he was prepared for the championship boxing match, he therefore spent his day off practicing and refining his strategies.
   (C) Feeling unsure that he was prepared for the championship boxing match, Carlos spent his day off practicing and refining his strategies.
   (D) Carlos felt unsure of being prepared for the championship boxing match, and this is why he spent his day off practicing and refining his strategies.
   (E) Practicing and refining his strategies is what Carlos did because he was unsure of being prepared for the championship boxing match.

8. <u>Marriage, often viewed as a legal contract, can be recognized</u> by the state, a religious authority, or both.

   (A) Marriage, often viewed as a legal contract, can be recognized
   (B) Marriage often being viewed as a legal contract, it can be recognized
   (C) Marriage is often viewed as a legal contract, it can be recognized
   (D) Often viewed as a legal contract, the recognition of marriage
   (E) The viewing of marriage is often done as a legal contract, this being recognized

9. <u>Having opened last year to glowing reviews, the quality of the food served at the café has since declined noticeably</u>.

   (A) Having opened last year to glowing reviews, the quality of the food served at the café has since declined noticeably.
   (B) The café opened last year to glowing reviews, but their food quality has declined noticeably since then.
   (C) Although the reviews given to it when it opened last year were glowing, the quality of the food served by the café has declined noticeably since then.
   (D) Although the café opened last year to glowing reviews, the quality of its food has since declined noticeably.
   (E) The café opened last year to glowing reviews, despite this the quality of its food has declined noticeably since that time.

10. <u>For all his claims</u> about improving schools, the mayor has done little to implement reforms demonstrated to increase students' knowledge.

   (A) For all his claims
   (B) In spite of him having claimed
   (C) Besides him having claimed
   (D) While he had claimed
   (E) Despite the fact of his claiming

11. The time devoted to books by publishing companies, experts suggest, has been reduced by both financial constraints <u>as well as an increase in the emphasis</u> on sales and marketing considerations.

   (A) as well as an increase in the emphasis
   (B) increasing the emphasis
   (C) and the emphasis increasing
   (D) and an increased emphasis
   (E) in addition to the emphasis increasing

The following sentences test your ability to recognize grammar and usage errors. Each sentence contains either a single error or none at all. No sentence contains more than one error. The error, if there is one, is underlined and lettered. If the sentence contains an error, select the one underlined part that must be changed in order to make the sentence correct. If the sentence is correct, select choice E. In choosing answers, follow the requirements of standard written English.

EXAMPLE:

Science fiction writer H.G. Wells, <u>the author of</u>
            A

more than 100 books, accurately <u>predicted</u> the
            B

the <u>invention</u> of television, the rise of the Internet,
   C

and <u>creating</u> the hydrogen bomb. <u>No error</u>
   D   E

○○○●○

12. Ethnomusicologist Alan Lomax, who <u>believed that</u>
               A

 poor and forgotten places contained <u>extraordinary</u>
                B

 <u>examples of</u> culture, <u>and traveling</u> the globe
  C   Ⓓ

 in search of traditional songs and stories. <u>No error</u>
               E

13. <u>Though</u> his paintings are considered iconic
  A

 <u>depictions of</u> everyday life, the painter lacks any sense
   B

 of either humor <u>and</u> self-awareness, relying instead <u>on</u>
       Ⓒ   D

 cliché. <u>No error</u>
    E

14. <u>According to</u> South African author Nadine Gordimer,
  A

 the process of writing fiction <u>is</u> unconscious, emerging
            B

 <u>from what</u> one learns and how <u>you live</u>. <u>No error</u>
  C   D   E

15. The <u>elimination of</u> poverty <u>ought to be</u> within our
    A   B

 grasp, <u>and yet</u> for hundreds of millions of people
    C

 across the globe, it remains <u>but</u> a dream. <u>No error</u>
           D   E

16. Though the book is <u>unexpected</u>/sober in tone for a
        Ⓐ ly

 biography of <u>so</u> forceful a personality, it nevertheless
      B

 does an excellent job <u>of emphasizing</u> its subject's <u>most</u>
         C   D

 important achievements. <u>No error</u>
         E

17. Homer's *Odyssey*, one of the most <u>extraordinary</u>
            A

 travel records of all time, <u>is about</u> one man's bravery,
          B

 cunning, and <u>he desires</u> to achieve his goal <u>at any cost</u>.
     Ⓒ   D

 <u>No error</u>
  E

18. <u>With</u> his prodigious talent, <u>adoring</u> parents, and
  A   B

 dedicated piano teacher named Marietta Clinkscales,
          double negative

 Duke Ellington could <u>not hardly</u> have failed to
        Ⓒ

 succeed as <u>a musician</u>. <u>No error</u>
     D   E

19. Easy communication between speakers <u>of</u> different
             A

 languages <u>are</u> a lovely ideal, but in reality <u>it could</u>
    Ⓑ   C

 <u>lead to</u> eternal confusion. <u>No error</u>
  D   E

20. In 1963, Lina Wertmüller <u>directed</u> her first film,
          A

 <u>whose</u> theme – the lives of impoverished people in
  B

 southern Italy – <u>will become</u> a recurring motif in her
        would Ⓒ

 <u>later</u> works. <u>No error</u>
  D   E

21. Though many have tried, instrument-makers are
    A
    unable to reproduce the precise sound of a Stradivarius
           B   ~its
    violin, so the quality of their tone remains a mystery.
           C   D
    No error
    E

22. Although Galileo is generally depicted as a strict
    proponent for rationalism and scientific thought, he
             (A)
    also derived much of his inspiration from works of art,
                   B   C
    particularly Dante's *Divine Comedy*. No error
    D   E

23. Introduced in 1678, the term "conscious" acquired
    A   B
    at least five definitions within fifty years, and its
                                                  C
                  has
    ambiguity had not faded in more recent times.
              D
    No error   continue
    E

24. In his novel *Parallel Stories*, Peter Nadas is
    A
    concerned not only with historical events but also
              B   influencing
    with their role to influence people's everyday lives
    C   (D)
    and emotions. No error
                  E

25. While modern technology offers remarkable
    A
    opportunities for self-expression and communication,
    B
    much of what new channels of communication bring
         C
    is mere distraction. No error
    D   (E)

26. According to entomologist Deborah Gordon, the
    popular image of ants as brave soldiers and dutiful
           A   B   is
    factory workers are a human fiction unrelated to true
                    C   D
    insect behavior. No error
                     E

27. Though no longer a household name, nineteenth
             A
    century English biologist Richard Owens published
                                      4o   B
    more than 600 articles and made discoveries that
                                    h   C
    rivaled Charles Darwin. No error
            (D)   E

28. Convinced of the artistic purity of their work, many
             A
    novelists have long dismissed the Internet as a means
                       B   C
    of distributing their writing and often sought to avoid
                                     D
    technology entirely. No error
                         E

                                            are
29. Hidden in the elegant structure of poetry is a
    A   (B)
    number of mathematical systems that include
                                   C
    fractal patterns, linear algebra, and Euclidean
                                     D
    geometry. No error
              E

Directions: The following passage is an early draft of an essay. Some parts of the passage need to be rewritten.

Read the passage and select the best answer for the questions that follow. Some questions are about particular sentences or parts of sentences and ask you to improve sentence structure or word choice. Other questions ask you to consider organization and development. In choosing you answer, follow the requirements of standard written English.

Questions 30-35 are based on the following passage.

(1) Protecting oneself in battle has always been one of the most important concerns of every soldier, including medieval knights. (2) The typical picture of a medieval knight depicts a figure covered from head to toe in gleaming metal. (3) Full suits of plate armor were not developed until the Middle Ages were almost over.

(4) The earliest type of armor to be invented was chain mail armor, which was made from thousands of interlocking metallic rings that a master craftsman and his apprentices had linked together by hand. (5) It was then placed over a "gambeson" – a jacket padded with wool or linen and worn on top of the knight's clothes. (6) Though very sturdy, full protection from an opponent's weapons was not offered, so a knight would often wear a helmet and carry a shield as well.

(7) As the Middle Ages progressed, new and more powerful weapons were created, as a result chain mail stopped being an effective form of protection. (8) Toward the end of the thirteenth century, the first plate armor was created. (9) At first, knights simply wore it around their chests and shoulders, but soon they were using it to cover nearly every inch of their bodies. (10) Being that it protected them so thoroughly, many found that their shields were no longer necessary.

(11) Knights wore armor not only as a way of protecting themselves in battle, in addition to showing off their high status. (12) Medieval society was highly stratified and consisted of a large underclass of serfs and a much smaller class of noble elites. (13) Because armor was so ornate and expensive, only the wealthiest members of society could afford to buy it, and they took every opportunity to show it off at ceremonies and banquets. (14) Gradually, though, armor became used only for show: when weapons based on gunpowder began to be used widely, armor became an ineffective defense. (15) Within a hundred years, it had disappeared from combat.

30. In context, what is the best way to revise the underlined portion of sentence 3 (reproduced below)?

    Full suits of plate armor were not developed until the Middle Ages were almost over.

    (A) Full suits of plate armor, however, did not develop
    (B) Furthermore, full suits of plate armor were not developed
    (C) Likewise, full suits of plate armor would not develop
    (D) For example, full suits of plate armor were not developed
    (E) In spite of this, full suits of plate armor had not been developed

31. Which of the following is the best way to revise the underlined portion of sentence 6 (reproduced below)?

    Though very sturdy, full protection from an opponent's weapons was not offered, so a knight would often wear a helmet and carry a shield as well.

    (A) Though very sturdy, full protection from an opponent's weapons not being offered; therefore
    (B) Though very sturdy, chain mail did not offer full protection from an opponent's weapon, and so
    (C) Though very sturdy, full protection from an opponent's weapons was not offered, therefore
    (D) In spite of it being very sturdy, chain mail did not offer full protection from an opponent's weapon, so
    (E) While it was very sturdy, full protection was not offered by it from an opponent's weapon, and

32. Which of the following is the best way to revise and combine the underlined portion of sentences 9 and 10?

At first, knights simply wore it around their chests and shoulders, but soon they were using it to cover nearly every inch of their bodies. Being that it protected them so thoroughly, many found that their shields were no longer necessary.

(A) (as it is now)
(B) but soon they were using it to cover nearly every inch of their bodies, it protected them so thoroughly that many found that their shields were
(C) but soon they were using it to cover nearly every inch of their bodies because of it protecting them so thoroughly and making their shields
(D) but soon they were using it to cover nearly every inch of their bodies since it protected them so thoroughly and made their shields
(E) but soon they were using it to cover nearly every inch of their bodies, while it protected them so thoroughly that many found that their shields were

33. In context, the fourth paragraph (sentences 11-15) would be most improved by the inclusion of

(A) a discussion of economic inequality in medieval England.
(B) the recipe for gunpowder used by fifteenth-century soldiers
(C) a description of the highly ornate armor typically worn by knights at ceremonies and banquets.
(D) an example of a knight who switched from chain mail to plate armor during the fourteenth century.
(E) a catalogue of the expenses incurred at a typical banquet during the late Middle Ages.

34. Which of the following is the best version of the underlined portion of sentence 11 (reproduced below)?

Knights wore armor not only as a way of protecting themselves in battle, in addition to showing off their high status.

(A) protecting themselves in battle so that they could show off their high status
(B) protecting themselves in battle and showing off their high status
(C) protecting themselves in battle, but also they wanted to show off their high status
(D) protecting themselves in battle and wanting to show off their high status
(E) protecting themselves in battle but also as a way of showing off their high status

35. Of the following, which sentence should be deleted because it interrupts the logical flow of the passage?

(A) Sentence 5
(B) Sentence 7
(C) Sentence 8
(D) Sentence 12
(E) Sentence 13

SECTION 2
Time – 10 Minutes
14 Questions

Directions: For each question in this section, select the best answer from among the choices given and fill in the corresponding circle on the answer sheet.

The following sentences test correctness and effectiveness of expression. Part of each sentence or the entire sentence is underlined; beneath each sentence are five ways of phrasing the underlined material. Choice A repeats the original phrasing; the other four choices are different. If you think the original phrasing produces a better sentence than any of the alternatives, select choice A; if not, select one of the other choices.

In making your selection, follow the requirements of standard written English; that is, pay attention to grammar, choice of words, sentence construction, and punctuation. Your selection should result in the most effective sentence—clear and precise, without awkwardness or ambiguity.

EXAMPLE:

○●○○○

Anna Robertson Moses completed her first painting <u>and she was seventy-six years old then</u>.

(A) and she was seventy-six years old then
(B) when she was seventy-six years old
(C) at age seventy-six years old
(D) upon arriving at the age of seventy-six
(E) at the time when she was seventy-six years old

1. <u>There has been many objections made</u> to the hospital's plan to construct its new infectious disease laboratories so close to the town center.

(A) There has been many objections made
(B) There has been many objections to make
(C) Many objections being made
(D) Many objections have been made
(E) The many objections that have been made

2. <u>In the recent consumer report, it being indicated by the market researchers</u> that food prices in economically depressed neighborhoods are frequently higher than in wealthier ones.

(A) In the recent consumer report, it being indicated by the market researchers
(B) The recent consumer report in which market researchers indicated
(C) The market researchers indicated in their recent consumer report
(D) The recent consumer report indicating by market researchers
(E) It being indicated by the market researchers in their recent consumer report

3. The Mississippi and the Nile <u>can be cited as an example</u> of rivers that form large deltas because of the large amount of sediment deposited at their mouths.

(A) can be cited as an example
(B) can be cited as examples
(C) are an example
(D) cited as an example
(E) which can be cited as an example

4. Both Rachel and Laetitia were disqualified from participating in the science fair after judges discovered <u>that she had fabricated a portion of her data</u>.

(A) that she had fabricated a portion of her data
(B) that a portion of the data having been fabricated by her
(C) that a portion of the data had been fabricated by her
(D) that Rachel would have fabricated a portion of her data
(E) that Rachel had fabricated a portion of her data

5. While erecting the new office building, <u>vandalism, graffiti, and litter were all problems that construction workers faced</u>.

   (A) vandalism, graffiti, and litter were problems that construction workers faced
   (B) problems faced by construction workers included vandalism, graffiti, and litter
   (C) construction workers faced problems including vandalism, graffiti, and litter
   (D) construction workers who faced problems including vandalism, graffiti, and litter
   (E) faced by the construction workers were problems including vandalism, graffiti, and litter

6. New Zealand has been so geographically isolated throughout its <u>history to a level at which</u> distinctive forms for fauna have arisen as a result.

   (A) history to a level at which
   (B) history, consequently
   (C) history, and
   (D) history, with
   (E) history that

7. <u>The beginning of the contemporary environmental movement was because</u> marine biologist and author Rachel Carson's book *Silent Spring* revealed the dangers of pesticides.

   (A) The beginning of contemporary environmental movement was because
   (B) The contemporary environmental movement beginning because
   (C) The beginning of the contemporary environmental movement has occurred because
   (D) The beginning of the contemporary environmental movement, which took place because
   (E) The contemporary environmental movement began when

8. The precocious son of an impoverished single mother, <u>W.E.B. Dubois' intellectual gifts were recognized by many of his high school teachers, who encouraged</u> him to further his education.

   (A) W.E.B. Dubois' intellectual gifts were recognized by many of his high school teachers, who encouraged
   (B) the intellectual gifts of W.E.B. Dubois had been recognized by many of his high school teachers, who encouraged
   (C) the intellectual gifts of W.E.B. Dubois were recognized by many of his high school teachers, who encouraged
   (D) W.E.B. Dubois was encouraged by many of his high school teachers, who recognized his intellectual gifts and urged
   (E) W.E.B. Dubois was encouraged by his many of his high school teachers, recognizing his intellectual gifts and urging

9. Passed in 1943 to make housing affordable for middle-class residents, <u>rents for some New York City apartments having remained stable because of rent control laws</u>.

   (A) rents for some New York City apartments having remained stable because of rent control laws
   (B) rents for some New York City apartments had remained stable because of rent control laws
   (C) rent control laws have stabilized rents for some New York City apartments
   (D) rent control laws having stabilized rents for some New York City apartments
   (E) some New York City apartments have rents that have remained stable, the reason being rent control laws

10. <u>Whaling, a risky pursuit that led sailors halfway across the world</u> and sometimes to the bottom of the sea, was centered in Nantucket during the early nineteenth century.

    (A) Whaling, a risky pursuit that led sailors halfway across the world
    (B) Whale being a risky pursuit that led sailors halfway across the world
    (C) Whaling, a risky pursuit for leading sailors halfway across the world
    (D) Whaling was a risky pursuit that led sailors halfway across the world
    (E) Whaling is a risky pursuit that led sailors halfway across the world

11. The highly textured bark and distinctive silhouette of the Dutch Elm <u>tree distinguishes</u> it from the equally common English Elm tree.

    (A) tree distinguishes
    (B) tree distinguish
    (C) tree, they distinguish
    (D) tree distinguishing
    (E) tree, which distinguish

12. As young children, most people are able to move effortlessly <u>between the worlds of the fantastic and reality</u>.

    (A) between the worlds of the fantastic and reality
    (B) between the worlds of the fantastic and the real
    (C) from the fantastic to reality and back again
    (D) back and forth between the world of fantasy and that of the real
    (E) from fantasy to the real, and then they return

13. In an attempt to boost school spirit, the university is <u>giving away tickets to athletic events, increasing support for student organizations, and holding a contest whereby a new mascot will be created</u>.

    (A) giving away tickets to athletic events, increasing support for student organizations, and holding a contest whereby a new mascot will be created
    (B) giving away tickets to athletic events, support for student organizations being increased, and holding a contest the creation of a new mascot
    (C) giving away tickets to athletic events, increasing support for student organizations, and holding a contest to create a new mascot
    (D) giving away tickets to athletic events, increasing support for student organizations, and a contest to create a new mascot will be held
    (E) giving away tickets to athletic events, support for student organizations is increased, and a contest is held to create a new mascot

14. A leading figure in the Pop Art movement, Andy Warhol was <u>at once</u> celebrated for his depictions of everyday objects <u>but he was denounced for his embrace of consumerist culture</u>.

    (A) but he was denounced for his embrace of consumerist culture
    (B) although they denounced him for his embrace of consumerist culture
    (C) and he was also denounced because he embraced consumerist culture
    (D) while being denounced for his embrace of consumerist culture
    (E) and denounced for his embrace of consumerist culture

Answers: Test 1, Section 1

1. C: Gerund required

The second clause explains *how* bats perceive and stalk their prey in complete darkness. The gerund phrase (*by using*) is therefore required to make the relationship clear. No other answer choice presents this possibility.

2. E: Improper use of gerund

In the original version of the sentence, the gerund *being* makes the phrasing unnecessarily awkward. The verb *were* by itself is sufficient to make clear that a continuing action is the past tense is being described. C and D both contain gerunds (*being, having*) that create sentence fragments, and B contains a gerund (*in discovering*) where an infinitive is required.

3. D: Subject-verb agreement

The sentence contains a plural subject (*altitude and proximity*) and therefore requires a plural verb. The original version contains a singular verb (*means*); B and C, and E all create fragments. D correctly supplies a plural verb (*create*) that agrees with the subject and obeys the rules of standard usage.

4. C: Tense consistency

The tense of the underlined verb must be consistent with the tense of the rest of the sentence. The verb *was* is in the simple past, so *turned* must be in the simple past as well – a condition met only by C. A contains the present perfect (*has turned*); C and E contain gerunds (*having, turning*) that create fragments; and D contains a verb in the present tense (*turns*).

5. E: Conjunction; semicolon

The two clauses in the sentence express contradictory ideas: the first tells us that Michel de Montaigne was famous; the second tells us that he has remained popular because he was ordinary. The sentence therefore requires a conjunction to express that contradiction. A and B can be eliminated because the conjunction *and* suggests that the two clauses contain the same idea. C contains a correctly used a comma + coordinating (FANBOYS) conjunction, but it also contains a gerund (*resting*). In, D the present progressive tense (*is resting*) is unnecessary and makes the sentence wordy and awkward. E correctly uses a semicolon before *however* and employs a conjugated verb (*rests*) instead of a gerund.

It is important to note that *enduring* is a participle rather than a gerund – even though it is an "-ing" word, it acts as an adjective modifying the noun *appeal* and in no way affects the correctness of the answers.

6. B: Fragment (non-essential clause)

The original version is a fragment because it lacks a main verb. The only verb that it contains (*has*) is part of the clause that begins with the word *previously*. In order to fix the sentence, it is necessary to create a non-essential clause that will make the verb *has* part of the main clause. C, D, and E all contain the original error. Only B correctly places the comma after *manner* and removes the excess words before the verb. Now when the non-essential clause is removed, the remaining sentence makes sense: *The senatorial candidate…has become increasingly evasive about his beliefs in recent weeks.*

7. C: Dangling modifier

Who was unsure that he was fully ready for the championship boxing match? Carlos. So *Carlos*, the subject, must come immediately after the comma – not *Carlos's day off*. (The original version implies that *the day off* was unsure that he was ready for the match, which is nonsense). Since C contains this construction, it is the correct answer.

8. A: No error; non-essential clause

On the SAT, an answer that contains a properly used non-essential clause will virtually always be correct, regardless of how unexpected the placement of the non-essential clause may be. Since the original version of the sentence makes sense when the non-essential clause is removed (*Marriage…can be recognized by the states, a religious authority, or both*), A is correct.

Here, the non-essential clause may sound odd because it is presented in appositive form – that is, it does not begin with *which*. Many test-takers will therefore want the sentence to read, *Marriage, **which is** often viewed as a legal contract, can be recognized…*" when in fact both ways are correct.

9. D: Dangling modifier

What opened last year to glowing reviews? *The café* (the subject), not the *quality of its food*. So the original version is a dangling modifier. B contains an incorrect pronoun-antecedent agreement (*it vs. their*); C also contains a dangling modifier and the passive voice (*the food **served by** the café*); and E contains a comma splice; D provides the subject in the first clause to eliminate the dangling modification.

10. A: No error; correctly used idiom

B, C, D, and E are all un-idiomatic and awkward.

11. D: Parallel structure; word pair

Both must go with *and*, which eliminates A, B, and E. Between C and D, only C correctly provides *adjective + noun* to make the structure parallel (*financial constraints…increased emphasis*).

12. D: Non-essential clause, tense consistency

When the non-essential clause (*who believed that poor and forgotten places contained extraordinary examples of culture*) is removed, the sentence does not make grammatical sense: *Ethnomusicologist Alan Lomax…and traveling the globe in search of songs and stories.* A verb must follow the non-essential clause, and the fact that the other verbs in the sentence are in the simple past (*believed, contained*) indicates that the underlined word should be in the simple past as well (*traveled*).

13. C: Word pair (either…or)

Either must be paired with *or*.

14. D: Pronoun Consistency (one vs. you)

The pronoun must remain consistent throughout the sentence: either *one…one* or *you…you*. Since *only you* live is underlined, it must be changed to *one lives* in order to avoid a pronoun switch.

15. E: No error

Although there are several constructions in this sentence that are likely to sound "off" to many test-takers, none is actually incorrect. There is nothing wrong with *ought*, and it is correctly followed by the infinitive (*to be*) rather than the gerund. Likewise, it is perfectly acceptable to have two seemingly contradictory conjunctions (*and + yet*) after the comma, and the phrase *but a dream* is well within the bounds of standard usage.

16. A: Adjective vs. adverb

The adverb *unexpectedly* rather than the adjective *unexpected* must be used to modify the adjective *sober*.

17. C: Parallel structure

All of the items in a list must be in the same format. The incorrect version of the sentence contains two items that are nouns (*bravery, cunning*), and a third that does not "match" because it is a verb (*he desires*). The verb must therefore be replaced by a noun alone (*desire*).

18. C: Double negative

Not hardly is a double negative; *hardly* should be used.

19. B: Subject-verb agreement (subject – prepositional phrase – verb)

Communication, the subject of the sentence, is singular and therefore requires a singular verb (*is* rather than *are*). Do not be fooled by the plural noun *languages*, which immediately precedes the verb. It is part of the prepositional phrase beginning with *between* that separates the subject from the verb.

20. C: Would vs. will

The inclusion a date (1963) indicates that the sentence is most likely testing verb tense. In this case, a sentence that contains a verb in the past (*directed*) should not also contain one in the future (*will become*) – the conditional (*would become*) is required instead.

21. D: Pronoun-antecedent

The plural pronoun *their* incorrectly refers to the singular noun *a Stradivarius*; the singular pronoun *its* should be used instead.

22. A: Preposition/idiom

The idiomatic phrase is a proponent *of*, not a proponent *for*.

23. D: Verb tense (present perfect vs. past perfect)

The past perfect (***had** not faded*) is used to refer to a finished action in the past that came before a second finished action in the past. The sentence clearly indicates, however, that the word's meaning is *still* ambiguous. The present perfect (***has** not faded*), which describes actions that continue into the present, is therefore required.

24. D: Gerund vs. infinitive

"Their role" requires a gerund rather than an infinitive: the sentence should correctly read, "...Peter Nadas is concerned not only with historical events but also with their role *in influencing* people's everyday lives and emotions." A is correct because "in" is the appropriate preposition to use when referring to a book; in B, "not only" is paired with "but also;" and C is correct because it maintains parallel structure (not only with...but with).

25. E: No error

The most likely error candidates in this sentence are C, which sounds awkward but is grammatically acceptable, and D, which suggests a subject-verb agreement problem. *Much*, the subject of *is*, takes a singular verb, however, and so the sentence is correct.

26. C: Subject-verb agreement (subject – prepositional phrase – verb)

Image, the subject of the sentence, is singular and therefore requires a singular verb (*is* rather than *are*). The plural noun (*workers*) that immediately precedes the verb is part of the prepositional phrase beginning with *of*.

27. D: Faulty comparison

The sentence incorrectly compares thing (*discoveries*) to a person (*Charles Darwin*) and must be rewritten so that a thing is compared to a thing. When this type of error appears in Fixing Sentences, the correct answer will usually be phrased as... *Richard Owens made discoveries that rivaled **those of** Charles Darwin*, NOT ...*Richard Owens made discoveries that rivaled Charles Darwin's discoveries.*

28. E: No error

There are two common trick answers in this question: B and C. Many test-takers believe that *a means* cannot be correct because the word *means* appears plural, and the article *a* can only be used in front of a singular noun. In fact, *means* is singular. As for C, ETS is fond of using the adjective *long* in a way that many test-takers are unaccustomed to hearing and thus believe is incorrect.

29. B: Subject-verb agreement (prepositional phrase – verb – subject)

The prepositional phrase at the beginning of the sentence (***in** the elegant structure of poetry*) signals that this question is testing subject-verb agreement. In such questions, the subject always immediately follows the verb, and in this case the subject (*a number*) is plural and thus requires a plural verb (*are* rather than *is*).

30. A: Paragraph organization

The two sentences express contrasting ideas: the first tells us that the *typical* image of a medieval knight involves a full suit of armor, while the second tells us that suits of armor were not *actually* invented until the end of the Middle Ages; consequently, the two clauses express opposing ideas. That eliminates B, C, and D, which would be used to join two clauses that express similar ideas. E can be eliminated because the two sentences are not contrasting two specific things.

31. B: Paragraph organization

The introductory clause (*Though very sturdy*) describes chain mail, but in the original version of the sentence, *chain mail* does not appear immediately afterward. The error to correct is therefore a dangling modifier, and of the choices, only B does so effectively. A, C, and E also contain dangling modifiers, and D contains the gerund *being*, which makes the sentence unnecessarily wordy and awkward and which virtually always signals an incorrect answer.

32. D: Gerund, conjunction

The shortcut to this question revolves around the phrase *being that*, which the College Board will always correct as either *because* or *since*. Only C and D contain those words, and B contains an unnecessary gerund, which leaves D. Otherwise, sentence 10 in the original version is a fragment, which eliminates A. B contains a comma splice, and E contains an illogical conjunction (*while*).

33. C: Paragraph organization

The focus of the third paragraph is the fact that armor had a social significance: knights used it a symbol of their high status. Although the passage does mention the existence of a class system in the Middle Ages, that is not its primary focus, and including A would distract from the point of the paragraph. Likewise, B can be eliminated because the medieval weaponry is not the focus of the paragraph, even though gunpowder is mentioned. The information in D would be an appropriate addition to the *second* paragraph, which does focus on the transition from chain mail to plate armor; and E is irrelevant to the focus of the paragraph. While the information in C is not crucial to the logic of the paragraph, it would enhance the author's point that armor reflected a knight's wealth.

34. E: Paragraph organization

This is a word pair/parallel structure question. *Not only* goes with *but also*, which narrows the options down to C and E, and E is correct because it provides a construction that is the same on both sides of the word pair (*a way of protecting…a way of showing off*).

35. D: Passage organization

The passage focuses on the development as well as the social function of armor during the Middle Ages, not on the class system of medieval society. Sentence 12 is therefore irrelevant to the focus of the passage.

Test 1, Section 2

1. D: Subject-verb agreement

Many objections is plural and therefore requires a plural verb (*have* rather than *has*). That eliminates A and B. C and E are both fragments, and D is correct.

2. C: Pronoun-antecedent; gerund

In the original version of the sentence, the pronoun *it* lacks an antecedent – that is, there is no noun or gerund that tells us exactly what *it* refers to. In addition, there is no main verb, only the gerund *being*, which creates a fragment. B, D, and E also contain fragments, and C correctly uses the pronoun *their* to refer to *market researchers*.

3. B: Noun agreement

Since there is more than one river – the Mississippi and the Nile – they must take a plural complement: they are *examples* (plural) rather than *an example* (singular).

4. E: Pronoun-antecedent (ambiguous antecedent)

In the original version of the sentence, the pronoun *her* is ambiguous: we do not know whether it refers to Rachel older sister or Laetitia; D and E both resolve the ambiguity by specifying that it was Rachel who fabricated her data; however, D contains an unnecessary tense switch (*would have fabricated*), while E keeps the tense consistent.

5. C: Dangling modifier

Who was erecting the new office building? The construction workers. So *the construction workers*, the subject, must immediately follow the comma. Only C and D begin that way, so A, B, and E can be eliminated. D is a fragment, and C is correct.

6. E: Word pair

So must be paired with *that*, making E the only option.

7. E: Miscellaneous

A noun cannot "be because" – it can only "happen" or "occur." That eliminates A. B contains a gerund (*beginning*) that turns the sentence into a fragment; the present perfect (*has occurred*) in choice C is incorrect because the sentence describes a finished action in the past, and the present perfect is used to describe an action that is continuing into the present; inserting D would turn the sentence into a fragment.

8. D: Dangling modifier

Who was the precocious son of an impoverished single mother? W.E.B. DuBois, not his intellectual gifts. Only D and E correctly place *W.E.B. DuBois*, the subject, immediately after the comma. E can be eliminated because it lacks a main verb, whereas D provides one (*recognized*).

9. C: Dangling modifier

What was passed in 1943 to make housing more affordable for middle-class residents? Rent control laws. So *rent control laws*, the subject, must immediately follow the comma. A, B, and E can therefore be eliminated. D contains a gerund (*having*) that creates a fragment, so the answer is C.

10. A: No error

The original version of the sentence contains a properly used non-essential clause (*a risky pursuit that led sailors halfway across the world and sometimes to the bottom of the sea*), and answer choices that contain this construction are virtually always correct.

When the non-essential clause is removed from the sentence, the information outside the commas (*Whaling…was centered on Nantucket during the early nineteenth century*) makes perfect grammatical sense.

The only other answer that does not create a fragment when plugged backed into the sentence is C, which contains an unnecessary gerund (*leading*).

11. B: Subject-verb agreement

The sentence contains a compound subject (*highly textured bark **and** distinctive silhouette*), which requires a plural verb (*distinguish* rather than *distinguishes*).

12. B: Parallel structure

B is the only option that keeps the construction at the end of the sentence parallel by using two nouns (*the fantastic…the real*).

13. C: Passive voice/parallel structure

The three items in the series must all be in the same form (gerund), which eliminates B, D, and E. A contains a passive and awkward construction (*whereby a new mascot **will be created***), while that in C (*to create a new mascot*) is much clearer and more concise.

14. E: Word pair/parallel structure

At once must be paired with *and*, eliminating A, B, and D. Of the remaining two choices, only E makes the structure of the sentence parallel (*celebrated for his depictions…denounced for his embrace*).

Test 2

Section 1

1. Ⓐ Ⓑ Ⓒ Ⓓ Ⓔ
2. Ⓐ Ⓑ Ⓒ Ⓓ Ⓔ
3. Ⓐ Ⓑ Ⓒ Ⓓ Ⓔ
4. Ⓐ Ⓑ Ⓒ Ⓓ Ⓔ
5. Ⓐ Ⓑ Ⓒ Ⓓ Ⓔ
6. Ⓐ Ⓑ Ⓒ Ⓓ Ⓔ
7. Ⓐ Ⓑ Ⓒ Ⓓ Ⓔ
8. Ⓐ Ⓑ Ⓒ Ⓓ Ⓔ
9. Ⓐ Ⓑ Ⓒ Ⓓ Ⓔ
10. Ⓐ Ⓑ Ⓒ Ⓓ Ⓔ
11. Ⓐ Ⓑ Ⓒ Ⓓ Ⓔ
12. Ⓐ Ⓑ Ⓒ Ⓓ Ⓔ
13. Ⓐ Ⓑ Ⓒ Ⓓ Ⓔ
14. Ⓐ Ⓑ Ⓒ Ⓓ Ⓔ
15. Ⓐ Ⓑ Ⓒ Ⓓ Ⓔ
16. Ⓐ Ⓑ Ⓒ Ⓓ Ⓔ
17. Ⓐ Ⓑ Ⓒ Ⓓ Ⓔ
18. Ⓐ Ⓑ Ⓒ Ⓓ Ⓔ
19. Ⓐ Ⓑ Ⓒ Ⓓ Ⓔ
20. Ⓐ Ⓑ Ⓒ Ⓓ Ⓔ
21. Ⓐ Ⓑ Ⓒ Ⓓ Ⓔ
22. Ⓐ Ⓑ Ⓒ Ⓓ Ⓔ
23. Ⓐ Ⓑ Ⓒ Ⓓ Ⓔ
24. Ⓐ Ⓑ Ⓒ Ⓓ Ⓔ
25. Ⓐ Ⓑ Ⓒ Ⓓ Ⓔ
26. Ⓐ Ⓑ Ⓒ Ⓓ Ⓔ
27. Ⓐ Ⓑ Ⓒ Ⓓ Ⓔ
28. Ⓐ Ⓑ Ⓒ Ⓓ Ⓔ
29. Ⓐ Ⓑ Ⓒ Ⓓ Ⓔ
30. Ⓐ Ⓑ Ⓒ Ⓓ Ⓔ
31. Ⓐ Ⓑ Ⓒ Ⓓ Ⓔ
32. Ⓐ Ⓑ Ⓒ Ⓓ Ⓔ
33. Ⓐ Ⓑ Ⓒ Ⓓ Ⓔ
34. Ⓐ Ⓑ Ⓒ Ⓓ Ⓔ
35. Ⓐ Ⓑ Ⓒ Ⓓ Ⓔ

Section 2

1. Ⓐ Ⓑ Ⓒ Ⓓ Ⓔ
2. Ⓐ Ⓑ Ⓒ Ⓓ Ⓔ
3. Ⓐ Ⓑ Ⓒ Ⓓ Ⓔ
4. Ⓐ Ⓑ Ⓒ Ⓓ Ⓔ
5. Ⓐ Ⓑ Ⓒ Ⓓ Ⓔ
6. Ⓐ Ⓑ Ⓒ Ⓓ Ⓔ
7. Ⓐ Ⓑ Ⓒ Ⓓ Ⓔ
8. Ⓐ Ⓑ Ⓒ Ⓓ Ⓔ
9. Ⓐ Ⓑ Ⓒ Ⓓ Ⓔ
10. Ⓐ Ⓑ Ⓒ Ⓓ Ⓔ
11. Ⓐ Ⓑ Ⓒ Ⓓ Ⓔ
12. Ⓐ Ⓑ Ⓒ Ⓓ Ⓔ
13. Ⓐ Ⓑ Ⓒ Ⓓ Ⓔ
14. Ⓐ Ⓑ Ⓒ Ⓓ Ⓔ

SECTION 1

Time – 25 Minutes
35 Questions

Directions: For each question in this section, select the best answer from among the choices given and fill in the corresponding circle on the answer sheet.

The following sentences test correctness and effectiveness of expression. Part of each sentence or the entire sentence is underlined; beneath each sentence are five ways of phrasing the underlined material. Choice A repeats the original phrasing; the other four choices are different. If you think the original phrasing produces a better sentence than any of the alternatives, select choice A; if not, select one of the other choices.

In making your selection, follow the requirements of standard written English; that is, pay attention to grammar, choice of words, sentence construction, and punctuation. Your selection should result in the most effective sentence—clear and precise, without awkwardness or ambiguity.

EXAMPLE:

○●○○○

Anna Robertson Moses completed her first painting and she was seventy-six years old then.

(A) and she was seventy-six years old then
(B) when she was seventy-six years old
(C) at age seventy-six years old
(D) upon arriving at the age of seventy-six
(E) at the time when she was seventy-six years old

1. Mountain-climbers wear different shoes and carry different equipment depending on whether their chosen route is over rock, snow, or is it ice.

(A) or is it ice
(B) or is it over ice
(C) or ice
(D) rather ice
(E) rather it is ice

2. Memoirs, which usually have different structure than autobiographies, and which follow the development of an author's personality rather than the writing of his or her works.

(A) and which follow
(B) they have followed
(C) and they have followed
(D) following
(E) follow

3. Originally founded in the seventeenth century, the success of the pharmaceutical company is well established.

(A) the success of the pharmaceutical company is well established
(B) the success of the pharmaceutical company being well established
(C) the pharmaceutical company having its success well established
(D) the pharmaceutical company is a well-established success
(E) what has been well established is the success of the pharmaceutical company

4. Choreographer and dancer Savion Glover aims to restore the African roots of tap dance by eliminating hand gestures and to return to a focus on the feet as the primary source of movement.

(A) gestures and to return
(B) gestures, they return
(C) gestures and returning
(D) gestures, he returns
(E) gestures having returned

185

5. In the past several years, the country's food <u>prices have increased dramatically, they are now at their highest rate</u> in two decades.

   (A) prices have increased dramatically, they are now at their highest rate
   (B) prices have increased dramatically and are now at their highest rate
   (C) prices, which have increased dramatically to their highest rate
   (D) prices, increasingly dramatically, and are now at
   (E) prices increase dramatically to their highest rate

6. Lyme disease <u>causes muscle aches in its early stages and nervous system problems in its later ones, and</u> it is so named because the first cases occurred in the town of Lyme, Connecticut.

   Parallel

   (A) causes muscle aches in its early stages and nervous system problems in its later ones, and
   (B) which causes muscle aches in its early stages and nervous system problems in its later ones, and
   (C) causes muscle aches in its early stages and has led to nervous system problems in its later ones, in addition
   (D) causing muscle aches in its early stages and leading to nervous system problems in its later ones, while
   (E) is caused as muscle aches in its early stages and nervous system problems in its later ones,

7. <u>Unable to work without listening to music, it was necessary for Anita to put on her headphones immediately</u> whenever she sat down to write a paper.

   (A) Unable to work without listening to music, it was necessary for Anita to put on her headphones immediately
   (B) Unable to work without listening to music, Anita's headphones were necessarily put on immediately
   (C) Anita's headphones that were immediately put on because she was unable to work without music
   (D) Because she was unable to work without listening to music, Anita found it necessary to put on her headphones immediately
   (E) Anita's headphones, necessary for her to work and listen to music, put on immediately

8. Entertainment sources such as movies and books are not, <u>some experts claim, responsible</u> for shaping a culture, only for reflecting it.

   (A) some experts claim, responsible
   (B) some experts claim that they are responsible
   (C) which some experts claim, responsible
   (D) there are some experts who claim that they may be responsible
   (E) being perhaps, according to the claims of some experts, responsible

9. Readers of the best-selling novel report that it is thrilling because of its many plot <u>twists, plus its happy ending makes it heartwarming</u>.

   (A) twists, plus its happy ending makes it heartwarming
   (B) twists, although heartwarming by having a happy ending
   (C) twists, and it is heartwarming with its happy ending
   (D) twists yet heartwarming by having a ending that makes it happy
   (E) twists and heartwarming because of its happy ending

   Parello

186

10. Because they often attracted uncontrollable crowds and led to rioting, the right to hold a fair could only be granted by royal charter during the Middle Ages.

   (A) Because they often attracted uncontrollable crowds and led to rioting, permission to hold a fair could only be granted by royal charter
   (B) Fairs often attracted uncontrollable crowds and led to rioting, and so permission to hold one could only be granted by royal charter
   (C) Because they often attracted uncontrollable crowds and led to rioting, it could only be permitted for a fair to be held by royal charter
   (D) When fairs were held, they often attracted uncontrollable crowds and led to rioting, so it could only be permitted by royal charter
   (E) Fairs, when held, often attracted uncontrollable crowds, and also rioting was caused, so they could only be permitted by royal charter

11. Although traditional Algonquin society was largely based on hunting and fishing, some of them practiced agriculture and cultivated corn, beans, and squash.

   (A) some of them practiced
   (B) some of them had practiced
   (C) some, who had practiced
   (D) some of them would practice
   (E) some of the Algonquins practiced

The following sentences test your ability to recognize grammar and usage errors. Each sentence contains either a single error or none at all. No sentence contains more than one error. The error, if there is one, is underlined and lettered. If the sentence contains an error, select the one underlined part that must be changed in order to make the sentence correct. If the sentence is correct, select choice E. In choosing answers, follow the requirements of standard written English.

EXAMPLE:

Science fiction writer H.G. Wells, the author of
                                    A
more than 100 books, accurately predicted the
                                    B
the invention of television, the rise of the Internet,
    C
and creating the hydrogen bomb. No error
    D   E

○ ○ ○ ● ○

12. Unlike Marco, both Heather and her older cousin
                    A
    Angela want to become an architect after they
          B   C
    graduate from college. No error
    D   E

13. Between around 500 and 900 AD, monks in
    A
    England, Ireland, and Scotland produced thousands of
                      B   C
    illuminated manuscripts. No error
    D   E

14. Measuring 250 square miles, Lake Tahoe, which
    A   B
    straddles the border between Nevada and California
                        C
    is more larger than any other alpine lake in North
       D
    America. No error
            E

15. Unlike many other inventions, which occurred
    A   B
    simultaneously in many different places, writing had

    only a few independent origins, and the alphabet arises
         C   D
    only once in history. No error
                          E

16. Having sought shelter in her car during the
    A   B
    thunderstorm, Anya and Imani stared out the foggy

    windows and waited for the rain to stop. No error
                        C   D   E

17. Many bird species worldwide become endangered as

    rapid modernizing societies expand roads, mines, and
    A   B
    chemical plants into environmentally sensitive areas.
                    C   D
    No error
    E

18. Though the play had received favorable reviews
                    A
    from critics, neither the lead actors or the supporting
    B   C
    players gave particularly memorable performances.
                   D
    No error
    E

19. When something goes wrong during a live
         A
    performance, the illusion of reality that audience
                                        B
    members have accepted can fall apart before his or her
            C   D
    eyes. No error
          E

20. Norman Rockwell's intricately conceived narrative
                       A
    paintings, widely reproduced in magazines, appealed
                      B
    to a vast audience of readers who recognized
    C   D
    themselves in the stories the images told. No error
                                              E

188

21. Even though the university <u>has been wracked</u> by
                              A
recent administrative scandals, <u>its</u> reputation is still
    reputation
<u>significantly</u> better than <u>most other schools</u> of
    C   D
comparable size and location. <u>No error</u>
                              E

22. <u>Throughout</u> his writings, the author manages to
    A
give the impression <u>of being</u> ready to commit to paper
                    B
his every thought, as if he <u>were attempting</u> to capture
                            C
the process of thinking <u>itself</u>. <u>No error</u>
                        D   (E)

23. Some planets <u>that are</u> very different from our own
                 A   *to turn*
<u>may have</u> the potential <u>for turning</u> current theories
    B   (C)
<u>of</u> solar system formation upside down. <u>No error</u>
D   E

24. <u>Because</u> each of the chapters in Annie Dillard's book
    A
Pilgrim at Tinker Creek <u>contain</u> a separate title, many
                          (B)
readers <u>mistakenly</u> believe that it is <u>a collection of</u>
        C   D
essays. <u>No error</u>
        E

25. During the Spanish Civil War, many Catalan writers
were <u>forced into</u> exile and, <u>with</u> the exception of
     A   B
Salvador Espriu, ceased <u>to publish</u> new works until
                        C
after democracy <u>had been</u> reestablished. <u>No error</u>
                D   E

26. Canberra's growth was hindered <u>by</u> the Great
                                   A
Depression, <u>which aggravated</u> a series of disputes over
            B
its management, but <u>they</u> began to thrive in the years
                    (C)
<u>following</u> World War II. <u>No error</u>
D   E

27. Though *Moby Dick* has <u>long been</u> considered
                          A
a classic work of literature, it was <u>published to</u>
                                     B
middling reviews, and <u>its</u> author, Herman Melville,
                      C
worked as a customs inspector for <u>most</u> of his life.
                                  D
<u>No error</u>
(E)

28. *Saint Maybe*, the twelfth novel by Pulitzer prize-
nominated author Anne Tyler, <u>revolves around</u> a
                             A
protagonist <u>whose efforts</u> to <u>compensate for</u> a single
            B   C
thoughtless act <u>dictates</u> the shape of his entire life.
                (D)
<u>No error</u>
E

29. The range of sounds perceptible to an owl is similar to
<u>a human being</u>, but an owl has <u>such acute</u> hearing that
(A)   B
<u>it is</u> often capable <u>of determining</u> the location of a
C   D
mouse covered by a foot of snow. <u>No error</u>
                                 E

Directions: The following passage is an early draft of an essay. Some parts of the passage need to be rewritten.

Read the passage and select the best answer for the questions that follow. Some questions are about particular sentences or parts of sentences and ask you to improve sentence structure or word choice. Other questions ask you to consider organization and development. In choosing you answer, follow the requirements of standard written English.

Questions 30-35 are based on the following passage

(1) When Henry Ford manufactured his first Model T at the Piquette Avenue plant in Detroit, Michigan in 1908, cars were a luxury that only the wealthy could afford. (2) The Model T changed all that. (3) By introducing the assembling line into the construction process, Ford reduced the amount of time necessary to produce a car from more than twelve hours to just over one hour, the price fell from several thousand dollars to just $825.

(4) The Model T wasn't just famous because it was affordable. (5) It was also famous for its color – or rather, its lack of color. (6) According to a popular story, Ford once said that people could buy the car known as the Model T in any color they wanted, as long as it was black. (7) However, this was only partially true. (8) During the early days of the Model T, it came in a variety of colors, including red, blue, gray, and green. (9) In 1913, Ford realized that it would be more efficient to produce cars in only one color, black being the most practical.

(10) For more than a decade, the Model T was only available in black. (11) Although many shades of black were actually used. (12) Almost thirty kinds of paint were used on each car because different types of paint dried more quickly on different parts. (13) In 1926, in response to increased competition from other car manufacturers, Ford decided to offer the Model T in other colors again. (14) Unfortunately, it was too late: the last Model T rolled off the assembly line the next year.

30. What is the best version of the underlined portion of sentence 3 (reproduced below)?

By introducing the assembling line into the construction process, Ford reduced the amount of time necessary to produce a car from more than twelve hours to just over one hour, the price fell from several thousand dollars to just $825.

(A) (as it is now)
(B) one hour and the price from several thousand dollars to just $825
(C) one hour; the price falling from several thousand dollars to just $825
(D) one hour, consequently the price fell from several thousand dollars to just $825
(E) one hour, and the price it fell from several thousand dollars to just $825

31. What is the best way to revise the underlined portion of sentence 6 (reproduced below)?

According to a popular story, Ford once said that people could buy the car known as the Model T in any color they wanted, as long as it was black.

(A) Change "people" to "one".
(B) Change "could buy" to "could have bought".
(C) Change "the car known as the Model T" to "the Model T".
(D) Delete "in any color they wanted".
(E) Change "it was" to "they were".

32. In context, what is the best revision of sentence 7 (reproduced below)?

However, this was only partially true.

(A) This statement was only partially true, though.
(B) On the other hand, this was partially true.
(C) Meanwhile, this did have some truth to it.
(D) Ford's claim, which was partially true.
(E) In fact, it was partially true.

33. What is the best way to revise and combine the underlined portion of sentences 8 and 9 (reproduced below)?

    During the early days of the Model T, it came in a variety of colors, including red, blue, gray, and green. In 1913, Ford realized

    (A) gray, and green, as a result, in 1913, Ford realized
    (B) gray, and green, while in 1913 Ford's realization
    (C) gray, and green; however, in 1913 Ford realized
    (D) gray, and green; and in 1913 Ford realized
    (E) gray, and green, but in 1913 Ford realizing

34. What is best to add to the beginning of sentence 13?

    (A) Ironically,
    (B) On the contrary,
    (C) For example,
    (D) In contrast,
    (E) Finally, though,

35. Which sentence is best inserted after sentence 14?

    (A) One famous photo from the 1920's shows Henry Ford standing next to a red Model T.
    (B) The Model-T assembly line had taken nearly a decade to for Ford and his partners to develop and refine.
    (C) Finally, the fifteen millionth Model T rolled off the assembly line on May 26th, 1927.
    (D) It would always be remembered as one of the most popular black cars ever produced.
    (E) In its last year of production, the assembly line produced a car every 24 seconds.

SECTION 2
Time – 10 Minutes
14 Questions

Directions: For each question in this section, select the best answer from among the choices given and fill in the corresponding circle on the answer sheet.

The following sentences test correctness and effectiveness of expression. Part of each sentence or the entire sentence is underlined; beneath each sentence are five ways of phrasing the underlined material. Choice A repeats the original phrasing; the other four choices are different. If you think the original phrasing produces a better sentence than any of the alternatives, select choice A; if not, select one of the other choices.

In making your selection, follow the requirements of standard written English; that is, pay attention to grammar, choice of words, sentence construction, and punctuation. Your selection should result in the most effective sentence—clear and precise, without awkwardness or ambiguity.

EXAMPLE:

○●○○○

Anna Robertson Moses completed her first painting and she was seventy-six years old then.

(A) and she was seventy-six years old then
(B) when she was seventy-six years old
(C) at age seventy-six years old
(D) upon arriving at the age of seventy-six
(E) at the time when she was seventy-six years old

1. In 60 B.C., Julius Caesar joined Crassus and Pompey in a political alliance that <u>would be dominating</u> Roman politics for several years.

   (A) would be dominating
   (B) would dominate
   (C) will dominate
   (D) was dominating
   (E) will be dominating

2. <u>John Breckinridge, who nearly defeated Abraham Lincoln in the 1860 election, held strong convictions, it being difficult for him</u> to navigate a moderate course.

   (A) John Breckinridge, who nearly defeated Abraham Lincoln in the 1860 election, held strong convictions, it being difficult for him
   (B) Nearly defeating Abraham Lincoln in the 1860 election, despite holding strong convictions, it was difficult for John Breckinridge
   (C) John Breckinridge, who nearly defeated Abraham Lincoln in the 1860 election, held strong convictions that made it difficult for him
   (D) Although he nearly defeated Abraham Lincoln in the 1860 election, John Breckinridge held strong convictions, it was difficult for him
   (E) Nearly defeating Abraham Lincoln and he held strong convictions, John Breckinridge, in the 1860 election, found it difficult

3. The discussion between Julia and her boss, Ms. Quintero, could only take place in the evening <u>because she had too much work</u> to finish before then.

   (A) because she had too much work
   (B) and she had too much work
   (C) because Julia had too much work
   (D) since Julia was having too much work
   (E) because she would have too much work

192

4. The Oxford English Dictionary was completed in the early nineteenth century, before that Samuel Johnson's *Dictionary of the English Language was* the most comprehensive British lexicon.

    (A) century, before that Samuel Johnson's *Dictionary of the English Language* was
    (B) century, replacing Samuel Johnson's *Dictionary of the English Language* as
    (C) century, Samuel Johnson's *Dictionary of the English Language* had previously been
    (D) century; Samuel Johnson's *Dictionary of the English Language* previously being
    (E) century; Samuel Johnson's *Dictionary of the English* Language having previously been

5. Depicting outdoor scenes, blending colors, rapid brushstrokes, and conveying a sense of immediacy were all important characteristics of the impressionist movement.

    (A) Depicting outdoor scenes, blending colors, rapid brushstrokes, and conveying
    (B) The depiction of outdoor scenes, the blending of colors, rapid brushstrokes, and conveying
    (C) To depict outdoor scenes, blend colors, make rapid brush strokes, and conveying
    (D) Depicting outdoor scenes, blending colors, making rapid brushstrokes, and conveying
    (E) Depicting outdoor scenes, blending colors, rapid brushstrokes, and to convey

6. Like theology and philosophy, scholars believe that neuroscience will change how people view both themselves and the world.

    (A) Like theology and philosophy, scholars believe that neuroscience
    (B) It is believed by scholars that to study neuroscience, like theology and philosophy,
    (C) Neuroscience, like philosophy and theology, scholars believe it
    (D) The study of neuroscience, like philosophy and theology, it is believed by scholars
    (E) Scholars believe that neuroscience, like philosophy and theology,

7. The only American president elected to more than two terms, Franklin D. Roosevelt created a durable coalition that would realign American politics for decades.

    (A) created a durable coalition that would realign
    (B) created a durable coalition that will realign
    (C) creates a durable coalition for realigning
    (D) created a durable coalition for that which will realign
    (E) would create a durable coalition whose realigning

8. Contrary to popular wisdom, test-taking not only promotes learning but is also more effective than to study repeatedly.

    (A) but is also more effective than to study repeatedly
    (B) but repeated studying showing less effectiveness
    (C) but repeatedly studying is something it is more effective than
    (D) but is also more effective than repeated studying
    (E) and studying repeatedly is not as effective as it

9. In his poems and essays, Dan Chiasson proves adept at both rigorously interrogating his own psychology and intellectually probing the outer world.

    (A) and intellectually probing the outer world
    (B) and he probes the outer world intellectually
    (C) and probing of the outer world intellectually
    (D) with intellectually probing the outer world
    (E) as well as an intellectual probing of the outer world

10. Because the lemur shares some traits also possessed by other primates, it is frequently mistaken for an ancestor of modern monkeys and apes.

    (A) Because the lemur shares some traits also possessed by other primates,
    (B) Because the lemur shares some traits with other primates,
    (C) Being that the lemur shares some traits that other primates have also had,
    (D) The lemur shares many traits that other primates also have, so
    (E) The lemur, which shares some traits with other primates

11. Grown in a variety of climates, the European chestnut tree produces fruit that is generally both larger and sweeter than the American chestnut tree.

(A) than the American chestnut tree
(B) than the American chestnut tree is
(C) than is the American chestnut tree
(D) than that of the American chestnut tree
(E) than the American chestnut tree, in terms of its edible parts

12. During the 1970's, the demand for long-lasting staple foods caused many manufacturers to add preservatives to previously simple dishes, whereby the quality of their flavor was reduced.

(A) dishes, whereby the quality of their flavor was reduced
(B) dishes, they reduced they quality of their flavor
(C) dishes, and this reduced the quality of their flavor
(D) dishes, with a reduction in its flavor occurring
(E) dishes, thus reducing the quality of their flavor

13. Used as both food and medicine in many cultures for thousands of years, garlic, a member of the onion family, dates to at least the time of the Giza Pyramids.

(A) garlic, a member of the onion family, dates to at least the time of the Giza Pyramids
(B) garlic is a member of the onion family, it dates to at least the time of the Giza Pyramids
(C) garlic's origins date to at least the time of the Giza Pyramids, and it is a member of the onion family
(D) the onion family counts garlic among its members; and it dates to at least the time of the Giza Pyramids
(E) as a member of the onion family, garlic dates to at least the time of the Giza Pyramids

14. Because most jurors are not compensated at rates sufficient to replace lost wages, many citizens seek to avoid jury duty by demonstrating financial hardship, and urgent commitments are claimed.

(A) hardship, and urgent commitments are claimed
(B) hardship, urgent commitments being claimed
(C) hardship or claiming urgent commitments
(D) hardship or else they claim urgent commitments
(E) hardship, they claim urgent commitments

Answers: Test 2, Section 1

1. C: Parallel structure

The two other items in the list each contain one noun; therefore, the third item must contain the same. That eliminates A, B, and E. The correct answer is C because *whether* should be paired with *or*.

2. E: Non-essential clause

The non-essential clause (*which usually have different structure than autobiographies*) must be followed by a verb in order to make the essential portion of the sentence grammatically logical (*Memoirs…follow the development of an author's personality rather than the writing of his or her works*). E is the only option that provides a verb.

3. D: Dangling modifier

What was founded in the seventeenth century? The pharmaceutical company, not the pharmaceutical company's success. So *the pharmaceutical company*, the subject, must appear immediately after the comma. The answer choices to this question follow the classic SAT pattern: of the five options, three (A, B, and E) retain the dangling modification, and two (C and D) correct it. C contains a gerund (*having*) rather than a main verb and is thus a fragment, so the answer is D.

4. C: Parallel structure

The non-underlined portion of the sentence contains a gerund (*by eliminating*), so to preserve parallel structure, the underlined portion of the sentence must contain a gerund as well. C correctly provides that gerund (*returning*).

5. B: Comma splice

The original version of the sentence contains two independent clauses separated by a comma. C and D contain fragments, and the use of the present tense in choice E (*increase*) is incorrect because the phrase *in the past several years* indicates that the present perfect (*have increased*) is necessary.

6. A: No error; parallel structure

The original version of the sentence is bit awkward because of the two *ands* (***and** nervous system problems in its later ones, **and***) but is correct because the essential structure is parallel: both effects of Lyme disease are listed in adjective + noun form (*muscle **aches**…and nervous system **problems***). B and D both create fragments; C contains an unnecessary tense switch creates a comma splice; and E is awkward and creates a comma splice as well.

7. D: Dangling modifier

Who was unable to work without listening to music? Anita. So *Anita*, the subject, must appear immediately after the comma. Only C provides this option.

8. A: No error; non-essential clause

The original version of the sentence contains a properly used non-essential clause, a construction that is virtually always correct. Many test-takers are likely to be thrown off by the placement of the non-essential clause, however. Although its location in the sentence may not feel natural, the sentence makes perfect sense when the non-essential clause is removed (*Entertainment sources such as movies and books are not…responsible for shaping a culture, only for reflecting it.*) B, C, D, and E are all unnecessarily wordy and awkward and do nothing to improve the information within the non-essential clause.

9. E: Parallel structure

The original version of the sentence contains two clauses whose construction does not match: we have *thrilling* (adjective) on one side, and on the other, *happy ending* (adjective + noun). Since the first side of the sentence is not underlined and therefore cannot be changed, we must find an option that includes a parallel construction for the second side. The first side contains the classic *x because of its y* structure, and so the easiest way to locate the correct answer is to look for an option that contains the words *because of its*. Only E fulfills that requirement.

10. B: Dangling Modifier

What often attracted uncontrollable crowds and led to rioting? Fairs, not the right to hold a fair. *So fairs*, the subject, must appear immediately after the comma. There is, however, no answer that provides that option. C also contains a dangling modifier; D contains a pronoun-antecedent disagreement (*fairs…it*); and E is awkward and contains the passive voice (*rioting was caused*).

11. E: Pronoun-antecedent: adjective as "trick" antecedent

In the original version of the sentence, the pronoun *them* refers to *the Algonquins*. In this case, however, Algonquin is used as an adjective that modifies *society*, and a pronoun cannot refer to an adjective – that is, an adjective cannot be the **antecedent** of a pronoun. Only a noun or a pronoun can be an antecedent. B and D both contain the same error as the original sentence, and C creates a fragment. Only E supplies the noun *Algonquins* to eliminate the problem of the missing antecedent.

12. C: Noun agreement

Since Heather and Marco are two people, they must want to become *architects*, not *an architect*.

13. E: No error; verb tense

The inclusion of dates (500 and 900 A.D.) indicates that the sentence is testing verb tense. The simple past ("produced") is correctly used here to describe completed events in the past, however, so C is correct. The only other strong possibility for an error is A (word pair), but *between* is correctly paired with *and*.

14. D: Double positive

The comparative form of *large* is *larger*; it is incorrect to include *more* in front of it.

15. D: Verb tense

The sentence clearly describes a finished event (the invention of writing) that occurred well in the past and that should therefore be referred to by a plural verb (*arose* not *arises*).

16. B: Pronoun-antecedent (ambiguous antecedent)

Since there are two female names (Anya and Imani), the pronoun *her* is ambiguous – we do not know which person it refers to.

17. A: Adjective vs. adverb

An adverb (*rapidly*) rather than an adjective (*rapid*) is required to modify the adjective *modernizing*.

18. C: Word pair

Neither must be paired with *nor*.

19. D: Pronoun-antecedent

His or her (singular) refers to *audience members* (plural). A plural pronoun (*they*) is therefore required.

20. E: No error

Possible error categories would be adjective vs. adverb (A); preposition (B and C); who vs. which (D); and verb tense (D). All are used correctly, however.

21. D: Faulty comparison

The sentence compares the *reputation* of the university to *most other schools*, whereas it should be compared to *the reputations* of most other schools.

22. E: No error

The most common error categories suggested by this question are preposition (A) and gerund vs. infinitive (B). The trick answers, however, are C and D. C includes the subjunctive (*as if he **were** attempting* rather than ***was** attempting*). Although this construction may sound odd, it is correct because it is used to refer to a hypothetical situation. D (*itself*) is simply placed at the end of the sentence for emphasis. While it too may sound strange, there is nothing grammatically wrong with it.

23. C: Gerund vs. infinitive

The phrase *to have the potential* should always be followed by the infinitive (*to turn*) rather than the gerund (*turning*).

24. B: Subject-verb agreement

Each is singular and therefore requires a singular verb (*is* rather than *are*). The plural noun *chapters* is part of the prepositional phrase *of the chapters in Annie Dillard's book Pilgrim at Tinker Creek*.

25. E: No error

Error categories include verb tense/form (A, C, D) and preposition (A), with many test-takers likely to pick either D because they are not sure when the past perfect (*had been published*) should be used or B because they think it sounds strange (it's fine). The past perfect is correct because it is used to refer to a finished action in the past (the reestablishment of democracy) that clearly came before a second action (Salvador Espriu ceased to publish new works)

26. C: Pronoun-antecedent

Canberra is a collective noun (*singular*) and should therefore be referred to by a singular pronoun (*it* rather than *they*).

27. E: No error

Error categories include verb tense (A and B); preposition (B); pronoun-antecedent (C); and comparative vs. superlative (D). The trick answer, however, is A, which many test-takers will pick because they think the phrase "long been" sounds odd.

28. D: Subject-verb agreement (subject – prepositional phrase – verb)

Efforts is plural and therefore requires a plural verb (*dictate* rather than *dictates*). The singular noun *act*, which immediately precedes the verb, is part of the prepositional phrase begun by *for*.

29. A: Faulty comparison

A range of sounds (thing) is being compared a human being (person). In order to correct the sentence, a thing must be compared to a thing: *The range of sounds perceptible to an owl is similar to **the range of sounds perceptible/that perceptible** to a human being…*

30. B: Parallelism

The construction *from…to* (*from more than twelve hours to just over one hour*) in the non-underlined portion of the sentence should be matched by an identical construction in the underlined portion. Only B correctly provides a parallel construction. In C, the semicolon does not separate two independent clauses; A and D contain comma splices; and in E, the use of *it* in the second clause is awkward and uncolloquial.

31. C: Wordiness

Changing people to one would (A) would create a pronoun-antecedent problem with they later in the sentence; since Ford was referring a current situation, there is no reason that the past conditional (*could have bought*) rather than the conditional (*could buy*) should be used (B); deleting *in any color they wanted* (D) would remove information crucial to the meaning of the sentence; and changing *it was* to *they were* creates an antecedent-pronoun disagreement with *the Model T* (singular). Only the information in C makes the sentence unnecessarily wordy.

32. A: Pronoun-antecedent

In the original version of the sentence, the pronoun *this* lacks an antecedent – it refers to Ford's *statement* about the color of the Model T, but the word *statement* does not appear. Only B provides an antecedent within a grammatically correct sentence. The word *assertion* in D would also be acceptable; however, that answer choice also contains a fragment.

33. C: Conjunction

The two sentences express opposing ideas, so a contradictor is required. Of the answers that contain such conjunctions (B, C, and E), B and E create fragments, and C correctly uses *however* preceded by a semicolon.

34. E: Conjunction

The sentence describes one of the last changes made to the Model T – the sentence clearly indicates that the car was discontinued the next year. In addition, the phrase *Finally, though* emphasizes the contrast between Ford's desire to manufacture the car only in black and his realization that he would have to manufacture it in other colors if he wished to remain competitive.

35. D: Passage organization

The passage as a whole focuses on the production of the *black* Model T. D appropriately concludes the passage by referring to this fact.

Test 2, Section 2

1. B: Verb tense

The sentence describes a continuing action in the past (Caeser, Crassus, and Pompey dominated *for several years*). Continuing actions in the past are described using *would* + past participle (*would dominate*), however, not the progressive (*would be dominating*) and not the future (*will dominate*). Thus B is the correct answer.

2. C: Non-essential clause

The original version of the sentence contains the gerund *being*, so it can be eliminated immediately. B contains a dangling modifier, B and D contain comma splices, and E is awkward.

2. **Shortcut:** C contains a properly-used non-essential clause (the remaining sentence, *John Breckenridge...held convictions that made it difficult for him to navigate a moderate course* makes perfect sense when the non-essential clause is removed). Sentences that contains properly used non-essential clauses are virtually always correct.

3. C: Ambiguous antecedent

Since the sentence clearly refers to two women (Julia and Ms. Quintero), we do not know which of them the pronoun *her* refers to. Only C specifies that information in a clear manner; D can be eliminated because it contains an unnecessary gerund.

4. B: Comma splice; semicolon; participle required

A and C contain comma splices, and the semicolons in D and E do not separate two independent clauses. The participle (*replacing*) in B correctly joins the two clauses without causing a punctuation error.

5. D: Parallel Structure

Only D keeps the form of all four items in the list consistent: *depicting, blending, making,* and *conveying.*

6. E: Faulty comparison; non-essential clause

The original version of the sentence compares theology and philosophy (things) to scholars (people); B contains the passive voice; C and D contain improperly used non-essential clauses (neither answer makes sense if the non-essential clause is removed); and E contains a properly used non-essential clause and corrects the faulty comparison.

7. A: Verb tense (would vs. will)

The sentence describes events that occurred in the past, and sentences that contain verbs in the past tense (*created*) should not typically contain verbs in the future tense (*will realign*). That eliminates B and D. The use of the present tense (*creates*) is C makes that option incorrect, and E contains a fragment.

8. D: Parallel structure; word pair

Not only must be paired with *but also*, which eliminates B, C, and E. The gerund *test-taking* in the non-underlined portion of the sentence must be matched be a gerund (*studying*) in the underlined-portion, which leaves D as the only option.

9. A: Parallel structure; word pair

Both must be paired with *and*, which eliminates D and E. Furthermore, the construction *adverb + gerund* (*rigorously constructing*) in the non-underlined portion of the sentence must be matched by an equivalent construction (*intellectually probing*) in the underlined portion. Only the original version of the sentence provides that construction.

10. B: Passive; wordiness

A and B are both grammatically correct, but A contains the passive voice (*also possessed by other primates*). C contains the gerund being; in D, *shared* should be followed by the preposition *with*; and E creates a fragment.

11. D: Faulty comparison

The original version of the sentence incorrectly compares the chestnut tree's *fruit* to the chestnut tree rather than the fruit to the fruit. Only D makes this relationship clear in a concise manner.

12. E: Passive voice; participle required

The original version of the sentence contains the passive voice (the *quality of their flavor **was reduced***). B contains a comma splice; the pronoun *this* in C lacks an antecedent; and the singular pronoun *its* in D disagrees with its plural antecedent (*dishes*).

13. A: Dangling modifier

What was used in both food and medicine in many cultures for thousands of years? Garlic. So *garlic*, the subject, must be placed immediately after the comma. Only A and B provide this option, and B creates a comma splice. Although D could potential fix the dangling modification as well, it incorrectly places a semicolon before a FANBOYS conjunction (*and*).

14. C: Parallel Structure

The gerund (*demonstrating*) in the non-underlined portion of the sentence must be matched by a gerund in the underlined portion (*claiming*). Only C provides that construction.

Test 3

Section 1

1. Ⓐ Ⓑ Ⓒ Ⓓ Ⓔ
2. Ⓐ Ⓑ Ⓒ Ⓓ Ⓔ
3. Ⓐ Ⓑ Ⓒ Ⓓ Ⓔ
4. Ⓐ Ⓑ Ⓒ Ⓓ Ⓔ
5. Ⓐ Ⓑ Ⓒ Ⓓ Ⓔ
6. Ⓐ Ⓑ Ⓒ Ⓓ Ⓔ
7. Ⓐ Ⓑ Ⓒ Ⓓ Ⓔ
8. Ⓐ Ⓑ Ⓒ Ⓓ Ⓔ
9. Ⓐ Ⓑ Ⓒ Ⓓ Ⓔ
10. Ⓐ Ⓑ Ⓒ Ⓓ Ⓔ
11. Ⓐ Ⓑ Ⓒ Ⓓ Ⓔ
12. Ⓐ Ⓑ Ⓒ Ⓓ Ⓔ
13. Ⓐ Ⓑ Ⓒ Ⓓ Ⓔ
14. Ⓐ Ⓑ Ⓒ Ⓓ Ⓔ
15. Ⓐ Ⓑ Ⓒ Ⓓ Ⓔ
16. Ⓐ Ⓑ Ⓒ Ⓓ Ⓔ
17. Ⓐ Ⓑ Ⓒ Ⓓ Ⓔ
18. Ⓐ Ⓑ Ⓒ Ⓓ Ⓔ
19. Ⓐ Ⓑ Ⓒ Ⓓ Ⓔ
20. Ⓐ Ⓑ Ⓒ Ⓓ Ⓔ
21. Ⓐ Ⓑ Ⓒ Ⓓ Ⓔ
22. Ⓐ Ⓑ Ⓒ Ⓓ Ⓔ
23. Ⓐ Ⓑ Ⓒ Ⓓ Ⓔ
24. Ⓐ Ⓑ Ⓒ Ⓓ Ⓔ
25. Ⓐ Ⓑ Ⓒ Ⓓ Ⓔ
26. Ⓐ Ⓑ Ⓒ Ⓓ Ⓔ
27. Ⓐ Ⓑ Ⓒ Ⓓ Ⓔ
28. Ⓐ Ⓑ Ⓒ Ⓓ Ⓔ
29. Ⓐ Ⓑ Ⓒ Ⓓ Ⓔ
30. Ⓐ Ⓑ Ⓒ Ⓓ Ⓔ
31. Ⓐ Ⓑ Ⓒ Ⓓ Ⓔ
32. Ⓐ Ⓑ Ⓒ Ⓓ Ⓔ
33. Ⓐ Ⓑ Ⓒ Ⓓ Ⓔ
34. Ⓐ Ⓑ Ⓒ Ⓓ Ⓔ
35. Ⓐ Ⓑ Ⓒ Ⓓ Ⓔ

Section 2

1. Ⓐ Ⓑ Ⓒ Ⓓ Ⓔ
2. Ⓐ Ⓑ Ⓒ Ⓓ Ⓔ
3. Ⓐ Ⓑ Ⓒ Ⓓ Ⓔ
4. Ⓐ Ⓑ Ⓒ Ⓓ Ⓔ
5. Ⓐ Ⓑ Ⓒ Ⓓ Ⓔ
6. Ⓐ Ⓑ Ⓒ Ⓓ Ⓔ
7. Ⓐ Ⓑ Ⓒ Ⓓ Ⓔ
8. Ⓐ Ⓑ Ⓒ Ⓓ Ⓔ
9. Ⓐ Ⓑ Ⓒ Ⓓ Ⓔ
10. Ⓐ Ⓑ Ⓒ Ⓓ Ⓔ
11. Ⓐ Ⓑ Ⓒ Ⓓ Ⓔ
12. Ⓐ Ⓑ Ⓒ Ⓓ Ⓔ
13. Ⓐ Ⓑ Ⓒ Ⓓ Ⓔ
14. Ⓐ Ⓑ Ⓒ Ⓓ Ⓔ

SECTION 1
Time – 25 Minutes
35 Questions

Directions: For each question in this section, select the best answer from among the choices given and fill in the corresponding circle on the answer sheet.

The following sentences test correctness and effectiveness of expression. Part of each sentence or the entire sentence is underlined; beneath each sentence are five ways of phrasing the underlined material. Choice A repeats the original phrasing; the other four choices are different. If you think the original phrasing produces a better sentence than any of the alternatives, select choice A; if not, select one of the other choices.

In making your selection, follow the requirements of standard written English; that is, pay attention to grammar, choice of words, sentence construction, and punctuation. Your selection should result in the most effective sentence—clear and precise, without awkwardness or ambiguity.

EXAMPLE:

Anna Robertson Moses completed her first painting and she was seventy-six years old then.

(A) and she was seventy-six years old then
(B) when she was seventy-six years old
(C) at age seventy-six years old
(D) upon arriving at the age of seventy-six
(E) at the time when she was seventy-six years old

1. Despite the poor economy, bank loans to small businesses have been increasing for the past few months.

   (A) have been increasing
   (B) increase
   (C) are increasing
   (D) will be increasing
   (E) increasing

2. Usually found in clear, shallow water, sunlight is what the most common kinds of coral require to grow.

   (A) sunlight is what the most common kinds of coral require to grow
   (B) sunlight being required to grow by the most common kinds of coral
   (C) and to require sunlight to grow by the most common kinds of coral
   (D) the most common kinds of coral require sunlight to grow
   (E) the most common kinds of coral requiring sunlight to grow

3. Goethe, an amateur scientist, was so impressed with the work of British chemist Luke Howard and deciding to publish, in German translation, an autobiographical letter that Howard had sent to him.

   (A) and deciding to publish
   (B) he decided to publish
   (C) as he decided to publish
   (D) that he decided to publish
   (E) and his decision to publish

4. Despite negotiations that were threatening to collapse, the senators were able to salvage the bill that they had worked so long to prepare.

   (A) negotiations that were threatening to collapse,
   (B) negotiations whose collapse was threatening,
   (C) negotiations and they threatened to collapse,
   (D) negotiations for which collapse was a threat,
   (E) negotiations where collapse was threatened,

5. Throughout history there have been many senatorial bodies, <u>two of them were the Spartan Gerousia and the Roman Senate</u>, but all of them were founded on similar principles.

(A) two of them were the Spartan Gerousia the Roman Senate,
(B) the Spartan Gerousia and Roman Senate were among them
(C) two of which were the Spartan Gerousia and the Roman Senate
(D) two early instances were the Spartan Gerousia and the Roman Senate
(E) the Spartan Gerousia and the Roman Senate being included among these

6. <u>The Iditarod dog sled race takes place</u> in Nome, Alaska each year, commemorates the dogsled teams that delivered a life-saving serum during the 1925 diphtheria epidemic.

(A) The Iditarod dog sled race takes place
(B) The Iditarod dog sled race, which takes place
(C) The Iditarod dog sled race taking place
(D) The Iditarod dog sled race, it takes place
(E) The Iditarod dog sled race, and this has taken place

7. Illegal logging in Mexican forests once came close to destroying the monarch butterfly's winter <u>habitat, however in recent years this has declined</u>.

(A) habitat, however in recent years this has declined
(B) habitat, with declines coming in recent years
(C) habitat that has declined in recent years
(D) habitat, in recent years it had declined, however
(E) habitat; in recent years, however, such threats have declined

8. A number of factors including <u>widespread social strife, a population that was exploding</u>, and economic stagnation conspired to weaken the Qing Dynasty in nineteenth century China.

(A) widespread social strife, a population that was exploding,
(B) social strife that was widespread, a population that was exploding,
(C) widespread social strife, the population explodes,
(D) widespread social strife, the population had exploded,
(E) widespread social strife, an exploding population,

9. Many of the experiments performed by cognitive psychologist Elizabeth Spelke <u>has been designed</u> to test how much babies and young children understand about the world around them.

(A) has been designed
(B) having been designed
(C) they were designed
(D) are designed
(E) designed them

10. Playwright and performance artist Anna Deveare Smith is primarily known for the one-woman "documentary plays" in which she plays <u>a wide variety of characters that are very different from one another</u>.

(A) a wide variety of characters that are very different from one another
(B) characters very different from one another and a wide variety of them
(C) many different characters, these being widely varied
(D) widely varying and differing characters
(E) a wide variety of characters

11. The terms abstract art, nonfigurative art, and non-representational art all have <u>similar, if not identical, meanings</u>.

(A) similar, if not identical, meanings
(B) similar meanings, but not being identical
(C) similar meanings, and they are not identical
(D) meanings that are similar, whereas they differ from one another
(E) meanings that are similar although differing somewhat

The following sentences test your ability to recognize grammar and usage errors. Each sentence contains either a single error or none at all. No sentence contains more than one error. The error, if there is one, is underlined and lettered. If the sentence contains an error, select the one underlined part that must be changed in order to make the sentence correct. If the sentence is correct, select choice E. In choosing answers, follow the requirements of standard written English.

EXAMPLE:

Science fiction writer H.G. Wells, the author of
                                    A
more than 100 books, accurately predicted the
                                  B
the invention of television, the rise of the Internet,
        C
and creating the hydrogen bomb. No error
      D   E

○○○●○

12. Puzzle-solving, an ancient and universal practice,
                         A
and it depends on the kind of creative insight that
 B   C
ignited the first campfires thousands of years ago.
                                                 D
No error
 E

13. The more precise form of timekeeper available,
         A   *most*
a cesium fountain atomic clock, is expected to
                                B
become inaccurate by less than a single second
                     C
over the next 50 million years. No error
 D   E

14. The diners, finding that the dish they had ordered
                A   B
tasted unexpectedly sourly, promptly requested that
                    C
the waiter remove it and replace it with a fresher
                    D
version. No error
         E

15. Some planets that are very different from our own
                 A   *to turn* B
may have the potential for turning current theories
                         C
about solar system formation upside down. No error
 D   E

16. In the early fifteenth century, Venice has drawn
    A   B
strivers from across the Mediterranean to build and
        C
run the guard fleets that kept the city-state's
adversaries in check. No error
            D   E

17. Several dozen boats are known to have sank off the
                                    sunk A
French Frigate Shoals or in neighboring atolls, now
                                               B
part of an enormous protected zone covering nearly
              C   D
150,000 square miles in the South Pacific. No error
                                            E

18. At the ceremony marking the Washington
                     A
Monument's opening, crowds gathered to see Dolly
                                        B
         because
Madison when she was one of the few public figures
        C
that remained from the revolutionary era. No error
 D   E

19. Although the southern part of Tunisia is covered by
    A   B
the Sahara Desert, the remaining areas of the country
                        C
contain exceptional fertile soil and hundreds of miles
         D
of coastline. No error
             E

20. Food historians claim that the Romans ate mixed
                                         A
greens with dressing, and the Babylonians are
                     B
known to have doused lettuce with oil and vinegar
 C   D
more than two thousand years ago. No error
                                  E

confidence

204

21. Many scientists, beginning with Darwin <u>himself,</u>
                                            A
<u>have asserted</u> that human mental capacities are simply
    B
<u>elaborations</u> on the faculties <u>found in</u> other apes.
    C   D
<u>No error</u>
    (E)

22. <u>Just who</u> inspired English painter John Constable's
    A
<u>marvelously</u> enigmatic cloud studies, <u>much prized by</u>
    B   C
collectors, <u>has</u> never been entirely clear. <u>No error</u>
            D   (E)

23. Dental problems such as impacted wisdom teeth

    <u>have arisen</u> only recently because people <u>now process</u>
        A   *they*   B
    their food so much that <u>we chew</u> with <u>too little</u> force.
                             (C)   D

    <u>No error</u>
        E

24. <u>When</u> the dust settled on the Napoleonic Wars, the
    A   *being*
    Spanish city of Cadiz held the distinction <u>to be</u> the
                                                (B)
    <u>only city in</u> continental Europe <u>to survive</u> a siege by
        C   D
    Napoleon. <u>No error</u>
                  E
                          single
25. What the advertising agency chooses to focus on for

    <u>their</u> next major campaign <u>will depend</u> upon the
    (A)   B
    interests and strengths of <u>those</u> responsible <u>for</u>
                                C   D
    overseeing the project. <u>No error</u>
                                E

26. In an effort <u>to attract</u> more patrons, the museum is
                     A
    venturing <u>in</u> the rapidly evolving field of "visitor
              (B)
    engagement," a social science <u>aimed at</u> trying to reach
                                      C
    everyone from children <u>to</u> seasoned scholars. <u>No error</u>
                            D   E

27. <u>Though</u> the buildings of architect Benjamin Marshall
    A
    <u>are</u> just as well known as <u>Frank Lloyd Wright,</u>
    B   C
    Marshall, <u>while much</u> admired by designers,
                  D
    has been largely forgotten by the general public.

    <u>No error</u>
        E

28. <u>For all</u> his fame and celebration, William
    A
    Shakespeare <u>remains</u> a mysterious figure because
                    B
    <u>so few</u> reliable sources about his personal life <u>exists.</u>
    C   (D)
    <u>No error</u>
        E

29. In ancient Rome, the first aquariums were created

    when <u>bringing sea barbels</u> indoors so that they <u>could</u>
         (A)   B
    be <u>housed in</u> tanks of marble and glass for houseguests
        C
    <u>to observe.</u> <u>No error</u>
        D   E

Directions: The following passage is an early
draft of an essay. Some parts of the passage need
to be rewritten.

Read the passage and select the best answer for the
questions that follow. Some questions are about
particular sentences or parts of sentences and ask
you to improve sentence structure or word choice.
Other questions ask you to consider organization
and development. In choosing you answer, follow
the requirements of standard written English.

Questions 30-35 refer to the following passage.

(1) Tomatoes are usually associated with Italian
cuisine, but before the sixteenth century, no one in Italy
even knew what a tomato looked like. (2) Native to the
South American continent, it had been grown for
thousands of years before the Spanish brought the first
tomatoes back to Europe in 1544. (3) Those tomatoes
hardly resembled the tomatoes found on the shelves of
most modern supermarkets: in the first place, they were
yellow. (4) They were also the size of berries.
(5) Tomatoes became an integral part of the Italian
diet almost as soon as they were introduced there, they
didn't fare so well elsewhere. (6) Resembling plants
known to be poisonous such as belladonna and mandrake,
people in Spain and England were initially hesitant to
consume tomatoes. (7) Instead, they used the tiny round
plants for decoration.
(8) Thomas Jefferson first brought them from France
in 1820, but they did not catch on immediately. (9) He had
served as the American ambassador there. (10) France had
undergone much political turmoil in the decades Jefferson
lived there. (11) Fifty years later, the tomato finally
acquired its modern form and flavor. (12) In 1870, the first
dark red tomato was introduced by a farmer named
Alexander Livingston. (13) Livingston had spent more than
two decades creating the tomato, which he named the
Paragon. (14) The Paragon quickly became popular and
has remained a staple of cooking in the United States ever
since.

30. In context, which of the following words would most
appropriately be inserted at the beginning of sentence
5?

(A) Although
(B) Despite
(C) Because
(D) When
(E) However

31. In context, which of the following is the best way to
revise the underlined portion of sentence 6
(reproduced below)?

Resembling plants known to be poisonous such as
belladonna and mandrake, people in Spain and
England were initially hesitant to consume tomatoes.

(A) people in Spain and England initially hesitating to
consume tomatoes
(B) at first people in Spain and England were hesitant
to consume tomatoes
(C) tomatoes initially made people in Spain and
England hesitant to consume them
(D) the consumption of tomatoes initially made
people in Spain and England hesitant
(E) people in Spain and England initially hesitated in
consuming tomatoes

32. The transition between the second and third
paragraphs would be most improved by inserting
which of the following sentences immediately before
sentence 8?

(A) In the eighteenth century, Linneaus classified the
tomato as a member of the genus *solanum*.
(B) In the United States, tomatoes were not
commonly eaten until the late nineteenth
century.
(C) Tomatoes have now become one of the most
popular garden plants grown in the United
States.
(D) Although the tomato is technically a fruit, it is
usually considered a vegetable because of its
low sugar content.
(E) By the early nineteenth century, the tomato had
become an important part of the cuisine of
many European countries.

33. In context, which of the following is the best way to combine and revise the underlined portion of sentences 8 and 9 (reproduced below)?

In 1820, Thomas Jefferson first brought them from France, but they did not catch on immediately. He had served as the American ambassador there.

(A) France, but they did not catch on immediately, having served as the American ambassador there
(B) France, where he had served as the American ambassador, although it did not catch on immediately
(C) France, he had served as the American ambassador there, but they did not catch on immediately
(D) France, which was where he had served as the American ambassador; however they did not catch on immediately
(E) France, where he had served as the American ambassador, but they did not catch on immediately

34. In context, what is the best way to deal with sentence 10 (reproduced below)?

France had undergone much political turmoil in the decades Jefferson lived there.

(A) Change "much" to "a significant amount".
(B) Change "France" to "the French".
(C) Change "Jefferson" to "he".
(D) Place it after sentence 8.
(E) Delete it from the passage.

35. In context, which of the following phrases is best to insert at the beginning of sentence 14?

(A) Because it had a sweeter taste and was more versatile than the varieties available at the time,
(B) Livingston was descended from several generations of farmers, but
(C) Although the tomato had already been important in European cooking for several centuries,
(D) While some Italian immigrants had brought tomato-based recipes with them to the United States,
(E) Although Livingston was an experienced farmer, the process was very difficult; therefore,

SECTION 2
Time – 10 Minutes
14 Questions

Directions: For each question in this section, select the best answer from among the choices given and fill in the corresponding circle on the answer sheet.

The following sentences test correctness and effectiveness of expression. Part of each sentence or the entire sentence is underlined; beneath each sentence are five ways of phrasing the underlined material. Choice A repeats the original phrasing; the other four choices are different. If you think the original phrasing produces a better sentence than any of the alternatives, select choice A; if not, select one of the other choices.

In making your selection, follow the requirements of standard written English; that is, pay attention to grammar, choice of words, sentence construction, and punctuation. Your selection should result in the most effective sentence—clear and precise, without awkwardness or ambiguity.

EXAMPLE:

○●○○○

Anna Robertson Moses completed her first painting <u>and she was seventy-six years old then</u>.

(A) and she was seventy-six years old then
(B) when she was seventy-six years old
(C) at age seventy-six years old
(D) upon arriving at the age of seventy-six
(E) at the time when she was seventy-six years old

1. In the United States, only a fraction as many students play on competitive squash <u>teams than</u> play on competitive tennis teams.

    (A) teams than
    (B) teams, and
    (C) teams as
    (D) teams when
    (E) teams whereas

2. Although they are typically powered by rowers, <u>canoes sometimes containing sails or electric motors</u>.

    (A) canoes sometimes containing sails or electric motors
    (B) sails or electronic motors sometimes being what canoes contain
    (C) canoes sometimes contain sails or electric motors
    (D) sails or electronic motors are what canoes sometimes contain
    (E) sails or electronic motors are what is sometimes contained in canoes

3. The words "buffalo" and "bison" are often used interchangeably, <u>but the North American animal is a bison while its cousins</u> in Asia and Africa are buffaloes.

    (A) but the North American animal is a bison while its cousins
    (B) but the North American animal is a bison, their cousins
    (C) the North American animal is a bison while their cousins
    (D) but the North American animal is a bison, its cousins, though,
    (E) and the North American animal is a bison and their cousins

4. More than just a way to communicate, writing by hand can improve both <u>the composition of ideas as well as how they are expressed</u>.

    (A) the composition of ideas as well as how they are expressed
    (B) how ideas are composed, and also their expression
    (C) composing ideas as well as expressing them
    (D) the composition and the expression of ideas
    (E) the composition of ideas and expressing them

5. The Philadelphia Zoo is the oldest zoo in the United States, it opened less than a decade after the end of the Civil War.

  (A) States, it opened
  (B) States, its opening
  (C) States, and it will open
  (D) States, they opened
  (E) States, having opened

6. Believing that real estate prices would not rise indefinitely, it was argued by the economist that housing costs would eventually plummet.

  (A) it was argued by the economist that housing costs would eventually plummet
  (B) it was argued by the economist that housing costs would have eventually plummeted
  (C) the economist argued that housing costs would eventually plummet
  (D) the economist's argument was that housing costs will eventually plummet
  (E) the argument of the economist was that housing costs would eventually plummet

7. While exploring the shipwreck, divers found several iron cauldrons used to boil whale blubber down into oil, which was the ultimate prize in the lucrative but highly speculative whaling trade.

  (A) divers found several iron cauldrons used to boil whale blubber down into oil, which
  (B) divers have found several iron cauldrons used to boil whale blubber down into oil, that
  (C) several iron cauldrons were found in which whale blubbered was boiled down into oil, because it
  (D) divers found about iron cauldrons used for boiling whale blubber down into oil, which
  (E) whale blubber was boiled down into oil in several iron cauldrons found by divers, which

8. By grounding planes and eliminating flights from schedules, airlines are reducing the number of seats available and passengers are forced to pay more.

  (A) passengers are forced
  (B) passengers will be forced
  (C) passengers would be forced
  (D) forcing passengers
  (E) this forces passengers

9. Throughout his novel *The Golden Gate*, Vikram Seth maintains a stubborn, if admirable, resistance to traditional structure.

  (A) if admirable
  (B) although being admirable
  (C) whereas it is also admirable
  (D) despite its being admirable
  (E) but it is also admirable

10. Cajun cuisine is predominantly rustic, relying on locally available ingredients and preparation of it is simple.

  (A) preparation of it is simple
  (B) preparation being simple
  (C) simple preparation
  (D) preparation as simple
  (E) simplicity in its preparation

11. Medications that are manufactured and sold without patent protection and that are known as generic drugs.

  (A) that are manufactured and sold without patent protection and that are
  (B) manufactured and sold without patent protection are
  (C) that are manufactured and sold without patent protection is
  (D) not having patent protection when they are manufactured and sold and that are
  (E) that are manufactured and sold without patent protection and

12. The maker of the documentary suggests that for all the hardships they endure, Tibetan nomads lead lives no more stressful than most city dwellers.

  (A) than most city dwellers
  (B) than what most city dwellers have
  (C) than those of most city dwellers
  (D) than most city dwellers have
  (E) than would be had by most city dwellers

13. <u>Were it to be proven</u>, the scientists' theory would confirm that the first life evolved on Earth shortly after the Late Heavy Bombardment, a period during which thousands of asteroids slammed into the young planet.

  (A) Were it to be proven
  (B) If it would have been proven
  (C) Was it to have been proven
  (D) If they were proven,
  (E) By having proven it,

14. Faculty members suspect that the university's new president will focus on promoting the <u>sciences, because of which the humanities will suffer</u>.

  (A) sciences, because of which the humanities will suffer
  (B) sciences, and therefore the humanities will suffer
  (C) sciences and causing the humanities to suffer
  (D) sciences, whereby the humanities would suffer
  (E) sciences at the expense of the humanities

Answers: Test 3, Section 1

1. A: Verb tense

The past perfect (*have been increasing*) is correctly used here to describe a situation that began in the past and that is continuing into the present. In addition, the word *for* indicates the need for this tense.

2. D: Dangling modifier

What is usually found in clear, shallow water? The most common kinds of coral, not sunlight. So *the most common kinds of coral* (the **complete subject**) must be the first words after the comma. Only D and E provide this construction; however, the gerund *requiring* in E creates a fragment, so the answer must be D.

3. D: Word pair

So must be paired with *that*. Because *so* appears in the non-underlined portion of the sentence, the fastest way to determine the answer is to simply look for an option containing *that*. Only D includes that word.

4. A: Essential clause

The fact that the negotiations were threatening to collapse is information essential to the meaning of the sentence, so in choice A, the use of "that" to begin an **essential clause** is correct. In B, the *collapse* was not threatening; C contains does not contain the correct logical relationship; D is uncolloquial; and in E, "where" should only be used to refer to places.

5. C: Comma splice

A, B, and D all contain comma splices, and E, while grammatically correct, unnecessarily contains the gerund *being*. C is the more concise grammatically correct option: it eliminates the comma splice by turning the beginning of the second independent clause into a non-essential clause that can be removed from the sentence without altering its fundamental meaning (*Throughout history there have been many senatorial bodies...but all of them were founded on similar principles.*)

6. B: Non-essential clause

The original version contains an illogically placed comma that separates an independent clause and a fragment whose relationship to the first clause is unclear. The most effective way to remedy this un-grammatical construction is to create a non-essential clause (*which takes place in Nome, Alaska*) at the beginning of the sentence.

7. E: Semicolon; antecedent-pronoun (missing antecedent)

In the original sentence, "however" is used to begin a clause but is incorrectly placed after a comma rather than a semicolon. In addition, the pronoun "this" lacks an antecedent (What has declined? Logging? The winter habitat?). Although B does not create a pronoun issue, the phrasing is awkward and the sentence never specifies what "declines" refers to. C creates a misplaced modifier that makes it sound as if the habitats has declined. D creates a comma splice, and E correctly uses a semicolon to separate two independent clauses and replaces the ambiguous pronoun with a noun ("threats").

8. E: Parallel structure

This questions is somewhat trickier than many parallelism questions because it is the second rather than the third item in the list that does not match the others. Since items one and three contain the essential construction adjective + noun (widespread social strife...economic stagnation), item two must contain the same construction, which is included only in E.

9. D: Subject-verb agreement

Many, the subject, is plural. Since there is no plural verb in the present perfect (*have been*), and the sentence does not require that the verb be in that tense, the only grammatically acceptable choice available is D.

10. E: Redundancy

By definition, "a wide array" means indicates many things that are different from one another; the original sentence is therefore redundant. Only E eliminates the redundancy in a clear and concise manner.

11. A: No error; non-essential clause

The non-essential clause is placed an unexpected point in the sentence but does not constitute an error.

12. B: Non-essential clause

Non-essential clauses should generally be followed by verbs; if the non-essential clause in this sentence is removed, what remains is ungrammatical (*Puzzle solving...and it depends on creative insight*). The words *and it* must be removed in order for the sentence to make sense.

13. A: More vs. most

More should be used only when two things are being compared; when more than two are being compared, *most* should be used instead. Since it can be logically understood that there are more than two forms of timekeeper in the world, *most* is the correct form.

14. C: Adjective vs. adverb

The verb *taste* should be followed by an adjective rather than an adverb. The dish that the diners ordered tasted *sour*, not *sourly*). The incorrect version implies that the *dish*, not the diners, was doing the tasting, and that it was doing so in a sour manner – a totally illogical implication.

15. C: Verb form (gerund vs. infinitive)

Standard usage requires that the infinitive (*to turn*) rather than the gerund (*for turning*) be used with the phrase *have the potential*. The gerund is un-idiomatic.

16. B: Verb tense (present perfect vs. simple past)

The sentence clearly describes a finished event in the past, as indicated by the phrase *In the fifteenth century*. The simple past (*drew*) rather than the present perfect (*has drawn*) is thus required.

17. A: Verb form (past participle vs. simple past)

The past participle (*sunk*) rather than the simple past (*sank*) is required after any form of the verb *to have*.

18. C: Conjunction

When should only be used to refer to times and time periods, but here it is incorrectly used to indicate an explanation. The conjunction serves to explain *why* crowds gathered to see Dolly Madison, so a transition such as *because* or *since* should be used instead.

19. D: Adjective vs. adverb

The adverb *exceptionally* should be used to modify the adjective *fertile*.

20. E: No error; verb tense

The appearance of the phrase *two thousand years ago* suggests that the sentence is testing verb test, but in A, the verb *ate* is in the simple past and therefore correct. The trick answer is C because many test-takers are likely to think that the construction *known to have* sound strange; however, it is perfectly acceptable. In B, the conjunction

and is correct because the two clauses express similar ideas; and in D, *with* is the correct proposition to use with *doused*.

21. E: No error

Because the sentence contains a non-essential clause, the most likely error candidate is B. In this case, however, the plural verb *have* agrees with the plural subject *scientists*, and there the present perfect tense (*have asserted*) is correct because it implies that scientists are still making this assertion. *Himself* in A is simply there for emphasis and is correct because it refers to Darwin; C is a noun, and nouns are virtually never incorrect (except in the case of faulty comparison and noun agreement questions); and the preposition *in* underlined in D is correct.

22. E: No error

Although the singular verb *has* may appear to incorrectly correspond with the plural noun *studies*, the subject is actually *who*, which always requires a singular verb (*has*) when it does not refer to a specific noun. Choice A could also be seen as a trick answer because the construction *Just who* at the beginning of the sentence could sound odd to some test-takers.

23. C: Pronoun-antecedent

The noun *people* corresponds to the pronoun *they*, not the pronoun *we*.

24. B: Verb form (gerund vs. infinitive)

The phrase *hold the distinction* must be followed by the preposition *of* + gerund (*of being*) rather than the infinitive (*to be*).

25. A: Pronoun-antecedent; collective noun

Agency is a collective noun (singular) and thus requires a singular pronoun (*its* rather than *they*).

26. B: Preposition/idiom

Venturing should be followed by the preposition *into* rather than just *in*.

27. C: Faulty comparison

The sentence compares the buildings of Benjamin Marshall (things) to Frank Lloyd Wright (a person), and things must be compared to things. The sentence should therefore read: *Though the buildings of architect Benjamin Marshall are just as well known as those of Frank Lloyd Wright* (or: *the buildings of Frank Lloyd Wright*)...

28. D: Subject-verb agreement (subject – prepositional phrase – verb)

The subject of *exists* (singular) is *sources* (plural), not *life*, which belongs to the prepositional phrase beginning with *about*. A is the trick answer because many test-takers will believe that the phrase *for all* sounds strange. It means *despite*, and it's perfectly acceptable.

29. A: Misplaced modifier; logical relationship

The sentence indicates that the *aquariums* were responsible for bringing the sea barbels inside to be observed – an extremely illogical implication. Since the sentence does not actually supply a subject and tell us *who* brought the sea barbels indoors, a passive construction is necessary to correct the error: *In ancient Rome, the first aquarium was created when sea barbells **were brought** indoors...*

30. A: Conjunction

The two clauses express contradictory ideas (tomatoes became popular in Italy vs. tomatoes didn't become popular elsewhere) and therefore require a conjunction that expresses that contrast. Only A does so in a grammatically acceptable manner.

31. C: Dangling modifier

What resembled plants known to be poisonous? Tomatoes, not people. Because *tomatoes*, the subject, must appear immediately after the comma, C is the only option.

32. B: Paragraph organization

The passage describes the tomato's introduction to the United States in the early nineteenth century, followed by its rise to popularity fifty years later. The statement that best states this general progression and serves as an appropriate topic sentence is B.

33. E: Pronoun-antecedent; non-essential clause

A creates a misplaced modifier (it sounds as if tomatoes had served as the ambassador); B contains a pronoun-antecedent disagreement (*it*, singular, refers to *tomatoes*, plural); C contains a comma splice; D is unnecessarily wordy although grammatically correct; and E expresses the information correctly and concisely by creating a non-essential clause.

34. E: Paragraph organization

The focus of the paragraph and the passage is the tomato, not political conditions in France. The sentence should therefore be deleted from the passage.

35. A: Paragraph organization

The sentence states that Livingston's tomato became popular but does not provide an explanation for why this occurred. The information in A clearly provides reasons (sweeter taste, more versatile) for that popularity.

Test 3, Section 2

1. C: Word pair

The *as* in the non-underlined portion of the sentence must match *as* in the underlined portion. Only C contains that construction.

2. C: Improper use of gerund

The original version contains a gerund (*containing*) rather than a conjugated verb (*contain*) and is therefore a fragment. C provides the conjugated verb.

3. A: No error; logical relationship; antecedent-pronoun

The two clauses describe opposing ideas (the words *buffalo* and *bison* are used interchangeably vs. they are actually different animals), making *but* the correct conjunction. That eliminates C and E. *Animal* is singular and should be referred to with the singular pronoun *its*, eliminating B. D contains a comma splice and is awkward, leaving A.

4. D: Parallel structure; word pair

Both must be paired with *and*, which eliminates A and C. In addition, the construction on either side of the conjunction *and* must match. Only D correctly provides two nouns (*the composition...the expression*).

5. E: Comma splice; participle required

The original sentence contains a comma splice: two independent clauses separated by a comma. B creates a fragment; C contains a verb in the wrong tense (future, when the sentence clearly describes events that occurred in the past); and D also contains a comma splice. Note that *having* does not violate the "no gerund" rule here because it is not a gerund but rather a participle that modifies the first clause.

6. C: Dangling modifier

Who believed that real estate prices would not rise indefinitely? The economist. So *the economist*, the subject, must appear immediately after the comma. Only E contains that construction.

7. A: No error; dangling modifier; pronoun-antecedent

Who was exploring the shipwreck? Divers. So *divers*, the subject, must come immediately after the comma. That eliminates C and E. In D, *found about* is un-colloquial, and E contains the passive voice (*whale blubber was boiled…found by divers*).

8. D: Parallel structure

The construction after the conjunction *and* must match the construction before the conjunction: *reducing = forcing*. All of the choices except D and E also contain unnecessary tense switches, and in E, the pronoun *this* does not have an antecedent. D correctly maintains parallel structure by providing the word *forcing*.

9. A: Non-essential clause

Although the non-essential clause is placed at an unexpected point in the sentence and may sound awkward to many test-takers, there is nothing inherently wrong with it, and the sentence makes perfect sense when it is crossed out (*Throughout his novel <u>The Golden Gate</u>, Vikram Seth maintains a stubborn resistance to traditional structure*). All of the other options are excessively wordy and awkward, leaving A as the only possibility.

10. C: Parallel structure

The presence of the conjunction *and* tells us that construction in the underlined portion of the sentence must match that in the non-underlined portion: adjective + noun. Only C provides that construction (*simple preparation*).

11. B: Fragment

The original version is a fragment because it lacks a main verb. The only verbs that appear in the sentence (*are manufactured…are sold*) are part of the relative clause begun by *that* rather than part of the sentence's main clause. In order to fix the sentence, it is necessary to remove the word *that* (and thus remove the relative clause) in order to make the verb correspond to the subject. Only B does so in a clear and concise manner.

12. C: Faulty comparison

The sentence incorrectly compares **the lives** of Tibetan nomads (things) to most city dwellers (people). In order for the sentence to be correct, things must be compared to things. In the correct version, the pronoun *those of* replaces the noun *lives*.

13. A: Subjunctive

In the original version of the sentence, the subjunctive is correctly used to indicate a hypothetical situation – the scientists' assertion has not actually been proven. When the subjunctive is tested, it will often be used correctly in the original version of the sentence, and test-takers will simply be responsible for recognizing that it is *not* incorrect.

14. E: Wordiness

E is the clearest and most concise option. Although it changes the phrasing, it retains the essential meaning while eliminating the wordiness of the other options.

Test 4

Section 1

1. Ⓐ Ⓑ Ⓒ Ⓓ Ⓔ
2. Ⓐ Ⓑ Ⓒ Ⓓ Ⓔ
3. Ⓐ Ⓑ Ⓒ Ⓓ Ⓔ
4. Ⓐ Ⓑ Ⓒ Ⓓ Ⓔ
5. Ⓐ Ⓑ Ⓒ Ⓓ Ⓔ
6. Ⓐ Ⓑ Ⓒ Ⓓ Ⓔ
7. Ⓐ Ⓑ Ⓒ Ⓓ Ⓔ
8. Ⓐ Ⓑ Ⓒ Ⓓ Ⓔ
9. Ⓐ Ⓑ Ⓒ Ⓓ Ⓔ
10. Ⓐ Ⓑ Ⓒ Ⓓ Ⓔ
11. Ⓐ Ⓑ Ⓒ Ⓓ Ⓔ
12. Ⓐ Ⓑ Ⓒ Ⓓ Ⓔ
13. Ⓐ Ⓑ Ⓒ Ⓓ Ⓔ
14. Ⓐ Ⓑ Ⓒ Ⓓ Ⓔ
15. Ⓐ Ⓑ Ⓒ Ⓓ Ⓔ
16. Ⓐ Ⓑ Ⓒ Ⓓ Ⓔ
17. Ⓐ Ⓑ Ⓒ Ⓓ Ⓔ
18. Ⓐ Ⓑ Ⓒ Ⓓ Ⓔ
19. Ⓐ Ⓑ Ⓒ Ⓓ Ⓔ
20. Ⓐ Ⓑ Ⓒ Ⓓ Ⓔ
21. Ⓐ Ⓑ Ⓒ Ⓓ Ⓔ
22. Ⓐ Ⓑ Ⓒ Ⓓ Ⓔ
23. Ⓐ Ⓑ Ⓒ Ⓓ Ⓔ
24. Ⓐ Ⓑ Ⓒ Ⓓ Ⓔ
25. Ⓐ Ⓑ Ⓒ Ⓓ Ⓔ
26. Ⓐ Ⓑ Ⓒ Ⓓ Ⓔ
27. Ⓐ Ⓑ Ⓒ Ⓓ Ⓔ
28. Ⓐ Ⓑ Ⓒ Ⓓ Ⓔ
29. Ⓐ Ⓑ Ⓒ Ⓓ Ⓔ
30. Ⓐ Ⓑ Ⓒ Ⓓ Ⓔ
31. Ⓐ Ⓑ Ⓒ Ⓓ Ⓔ
32. Ⓐ Ⓑ Ⓒ Ⓓ Ⓔ
33. Ⓐ Ⓑ Ⓒ Ⓓ Ⓔ
34. Ⓐ Ⓑ Ⓒ Ⓓ Ⓔ
35. Ⓐ Ⓑ Ⓒ Ⓓ Ⓔ

Section 2

1. Ⓐ Ⓑ Ⓒ Ⓓ Ⓔ
2. Ⓐ Ⓑ Ⓒ Ⓓ Ⓔ
3. Ⓐ Ⓑ Ⓒ Ⓓ Ⓔ
4. Ⓐ Ⓑ Ⓒ Ⓓ Ⓔ
5. Ⓐ Ⓑ Ⓒ Ⓓ Ⓔ
6. Ⓐ Ⓑ Ⓒ Ⓓ Ⓔ
7. Ⓐ Ⓑ Ⓒ Ⓓ Ⓔ
8. Ⓐ Ⓑ Ⓒ Ⓓ Ⓔ
9. Ⓐ Ⓑ Ⓒ Ⓓ Ⓔ
10. Ⓐ Ⓑ Ⓒ Ⓓ Ⓔ
11. Ⓐ Ⓑ Ⓒ Ⓓ Ⓔ
12. Ⓐ Ⓑ Ⓒ Ⓓ Ⓔ
13. Ⓐ Ⓑ Ⓒ Ⓓ Ⓔ
14. Ⓐ Ⓑ Ⓒ Ⓓ Ⓔ

SECTION 1
Time – 25 Minutes
35 Questions

Directions: For each question in this section, select the best answer from among the choices given and fill in the corresponding circle on the answer sheet.

The following sentences test correctness and effectiveness of expression. Part of each sentence or the entire sentence is underlined; beneath each sentence are five ways of phrasing the underlined material. Choice A repeats the original phrasing; the other four choices are different. If you think the original phrasing produces a better sentence than any of the alternatives, select choice A; if not, select one of the other choices.

In making your selection, follow the requirements of standard written English; that is, pay attention to grammar, choice of words, sentence construction, and punctuation. Your selection should result in the most effective sentence—clear and precise, without awkwardness or ambiguity.

EXAMPLE:

Anna Robertson Moses completed her first painting and she was seventy-six years old then.

(A) and she was seventy-six years old then
(B) when she was seventy-six years old
(C) at age seventy-six years old
(D) upon arriving at the age of seventy-six
(E) at the time when she was seventy-six years old

1. Accused of running his campaign with donations from convicted embezzlers, the mayor offering an apology.

(A) offering
(B) offered
(C) having offered
(D) who offered
(E) who will offer

3. Hersheypark was created in 1907 as a leisure park for Hershey Chocolate Company employees; however, it was later opened to the general public.

(A) employees; however, it was later opened to the general public
(B) employees; it was, however, later generally opened publicly
(C) employees; however, it was later opening to the general public
(D) employees, despite its later being opened to the general public
(E) employees but later opening to the public generally

2. Because of his staunchly refusing to swear an oath of allegiance to the king, John Dryden was removed from the post of British poet laureate – a post that was normally held for life.

(A) Because of his staunchly refusing to swear an oath of allegiance to the king,
(B) Because he staunchly refused to swear an oath of allegiance to the king,
(C) He refused staunchly to swear allegiance to the king, then
(D) Staunchly refusing to swear allegiance to the king, this was why
(E) While he staunchly refuses to swear allegiance to the king,

4. Renowned for the originality of their works, George Balanchine and Mikhail Baryshnikov <u>are widely acknowledged as a choreographer responsible</u> for shaping the course of twentieth-century ballet.

(A) are widely acknowledged as a choreographer responsible
(B) are acknowledged widely in that they are a choreographer responsible for
(C) are widely acknowledged as choreographers responsible
(D) acknowledged widely as choreographers responsible for
(E) are acknowledged widely as choreographers responsible in

5. The average family size in most countries has been steadily <u>decreasing, as a result, there are</u> fewer children than there used to be.

(A) decreasing, as a result, there are
(B) decreasing; however, there has been
(C) decreasing, there are consequently
(D) decreasing; consequently, there are
(E) decreasing by their having

6. Romantic poetry emphasized intuition over <u>reason, plus it has promoted</u> the use of everyday language over that of typically poetic language.

(A) reason, plus it has promoted
(B) reason, moreover it has promoted
(C) reason and promoted
(D) reason, and, furthermore they often promoted
(E) reason, it promoted

7. Over the past several decades, traditional African instruments such as the kora, the balafon, and the ngoni <u>has strongly influenced</u> the sound of rap music.

(A) has strongly influenced
(B) would have strongly influenced
(C) will strongly influence
(D) which strongly influenced
(E) have strongly influenced

8. With fifteen percent of the vote, <u>the title of most important African-American leader was won by Jesse Jackson</u> in a 2006 survey.

(A) the title of most important African-American leader was won by Jesse Jackson
(B) the title of most important African-American leader won by Jesse Jackson
(C) Jesse Jackson's title of most important African-American leader was won
(D) Jesse Jackson won the title of most important African-American leader
(E) Jesse Jackson, having won the title of most important African-American leader,

9. Human computers, who performed numerical analysis for laboratories before computers became widespread, <u>and</u> behind the calculations for both the return of Halley's Comet and the Manhattan Project.

(A) and
(B) and who have been
(C) also have been
(D) were
(E) having been

10. The World Health Organization <u>clearly states in its constitution</u> the goal of eradicating infectious diseases and promoting the general health of people everywhere.

    (A) clearly states in its constitution
    (B) clearly states in their constitution
    (C) stated in its constitution clearly
    (D) stated in their constitution in a clear way
    (E) has stated in a straightforward manner in its constitution

11. Just <u>as</u> the machine age transformed an economy of farm laborers into one of assembly lines, <u>but the technology revolution is replacing factory workers with robots, and clerks are being replaced with computers.</u>

    (A) but the technology revolution is replacing factory workers with robots, and clerks are being replaced with computers
    (B) so the technology revolution is replacing factory workers with robots and clerks with computers
    (C) the technology revolution is now replacing factory workers with robots, and clerks are replaced with computers
    (D) and the technology revolution has replaced factory workers with robots and replaced clerks with computers
    (E) likewise, the technology revolution is replacing factory workers with robots, and clerks will be replaced with computers

The following sentences test your ability to recognize grammar and usage errors. Each sentence contains either a single error or none at all. No sentence contains more than one error. The error, if there is one, is underlined and lettered. If the sentence contains an error, select the one underlined part that must be changed in order to make the sentence correct. If the sentence is correct, select choice E. In choosing answers, follow the requirements of standard written English.

EXAMPLE:

Science fiction writer H.G. Wells, <u>the author of</u>
                                        A
more than 100 books, accurately <u>predicted</u> the
                                     B
the <u>invention</u> of television, the rise of the Internet,
       C
and <u>creating</u> the hydrogen bomb. <u>No error</u>
        D   E

○○○●○

12. Thomas Brussig, a German writer <u>best known for</u>
                                          A
his satirical novels, <u>worked as</u> a cleaner, museum
                          B
guard, and <u>he was also</u> a builder, <u>before studying</u> film-
              C   D
making in Berlin. <u>No error</u>
                      E

13. Nikolai Tesla's inventions, <u>which include</u> fluorescent
                                     A
lighting <u>and</u> the modern radio, are still considered just
            B
<u>as</u> important as <u>Thomas Edison</u>. <u>No error</u>
 C   D   E

14. Spiders are found on every continent <u>other than</u>
                                              A
        are ~~its~~
Antarctica and <u>being</u> established in <u>nearly every</u>
                   B   C
habitat with the <u>exception of</u> the air and the sea.
                     D
<u>No error</u>
 E

15. The presence of mysterious cave paintings <u>have</u>
                                                   A
puzzled archaeologists <u>studying</u> images created <u>by</u>
                           B   C
ancient <u>residents of</u> the Mississippi Valley. <u>No error</u>
            D   E

16. The Hale–Bopp comet <u>received</u> so much media
                            A
        so ---- that
coverage <u>becoming</u> one of the <u>most highly</u> observed
            B   C
astronomical bodies <u>in history</u>. No error
                        E

17. <u>Even after</u> weeks of protests, the workers <u>would</u>
     A   B
agree <u>to discuss</u> the overtime dispute with neither
          C
outside mediators <u>or</u> company officials. <u>No error</u>
                     D   E

18. The compositions <u>of</u> jazz musician Thelonius Monk
                        A
<u>seem</u> to evoke a self-enclosed world, one with <u>its</u> own
 B   C
telltale harmonies <u>and</u> rhythms. <u>No error</u>
                       D   E

19. Anchors, like many other types of maritime
technology, <u>has evolved</u> significantly since the
               A
nineteenth century, <u>making</u> it easier to identify <u>their</u>
                        B   C
approximate date <u>of</u> manufacture. <u>No error</u>
                     D   E

20. In the early nineteenth century, <u>contact with</u>
                                          A
Europeans <u>led</u> Native Americans <u>to adopt</u> new
              B   C
materials, including glass beads and copper, and
to incorporate <u>this</u> into existing styles of clothing.
                   D
<u>No error</u>
 E

221

21. Recent studies <u>have shown</u> that in comparison to
                  A

    another popular decongestant, zinc is <u>most</u> effective
                                    B

    <u>at curing</u> symptoms <u>associated with</u> the common cold.
      C   D

    <u>No error</u>
      E

22. When the jury <u>retreated into</u> a locked room to
               A

    deliberate, <u>it</u> left behind a courtroom of fascinated
            B

    onlookers, <u>all eager</u> to learn the outcome <u>of</u> the trial.
             C   D

    <u>No error</u>
      E

23. The study of meteorology began centuries ago,

    <u>and</u> it was not until the eighteenth century <u>that</u>
    A   B

    technology became <u>sufficiently</u> advanced to
                  C

    permit <u>any</u> real breakthroughs. <u>No error</u>
          D   E

24. Members of the Nagapuhi, a Maori tribe indigenous

    <u>to</u> New Zealand, <u>have adopted</u> muskets after European
    B   C

    traders <u>arrived</u> to conquer them in 1818. <u>No error</u>
          D   E

25. By the end <u>of</u> the seventeenth century, the tragedies
           A

    of French playwright Jean Racine <u>had become</u>
                              B

    <u>considerably</u> more successful than <u>his main rival,</u>
      C   D

    Pierre Corneille. <u>No error</u>
               E

26. In 1610, the year Galileo <u>began</u> viewing the
                    A

    sky <u>through</u> the lens of a telescope, he <u>had become</u>
        B   C

    the first person <u>to observe</u> Saturn's rings. <u>No error</u>
             D   E

27. <u>Although</u> apes are generally able to recognize
    A

    themselves <u>when shown</u> a mirror, monkeys are unable
                 B

    to <u>do it</u> and perceive a stranger in <u>their</u> reflections.
        C   D

    <u>No error</u>
      E

28. The construction of the Panama Canal <u>marked</u> a
                              A

    shift <u>from</u> the great ancient public works <u>built by</u>
        B   C

    backbreaking labor to the <u>far more</u> mechanized
                      D

    triumphs of the twentieth century. <u>No error</u>
                        E

29. Though <u>its</u> use has now been banned in many
        A

    countries, asbestos, <u>formerly</u> used widely in industrial
                  B

    and domestic environments in the past, <u>has left</u>
                             C

    <u>potentially</u> dangerous material in many buildings.
      D

    <u>No error</u>
      E

Directions: The following passage is an early draft of an essay. Some parts of the passage need to be rewritten.

Read the passage and select the best answer for the questions that follow. Some questions are about particular sentences or parts of sentences and ask you to improve sentence structure or word choice. Other questions ask you to consider organization and development. In choosing you answer, follow the requirements of standard written English.

Questions 30-35 refer to the following passage.

(1) While people have been inventing calculating machines for thousands of years, the history of the computer is relatively short. (2) The ENIAC, one of the precursors to the modern computer, was built less than a century ago. (3) Developed in the 1940s by John Mauchley and J. Presper Eckert, the ENIAC was capable of adding 5,000 numbers in a second, this being a remarkable achievement for a machine at that time. (4) With thousands of vacuum tubes, diodes, and other parts, it weighed thousands of tons and took up nearly 2,000 square feet. (5) There were dozens of panels, each of which performed a different function. (6) It could also take weeks for a program to be entered into the machine.

(7) It broke down very often. (8) When it was first built, there were critics who said that it could never be used. (9) its vacuum tubes would constantly be burning out. (10) Although this prediction turned out to false, in the beginning several tubes did fail every day and needed to be replaced. (11) Finally, engineers realized that if they never turned the computer off, the tubes burned out less often.

(12) The limitations of the ENIAC were always clear, and in 1944, Eckert and Mauchley began work on a new computer, which became known as the EDVAC. (13) Though still very large, the EDVAC was smaller and more powerful than the ENIAC. (14) It was also much more reliable, and ten years after its construction, it was still being used.

30. In context, which of the following phrases would most appropriately be inserted at the beginning of sentence 2?

(A) Nevertheless,
(B) In the beginning,
(C) In fact,
(D) On the other hand,
(E) Regardless of this fact,

31. In context, which is the best revision of the underlined portion of sentence 3 (reproduced below)?

Developed in the 1940s by John Mauchley and J. Presper Eckert, the ENIAC was capable of adding 5,000 numbers in a second, this being a remarkable achievement for a machine at that time.

(A) numbers in a second, this was a remarkable achievement for a machine at that time
(B) numbers in a second, a remarkable achievement for a machine at that time
(C) numbers in a second, although this was a remarkable achievement for a machine then
(D) numbers in a second, it has made a remarkable achievement for a machine at that time
(E) numbers in a second, and this was a remarkable achievement for a machine then

32. In context, which of the following phrases would most appropriately be inserted at the beginning of sentence 7?

(A) In spite of the ENIAC's numerous problems,
(B) Mauchley and Eckert's work paid off since
(C) As engineers familiarized themselves with the ENIAC
(D) While computers did not play a large role in everyday life in the 1940s,
(E) Not only was the ENIAC large and difficult to handle, but

33. In context, what is the best way to revise and combine the underlined portions of sentences 8 and 9 (reproduced below)?

When the ENIAC was first built, there were critics who said that it could never be used. Its vacuum tubes would constantly be burning out.

(A) there were critics who said that it could never be used, and this was because it vacuum tubes would constantly burn

(B) some critics who said that it could never be used because of its vacuum tubes constantly burning out

(C) there were critics who said that it could never be used; its vacuum tubes constantly burning out

(D) some critics said that it could never be used since its vacuum tubes would constantly burn out

(E) there were critics who said that it could never be used, and their vacuum tubes would burn out constantly.

34. The second paragraph would be most improved by inserting which of the following sentences immediately after sentence 11?

(A) Each vacuum tube contained several electrodes inside an airtight enclosure.

(B) Waiting for the computer to shut down could be a lengthy process.

(C) Whenever a tube failed, the machine needed to be turned off so that it could be replaced.

(D) Once, they even functioned continuously for almost five days.

(E) In the 1940s, vacuum tubes were also less reliable than they are today.

35. In context, where is the best place to put the following sentence?

However, the ENIAC had few of the capacities that people taken for granted in computers today.

(A) Immediately before sentence 4

(B) Immediately before sentence 6

(C) Immediately before sentence 8

(D) Immediately before sentence 10

(E) Immediately before sentence 11

SECTION 2

Time – 10 Minutes
14 Questions

Directions: For each question in this section, select the best answer from among the choices given and fill in the corresponding circle on the answer sheet.

The following sentences test correctness and effectiveness of expression. Part of each sentence or the entire sentence is underlined; beneath each sentence are five ways of phrasing the underlined material. Choice A repeats the original phrasing; the other four choices are different. If you think the original phrasing produces a better sentence than any of the alternatives, select choice A; if not, select one of the other choices.

In making your selection, follow the requirements of standard written English; that is, pay attention to grammar, choice of words, sentence construction, and punctuation. Your selection should result in the most effective sentence—clear and precise, without awkwardness or ambiguity.

EXAMPLE:

○●○○○

Anna Robertson Moses completed her first painting <u>and she was seventy-six years old then</u>.

(A) and she was seventy-six years old then
(B) when she was seventy-six years old
(C) at age seventy-six years old
(D) upon arriving at the age of seventy-six
(E) at the time when she was seventy-six years old

1. As the cost of space travel decreases, scientists <u>expect that more experiments will be conducted in weightless environments</u>.

  (A) expect that more experiments will be conducted in weightless environments
 (B) have the expectation of conducting more experiments in weightless environments
 (C) expect, they would conduct more experiments in weightless environments
 (D) expected, more experiment would be conducted in weightless environments by them
 (E) would conduct in weightless environments more experiments

2. <u>The sailing trip, which had begun in ideal weather conditions rapidly turning</u> frightening after storm clouds gathered above the boat.

 (A) The sailing trip, which had begun in ideal weather conditions rapidly turning
 (B) The sailing trip, which had begun in ideal weather conditions, rapidly turned
 (C) The sailing trip being begun in ideal weather conditions rapidly turned
 (D) The sailing trip began in ideal weather and conditions rapidly turning
 (E) The sailing trip's beginning in ideal weather conditions having rapidly turned

3. <u>The almond is usually being thought of as a nut, but</u> it is actually the edible seed of a fruit.

 (A) The almond is usually being thought of as a nut, but
 (B) The almond is usually thought of a nut,
 (C) Although the almond is usually thought of as a nut,
 (D) Despite the almond's usually being thought of as a nut,
 (E) Whereas the almond is usually thought of as a nut, but

4. In 1858, architects Frederick Law Olmsted and Calvert Vaux won the commission to beautify Manhattan's Central <u>Park, to be beginning</u> construction on it the same year.

 (A) Park, to be beginning
 (B) Park, and they were beginning
 (C) Park, they began
 (D) Park and began
 (E) Park, to have begun

225

5. Elizabeth Barrett Browning's "Cry of the Children," published in 1842, denounced the use of child labor and also helping bring about legislation to prevent it.

 (A) denounced the use of child labor and also helping bring about legislation to prevent it
 (B) denouncing the use of child labor and also helping to bring about legislation to prevent it
 (C) both denounced the use of child labor and helped bring about legislation to prevent it
 (D) has been denouncing the use of child labor and also helped bring about legislation to prevent it
 (E) denounced the use of child labor and has also helped bring about legislation to prevent it

6. Farmers in many parts of Brazil have succeeded in reducing the acidity of their soil, in recent years they have substantially increased their production of food.

 (A) soil, in recent years they have substantially increased their production of food
 (B) soil, and in recent years increasing their production of food substantially
 (C) soil; and they have substantially increased their food production in recent years
 (D) soil and, in recent years, have substantially increased their production of food
 (E) soil, their food production having substantially increased in recent years

7. Although several architectural awards had been won by it, the university's new dormitory was criticized for its impractical layout.

 (A) Although several architectural awards had been won by it, the university's new dormitory was
 (B) Although it won several architectural awards, the university's new dormitory was
 (C) It won several architectural awards, but the university's new dormitory being
 (D) It won several architectural awards, despite this, the university's new dormitory
 (E) Several architectural awards were won by it, however the university's new dormitory was

8. People living cities tend to eat more processed foods than those living in rural areas, and more health problems are had by them because of that.

 (A) areas, and more health problems are had by them because of that
 (B) areas, and more health problems are thereby had by them
 (C) areas; consequently, they have more health problems
 (D) areas, thereby having more health problems
 (E) areas, so more health problems are had by them

9. From the frigid lakes of the Himalayas and the tropical forests that lie hundreds of miles to the south, India's natural resources host an astounding variety of birds and other animals.

 (A) and the tropical forests that lie
 (B) and the tropical forests lying
 (C) and the tropical forests, they lie
 (D) to the tropical forests, and they lie
 (E) to the tropical forests that lie

10. <u>Because most of the coral reefs off the coast of the Philippines have disappeared is why</u> the Filipino government has outlawed certain kinds of fishing destructive to marine life.

    (A) Because most of coral reefs off the coast of the Philippines have disappeared is the reason why
    (B) Because most of coral reefs off the coast of the Philippines have disappeared,
    (C) Most of the coral reefs off the coast of the Philippines have disappeared is the reason why
    (D) As a consequence of most of the coral reefs off the coast of the Philippines disappearing;
    (E) The disappearance of most of the coral reefs off the coast prompting

11. <u>Ronald Joffrey and Gerald Arpino founded the Joffrey Ballet School in 1953; it has since become</u> one of the world's most prestigious training centers for dance.

    (A) Ronald Joffrey and Gerald Arpino founded the Joffrey Ballet School in 1953; it has since become
    (B) Ronald Joffrey and Gerald Arpino founded the Joffrey Ballet School in 1953, and has since become
    (C) Ronald Joffrey and Gerald Arpino founded the Joffrey Ballet School in 1953; and it has since become
    (D) The Joffrey Ballet School was founded by Ronald Joffrey and Gerald Arpino in 1953, which has since become
    (E) Founded by Ronald Joffrey and Gerald Arpino, since 1953 the Joffrey Ballet school has become

12. The first boardwalk in <u>Atlantic City served as the inspiration</u> for the board game Monopoly, was constructed toward the end of the nineteenth century.

    (A) Atlantic City served as the inspiration
    (B) Atlantic City serves as the inspiration
    (C) Atlantic City, serving as the inspiration
    (D) Atlantic City, which was inspiring
    (E) Atlantic City, the inspiration

13. Europeans began to consume many new <u>food products, like eating chili peppers,</u> after trade between Europe and the Americas began in the sixteenth century.

    (A) food products, like eating chili peppers,
    (B) food products, these included chili peppers,
    (C) food products, for example when they ate chili peppers,
    (D) food products, one of these was the chili pepper,
    (E) food products, including chili peppers,

14. The majority of rebellions that occurred in Tudor England did not achieve their objectives because of the weakness of the rebels <u>and the extreme power of the reigning monarchs.</u>

    (A) and the extreme power of the reigning monarchs
    (B) and the reigning monarchs were extremely powerful
    (C) and extreme power was held by the reigning monarchs
    (D) and the reigning monarchs would hold extreme power
    (E) with reigning monarchs having extreme power

Answers: Test 4, Section 1

1. B: Fragment

The original version uses the gerund *offering* instead of a main verb and thus creates a fragment. B supplies a verb (*offered*), creating a complete sentence.

2. B: Unnecessary gerund

The construction *Because of his staunchly refusing* in the original sentence contains the gerund *refusing*, which makes the sentence unnecessarily wordy and awkward; B presents the same information in a much cleaner way by using the verb *refused*. C and D create comma splices, and E provides an incorrect logical relationship (Dryden's removal from office was a *result* of his refusal to swear allegiance; it did not occur *despite* his refusal) and includes a verb in the present tense, *refuses*, which is inconsistent with the past tense of the other verbs in the sentence (*was removed...was held*).

3. A: No error; semicolon

The original version correctly uses a semicolon to separate an independent clause and a clause begun by *however* and conveys the contrasting relationship between the two clauses (Hersheypark was first open only to employees **but** later to everyone).

4. C: Noun agreement

Since George Balanchine and Mikhail Baryshnikov are two people, they should be referred to as *choreographers*, plural, rather than *a choreographer*, singular. Although C, D, and E correctly provides the plural, D is missing a main verb, *was*, and E contains an un-colloquial construction: *responsible* is followed by the preposition *in* rather than *for*.

5. D: Comma splice; conjunction

The original version of the sentence contains two independent clauses separated by a comma – a construction that is always incorrect. B correctly places *however* after a semicolon, but it indicates a contrasting relationship between the two clauses when in fact the second clause explains the consequences of the first. C also contains a comma splice, and E includes the gerund *having*, which creates awkwardness, and fails to provide a plural noun to serve as the antecedent for the plural pronoun *their*. D correctly uses a semicolon to separate two independent clauses and conveys the correct logical relationship of consequence between the clauses.

6. C: Tense consistency

Tenses within a sentence should generally remain consistent unless there is information that clearly indicates that different events occurred at different times. In this case, the non-underlined portion of the sentence includes a verb in the simple past (*emphasized*); thus, the verb in the underlined portion must "match." C, D, and E include a verb in the correct form, *promoted*; however, D is wordy and contains a pronoun-antecedent disagreement (*they* is plural whereas *poetry* is singular), and E contains a comma splice.

7. E: Subject-verb agreement

Instruments, the subject, is plural and therefore requires a plural verb (*have* rather than *has*). Although B, C, and D present verbs in different tenses, this is not fundamentally a tense question. The present perfect (*has influenced*) in the original version of the sentence is correct because it describes a situation that began in the past and that continues into the present; only the *number* of the verb (singular *has* vs. plural *have*) is incorrect.

8. D: Dangling modifier

Who got fifteen percent of the vote? Jesse Jackson. So *Jesse Jackson*, the subject, must appear immediately after the comma. Only D and E include this construction, and E includes the gerund *having* that creates a fragment when plugged back into the sentence.

9. D: Non-essential clause

The commas around the clause *who performed...widespread* indicate that the clause can be removed from the sentence. When it is removed, however, the remainder of the sentence clearly does not make sense: *Human computers...and behind the calculations for both the return of Halley's Comet and the Manhattan Project.* In order for the sentence to make grammatical sense, a verb (*were*) must be placed immediately after the second comma. Only D contains this construction.

10. A: No error; pronoun-antecedent

Organization is a collective noun (singular) that requires a singular pronoun (*its* rather than *their*). That eliminates B and D. Of the remaining options, A is the clearest and most concise answer.

11. B: word pair

Although the original version of the sentence may seem exceedingly complicated, the question can be solved by simple recognition of the word pair *just as...so*. Since the sentence begins with *just as*, the correct answer must begin with *so*. B is the only choice that includes that word, making it the only possible answer.

12. C: Parallel structure

The two other items in the list are both nouns (*cleaner, museum guard*), so the third item should contain only a noun (*builder*) as well.

13. D: Faulty comparison

The sentence compares inventions (things) to Thomas Edison (person). In order for the sentence to be correct, things must be compared to things (*...just as important as Thomas Edison's inventions*, OR *....just as important as **those of** Thomas Edison*).

14. B: Verb consistency

The form of all the verbs in the sentence must stay consistent: since there is already one verb in the present tense (*are found*), it is incorrect for the second verb to appear as a gerund (*being*). Instead, it must match the first verb (*are established*).

15. A: Subject-verb agreement (subject – prepositional phrase – verb)

Presence, the subject, is singular and therefore requires a singular verb (*has* rather than *have*). The plural noun *paintings* before the verb is part of the prepositional phrase begun by *of*.

16. B: Word pair; verb form

So must be paired with *that*, and the sentence contains a non-underlined verb in the past tense (*received*) that the underlined verb much match. The sentence should correctly read: *The Hale-Bopp comet received **so much attention that it became** one of the most highly observed astronomical bodies in history.*

17. D: Word pair

Neither must always be paired with *nor*; here it is incorrectly paired with *or*.

18. E: No error

Because this sentence contains a subject and a verb separated from one another by a prepositional phrase, it suggests that there is a subject-verb agreement error. The plural verb *seem* agrees with the plural subject *compositions*, however. The singular pronoun *its* is also a likely error candidate; however, it correctly refers to the singular noun *world*.

19. A: Subject-verb agreement (subject – non-essential clause – verb)

The plural subject *anchors* requires a plural verb (*have* rather than *has*). The singular noun *technology*, which comes before the verb, belongs to the non-essential clause beginning with *like*.

20. D: Pronoun-antecedent

The singular pronoun *this* incorrectly refers to the plural noun *materials*. A plural pronoun (*they*) is needed instead.

21. B: More vs. most

Since two things are being compared (zinc vs. another popular decongestants), *more* rather than *most* must be used.

22. E: No error; pronoun-antecedent (collective noun)

The major concept that this question tests is pronoun agreement with a collective noun (*jury*). Since *jury* is singular, a singular pronoun (*it*) should be used. C could also be considered a trick answer since some test-takers may consider *all eager* odd, but there is nothing wrong with the construction.

23. A: Conjunction

The two clauses express opposing ideas (the study of meteorology is extremely old vs. no advances were made for a very long time). A contradictor such as *but* is therefore required.

24. C: Verb tense

The sentence clearly describes a completed action in the past, as indicated by the date 1818. The simple past (*adopted*) rather than the present perfect (*have adopted*) is therefore required.

25. D: Faulty comparison

The sentence compares tragedies (things) to a rival (person). In order to be correct, the sentence must compare things to things: *...the tragedies of Jean Racine had become considerably more successful than his rival's* **tragedies** (or: **those of** *his rival*).

26. C: Verb tense

The past perfect (*had become*) should only be used to describe an event in the past that took place *before* a second event in the past. Logically, however, Galileo could have not have become to first person to view Saturn's rings *before* he began viewing the sky through a telescope. The simple past (*became*) should thus be used instead.

27. C: Pronoun-antecedent

The pronoun *it* refers to monkeys *recognizing* themselves when they are shown a mirror. But the gerund *recognizing*, the true antecedent, doesn't appear in the sentence – only to verb *recognize*. And since a pronoun cannot refer to a verb, only a (pro)noun or gerund, *it* lacks an antecedent. The correct phrase is therefore *do so*.

28. E: No error; verb tense

The sentence includes a time period (*twentieth century*), which indicates a verb tense question; however, the only underlined verb (*marked*) is correct because it refers to a finished event in the past (the construction of the Panama Canal).

29. B: Redundancy

Formerly and *in the past* have the same meaning, so it is redundant to include both. Since *formerly* is underlined, it should be eliminated from the sentence.

30. C: Transition; logical relationship

The information in sentence 2 emphasizes the idea that the history of the computer is "relatively short" by stating that the first modern computer "was built less than a century ago." *In fact* is the most appropriate transition because its function is to emphasize.

31. B: Pronoun-antecedent; gerund

The original version of the sentence contains the gerund *being* and lacks an antecedent for the pronoun *this* – it refers to *the fact that* the ENIAC was capable of adding 5,000 numbers in a sentence, but the sentence does not contain the phrase *the fact that*; C and E both contain the same error and A; and D creates a comma splice and contains a verb (*has made*) whose tense is not consistent with the tense of the sentence's other verb, *was*. Only B eliminates the pronoun-antecedent and verb-tense problems entirely.

32. E: Paragraph organization

The previous sentence describes the ENIAC as being large and complicated; the following sentence builds on that idea by describing its unreliability. The transitional phrase in E acknowledges the idea in the previous sentence and creates a logical bridge to the following thought.

33. D: Conjunction

The second sentence provides an explanation for the first sentence; a conjunction such as *because* or is *since* is therefore required. Only B and D provide such conjunctions, and B contains a gerund (*burning*) that makes the sentence unnecessarily wordy.

34. D: Paragraph organization

Sentence 10 describes how engineers discovered a way to keep the ENIAC's vacuum tubes from burning out; the sentence in D logically expands on that idea by explaining the result of that discovery – the vacuum tubes were able to function for a longer period of time.

35. A: Paragraph organization

The sentence should be inserted before sentence 4 because it sets up the general idea (the ENIAC was an unsophisticated machine by modern standards) that is supported by specific details in the following lines (it was very heavy, it had many parts, it was difficult to program).

Test 4, Section 2

1. A: No error; would vs. will

Sentences that contain verbs in the present tense should generally contain *will* (future tense) rather than *would* (conditional). The non-underlined portion of the sentence contains a verb in the present tense (*decreases*), and so the original version, which contains *will* is correct. That eliminates C, D, and E. B contains a gerund (*conducting*), so that option can be eliminated as well.

2. B: Fragment/non-essential clause

The original version contains a gerund (*turning*) that turns the sentence into a fragment. C, D, and E also contain this error. In order to create a sentence, it is necessary to provide a conjugated verb (*turn*) and create a non-essential clause.

3. C: Unnecessary gerund; comma splice; conjunction

A and D contain the gerund *being* and can thus be eliminated; B creates a comma splice and can be eliminated as well; and E incorrectly contains a conjunction in both clauses (*whereas, but*). C correctly separates a dependent clause and an independent clause with a comma.

4. D: Verb consistency

The non-underlined portion of the sentence contains a verb in the simple past (*won*), so the verb in the underlined portion of the sentence must also be in the simple past rather than in gerund form (*began* rather than *beginning*).

5. C: Verb consistency

The phrase *published in 1842* indicates that the sentence is describing a finished action in the past and that the simple past (*denounced...helped*) is needed for both verbs. In addition, the conjunction *and* indicates that both verbs in the underlined portion of the sentence indicates that both verbs should be in the same form.

6. D: Comma splice; non-essential clause

The original version contains two independent clauses separated by a comma (comma splice) and can thus be eliminated; B and E contain unnecessary gerunds (*increasing, having*); and C incorrectly places a semicolon before *and*. Although the non-essential clause in D is placed at an unexpected point in the sentence, the remaining sentence, *Farmers in many parts of Brazil have succeeded in reducing the acidity of their soil and....have substantially increased their production of food,* makes perfect sense.

7. B: Passive voice

Both the original version and E contain a passive construction (*several architectural awards **had been/were won by it***) that is unnecessarily wordy and awkward. C contains the gerund *being*, which turns the second clause into a fragment; and D contains a comma splice. B is grammatically correct and is the clearest and most concise option.

8. C: Passive voice

A, B, and E all contain passive construction (*health problems **are had by them***), and D contains an unnecessary gerund (*having*). Although C is longer than D, it contains a conjugated verb (*have*) rather than a gerund and correctly places *consequently* after a semicolon.

9. E: Word pair

From must be paired with *to*, so A, B, and C can be eliminated. Between D and E, D creates an illogical break in the sentence, while E is clear, concise, and logical.

10. B: Redundancy

The phrase *the reason why* is redundant (if something is a reason, then by definition it is *why*). A not only contains this phase but also *because*, so it is doubly redundant and can immediately be eliminated. C is extremely awkward and also contains *the reason why*, so it can be eliminated as well. D incorrectly contains a fragment rather than an independent clause before the semicolon; and E contains a gerund (*prompting*) that creates a fragment. B is grammatically correct and is the clearest, most concise option.

11. A No error; semicolon

The original version of the sentence correctly uses a semicolon to separate two independent clauses. B does not make sense because it omits the subject in the second clause; C incorrectly uses a semicolon before *and*; in D, the pronoun *which* appears to refer to 1953 rather than to the Joffrey Ballet School; and E creates a comma splice.

12. E: Non-essential clause

The original version of the sentence contains an independent clause (*The first boardwalk in Atlantic City served as the inspiration for the board game Monopoly*) and a clause that is missing a subject (*was constructed toward the end of the nineteenth century*) – a construction that is grammatically unacceptable. B contains the same problem; C and D contain gerunds (*serving, inspiring*) that make the sentence unnecessarily wordy; and E is correct because it is clear, concise, and creates a non-essential clause that makes the sentence grammatically logical.

13. E: Logical relationship; comma splice

In the original version of the sentence, the phrase **eating** *chili peppers* is an action, not an example of a food product and is thus illogical. B and D create comma splices; C is wordy and awkward; and E correctly provides an example of a food product in a concise manner.

14. A: No error; parallel structure

The original version of the sentence is correct because the construction on either side of the conjunction *and* is fundamentally the same: *weakness **of the** rebels* vs. *extreme power **of the** reigning monarchs*. No other option contains this construction.

Test 5

Section 1

1. Ⓐ Ⓑ Ⓒ Ⓓ Ⓔ
2. Ⓐ Ⓑ Ⓒ Ⓓ Ⓔ
3. Ⓐ Ⓑ Ⓒ Ⓓ Ⓔ
4. Ⓐ Ⓑ Ⓒ Ⓓ Ⓔ
5. Ⓐ Ⓑ Ⓒ Ⓓ Ⓔ
6. Ⓐ Ⓑ Ⓒ Ⓓ Ⓔ
7. Ⓐ Ⓑ Ⓒ Ⓓ Ⓔ
8. Ⓐ Ⓑ Ⓒ Ⓓ Ⓔ
9. Ⓐ Ⓑ Ⓒ Ⓓ Ⓔ
10. Ⓐ Ⓑ Ⓒ Ⓓ Ⓔ
11. Ⓐ Ⓑ Ⓒ Ⓓ Ⓔ
12. Ⓐ Ⓑ Ⓒ Ⓓ Ⓔ
13. Ⓐ Ⓑ Ⓒ Ⓓ Ⓔ
14. Ⓐ Ⓑ Ⓒ Ⓓ Ⓔ
15. Ⓐ Ⓑ Ⓒ Ⓓ Ⓔ
16. Ⓐ Ⓑ Ⓒ Ⓓ Ⓔ
17. Ⓐ Ⓑ Ⓒ Ⓓ Ⓔ
18. Ⓐ Ⓑ Ⓒ Ⓓ Ⓔ
19. Ⓐ Ⓑ Ⓒ Ⓓ Ⓔ
20. Ⓐ Ⓑ Ⓒ Ⓓ Ⓔ
21. Ⓐ Ⓑ Ⓒ Ⓓ Ⓔ
22. Ⓐ Ⓑ Ⓒ Ⓓ Ⓔ
23. Ⓐ Ⓑ Ⓒ Ⓓ Ⓔ
24. Ⓐ Ⓑ Ⓒ Ⓓ Ⓔ
25. Ⓐ Ⓑ Ⓒ Ⓓ Ⓔ
26. Ⓐ Ⓑ Ⓒ Ⓓ Ⓔ
27. Ⓐ Ⓑ Ⓒ Ⓓ Ⓔ
28. Ⓐ Ⓑ Ⓒ Ⓓ Ⓔ
29. Ⓐ Ⓑ Ⓒ Ⓓ Ⓔ
30. Ⓐ Ⓑ Ⓒ Ⓓ Ⓔ
31. Ⓐ Ⓑ Ⓒ Ⓓ Ⓔ
32. Ⓐ Ⓑ Ⓒ Ⓓ Ⓔ
33. Ⓐ Ⓑ Ⓒ Ⓓ Ⓔ
34. Ⓐ Ⓑ Ⓒ Ⓓ Ⓔ
35. Ⓐ Ⓑ Ⓒ Ⓓ Ⓔ

Section 2

1. Ⓐ Ⓑ Ⓒ Ⓓ Ⓔ
2. Ⓐ Ⓑ Ⓒ Ⓓ Ⓔ
3. Ⓐ Ⓑ Ⓒ Ⓓ Ⓔ
4. Ⓐ Ⓑ Ⓒ Ⓓ Ⓔ
5. Ⓐ Ⓑ Ⓒ Ⓓ Ⓔ
6. Ⓐ Ⓑ Ⓒ Ⓓ Ⓔ
7. Ⓐ Ⓑ Ⓒ Ⓓ Ⓔ
8. Ⓐ Ⓑ Ⓒ Ⓓ Ⓔ
9. Ⓐ Ⓑ Ⓒ Ⓓ Ⓔ
10. Ⓐ Ⓑ Ⓒ Ⓓ Ⓔ
11. Ⓐ Ⓑ Ⓒ Ⓓ Ⓔ
12. Ⓐ Ⓑ Ⓒ Ⓓ Ⓔ
13. Ⓐ Ⓑ Ⓒ Ⓓ Ⓔ
14. Ⓐ Ⓑ Ⓒ Ⓓ Ⓔ

SECTION 1
Time – 25 Minutes
35 Questions

Directions: For each question in this section, select the best answer from among the choices given and fill in the corresponding circle on the answer sheet.

The following sentences test correctness and effectiveness of expression. Part of each sentence or the entire sentence is underlined; beneath each sentence are five ways of phrasing the underlined material. Choice A repeats the original phrasing; the other four choices are different. If you think the original phrasing produces a better sentence than any of the alternatives, select choice A; if not, select one of the other choices.

In making your selection, follow the requirements of standard written English; that is, pay attention to grammar, choice of words, sentence construction, and punctuation. Your selection should result in the most effective sentence—clear and precise, without awkwardness or ambiguity.

EXAMPLE:

Anna Robertson Moses completed her first painting <u>and she was seventy-six years old then</u>.

(A) and she was seventy-six years old then
(B) when she was seventy-six years old
(C) at age seventy-six years old
(D) upon arriving at the age of seventy-six
(E) at the time when she was seventy-six years old

1. <u>Ms. Prakash has imposed a new set of research guidelines in her classroom that is designed to prevent plagiarism.</u>

   (A) Ms. Prakash has imposed a new set of research guidelines in her classroom that is designed to prevent plagiarism.
   (B) Ms. Prakash has imposed a new set of research guidelines in her classroom for preventing plagiarism.
   (C) In order to prevent plagiarism in her classroom, Ms. Prakash has imposed a new set of research guidelines.
   (D) The prevention of plagiarism in her classroom being why Ms. Prakash has imposed a new set of research guidelines.
   (E) Wanting to prevent plagiarism has caused Ms. Prakash's imposing a new set of research guidelines.

2. A number of Mary Shelley's works suggest that the act of cooperation among <u>women, representing</u> a way to improve society.

   (A) women, representing
   (B) women, it represents
   (C) women and represent
   (D) women represents
   (E) women, which represent

3. Pablo Picasso founded the cubist <u>movement in the first half of the twentieth century to revolutionize art</u>.

   (A) movement in the first half of the twentieth century to revolutionize art
   (B) movement, and so art was revolutionized in the first half of the twentieth century
   (C) movement, which revolutionized art in the first half of the twentieth century
   (D) movement in the first half of the twentieth century, art being revolutionized by this
   (E) movement in the first half of the twentieth century and caused them to revolutionize art

236

4. Doris Lessing learned that she had been awarded the Nobel Prize for <u>Literature when she has returned</u> from grocery shopping to find reporters on her lawn.

   (A) Literature when she has returned
   (B) Literature; when she has returned
   (C) Literature when she returned
   (D) Literature; upon her return
   (E) Literature, but she would return

5. <u>The production of ceramics began in China during the Neolithic period, and continuing</u> to the present day.

   (A) The production of ceramics began in China during the Neolithic period, and continuing
   (B) The production of ceramics beginning in China during the Neolithic period and continuing
   (C) The production of ceramics, which began in China during the Neolithic period, continuing
   (D) The production of ceramics, it began in China during the Neolithic period, and has continued
   (E) The production of ceramics, having begun in China during the Neolithic period, has continued

6. <u>Former space shuttle commander Pamela Melroy retired from NASA in 2007,</u> she had successfully logged close to forty days in orbit.

   (A) Former space shuttle commander Pamela Melroy retired from NASA in 2007,
   (B) When former space shuttle commander Pamela Melroy retired from NASA in 2007,
   (C) Former space shuttle commander Pamela Melroy, who retired from NASA in 2007,
   (D) Former space shuttle commander Pamela Melroy, who retired from NASA in 2007, and
   (E) Because space shuttle commander Pamela Melroy retired from NASA in 2007,

7. 主语
<u>Opposition</u> to rodeos by animal-rights workers <u>have centered primarily on their</u> poor treatment and living conditions of the horses used in competitions.

   (A) have centered primarily on their
   (B) have centered primarily on the
   (C) have primarily centered on its
   (D) has primarily centered on its
   (E) has primarily centered on the

8. Formed by volatile compounds that can easily disintegrate, <u>outside of people's memories odors are often ephemeral.</u>

   (A) outside of people's memories odors are often ephemeral
   (B) outside of people's memories are odors that are
   (C) people's memories contain odors that are often ephemeral
   (D) odors are often ephemeral outside of people's memories
   (E) odors often being ephemeral outside of people's memories

9. It is necessary that the committee responsible for organizing the outdoor <u>concert obtain permission</u> from the city council because thousand of listeners are expected to attend.

   (A) concert obtain permission
   (B) concert obtaining permission
   (C) concert has to obtain permission
   (D) concert is granted permission
   (E) concert, who must obtain permission

10. Often advertised to promote health and reduce stress, <u>some doctors warn that dietary supplements can have harmful effects, even though they are easy to purchase</u>.

    (A) some doctors warn that dietary supplements can have harmful effects, even though they are easy to purchase

    (B) dietary supplements are easy to purchase, but it is warned by some doctors that they can have harmful effects

    (C) dietary supplements are easy to purchase, yet some doctors warn they can have harmful effects

    (D) harmful effects can be had by dietary supplements, even though they are easy to purchase, some doctors warn

    (E) the effects of some dietary supplements can be harmful some doctors warn, although they are easy to purchase

11. Sources of entertainment such as movies and books <u>are not, according to some critics, responsible for shaping a culture, only for reflecting it</u>.

    (A) are not, according to some critics, responsible for shaping a culture, only for reflecting it

    (B) not being responsible for shaping a culture, some critics say, they only reflect it

    (C) are not responsible for shaping a culture, with some critics saying they are responsible only for reflecting it

    (D) are not responsible for shaping a culture some critics say, on the contrary, they only reflect it

    (E) cannot be held responsible for shaping a culture, according to some critics; only reflecting it

The following sentences test your ability to recognize grammar and usage errors. Each sentence contains either a single error or none at all. No sentence contains more than one error. The error, if there is one, is underlined and lettered. If the sentence contains an error, select the one underlined part that must be changed in order to make the sentence correct. If the sentence is correct, select choice E. In choosing answers, follow the requirements of standard written English.

EXAMPLE:

Science fiction writer H.G. Wells, <u>the author of</u>
                                          A
more than 100 books, accurately <u>predicted</u> the
                                          B
the <u>invention</u> of television, the rise of the Internet,
        C
and <u>creating</u> the hydrogen bomb. <u>No error</u>
        D   E

○○○●○

12. Although procrastination is a <u>fundamental</u> human
                                           A
    drive, <u>but</u> anxiety about <u>it appears</u> to have arisen
             B   C
    <u>only</u> a few hundred years ago. <u>No error</u>
      D   E

13. Like William Dean Howells and Mark Twain, Henry
                    made
    James <u>makes</u> important <u>contributions to</u> the field of
            A   B
    literary theory <u>in</u> his <u>renowned</u> 1884 essay, "The Art
                      C   D
    of Fiction." <u>No error</u>
                       E

14. Lana and Tom discovered a large cave <u>exploring</u> a
                                                    A
    <u>remote</u> corner of the national park <u>whose</u> ecosystem
      B   C
    <u>they were studying</u> for a science project. <u>No error</u>
          D   E

15. <u>Because</u> prices are continuing <u>to rise</u>, the country's
       A   B
    citizens <u>have begun</u> to hoard light bulbs and canned
                  C
    food for fear that these products <u>will become</u>
                                           D
    unaffordable. <u>No error</u>
                        E

16. While doctors must <u>increasingly</u> <u>depend on</u>
                                              A
    computers <u>more often</u>, they can also <u>use</u> such devices
                  B   C
    <u>to help</u> patients in new and unforeseen ways. <u>No error</u>
      D   E

17. Just <u>being</u> exposed to words <u>associated with</u> money
           A   B
    <u>seems</u> to cause people to become more independent
      C   *to help*
    and less inclined <u>in helping</u> others. <u>No error</u>
                          D   E

18. Geneticist Barbara McClintock <u>won</u> the 1983 Nobel
                                      A
    Prize in Physiology or Medicine <u>for</u> her discovery of
                                        B
    the process <u>by which</u> chromosomes exchange
                    C
    information <u>during</u> cell division. <u>No error</u>
                    D   E

19. Louise Erdrich's fiction and poetry <u>draws on</u> her
                                            A
    Chippewa heritage <u>to examine</u> complex familial
                          B
    relationships <u>among</u> Native Americans as they reflect
                      C
    <u>on</u> issues of identity in American culture. <u>No error</u>
      D   E

20. Pharmacists <u>typically</u> recommend that medications
                    A   *these*
    <u>not be stored</u> at high temperatures <u>because this</u> can
          B   C
    cause their active ingredients to lose <u>their</u> potency.
                                              D
    <u>No error</u>
        E

21. Better remembered <u>for ending</u> slavery, Abraham
A
to impose
   Lincoln <u>was</u> also the first president <u>imposing</u> an
B   C
   income tax and issue currency <u>not backed by</u> gold or
D
   silver. <u>No error</u>
E

22. Unlike <u>other organisms</u>, the eyes of many predatory
A
   animals are designed <u>to enhance</u> depth perception
B
   <u>rather than</u> to maximize the field <u>of</u> vision. <u>No error</u>
C   D   E

23. Legendary horseback rider Frank Hopkins claimed

   <u>to have won</u> over four hundred races, many <u>of which</u>
A   B
   <u>were invented</u> by Hopkins <u>himself</u>. <u>No error</u>
C   D   E

24. Before playwright Lynn Nottage <u>has been</u> awarded
A
   a Pulitzer Prize <u>in</u> 2009, seven of her plays <u>were</u>
B   C
   <u>successfully</u> produced in off-Broadway theaters.
D
   <u>No error</u>
E

25. Snowbush, which can lie <u>dormant</u> in soil for centuries,
A
   has <u>so adapted to</u> extreme weather conditions that
B
is
   neither intense heat nor bitter cold <u>are</u> capable of
C
   destroying <u>it</u>. <u>No error</u>
D   E

26. The origins <u>of</u> the <u>koala bear</u> <u>are</u> unclear, although
it   A   B
   <u>they</u> almost certainly descended <u>from</u> a terrestrial
C   D
   wombat-like animals millions of years ago. <u>No error</u>
E

27. Eugene O'Neill <u>hardly began</u> his career <u>as</u> a
had
A   B
   playwright <u>when</u> in 1920 he was awarded the Pulitzer
C
   Prize for *Beyond the Horizon*, his first <u>published</u> play.
D
   <u>No error</u>
E

28. Though <u>neither had</u> originally planned to <u>do so</u>,
A   B
   Cranston and Nathaniel Paschall began <u>working for</u>
C
   their family's airplane manufacturing company
who?
   company following <u>his decision</u> to train as an aviation
D
   engineer. <u>No error</u>
E

29. <u>According to</u> many economists, statistics can
A
   frequently be useful <u>in revealing</u> phenomena that
B
perceptible   *merely*
   would not otherwise be <u>perceptive</u> from <u>mere</u>
C   D
   observation. <u>No error</u>
E

Directions: The following passage is an early draft of an essay. Some parts of the passage need to be rewritten.

Read the passage and select the best answer for the questions that follow. Some questions are about particular sentences or parts of sentences and ask you to improve sentence structure or word choice. Other questions ask you to consider organization and development. In choosing you answer, follow the requirements of standard written English.

Questions 30-35 refer to the following passage.

My grandfather is the most formal person I have ever met. (1) He still put on a three-piece suit and tie every day. (2) This is despite the fact that he retired from his job almost ten years ago. (3) It doesn't matter to him because he wants to look "presentable," as he says, and it doesn't matter to him if he's the only person in the room who's dressed up. (4) Sometimes I think it drives my grandmother crazy because she wants him to be more relaxed, but I can't imagine him wearing jeans and a t-shirt. (5)

Even though I find some of my grandfather's habits odd, I understand that they're an important part of who he is. (6) For example, every morning he lines up all his pairs of shoes and polishes them one by one. (7) Ever since I was little, I've always associated the odor of shoe polish with my grandfather. (8) Whenever I smell it, I can't help but remember how, when I was five years old, I was always being really excited to help him to do it. (9) I don't think that polishing shoes is so exciting now. (10) Nevertheless, I can see how comforting the ritual is to my grandfather.

(11) I see that people respect him because he is so polite. (12) When my grandfather takes me out to dinner at the same restaurant he's been going to for forty years and shakes hands with the owner, it's obvious that he appreciates being treated so courteously. (13) I might never be as formal as my grandfather, but watching him has taught me a lot about how to treat other people.

30. Which of the following is the best way to revise and combine the underlined portion of sentences 2 and 3 (reproduced below)?

    He still put on a three-piece suit and tie every day. This is despite the fact that he retired from his job almost ten years ago.

    (A) every day, in spite of his retiring from his job almost ten years ago
    (B) every day, even though he retired from his job almost ten years ago
    (C) every day, however he retired from his job almost ten years ago
    (D) every day, with his retirement from his job now occurring almost ten years ago
    (E) every day, but ten years ago is when his retirement from his job happened

31. In context, which of the following is best to use instead of "it" in sentence 4?

    (A) his wardrobe
    (B) the room
    (C) his job
    (D) the person
    (E) the polish

32. In context, which is the best version of sentence 8 (reproduced below)?

    Whenever I smell it, I can't help but remember how, when I was five years old, I was always being really excited to help him to do it.

    (A) when I was five years old and always really excited to help him do it
    (B) when I was five years old, it was exciting to me to help him do it
    (C) at five years old, it was always really exciting to help him do it
    (D) at five years old, polishing his shoes was really exciting to me
    (E) at the age of five, I was always really excited to help him polish his shoes

241

33. An important strategy used in the second paragraph is to

    (A) offer an detailed criticism of an offensive habit
    (B) suggest a novel response to a unexpected occurrence
    (C) describe a personal recollection to illustrate a theme of the essay
    (D) compare and contrast reactions to a difficult situation
    (E) indicate that a particular response was uncalled for

34. Which of the following would be best to insert after sentence 10?

    (A) My grandfather prefers to wear leather shoes because he is convinced that other kinds are too casual.
    (B) Sometime in the 1950s was when my grandfather bought his first jar of shoe polish.
    (C) I think that my grandmother is often tempted to leave when he opens the jar because the smell is so strong.
    (D) Nowadays, I prefer to help him work in the garden or cook dinner instead.
    (E) He closes his eyes and hums, looking more relaxed than I've ever seen him.

35. Which of the following is the best way to revise the underlined portion of sentence 12 (reproduced below)?

    I see that people respect him because he is so polite.

    (A) On the other hand, I see that people respect him
    (B) I also see that people respect him
    (C) I see, however, that people would respect him
    (D) Nonetheless, I think that people will respect him
    (E) Similarly, people respected him

SECTION 2
Time – 10 Minutes
14 Questions

Directions: For each question in this section, select the best answer from among the choices given and fill in the corresponding circle on the answer sheet.

The following sentences test correctness and effectiveness of expression. Part of each sentence or the entire sentence is underlined; beneath each sentence are five ways of phrasing the underlined material. Choice A repeats the original phrasing; the other four choices are different. If you think the original phrasing produces a better sentence than any of the alternatives, select choice A; if not, select one of the other choices.

In making your selection, follow the requirements of standard written English; that is, pay attention to grammar, choice of words, sentence construction, and punctuation. Your selection should result in the most effective sentence—clear and precise, without awkwardness or ambiguity.

EXAMPLE:

○●○○○

Anna Robertson Moses completed her first painting <u>and she was seventy-six years old then</u>.

(A) and she was seventy-six years old then
(B) when she was seventy-six years old
(C) at age seventy-six years old
(D) upon arriving at the age of seventy-six
(E) at the time when she was seventy-six years old

1. Many people who stutter find that their speech problems are aggravated <u>and they find themselves</u> in stressful situations.

   (A) and they find themselves
   (B) and their finding themselves
   (C) when they find themselves
   (D) with their finding themselves
   (E) they find themselves

2. My cousin Alexa's dog knows far more tricks than mine because <u>she has been working on this</u> since the beginning of last summer.

   (A) she has been working on this
   (B) she has been teaching him to talk
   (C) of her doing it
   (D) of teaching him to talk
   (E) she has been teaching him to do it

3. Because it is located in a densely populated area of the city, <u>the stadium has undergone numerous renovations over the years not originally foreseen</u>.

   (A) the stadium has undergone numerous renovations over the years not originally foreseen
   (B) the stadium has undergone numerous renovations over the years, but this was not originally foreseen
   (C) numerous unforeseen renovations being made to the stadium over the years
   (D) numerous unforeseen renovations having been made to the stadium over the years
   (E) the stadium has, over the years, undergone numerous unforeseen renovations

4. Gravity is the dominant force on <u>earth, without it many common chemical processes would behave very differently</u>.

   (A) earth, without it many common chemical processes would behave very differently
   (B) earth, without this many common chemical processes would behave very differently
   (C) earth; many common chemical processes would behave very differently without it
   (D) earth, without it many common chemical processes will behave very differently
   (E) earth; without this many common chemical processes being very different

243

5. As a student, paleontologist Roy Chapman rarely participated in excavations but instead studied piles of fossils <u>and he gained a thorough understanding of dinosaur bone structure</u>.

    (A) and has gained a thorough understanding of dinosaur bone structure
    (B) before his thorough understanding of dinosaur bone structure was gained
    (C) and gaining a thorough understanding of dinosaur bone structure
    (D) but a thorough understanding of dinosaur bone structure was gained by him
    (E) in order to gain a thorough understanding of dinosaur bone structure

6. Often nicknamed the daddy longlegs, the harvestman has limbs that are nearly twice as long <u>as those of other spiders</u>.

    (A) as those of other spiders
    (B) like those of other spiders are long
    (C) just as other spiders have long legs
    (D) as other spiders, who also have long legs
    (E) as those of other spiders' legs

7. <u>There are numerous kinds of redwoods, the shortest of these are</u> still capable of growing to more than two hundred feet tall.

    (A) There are numerous kinds of redwoods, the shortest of these are
    (B) Numerous kinds of redwoods, of which the shortest are
    (C) There are numerous kinds of redwoods; the shortest of them being
    (D) There are numerous kinds of redwoods, the shortest of which is
    (E) Although there are numerous kinds of redwoods, the shortest of which is

8. Computer programs devoted to facial recognition can determine human emotions by following face movements <u>and linking its readings</u> with a database of expressions.

    (A) and linking its readings
    (B) and linking their readings
    (C) and they link their readings
    (D) and its readings are thereby linked
    (E) and their readings, which are linked

9. George Westinghouse, a pioneer in the electrical industry, <u>created his first major invention, the rotary steam engine,</u> before the age of twenty.

    (A) created his first major invention, the rotary steam engine,
    (B) created his first major invention, it was the rotary steam engine,
    (C) the rotary steam engine was his invention and was created
    (D) the rotary steam engine created by him, his first major invention
    (E) his first major invention, the rotary steam engine, was created

10. Precise, unforgiving, and frequently unnatural, <u>no artistic pursuit is more physically or mentally demanding than ballet.</u>

    (A) no artistic pursuit is more physically or mentally demanding than ballet
    (B) the physical and mental demands of ballet making it the most demanding of artistic pursuits
    (C) ballet's physical and mental challenges have made it the most demanding artistic pursuit
    (D) ballet, which is more physically and mentally demanding than any other artistic pursuit
    (E) ballet is the most physically and mentally demanding of artistic pursuits

11. In Medieval Europe, the Black Plague <u>so devastated the working population, therefore wages were forced to rise and the middle class began</u> to emerge.

(A) so devastated the working population, therefore wages were forced to rise and the middle class began
(B) devastated the working population and so forcing wages to rise and the middle class beginning
(C) was so devastating to the working population; in this regard, it forced wages to rise and the middle class had begun
(D) was so devastating to the working population, it forced wages to rise and the middle class began
(E) devastated the working population; wages were thus forced to rise and the middle class began

12. Higher education in the United States has undergone radical changes over the past hundred <u>years, being that it evolved from a system consisting primarily of rote memorization of classics to one covering</u> a vast number of disciplines.

(A) years, being that it evolved from a system consisting primarily of rote memorization of classics to one covering
(B) years because of it evolving from a system consisting primarily of rote memorization of classics with one covering
(C) years; in this sense, it evolved from a system consisting primarily of rote memorization of classics to one covering
(D) years: it evolved from a system consisting primarily of rote memorization of classics to one covering
(E) years because it evolved from a system that consisted primarily of rote memorization of classics to one having covered

13. The dam was declared a threat to the region <u>because, if it eroded internally, they could be put in danger</u>.

(A) because, if it eroded internally, they could be put in danger
(B) because its eroding internally could be dangerous to them
(C) and if it eroded internally, they would be endangered by this
(D) for its internal erosion might possibly pose a danger to them
(E) because its internal erosion could endanger residents of surrounding areas

14. Some of the artist's ideas seem mainly intended to challenge conventional wisdom about painting, <u>and many critics insist that they can be</u> implemented in a practical way.

(A) and many critics insist that they can be
(B) many critics insist they can be
(C) not, as many critics insist, to be
(D) not what many critics insist, it can be
(E) but many critics insist it can be

Answers: Test 5, Section 1

1. C: Misplaced modifier

The original version implies that the *classroom* was intended to prevent plagiarism; C makes clear that the *guidelines* were actually intended to do so.

2. D: Gerund

The original version is a fragment because it contains a gerund (*representing*) rather than a conjugated verb (*represents*). It also contains an comma that incorrectly separates the subject from the verb. D correctly provides a conjugated verb and removes the comma.

3. C: Misplaced modifier

The original version of the sentence implies that that the purpose of the *twentieth century* was to revolutionize art. C makes clear that this was the purpose of the *cubist movement*. Although answer containing *which* are often wrong, in this case *which* is correct because it refers to the singular noun (*movement*) that appears immediately before it.

4. C: Verb tense

The sentence describes a finished action in the past, and so a verb in the simple past (*returned*) is required.

5. E: Verb consistency; non-essential clause

The original version of the sentence contains an unnecessary verb shift (*began...continuing*) and thus creates an non-parallel structure. The correct version, E, fixes this error by rearranging the sentence to create a non-essential clause. Although the non-essential clause contains a gerund (*having*), the rest of the sentence makes grammatical sense when the clause is removed: *The production of ceramics...has continued to the present day.*

6. B: Comma splice

The original version of the sentence incorrectly contains two independent clauses separated by a comma; C and D contain improperly used non-essential clauses; E makes the first clause dependent by adding the conjunction *because*, but it does not create a logical relationship between the two clauses; and B is correct because it creates a logical relationship between the two clauses while eliminating the comma splice and creating a dependent clause (*When former space shuttle commander Pamela Melroy retired from NASA in 2007*).

7. E: Subject-verb agreement

Opposition, the subject of the sentence, is singular and requires a singular verb (*has* rather than *have*), eliminating A, B, and C. The singular pronoun *its* in D is incorrect because it refers to the plural noun *rodeos*.

8. D: Dangling Modifier

What is formed by volatile compounds that can easily disintegrate? Odors. So *odors*, the subject, must appear immediately after the comma. That leaves D and E; however, E contains the gerund *being*, which creates a fragment.

9. A: Subjunctive

The original version of the sentence correctly uses the subjunctive to indicate necessity (*it is necessary that the committee **obtain***, NOT *the committee **obtains***). The original version of the sentence is therefore correct, as is often the case when the subjunctive is tested. The trick answer is D because *committee* (singular) would typically require the verb *obtains*. The *–s* at the end of the verb is incorrect only because the subjunctive is required.

10. C: Dangling modifier

What is often advertised to promote health and reduce stress? Dietary supplements. So *dietary supplements*, the subject, must appear immediately after the comma. The leaves B and C, but B contains a wordy and passive construction (*it **is** warned **by** some doctors*).

11. A: Non-essential clause

The original version contains a non-essential clause at an unexpected point in the sentence but is the most concise and grammatically correct option. B contains a fragment; C is unnecessarily wordy and contains an ambiguous pronoun (*they* could refer to either *sources of entertainment* or to *critics*) D contains a comma splice; and the semicolon in E does not separate two independent clauses.

12. B: Double conjunction

Only one conjunction (*although* or *but*) should be used in the sentence. The underlined conjunction, B, should therefore be eliminated entirely.

13. A: Verb tense

The date *1884* clearly indicates that a verb in the past (*made*) rather than the present (*makes*) is required.

14. A: Misplaced modifier

Because *exploring* is placed immediately after *cave*, it sounds as if the cave – rather than Lana and Tom – were exploring the national park. In order to fix the sentence, it would be necessary to make clear that Lana and Tom were the ones doing the exploring: *Lana and Tom discovered a large cave while **they were** exploring a remote corner of the national park...*

15. E: No error

The conjunction *because* in A provides an appropriate logical relationship – it provides an explanation for the information in the second clause; in B, the infinitive *to increase* rather than the gerund *increasing* is correctly used after *continuing*; the present perfect (*have begun*) in C is correct because the sentence describes an event that is continuing into the present; and *will* rather than *would* is correctly used in D.

16. B: Redundancy

Increasingly and *more often* mean the same thing, so it is unnecessary to include both in the sentence.

17. D: Gerund vs. infinitive

Inclined should always be followed by an infinitive (*to help*) rather than a gerund (*helping*).

18. E: No error

The inclusion of the date 1983 in the sentence suggests a verb-tense error. Since the verb *won* is correctly given in the simple past, however, the answer is likely to be E. The trick answer is C, *by which*, because many test-takers will believe that it sounds odd. In fact, answers that include the construction *preposition + which* are typically correct.

19. A: Subject-verb agreement

The sentence contains a compound subject (*fiction **and** poetry*), which requires a plural verb (*draw*) rather than a singular verb (*draws*).

20. C: Antecedent-pronoun

The pronoun *this* (singular) refers to *high temperatures* (plural). In order to fix the sentence, the pronoun must be made plural (*these*), or for maximum clarity, removed entirely and replaced with the noun it refers to (*the heat*).

21. C: Gerund vs. infinitive

Standard usage requires that the infinitive (*to impose*) rather than the gerund (*imposing*) be used.

22. A: Faulty comparison

The sentence incorrectly compares *eyes* (things) to *other organisms* (living creatures). In order for the sentence to be made correct, eyes must be compared to eyes. The sentence should thus read, *Unlike **the eyes of** other organisms...* (or: *Unlike **those of** other organisms...*)

23. E: No error

This sentence contains several potentially tricky answers: A, B, and D could all be heard as sounding slightly "off." A contains an infinitive (*to have*), however, and when the gerund (*having*) is plugged in, it sounds distinctly worse; B contains the construction *preposition + which*, which may sound odd but is typically correct; and *himself* in D is simply there for emphasis.

24. A: Verb tense (present perfect vs. simple past)

The description of a finished action in the past (Lynn Nottage's reception of the Pulitzer Prize occurred once) indicates that the simple past (*was*) rather than the present perfect (*has been*) is required.

25. B: Subject-verb agreement

When *neither...nor* is tested with subject-verb agreement, the rule is that the verb always agrees with the noun after *nor*. Since *bitter cold* is singular, the verb that follows it should be singular as well (*is* rather than *are*).

26. C: Pronoun-antecedent: agreement

The plural pronoun *they* incorrectly refers to the singular noun *koala bear*; the singular *it* is required instead.

27. A: Verb tense

Eugene O'Neill clearly began his career as a playwright before he won the Pulitzer Prize; the past perfect (*had begun*

28. D: Ambiguous antecedent

The pronoun *his* could refer to either Nathaniel or Cranston, but the sentence does not make clear which one.

29. D: Diction

Perceptive means "able to perceive well" and is generally used to describe a person -- statistics themselves cannot possess this quality. The correct word is *perceptible*, which means *able to be perceived*. This makes sense because the sentence refers to *subtle phenomena*, which would normally be difficult to perceive.

30. B: wordiness

B is the most concise grammatically correct option. A and D contain unnecessary gerunds (*retiring, occurring*); B incorrectly places a comma rather than a semicolon before *however*; and E incorrectly contains a verb in the present (*is*) to refer to an event in the past.

31. A: Paragraph organization

The first paragraph presents the idea that the author's grandfather likes to dress formally, and the preceding sentence includes the words *dressed up* – the word *it* in sentence 4 thus refers to the grandfather's clothing, i.e. his wardrobe.

32. E: Antecedent-pronoun; dangling modifier

The pronoun *it* in A, B, and C lacks an antecedent – it refers to the act of *polishing his shoes*, but that phrase does not actually appear in the sentence. In addition, C and D contain dangling modifiers (who was five years old? I. But *I* does not appear immediately after the comma). E eliminates both the dangling modification and the missing antecedent.

33. C: Paragraph organization

In the second paragraph, the author describes a specific memory – helping to polish his grandfather's shoes – to support the idea that the grandfather takes great care of his appearance, and that making sure he appears well-dressed is a significant part of who he is -- in other words, a major theme of the essay.

34. D: Paragraph organization

In sentence 10, the author states that (s)he no longer wants to help polish shoes; D provides an example of another activity that the author would rather help his/her grandfather with.

35. B: Paragraph organization

The main idea of the third paragraph simply continues the main idea of the essay – that the grandfather's sense of formality plays a positive role in his life. Since there is no contradiction between the end of the second paragraph and the beginning of the third, A, C, and D can be eliminated. E does not make sense because the word *similarly* implies a comparison where none is being made, and the verb *respected* (past tense) does not match the tense of the rest of the passage (present tense).

Test 5, Section 2

1. C: Conjunction

The conjunction *when* is necessary to specify the relationship between the two clauses. The original version of the sentence is also a run-on because no comma is provided before the coordinating conjunction *and*.

2. B: Antecedent-pronoun

In the original version of the sentence, the pronoun *this* lacks an antecedent – although it is implied that Alexa has been *teaching her dog tricks* since last summer, that phrase never actually appears in the sentence. Only B and D include the phrase, and D includes an unnecessary gerund (*teaching*).

3. E: Misplaced modifier

The original version of the sentence implies that the *years* rather than the *renovations* were unforeseen. E corrects this error in logic. The singular pronoun *this* in B disagrees with its plural antecedent (*renovations*); and C and D both contain gerunds (*being, having*) that create fragments.

4. C: Comma splice

The original version of the sentence incorrectly uses a comma to separate two independent clauses, whereas C correctly uses a semicolon to separate the clauses. B and D also contain comma splices, and D also contains a verb in the wrong tense (*will*); the semicolon in E does not separate two independent clauses.

5. E: Run-on; passive voice

A, C, and D create run-on sentences (two independent clauses joined by a FANBOYS conjunction but lacking a comma before the conjunction), and B contains the passive voice (*understanding was gained*). E makes clear the relationship between the two parts of the sentence: Chapman studied piles of bones because he wanted to gain a thorough understanding of bone structure.

6. A: No error; faulty comparison

The original version of the sentence correctly compares **the limbs** *of the harvestman* to **the limbs** of other spiders.

7. D: Comma splice

The original version of the sentence incorrectly uses a comma to separate two independent clauses; D remedies this error by transforming the second clause into a dependent clause. B and E create fragments; and the semicolon is C does not separate two independent clauses.

8. B: Antecedent-pronoun

In the original version of the sentence, the singular pronoun *it* is incorrectly used to refer to the plural noun *programs*. The plural pronoun *they* is required instead. B is correct because it keeps *linking* parallel to *following* and provides the correct pronoun.

9. A: Non-essential clause

The sentence contains two non-essential clauses (*One of Thomas Edison's main rivals…the rotary steam engine*), making it somewhat wordy but grammatically correct. Answer choices that contain properly used non-essential clauses are generally correct.

10. E: Dangling modifier

What is precise, unforgiving, and frequently unnatural? Ballet. So *ballet*, the subject, must follow the comma. That eliminates A, B, and C; D can also be eliminated because it creates a fragment.

11. E: Comma/semicolon

In the original version of the sentence, a comma rather than a semicolon is used to separate two independent clauses; B contains two unnecessary gerunds (*forcing, beginning*); C is excessively wordy and does not keep the tense of the verbs consistent (*forced* vs. *had begun*); and D incorrectly places a comma between two independent clauses. Only E correctly uses a semicolon to separate two independent clauses.

12. D: Parallel structure; unnecessary use of gerund

The original version of the sentence can be eliminated because it contains the gerund *being*. B and E can also be eliminated because they contain unnecessary gerunds (*evolving, having*). Although C and D are both grammatically acceptable, D is correct because it is more concise: the phrase *in this sense* in C is simply unnecessary. In D, the colon, which appears very occasionally in answer choices, is here used correctly to both to set off an explanation (colons are not only for lists!) and to follow a full sentence. It also contains the most common correction (*because*) for the awkward phrasing *being that*.

13. E: Pronoun-antecedent: missing antecedent

In the original version of the sentence, it is implied that *they* refers to the residents of surrounding areas, but those words do not actually appear in the sentence. Only E states precisely who "they" are.

14. C: Conjunction; non-essential clause

The original version of the sentence provides an illogical relationship between the clauses: they clearly contradict one another, so the conjunction *and* is inappropriate. E contains a more logical conjunction but creates a pronoun-antecedent disagreement (the singular *it* refers to the plural noun *ideas*). B contains a comma splice and is excessively awkward. C is the clearest, most concise version of the sentence; it also contains properly used non-essential clause, which typically signals a correct answer.

Test 6

Section 1

1. Ⓐ Ⓑ Ⓒ Ⓓ Ⓔ
2. Ⓐ Ⓑ Ⓒ Ⓓ Ⓔ
3. Ⓐ Ⓑ Ⓒ Ⓓ Ⓔ
4. Ⓐ Ⓑ Ⓒ Ⓓ Ⓔ
5. Ⓐ Ⓑ Ⓒ Ⓓ Ⓔ
6. Ⓐ Ⓑ Ⓒ Ⓓ Ⓔ
7. Ⓐ Ⓑ Ⓒ Ⓓ Ⓔ
8. Ⓐ Ⓑ Ⓒ Ⓓ Ⓔ
9. Ⓐ Ⓑ Ⓒ Ⓓ Ⓔ
10. Ⓐ Ⓑ Ⓒ Ⓓ Ⓔ
11. Ⓐ Ⓑ Ⓒ Ⓓ Ⓔ
12. Ⓐ Ⓑ Ⓒ Ⓓ Ⓔ
13. Ⓐ Ⓑ Ⓒ Ⓓ Ⓔ
14. Ⓐ Ⓑ Ⓒ Ⓓ Ⓔ
15. Ⓐ Ⓑ Ⓒ Ⓓ Ⓔ
16. Ⓐ Ⓑ Ⓒ Ⓓ Ⓔ
17. Ⓐ Ⓑ Ⓒ Ⓓ Ⓔ
18. Ⓐ Ⓑ Ⓒ Ⓓ Ⓔ
19. Ⓐ Ⓑ Ⓒ Ⓓ Ⓔ
20. Ⓐ Ⓑ Ⓒ Ⓓ Ⓔ
21. Ⓐ Ⓑ Ⓒ Ⓓ Ⓔ
22. Ⓐ Ⓑ Ⓒ Ⓓ Ⓔ
23. Ⓐ Ⓑ Ⓒ Ⓓ Ⓔ
24. Ⓐ Ⓑ Ⓒ Ⓓ Ⓔ
25. Ⓐ Ⓑ Ⓒ Ⓓ Ⓔ
26. Ⓐ Ⓑ Ⓒ Ⓓ Ⓔ
27. Ⓐ Ⓑ Ⓒ Ⓓ Ⓔ
28. Ⓐ Ⓑ Ⓒ Ⓓ Ⓔ
29. Ⓐ Ⓑ Ⓒ Ⓓ Ⓔ
30. Ⓐ Ⓑ Ⓒ Ⓓ Ⓔ
31. Ⓐ Ⓑ Ⓒ Ⓓ Ⓔ
32. Ⓐ Ⓑ Ⓒ Ⓓ Ⓔ
33. Ⓐ Ⓑ Ⓒ Ⓓ Ⓔ
34. Ⓐ Ⓑ Ⓒ Ⓓ Ⓔ
35. Ⓐ Ⓑ Ⓒ Ⓓ Ⓔ

Section 2

1. Ⓐ Ⓑ Ⓒ Ⓓ Ⓔ
2. Ⓐ Ⓑ Ⓒ Ⓓ Ⓔ
3. Ⓐ Ⓑ Ⓒ Ⓓ Ⓔ
4. Ⓐ Ⓑ Ⓒ Ⓓ Ⓔ
5. Ⓐ Ⓑ Ⓒ Ⓓ Ⓔ
6. Ⓐ Ⓑ Ⓒ Ⓓ Ⓔ
7. Ⓐ Ⓑ Ⓒ Ⓓ Ⓔ
8. Ⓐ Ⓑ Ⓒ Ⓓ Ⓔ
9. Ⓐ Ⓑ Ⓒ Ⓓ Ⓔ
10. Ⓐ Ⓑ Ⓒ Ⓓ Ⓔ
11. Ⓐ Ⓑ Ⓒ Ⓓ Ⓔ
12. Ⓐ Ⓑ Ⓒ Ⓓ Ⓔ
13. Ⓐ Ⓑ Ⓒ Ⓓ Ⓔ
14. Ⓐ Ⓑ Ⓒ Ⓓ Ⓔ

SECTION 1
Time – 25 Minutes
35 Questions

Directions: For each question in this section, select the best answer from among the choices given and fill in the corresponding circle on the answer sheet.

The following sentences test correctness and effectiveness of expression. Part of each sentence or the entire sentence is underlined; beneath each sentence are five ways of phrasing the underlined material. Choice A repeats the original phrasing; the other four choices are different. If you think the original phrasing produces a better sentence than any of the alternatives, select choice A; if not, select one of the other choices.

In making your selection, follow the requirements of standard written English; that is, pay attention to grammar, choice of words, sentence construction, and punctuation. Your selection should result in the most effective sentence—clear and precise, without awkwardness or ambiguity.

EXAMPLE:

○●○○○

Anna Robertson Moses completed her first painting and she was seventy-six years old then.

(A) and she was seventy-six years old then
(B) when she was seventy-six years old
(C) at age seventy-six years old
(D) upon arriving at the age of seventy-six
(E) at the time when she was seventy-six years old

1. Florida was the site of some of the first European settlements in North America yet increasing its population very slowly after it became a state.

(A) yet increasing
(B) yet has increased
(C) and increases
(D) but increased
(E) it increased

2. The designers of Disney's Animal Kingdom left the parking lots as bleak as possible because of wanting to deliberately heighten the contrast visitors felt when entering the lush, wooded zoo.

(A) because of wanting to deliberately heighten the contrast
(B) and they wanted to heighten the contrast deliberately
(C) because they deliberately wanted to heighten the contrast
(D) for they deliberately want to heighten the contrast
(E) because it was deliberately wanted by them to heighten the contrast

3. Psychology professor Daryl Bem insists that ESP does exist, which has led to his becoming a highly controversial figure in the scientific community.

(A) exist, which has led to his becoming
(B) exist and becoming
(C) exist and his becoming
(D) exist, this has caused his becoming
(E) exist; therefore, he has become

253

4. Before they became a team, Richard Rogers and Oscar <u>Hammerstein, writing hit musicals in the 1950s and collaborating</u> with other partners: Rogers with Lorenz Hart and Hammerstein with Jerome Kern.

   (A) Hammerstein, writing hit musicals in the 1950s and collaborating
   (B) Hammerstein not only wrote hit musicals in the 1950s, in addition they collaborated
   (C) Hammerstein wrote hit musicals in the 1950s, but they also collaborate
   (D) Hammerstein, writing hit musicals in the 1950s, and they also collaborated
   (E) Hammerstein, who wrote hit musicals in the 1950s, had collaborated

5. One major difference between lowland Mayan rituals <u>and other ancient peoples</u>, some scholars believe, is that the former developed in relative isolation.

   (A) and other ancient peoples
   (B) and the rituals of other ancient peoples
   (C) as compared to other ancient people
   (D) with that of other ancient peoples
   (E) with other ancient peoples

6. The city's industrial economy has weakened significantly over the past decade, <u>leading to an overwhelming loss of manufacturing jobs</u>.

   (A) leading to an overwhelming loss of manufacturing jobs
   (B) overwhelmingly this led to a loss of manufacturing jobs
   (C) as a result there was an overwhelming loss of manufacturing jobs
   (D) the loss of manufacturing jobs was thus overwhelming
   (E) consequently an overwhelming loss of manufacturing jobs had resulted

7. Several recent modifications made to fishing gear <u>has helped to limit</u> accidental catches of endangered marine animals.

   (A) has helped to limit
   (B) have helped to limit
   (C) has helped in limiting
   (D) have helped with limiting
   (E) helping to limit

8. At the beginning of every rehearsal, the actors prepare by warming up their voices, stretching their bodies, and <u>he or she imagines how their characters would move</u>.

   (A) he or she imagines how their characters would move
   (B) they imagine how their characters would move
   (C) their imagination of their characters' movements
   (D) imagining their characters' movements
   (E) their characters' movements are imagined by them

9. Gloria Steinem has often been singled out for her work in the women's <u>movement, in reality</u> she was just one of many leaders.

   (A) movement, in reality
   (B) movement, however in reality
   (C) movement; in reality
   (D) movement, and in reality
   (E) movement; but in reality

10. <u>The health insurance package proposed by the company has been tentatively approved by their union leaders</u>.

   (A) The health insurance package proposed by the company has been tentatively approved by their union leaders.

   (B) The health insurance package proposed by the company having been tentatively approved by their union leaders.

   (C) The company has proposed a health insurance package, and their union leaders have tentatively approved this.

   (D) The health insurance package proposed by the company, which has been tentatively approved by union leaders.

   (E) Union leaders have tentatively approved the health insurance package proposed by the company.

11. Once known to live throughout much of Europe and North America, <u>the destruction of the gray wolf's natural habitat has caused its population to decline</u>.

   (A) the destruction of its natural habitat has caused the number of gray wolves to decline

   (B) the decline of the gray wolf population is attributable to the destruction of its habitat

   (C) the gray wolf has seen its population decline because of the destruction of its habitat

   (D) the population of the gray wolf has declined, and this is because their natural habitat has been destroyed

   (E) the gray wolf's population has declined because they destroyed its natural habitat

The following sentences test your ability to recognize grammar and usage errors. Each sentence contains either a single error or none at all. No sentence contains more than one error. The error, if there is one, is underlined and lettered. If the sentence contains an error, select the one underlined part that must be changed in order to make the sentence correct. If the sentence is correct, select choice E. In choosing answers, follow the requirements of standard written English.

EXAMPLE:

Science fiction writer H.G. Wells, <u>the author of</u>
                          A

more than 100 books, accurately <u>predicted</u> the
                             B

the <u>invention</u> of television, the rise of the Internet,
    C

and <u>creating</u> the hydrogen bomb. <u>No error</u>
      D   E

○○○●○

12. While <u>there is</u> few new facts remaining <u>to be</u>
          A   B

unearthed about Abraham Lincoln, analyses of his

presidency <u>continue</u> to appear very <u>frequently</u>.
              C   D

<u>No error</u>
   E

13. <u>Along</u> the banks of the Mississippi are levees <u>they</u>
    A   B

remove the natural <u>protection of</u> the wetlands and
                   C

<u>cause</u> severe flooding. <u>No error</u>
   D   E

14. Economist George Akerlof has <u>argued that</u>
                          A

procrastination reveals the <u>limits of</u> rational thinking
                    B

and <u>can</u> teach useful lessons about phenomena
      C

as diverse as overeating and <u>to save</u> money. <u>No error</u>
                       D   E

15. The original British settlements in Australia, chosen

<u>only</u> for their strategic locations, <u>had</u> rocky soil and
 A   B

were able to produce <u>scarcely no</u> food to support <u>their</u>
                   C   D

inhabitants. <u>No error</u>
           E

16. Shakespeare's writing <u>itself is</u> undeniably original, <u>and</u>
                  A   *but* B

the plots of many of his <u>most famous</u> plays were
                   C

borrowed from classical works <u>familiar to</u> Elizabethan
                       D

audiences. <u>No error</u>
         E

17. <u>Many</u> bird species <u>become</u> endangered when
   A   B

<u>rapid</u> modernizing societies expand roads, mines,
   C

and chemical plants <u>into</u> environmentally sensitive
               D

areas. <u>No error</u>
      E

18. Historians Daniel Smail and Andrew Shyrock are

regarded <u>as an expert</u> in deep history, a <u>novel</u> field that
         A   B

<u>focuses on</u> the development of trends and processes
   C

<u>over</u> hundreds of thousands of years. <u>No error</u>
   D   E

19. <u>Although</u> most of the world's wealthiest countries
   A

<u>have</u> democratic governments, democracy is neither
   B

necessary <u>or</u> sufficient for a country's long-term
          C

economic <u>growth</u>. <u>No error</u>
          D   E

20. A collection of stone tools <u>found</u> on the Arabian
                   A

Peninsula's eastern shores <u>has reopened</u> the critical
                 B

question <u>of when</u> modern humans escaped <u>from their</u>
       C   D

ancestral homeland in Africa. <u>No error</u>
                      E

21. <u>As</u> agriculture spread <u>into</u> Neolithic Europe, it <u>gave</u>
    A   B   C
hunter-gatherer societies not only milk <u>as well as</u>
                                              D
wheat and barley. <u>No error</u>
                       E

22. <u>To isolate</u> his subjects in a space free of distracting
    A
elements, the artist <u>used</u> a series of blank folding
                          B
screens <u>more</u> frequently than <u>any backdrop</u>. <u>No error</u>
         C   D   E

23. Although Andrew Carnegie and Cornelius Vanderbilt
<u>eventually</u> became two of <u>most powerful</u> figures
 A   B
in business, neither <u>were</u> born <u>into</u> a wealthy family.
                        C   D
<u>No error</u>
 E

24. The conference between my professor and <u>I</u> went
                                             A
<u>surprisingly</u> well, despite the anxiety I had felt <u>about it</u>
 B   B
<u>earlier</u> in the week. <u>No error</u>
 C   E

25. Endorphins have traditionally been credited <u>to produce</u>
                                                 A
"runner's high," the <u>fleeting</u> sense of euphoria and
                      B
calm <u>that many</u> athletes report <u>experiencing</u> after
      C   D
prolonged exercise. <u>No error</u>
                         E

26. Unlike <u>a bumble bee colony</u>, the life of a honey bee
           A
colony can last <u>for many</u> years <u>and can include</u>
                 B   C
<u>thousands of</u> generations of queens, drones, and
 D
workers. <u>No error</u>
          E

27. Mobile phone manufacturers' attempts <u>to make</u>
                                          A
<u>their</u> products <u>more appealing</u> by implementing new
 B   C
forms of technology <u>has led</u> to great innovations in
                      D
phone development. <u>No error</u>
                        E

28. Tarsiers, five-inch tall primates <u>that inhabit</u> the
                                       A
islands of Southeast Asia, are unusual <u>in that</u> they
                                         B
<u>omit</u> sounds <u>whose frequencies</u> are entirely above
 C   D
the range that the human ear can perceive. <u>No error</u>
                                             E

29. Most people think of hobbits as <u>fictional creatures</u>,
                                     A
but <u>they actually</u> existed as *homo floresiensis*, a
     B
<u>long extinct species</u> that <u>once</u> lived among human
 C   D
beings. <u>No error</u>
         E

Directions: The following passage is an early draft of an essay. Some parts of the passage need to be rewritten.

Read the passage and select the best answer for the questions that follow. Some questions are about particular sentences or parts of sentences and ask you to improve sentence structure or word choice. Other questions ask you to consider organization and development. In choosing you answer, follow the requirements of standard written English.

Questions 30-35 refer to the following passage.

(1) Between World War I and the 1950's, more than six million African-Americans relocated from the rural South to the industrialized cities of the North and Midwest. (2) This became known as the Great Migration. (3) Beginning in 1941, it was captured by Jacob Lawrence, one of the most renowned artists of the twentieth century.

(4) In a series composed of sixty paintings, Lawrence depicted the discrimination that African Americans encountered at home and their gradual movement northward in search of a better life. (5) In one panel, he showed people eating in a restaurant that had clearly marked sections for black patrons and white patrons. (6) In numerous other panels, he showed people on a train going from south to north. (7) And finally, he painted scenes of people working in cities such as Chicago and Detroit in factories.

(8) Completing the project was difficult for Lawrence because there were so many paintings. (9) To make sure that the colors were same in each work, he put up all sixty boards at the same time, next he painted a single shade onto each board. (10) When that color was dry, he would paint another one, continuing on like this until all the paintings were complete. (11) The series was immediately recognized as a masterpiece, with the Museum of Modern Art (MoMA) and the Phillips Collection agreeing to split it between them. (12) Initially they were unable to decide who would receive which paintings, but ultimately they reached a compromise: Phillips would get the odd-numbered paintings, and MoMA would get the even.

30. In context, what is the best way to revise and combine the underlined portion of sentences 1 and 2 (reproduced below)?

    Between World War I and the 1950's, more than six million African-Americans relocated from the rural South to the industrialized cities of the North and Midwest. This became known as the Great Migration.

    (A) Midwest, with this becoming known
    (B) Midwest, this movement became known
    (C) Midwest, a movement that became known
    (D) Midwest, which became known
    (E) Midwest, having become known

31. Which of the following is best to insert at the beginning of sentence 5?

    (A) For instance,
    (B) Nevertheless,
    (C) Finally,
    (D) On the other hand,
    (E) Moreover,

32. Which of the following would most improve sentence 7 (reproduced below)?

    And finally, he painted scenes of people working in cities such as Chicago and Detroit in factories.

    (A) Insert "vivid" before "painted"
    (B) Move "in factories" to after "working"
    (C) Change "such as" to "like"
    (D) Change "he" to "Lawrence"
    (E) Delete "scenes of"

33. What is the primary purpose of sentence 8?

    (A) To refute an argument presented earlier in the passage
    (B) To present a controversial point of view
    (C) To promote an appreciation of African American artists
    (D) To elicit admiration from the reader
    (E) To describe a challenging situation

34. In context, which is the best revision of the underlined portion of sentence 9?

To make sure that the colors were same in each work, he put up all sixty boards at the same time, next he painted a single shade onto each board.

(A) time, painting next
(B) time, after this he painted
(C) time; he then painted
(D) time and painting
(E) time; however, he painted

35. Where is the best place to begin a new paragraph?

(A) after sentence 5
(B) after sentence 6
(C) after sentence 9
(D) after sentence 10
(E) after sentence 11

SECTION 2

Time – 10 Minutes

14 Questions

Directions: For each question in this section, select the best answer from among the choices given and fill in the corresponding circle on the answer sheet.

The following sentences test correctness and effectiveness of expression. Part of each sentence or the entire sentence is underlined; beneath each sentence are five ways of phrasing the underlined material. Choice A repeats the original phrasing; the other four choices are different. If you think the original phrasing produces a better sentence than any of the alternatives, select choice A; if not, select one of the other choices.

In making your selection, follow the requirements of standard written English; that is, pay attention to grammar, choice of words, sentence construction, and punctuation. Your selection should result in the most effective sentence—clear and precise, without awkwardness or ambiguity.

EXAMPLE:

○●○○○

Anna Robertson Moses completed her first painting <u>and she was seventy-six years old then</u>.

(A) and she was seventy-six years old then
(B) when she was seventy-six years old
(C) at age seventy-six years old
(D) upon arriving at the age of seventy-six
(E) at the time when she was seventy-six years old

1. Playwright Evan Jones is well-known in the United Kingdom <u>because of writing</u> a script for the television program that featured Bob Dylan's acting debut.

   (A) because of writing
   (B) because he wrote
   (C) and he wrote
   (D) for his writing
   (E) and he would write

2. Because Portugal is a seafaring nation with a well-developed fishing industry, <u>this is why they typically eat</u> large amounts of fish and seafood.

   (A) this is why they typically eat
   (B) this being why they typically eat
   (C) for this reason they typically eat
   (D) so the Portuguese typically eat
   (E) the Portuguese typically eat

3. Henry James never achieved the kind of popularity enjoyed by Dickens because <u>there was a refusal by himself of writing</u> the kind of sprawling, melodramatic novels that nineteenth century readers had come to expect.

   (A) there was a refusal by himself of writing
   (B) his refusal of writing
   (C) he refused to write
   (D) he has refused to write
   (E) refusals of writing were made by him

4. In order to be an effective driver, one must have an intuitive understanding of how to handle a vehicle <u>and you should be willing</u> to obey traffic laws strictly.

   (A) and you should be willing
   (B) as well as being willing
   (C) and having a willingness
   (D) and a willingness
   (E) plus being willing

5. In 1709, Great Britain established the world's first copyright law to formally protect books <u>about their being copied illegally</u>.

   (A) about their being copied illegally
   (B) from being copied illegally
   (C) and they were copied illegally
   (D) to be illegally copied
   (E) that they would copy illegally

6. Speed bumps are used in many countries around the world, and they are found most frequently in places <u>where speed limits are legally imposed</u>.

   (A) where speed limits are legally imposed
   (B) where they illegally impose speed limits
   (C) in which speed limits are being imposed
   (D) where speed limits that are legally imposed
   (E) in which they are legally imposing speed limits

7. Copper, a metal widely used by the ancient Greeks, <u>had great significance because of its association with Cyprus, it was considered</u> a sacred island.

   (A) had great significance because of its association with Cyprus, it was considered
   (B) and it had great significance because of their association with Cyprus, this was considered
   (C) had great significance because of its association with Cyprus, which was considered
   (D) having great significance because of its association with Cyprus, which was considered
   (E) had great significance because of being associated with Cyprus, this was considered

8. Universally concerned with the representation of the human form, <u>the inheritance of the classical tradition belongs to today's comic artists</u>.

   (A) the inheritance of the classical tradition belongs to today's comic artists
   (B) the inheritance of the classical tradition, which belongs to today's comic artists
   (C) the classical tradition belonging to today's comic book artists
   (D) today's comic artists are the inheritors of the classical tradition
   (E) today's comic artists, who inherited the classical tradition

9. Over the course of the novel, the author's prose, <u>already known for its sharpness and incisiveness, becomes</u> increasingly spare.

   (A) already known for its sharpness and incisiveness, becomes
   (B) which is already known for its sharpness and incisiveness, and becomes
   (C) already known for its sharpness and incisiveness, becoming
   (D) already known for its sharpness and incisiveness, which becomes
   (E) already known for its sharpness and incisiveness, it becomes

10. The founding of the *Chicago Tribune* by friends James Kelly, John Wheeler and Joseph Forrest <u>were prompted by the desire for creating</u> a world-class newspaper in a region lacking in serious journalism.

   (A) were prompted by the desire for creating
   (B) were prompted by the desire to create
   (C) was prompted by the desire to create
   (D) were prompted by the desire for creating
   (E) was prompted by the desire in creating

11. Long after ancient warriors had ceased to use chariots in warfare, ordinary citizens continued to rely on them for traveling over long distances, celebrating during festivals, <u>and the racing of</u> them in sporting events.

   (A) and the racing of
   (B) and they would race
   (C) and they had raced
   (D) and to race
   (E) and racing

12. Joyce Carol Oates is better known <u>for the large quantity of writing she has produced than because of its quality, which is lower</u>.

   (A) for the large quantity of writing she has produced than because of its quality, which is lower
   (B) for the large quantity of her writing as opposed to its quality because this is lower
   (C) for quantity of her writing rather than its being high in quality
   (D) because of the large quantity of her writing and not the quality of it
   (E) for the quantity than for the quality of her writing

13. <u>Jane Goodall became</u> the world's foremost expert on chimpanzees was hardly a surprise to those who had observed her childhood fascination with animals.

  (A) Jane Goodall became
  (B) That Jane Goodall became
  (C) Because Jane Goodall became
  (D) Jane Goodall, who would become
  (E) Jane Goodall, whose becoming

14. A recipient of the Presidential Medal of Freedom, <u>Barbara Jordan's election to Congress made her one of the most politically accomplished African-American women</u>.

  (A) Barbara Jordan's election to Congress made her one of the most politically accomplished African American women
  (B) the election of Barbara Jordan to Congress made her one of the most politically accomplished African American women
  (C) Congress elected Barbara Jordan, thereby making her one of the most politically accomplished African American women
  (D) Barbara Jordan became one of the most politically accomplished African American women when she was elected to Congress
  (E) Barbara Jordan's election to Congress had made her one of the most politically accomplished African American women

Answers: Test 6, Section 1

1. D: Tense consistency

The original version of the sentence contains verbs whose forms are not consistent (*was* vs. *increasing*); D corrects this error in parallelism (*was...increased*) and puts both verbs in the simple past tense.

2. C: Unnecessary use of gerund

The original version of the sentence provides a gerund (*because of deliberately wanting*) where none is necessary. C provides the clearer conjugated form of the verb (*because they wanted*).

3. E: Antecedent-pronoun

In the original version of the sentence, the pronoun *which* lacks an antecedent – it refers to Daryl Bem's insistence that ESP does exist, but the noun *insistence* does not actually appear in the sentence. B and C contain unnecessary gerunds; D creates the same problem as A and B, only using a different pronoun (*this*); and E corrects the sentence by eliminating the ambiguous pronoun entirely and correctly placing a semicolon before *therefore*.

4. E: Gerund; non-essential clause

A verb rather than a gerund (*collaborating*) must immediately follow the non-essential clause; otherwise, there is a fragment. only E provides a verb (*had*).

5. B: Faulty comparison

The original version of the sentence compares rituals (things) to peoples. In order for the sentence to be correct, *rituals* must be compared to *rituals*; only B provides the correct form of the comparison and the correct completion of the word pair *between...and*.

6. A: Participle required; comma splice

The participle *leading* correctly modifies the previous clause and makes the second clause dependent – since it is correct to use a comma between a dependent and an independent clause, there is no error. On the other hand, B, C, D, and E all create comma splices because they use a comma to separate two independent clauses.

7. B: Subject-verb agreement

Modifications, the subject of the sentence, is plural and thus requires a plural verb (have rather than have). Only B and D provide the correct form of the verb, and D

incorrectly uses the gerund *limiting* rather than the infinitive *to limit* after the verb *help*.

8. D: Parallel structure

The two non-underlined items in the list are both gerunds (*warming...stretching*), so the third item must also be a gerund (*imagining*).

9. C: Comma splice

The original version of the sentence contains two independent clauses separated by a comma; C corrects this error by providing a semicolon between the two independent clauses. Although the conjunctions *however* and *but* in B and E respectively also provide the correct logical relationship, *however* must be preceded by a semicolon when used to begin a clause, and *but* must be preceded by a comma. The conjunction *and* in D does not create the correct logical relationship.

10. E: Passive voice; pronoun-antecedent

The original version of the sentence contains two passive constructions (*proposed by the company...approved by their union leaders*) and an antecedent-pronoun disagreement: *union* = collective noun (singular) = *its*, not *their*. E makes both of the passive constructions active and eliminates the antecedent-pronoun disagreement.

11. C: Dangling modifier

What was once known to live throughout much of Europe and North America? The gray wolf. So *the gray wolf*, the subject, must come immediately after the comma. Only C provides that construction.

12. A: Subject-verb agreement: there is/there are

Since *few* is plural and thus requires a plural verb, *there are* rather than *there is* should be used.

13. B: Pronoun; fused sentence

The pronoun *they* creates a fused sentence: two independent clauses placed back-to-back without any punctuation between them. The simplest way to fix this error is to insert the pronoun *that*.

14. D: Parallel structure; gerund vs. infinitive

The infinitive *to save* must be changed to *saving* in order to make it parallel to the gerund *overeating*.

263

15. C: Double negative

Scarcely no is a double negative; *scarcely any* is correct.

16. B: Conjunction

The two clauses present contrasting ideas (the originality of Shakespeare's writing vs. the audience's familiarity with his stories) and thus require a contradictor such as *but* or *yet* rather than *and*.

17. C: Adjective vs. adverb

The adverb *rapidly* rather than the adjective *rapid* is required to modify the participle *modernizing*.

18. A: Noun agreement

Since Daniel Smail and Andrew Shyrock are two people, they are as *experts* (plural) rather than *an expert* (singular).

19. C: Word pair

Neither must always be paired with *nor*.

20. E: No error; subject-verb agreement

The most likely candidate for an error in this sentence is B because it is a verb that is separated from its subject by a prepositional phrase; however, *collection*, the subject, is singular, so there is no disagreement. C is the trick answer because it sounds slightly awkward but is grammatically acceptable.

21. D: Word pair (not only…but also)

Not only must be paired with *but also*.

22. D: Faulty comparison/logical relationship

Since *a series of blank folding screens* is itself a type of backdrop, it must have been used more than *any other backdrop*. To say that it was used more than *any backdrop* would imply that *a series of folding screens* is not a type of backdrop.

23. C: Subject-verb agreement: neither…nor

When *neither* appears without *nor* but refers to two singular subjects (Andrew Carnegie and Cornelius Vanderbilt), a singular verb should be used (*was* rather than *were*).

24. A: Pronoun case

The preposition *between* is always used with *me*, never *I*.

25. A: Gerund vs. infinitive

Credited should always be followed by *with + gerund* (*with producing*) rather than the infinitive (*to produce*).

26. A: Faulty comparison

The life of a bumblebee colony (thing) is being incorrectly compared to a honeybee colony (animals). In order for the sentence to be correct, *the life of a bumblebee colony* must be compared to *the life of a honeybee colony*.

27. D: Subject-verb agreement (subject – prepositional phrase – verb)

Attempts, the subject of the sentence, is plural and therefore requires a plural verb (*have* rather than *has*). The singular noun *technology*, which precedes the verb, is part of the prepositional phrase beginning with *of*.

28. C: Diction

Omit means *to deliberately leave out*, whereas the correct word, *emit*, means *utter* or *produce (a sound)*. Based on the context of the sentence, tarsiers would logically *emit* or *let out* a sound that is above the range that the human ear can perceive – *omit* does not make sense in context, even thought the two words sound very similar. B is the trick answer because many test-takers will believe that *in that* sounds odd. In reality, it's simply a synonym for *because*; while there may be more concise options, it is not inherently wrong.

29. E: No error

There are multiple underlined words/phrases that correspond to error categories: A suggests a noun agreement problem, but *creatures* (plural) agrees with *hobbits* (plural); *they* in B suggests a pronoun-antecedent agreement problem, but both the pronoun and its antecedent (*hobbits*) are plural. C and D are underlined because they have the potential to sound odd, but both are grammatically correct.

Shortcut: the sentence includes the adjective *long* in a way that many test-takers might not be accustomed to hearing (*long extinct*). The SAT often tests the use of *long* in this particular way; when it appears, it is virtually always correct, and the sentence in which it appears will often not contain another error.

30. C: Pronoun-antecedent

The original version of the sentence as well as B, C, and D all contain pronouns (*this* and *which*) that lack antecedents – the pronouns refer to *the movement*, but that noun does not actually appear in the sentence. Only C provides the noun. E is incorrect because the placement of the gerund *having* implies that the cities of the North and Midwest – rather than the movement itself – became known as the Great Migration.

31. A: Transition/logical relationship

Sentence 4 provides a general description of Lawrence's paintings (*they depicted the discrimination that African Americans encountered at home*), and sentence 5 provides a specific example (*eating in a restaurant that had clearly marked sections for black and white patrons*). *For instance* correctly conveys that relationship.

32. B: Misplaced modifier

The original version of the sentence states that Chicago and Detroit were *in* factories, whereas the factories were where the people worked. Placing the phrase *in factories* after *working* makes that fact clear.

33. E: Paragraph organization

Sentence 8 tells us that it was *difficult* for Lawrence to complete the paintings and then provides an explanation for that statement – in other words, it indicates a *challenge* that he faced.

34. C: Comma splice

Both the original version of the sentence and B contain two sentences separated by a comma; D contains a gerund (*painting*) that is not parallel to the verb *put*; and E contains an incorrect logical relationship because the two clauses do not contradict one another.

35. D: Paragraph organization

The most logical place to begin a new paragraph is after sentence 10 because sentence 11 marks a shift from the description of Lawrence's working method to its reception and display after it was completed.

Test 6, Section 2

1. B: Gerund

The sentence contains an unnecessary gerund (*writing*) rather than conjugated verb (*wrote*). B retains the conjunction *because*, which provides a logical relationship between the clauses as well as a conjugated verb.

2. E: Pronoun-antecedent

The pronoun *they* in A, B, and C refers to the Portuguese, but *the Portuguese* does not actually appear in the sentence. In D, *so* is unnecessary because the first clause contains *because*. E provides the phrase *the Portuguese* and avoids the double conjunction.

3. C: Passive voice; gerund vs. infinitive

The original version contains a passive and wordy construction made more awkward and uncollaquial by the gerund *writing*. C makes the sentence active and concise, and it replaces the gerund with the infinitive *to write*.

4. D: Parallel structure

The two qualities necessary to be a good driver must be presented in the same form: since the first is a noun (*an understanding*), the second must be a noun as well (*a willingness*). Only D provides that parallel construction.

5. B: Preposition/idiom

Something is prevented *from* being, not *about* being. Only B provides the correct preposition. Although answers with *being* are usually wrong, this one is correct because *prevent from being* is standard idiomatic usage.

6. A: No error

The original version of the sentence is correct; in B and E, the pronoun *they* lacks an antecedent; C contains an unnecessary gerund (*being*); and D creates a fragment.

7. C: Comma splice

A, B and E, contain two sentences separated by only a comma; and D creates a fragment by replacing the main verb with a gerund (*having*). C is correct because it provides a main verb (*had*) and uses the pronoun *which* to make the last clause dependent, thus eliminating the comma splice. Although the presence of *which* often signals an incorrect answer, in this case it is correct because it refer to the noun (*Cyprus*) that immediately precedes it.

8. D: Dangling modifier

Who was universally concerned with the representation of the human form? Today's comic artists. So *today's comic artists*, the subject, must appear immediately after the comma. Only D and E contain this construction, and E creates a fragment.

9. A: No error; non-essential clause

The original version of the sentence contains a properly used non-essential clause, indicating a correct answer. All of the other answers fail to place a verb immediately after the comma signaling the end of the non-essential clause.

10. C: Subject-verb agreement

Founding, the subject of the sentence, is singular and thus requires a singular verb, *was*. That eliminates A, B, and D. In E, the phrase *in creating* is un-colloquial: *the desire* should be followed by the infinitive, *to create*.

11. E: Parallel structure

The two non-underlined items in the list both begin with a gerund (*traveling, celebrating*), and so the third item must begin with a gerund (*racing*) as well. Only E contains that construction.

12. E: Parallel structure

The construction in the underlined portion of the sentence must match the construction in the non-underlined part: ***for** the quantity* = ***for** the quality*. E is the only answer choice that contains *for*. In addition, *better* must be paired with *than*, also making E the only option.

13. B: *That* as a subject

Although B may sound strange when plugged into the sentence, it is perfectly correct to use *that* , the shortened version of *the fact that*, as part of a subject. With the complete version, the sentence would sound much less odd: *The fact that Jane Goodall became the world's foremost expert on chimpanzees was hardly a surprise…* The two constructions, however, are interchangeable. All of the other answer choices create ungrammatical nonsense when plugged back into the sentence.

14. D: Dangling modifier

Who was a recipient of the Presidential Medal of Freedom? Barbara Jordan. So *Barbara Jordan*, the subject must appear immediately after the comma. Only D provides that construction.

Test 7

Section 1

1. Ⓐ Ⓑ Ⓒ Ⓓ Ⓔ
2. Ⓐ Ⓑ Ⓒ Ⓓ Ⓔ
3. Ⓐ Ⓑ Ⓒ Ⓓ Ⓔ
4. Ⓐ Ⓑ Ⓒ Ⓓ Ⓔ
5. Ⓐ Ⓑ Ⓒ Ⓓ Ⓔ
6. Ⓐ Ⓑ Ⓒ Ⓓ Ⓔ
7. Ⓐ Ⓑ Ⓒ Ⓓ Ⓔ
8. Ⓐ Ⓑ Ⓒ Ⓓ Ⓔ
9. Ⓐ Ⓑ Ⓒ Ⓓ Ⓔ
10. Ⓐ Ⓑ Ⓒ Ⓓ Ⓔ
11. Ⓐ Ⓑ Ⓒ Ⓓ Ⓔ
12. Ⓐ Ⓑ Ⓒ Ⓓ Ⓔ
13. Ⓐ Ⓑ Ⓒ Ⓓ Ⓔ
14. Ⓐ Ⓑ Ⓒ Ⓓ Ⓔ
15. Ⓐ Ⓑ Ⓒ Ⓓ Ⓔ
16. Ⓐ Ⓑ Ⓒ Ⓓ Ⓔ
17. Ⓐ Ⓑ Ⓒ Ⓓ Ⓔ
18. Ⓐ Ⓑ Ⓒ Ⓓ Ⓔ
19. Ⓐ Ⓑ Ⓒ Ⓓ Ⓔ
20. Ⓐ Ⓑ Ⓒ Ⓓ Ⓔ
21. Ⓐ Ⓑ Ⓒ Ⓓ Ⓔ
22. Ⓐ Ⓑ Ⓒ Ⓓ Ⓔ
23. Ⓐ Ⓑ Ⓒ Ⓓ Ⓔ
24. Ⓐ Ⓑ Ⓒ Ⓓ Ⓔ
25. Ⓐ Ⓑ Ⓒ Ⓓ Ⓔ
26. Ⓐ Ⓑ Ⓒ Ⓓ Ⓔ
27. Ⓐ Ⓑ Ⓒ Ⓓ Ⓔ
28. Ⓐ Ⓑ Ⓒ Ⓓ Ⓔ
29. Ⓐ Ⓑ Ⓒ Ⓓ Ⓔ
30. Ⓐ Ⓑ Ⓒ Ⓓ Ⓔ
31. Ⓐ Ⓑ Ⓒ Ⓓ Ⓔ
32. Ⓐ Ⓑ Ⓒ Ⓓ Ⓔ
33. Ⓐ Ⓑ Ⓒ Ⓓ Ⓔ
34. Ⓐ Ⓑ Ⓒ Ⓓ Ⓔ
35. Ⓐ Ⓑ Ⓒ Ⓓ Ⓔ

Section 2

1. Ⓐ Ⓑ Ⓒ Ⓓ Ⓔ
2. Ⓐ Ⓑ Ⓒ Ⓓ Ⓔ
3. Ⓐ Ⓑ Ⓒ Ⓓ Ⓔ
4. Ⓐ Ⓑ Ⓒ Ⓓ Ⓔ
5. Ⓐ Ⓑ Ⓒ Ⓓ Ⓔ
6. Ⓐ Ⓑ Ⓒ Ⓓ Ⓔ
7. Ⓐ Ⓑ Ⓒ Ⓓ Ⓔ
8. Ⓐ Ⓑ Ⓒ Ⓓ Ⓔ
9. Ⓐ Ⓑ Ⓒ Ⓓ Ⓔ
10. Ⓐ Ⓑ Ⓒ Ⓓ Ⓔ
11. Ⓐ Ⓑ Ⓒ Ⓓ Ⓔ
12. Ⓐ Ⓑ Ⓒ Ⓓ Ⓔ
13. Ⓐ Ⓑ Ⓒ Ⓓ Ⓔ
14. Ⓐ Ⓑ Ⓒ Ⓓ Ⓔ

SECTION 1
Time – 25 Minutes
35 Questions

Directions: For each question in this section, select the best answer from among the choices given and fill in the corresponding circle on the answer sheet.

The following sentences test correctness and effectiveness of expression. Part of each sentence or the entire sentence is underlined; beneath each sentence are five ways of phrasing the underlined material. Choice A repeats the original phrasing; the other four choices are different. If you think the original phrasing produces a better sentence than any of the alternatives, select choice A; if not, select one of the other choices.

In making your selection, follow the requirements of standard written English; that is, pay attention to grammar, choice of words, sentence construction, and punctuation. Your selection should result in the most effective sentence—clear and precise, without awkwardness or ambiguity.

EXAMPLE:

○ ● ○ ○ ○

Anna Robertson Moses completed her first painting <u>and she was seventy-six years old then</u>.

(A) and she was seventy-six years old then
(B) when she was seventy-six years old
(C) at age seventy-six years old
(D) upon arriving at the age of seventy-six
(E) at the time when she was seventy-six years old

1. By the mid-1950s, Frank Sinatra <u>becomes</u> successful as a singer, having released several albums to great critical acclaim.

(A) becomes
(B) will become
(C) could become
(D) had become
(E) having become

2. June Mathis, who was one of the first screenwriters to include details such as stage directions in her work, <u>and she helped make</u> film into an art form.

(A) and she helped make
(B) this helped that it would make
(C) helped make
(D) which had helped make
(E) also she was helping make

3. Members of the local arts council have recently commissioned the construction of a massive <u>sculpture, which will be placed in the city's main square</u>.

(A) sculpture, which will be placed in the city's main square
(B) sculpture; the city's main square is where it will be placed by them
(C) sculpture, that is what will be placed in the city's main square
(D) sculpture, it will be placed in the city's main square
(E) sculpture, and they will be placed in the city's main square

4. Following his release from captivity, King Louis IX of France used his influence to show crusaders <u>about how they could rebuild</u> their defenses and conduct diplomacy.

(A) about how they could rebuild
(B) about how they rebuild
(C) about their rebuilding
(D) that they could rebuild
(E) that they can rebuild

5. When the *Mona Lisa*, already the most famous painting in the world, had its first exhibition in the United States, thousands of viewers flocked to Washington, D.C. to attend that.

   (A) to attend that
   (B) for its attendance
   (C) to attend
   (D) for the attendance at it
   (E) for attending

6. In places far removed from modern conveniences, plants play a key role in survival, providing shelter, food, and clothing for people as well as animals.

   (A) In places far removed from modern conveniences, plants play a key role in survival, providing
   (B) In places being far removed from modern conveniences, plants play a key role in survival, providing
   (C) In places far removed from modern conveniences, plants play a key role in survival, they provide
   (D) In places far removed from modern conveniences, plants play a key role in survival, because of it providing
   (E) In places far removed from modern conveniences, plants playing a key role in survival by providing

7. According to most travel agents, before you leave for a trip, people should confirm all of the reservations that one has made.

   (A) before you leave for a trip, people should confirm all of the reservations that one has
   (B) before you leave for a trip, people should confirm all of the reservations that you have
   (C) before one leaves for a trip, people should confirm all of the reservations that they have
   (D) before one leaves for a trip, he or she should confirm all of the reservations that they have
   (E) before people leave for a trip, they should confirm all of the reservations that they have

8. There has been many debates over various methods of dog training as well as the describing of those methods.

   (A) There has been many debates over various methods of dog training as well as the describing
   (B) There have been many debates over various methods of dog training as well as the descriptions
   (C) For dog training, there have been many debates over various methods as well as the describing
   (D) There has been many debates over various methods of dog training as well as how to describe
   (E) Many debates, which have been held over various methods of dog training as well as the descriptions

9. Whales and dolphins breathe through their blowholes and then seal their nostrils as they dive, nevertheless they make powerful sounds underwater.

   (A) dive, nevertheless they make
   (B) dive but making
   (C) dive, despite this they make
   (D) dive; nevertheless they make
   (E) dive, however they make

10. In similarity to bears, coyotes are expanding into new habitats in recent decades because human settlements have encroached upon the wooded areas where they once lived.

    (A) In similarity to
    (B) As
    (C) As with what happened to
    (D) Like with
    (E) Like

11. A classic diplomatic manual affirmed that negotiations between countries should be conducted with honor, and that deceit should not be used in any form.

    (A) honor, and that deceit should not be used in any form
    (B) honor, moreover it should not include any form of deceit
    (C) honor and without any form of deceit
    (D) honor, also no form of deceit should be used
    (E) honor, plus deceit should not in any form be used

The following sentences test your ability to recognize grammar and usage errors. Each sentence contains either a single error or none at all. No sentence contains more than one error. The error, if there is one, is underlined and lettered. If the sentence contains an error, select the one underlined part that must be changed in order to make the sentence correct. If the sentence is correct, select choice E. In choosing answers, follow the requirements of standard written English.

EXAMPLE:

Science fiction writer H.G. Wells, the author of
                                    A
more than 100 books, accurately predicted the
                                    B
the invention of television, the rise of the Internet,
    C
and creating the hydrogen bomb. No error
    D   E

○○○●○

12. The largest gecko ever found was nearly four times
                     A   B
    larger than the smallest known gecko, the Jaragua
    C
    Sphaero, what measured a mere sixteen millimeters
            D
    long. No error
         E

13. Johanes Kepler, the astronomer which published the
                                   A
    first defense of Copernican theory, was introduced to
                 B
    astronomy at an early age and developed a fascination
                                   C
    with it that lasted his entire life. No error
    D   E

14. Feudalism, a total organization of social hierarchies,
                                   A
    specify the status of the individual and his or her
    B   C
    relations with other members of a society. No error
    D   E

15. Despite the term "Harlem Renaissance," the famed
    A
    artistic movement took place in many African-
            B
    American communities and has represented a whole
                            C
    new set of opportunities rather than a rebirth. No error
                            D   E

16. The success of some Broadway plays are,
                   A   B
    unsurprisingly, matched by an equal amount
                   C
    of success in regional theaters. No error
    D   E

17. The designer of Central Park in New York City,
        A
    Frederick Law Olmsted initially worked as a clerk, a
                         B   C
    sailor, and numerous other fields. No error
                D   E

18. Since 1987, physician Jaime Guevara has studied the
                                      A
    residents of a remote village, many of whom have a
                                      B
    rare genetic condition that inhibit the development of
                             C
    certain common diseases. No error
    D   E

19. The 1970s energy crisis was a period in which it was
                                      A
    revealed that the world's largest industrialized nations
    B   C
    faced substantial shortages of crude oil. No error
    D   E

20. When the Stanford Artificial Intelligence Laboratory
    A
    opened in 1963, its founders mistaken believed that it
                                B
    would only take ten years to create a thinking
    C   D
    machine. No error
            E

21. Before suffragist Elizabeth Cady Stanton <u>narrowed</u> her
                                              A
    political focus almost <u>exclusively to</u> women's rights,
                           B
    she <u>had been</u> an active <u>member of</u> the abolitionist
         C   D
    movement. <u>No error</u>
               E

22. <u>Although they</u> initially gave her <u>unfavorable</u> reviews
        A   B
    and expressed skepticism <u>with</u> her literary abilities,
                             C
    critics now <u>view</u> Emily Dickinson as a major poet.
                 D
    <u>No error</u>
    E

23. The <u>development of</u> new forms of digital technology
            A
    <u>have allowed</u> acoustic engineers to create entirely new
        B
    sounds and filter unwanted noise <u>with</u> a precision
                                      C
    <u>never before</u> possible. <u>No error</u>
        D   E

24. Greek historians such as Strabo <u>regarded</u> the hanging
                                     A
    gardens of Babylon <u>to be</u> one of the seven wonders
                        B
    of the ancient world <u>because they were</u> believed
                          C
    <u>to have towered</u> hundreds of feet in the air. <u>No error</u>
        D   E

25. <u>Because</u> other patrons in the gallery <u>had begun</u> to
        A   B
    complain, the guide asked <u>Corey and I</u> to lower our
                              C
    voices <u>as</u> we walked through the museum. <u>No error</u>
           D   E

26. Sociologist Sherry Turkle <u>has argued</u> that the
                              A
    growing trend <u>toward</u> creating machines that act as if
                  B
    <u>they were</u> alive could lead people to place machines in
        C
    roles <u>better</u> occupied by humans. <u>No error</u>
          D   E

27. <u>Once common</u> across southwest Asia, the Indian
        A
    cheetah was driven <u>nearly to</u> extinction during the late
                       B
    twentieth century <u>and now</u> resides in the fragmented
                      C
    pieces of <u>their</u> remaining habitat. <u>No error</u>
              D   E

28. After <u>discovering</u> that both events were <u>scheduled for</u>
          A   B
    the same night, Ricardo found it difficult <u>to decide</u>
                                                C
    between attending the dance <u>or</u> watching his sister's
                                D
    recital. <u>No error</u>
             E

29. The <u>increasingly</u> global character of publishing
            A
    <u>has caused</u> editors to be simultaneously pulled in
        B
    many different directions <u>at once</u>, with authors in
                              C
    multiple countries <u>making</u> competing demands.
                       D
    <u>No error</u>
    E

Directions: The following passage is an early draft of an essay. Some parts of the passage need to be rewritten.

Read the passage and select the best answer for the questions that follow. Some questions are about particular sentences or parts of sentences and ask you to improve sentence structure or word choice. Other questions ask you to consider organization and development. In choosing you answer, follow the requirements of standard written English.

Questions 30-35 refer to the following passage.

(1) The discovery of penicillin was among the most famous accidents in medical history. (2) This was the first antibiotic. (3) When British scientist Alexander Fleming arrived in his laboratory one morning in September of 1928, he had no idea that he was about to make a discovery that would alter the course of medical history. (4) Fleming had recently spent several weeks away, and not being the neatest worker, a stack of cultures containing the bacteria *staphylococcus* was left in a corner of the lab. (5) When Fleming examined the cultures, he discovered that one had been contaminated with a fungus. (6) Fleming noticed that all of the *staphylococcus* bacteria immediately surrounding the fungus had been destroyed, but that the bacteria further away from the fungus was not affected. (7) This suggested that the fungus was responsible for destroying the potentially lethal bacteria.

(8) Fleming didn't think about the possibilities. (9) It was actually his assistant, Merlin Price, who came up with the idea to test the fungus. (10) Price knew that Fleming had already made another major discovery by accident, he urged his supervisor to see if the fungus, *penicillum*, might have some use. (11) Fleming took his advice and tested the fungus, it was revealed that the fungus was capable of destroying a number of disease-causing bacteria. (12) At that time, however, the fungus was difficult to produce in large quantities; consequently, Fleming abandoned the project. (13) Almost fifteen years later, Ernst Chain and Howard Florey succeeded in making the first purified form of penicillin that could be easily distributed. (14) Their achievement, which they admitted would have been impossible without Fleming, came just in time to save the lives of thousands of soldiers during World War II.

30. In context, what is the best way to revise and combine sentences 1 and 2 (reproduced below) at the underlined portion?

    The discovery of penicillin was among the most famous accidents in medical history. This was the first antibiotic.

    (A) penicillin was among the most famous accidents in medical history and was the first antibiotic
    (B) penicillin, which was among the most famous accidents in medical history, was the first antibiotic
    (C) penicillin, which was the first antibiotic, it was one of the most famous accidents in medical history
    (D) penicillin was among the most famous accidents in medical history, moreover it was the first antibiotic
    (E) penicillin, the first antibiotic, was among the most famous accidents in medical history

31. In context, which is the best version of the underlined portion of sentence 4 (reproduced below)?

    Fleming had recently spent several weeks away, and not being the neatest worker, a stack of cultures containing the bacteria staphylococcus were left in a corner of the lab.

    (A) a stack of cultures containing the bacteria *staphylococcus* had been left in a corner of the lab
    (B) a stack of cultures containing the bacteria *staphylococcus* having been left in a corner of the lab
    (C) he had left a stack of cultures containing the bacteria *staphylococcus* in a corner of the lab
    (D) cultures containing the bacteria *staphylococcus* had been left by him in a stack in a corner of the lab
    (E) a stack of cultures in a corner of the lab that contained the bacteria *staphylococcus* had been left

32. In context, which of the following phrases would best be inserted at the beginning of sentence 8?

   (A) Because he was intrigued,
   (B) Despite this exciting development,
   (C) In the meantime,
   (D) Immediately seeing the possibilities,
   (E) Although he was puzzled by the situation,

33. In context, which of the following would be the best way to revise the underlined portion of sentence 10?

   Price knew that Fleming had already made another major discovery by accident, he urged his supervisor to see if the fungus, penicillum, might have some use.

   (A) accident, therefore he urged
   (B) accident and thus urging
   (C) accident, so he urged
   (D) accident; however, he urged
   (E) accident; he likewise urged

34. In context, what is the best revision of the underlined portion of sentence 11 (reproduced below)?

   Fleming took his advice and tested the fungus, it was revealed that the fungus was capable of destroying a number of disease-causing bacteria.

   (A) fungus, they revealed that it was capable of destroying
   (B) fungus, and it was revealed that this was capable to destroy
   (C) fungus, it was revealed as being capable of destroying
   (D) fungus, which was revealed to be capable of destroying
   (E) fungus; however, it was revealed that the fungus was capable of destroying

35. What is the best place for sentence 12?

   (A) where it is now
   (B) after sentence 8
   (C) after sentence 9
   (D) after sentence 13
   (E) after sentence 14

SECTION 2
Time – 10 Minutes
14 Questions

Directions: For each question in this section, select the best answer from among the choices given and fill in the corresponding circle on the answer sheet.

The following sentences test correctness and effectiveness of expression. Part of each sentence or the entire sentence is underlined; beneath each sentence are five ways of phrasing the underlined material. Choice A repeats the original phrasing; the other four choices are different. If you think the original phrasing produces a better sentence than any of the alternatives, select choice A; if not, select one of the other choices.

In making your selection, follow the requirements of standard written English; that is, pay attention to grammar, choice of words, sentence construction, and punctuation. Your selection should result in the most effective sentence—clear and precise, without awkwardness or ambiguity.

EXAMPLE:

○●○○○

Anna Robertson Moses completed her first painting <u>and she was seventy-six years old then.</u>

(A) and she was seventy-six years old then
(B) when she was seventy-six years old
(C) at age seventy-six years old
(D) upon arriving at the age of seventy-six
(E) at the time when she was seventy-six years old

1. <u>It having been discovered by researchers in Texas</u> that the heart of a newborn mouse is capable of regenerating itself without surgical intervention.

(A) It having been discovered by researchers
(B) The discovery by researchers in Texas
(C) Researchers in Texas discovering
(D) Researchers in Texas have discovered
(E) The discovery by researchers in Texas having been made

2. Although desserts <u>typically known</u> for their sweetness, pastry chefs are now creating ones that feature unexpected mixtures of sweet and savory.

(A) typically known
(B) having typically been known
(C) are typically known
(D) that are typically known
(E) typically would be known

3. Leisure gardens, the predecessors of modern amusement parks, became popular refuges for nineteenth-century <u>workers, and they provided</u> an escape from the grim urban environments.

(A) workers, and they provided
(B) workers; their providing
(C) workers, they provided
(D) workers by providing
(E) workers when they provided

4. Most parrot species spend their time perching on the limbs of trees, climbing by hooking their beaks onto rocks and branches, <u>or else they forage</u> for seeds and flowers.

(A) or else they forage
(B) or to forage for
(C) otherwise they forage
(D) and to forage
(E) and foraging

5. Despite the destruction of its original auditorium in 1951, <u>performances have been staged continuously by the Abbey Theatre since the early twentieth century</u>.

(A) performances have been staged continuously by the Abbey Theatre since the early twentieth century
(B) performances having been staged continuously by the Abbey Theatre since the early twentieth century
(C) the continuous staging of performances at the Abbey Theatre has taken place since the twentieth Century
(D) the Abbey Theatre has staged performances continuously since the early twentieth century
(E) the Abbey Theatre had staged their performances continuously since the early twentieth century

6. <u>Known not only for their elegance and grace but also for their rowdy behavior,</u> flamingoes have recently become the subject of serious scientific examination.

(A) Known not only for their elegance and grace but also for their rowdy behavior,
(B) While they are known not only for their elegance and grace but they also have rowdy behavior,
(C) They are known not only for their elegance and grace as well as their rowdy behavior,
(D) Being known for their elegance and grace plus having rowdy behavior,
(E) They are known not only for their elegance and grace but also having rowdy behavior,

7. The poet's works are unusual for the era <u>where they were written because they frequently include</u> elements such as short lines and unconventional punctuation.

(A) where they were written because they frequently include
(B) when they were written because they frequently include
(C) where they were written because of their frequently including
(D) in which they were written because of frequently including
(E) in which it was written because of their frequent inclusion of

8. Conductor Marin Alsop is a consummate musician whose every gesture reveals her <u>commitment and passion for</u> her art.

(A) commitment and passion for
(B) commitment and passion
(C) commitment to and passion
(D) commitment to and passion for
(E) commitment to and having passion

9. Despite technological advances, weather forecasting is far better at estimating <u>where a storm will move than their level of intensity</u>.

(A) where a storm will move than their level of intensity
(B) where a storm will move and not its level of intensity
(C) a storm's movement but not how intense it will be
(D) the movement of a storm but not how intense they will be
(E) the movement of a storm than the level of its intensity

10. Often thought of as a modern sport, one that has only gained popularity over the last fifty years, <u>but surfing was an important activity</u> in Polynesian culture long before Europeans first observed it.

(A) but surfing was an important activity
(B) but surfing had been an important activity
(C) surfing was an important activity
(D) surfing, which had been an important activity
(E) and surfing was an important activity

11. Renowned by his contemporaries for his virtuosic skill as a performer, <u>it was often said that Liszt was the most technically advanced pianist of his age</u> and perhaps of all time.

    (A) it was often said that Liszt was the most technically advanced pianist of his age
    (B) it has often been said that Liszt was the most technically advanced pianist of his age
    (C) the most technically advanced pianist of his age, Liszt, it was often said,
    (D) Liszt was often said to be the most technically advanced pianist of his age
    (E) Liszt often said to be the most technically advanced pianist of his age

12. <u>Although her academic credentials were far less impressive than her male colleagues,</u> Austrian-born psychoanalyst Melanie Klein became known as an innovator for her work with young children.

    (A) Although her academic credentials were far less impressive than her male colleagues,
    (B) Although her academic credentials were far less impressive than those had by her male colleagues,
    (C) While her academic credentials were far less impressive than what her male colleagues had,
    (D) Although her academic credentials were not as impressive as her male colleagues,
    (E) Her academic credentials were far less impressive than those of her male colleagues,

13. The retailer has attributed its declining sales to the high rate of unemployment and <u>the inclination of shoppers to make their purchases online</u>.

    (A) the inclination of shoppers to make their purchases online
    (B) shoppers are inclined to make their purchases online
    (C) online purchases are shoppers' inclination
    (D) purchasing online is a shoppers' inclination
    (E) shoppers being inclined to make purchases online

14. Many parrot species are capable of using their feet to manipulate food and other objects with a high degree of dexterity, <u>much like a person using their</u> hands.

    (A) much like a person using their
    (B) much like a person using his or her
    (C) which is similar to a person using their
    (D) and this is like a person using his or her
    (E) similar to when a person uses their

Answers: Test 7, Section 1

1. D: Verb tense

The date mid-1950s indicates that the sentence is describing an action that occurred in the past, and D is the only option that provides a verb in the past tense (*had become*).

2. C: Non-essential clause

The original version of the sentence fails to place a verb after the non-essential clause *who was one of the first screenwriters to include details such as stage directions in her work*. When that clause is removed from the sentence, what remains does not make sense: *June Mathis...and she helped make film into an art form*. Only C provides a verb (*helped*).

3. A: No error; pronoun-antecedent

In the original version of the sentence, the pronoun *which* is correctly used to modify the noun (*sculpture*) that immediately precedes it. B contains a passive construction (*it **will be** placed **by** them*); C and D create comma splices; and E incorrectly contains a plural pronoun (*they*).

4. D: Preposition/idiom

Standard usage requires that the verb *show* be followed by *that* rather than *about*, eliminating A, B, and C. E can be eliminated as well because it contains a verb in the present (*can*), and the sentence clearly describes events that took place in the past.

5. C: Pronoun

The pronoun *that* is unnecessary at the end of the sentence.

6. A: Participle required

The participle phrase *providing food, shelter, and clothing for people as well as animals* is correctly used to modify the statement *plants play a key role in survival*. Although *providing* ends in "-ing," it is a participle rather than a gerund and not problematic in any way. B, D, and E do include unnecessary gerunds, however, and C creates a comma splice.

7. E: Pronoun-antecedent

The pronoun should stay consistent and match its antecedent throughout the sentence: *one* goes with *one*; *you* goes with *you*; and *people* goes with *they*. Only D provides a matching pronoun-antecedent pair.

8. B: Subject-verb agreement; parallel structure

Many debates is plural and must take a plural verb (*have* rather than *has*), eliminating A and D. In addition, the two items must be presented in parallel form: C mixes a noun (*methods*) with a gerund (*describing*), and D mixes the same noun with a relative pronoun + infinitive (*how to describe*). Only B correctly pairs the noun with another noun (*descriptions*).

9. D: Comma splice; semicolon

When it is used to begin a clause, *nevertheless* should be preceded by a semicolon rather than a comma. D correctly provides a semicolon.

10. E: Idiom

The more concise, idiomatic construction is, **Like** bears, coyotes are... In general, *like* is used to compare nouns while *as* is used to compare adjectives.

11. C: Parallel structure

C makes the construction *with* + *noun* (*honor*) in the non-underlined portion of the sentence parallel to *without* + *noun* (*deceit*) in the underlined portion. The original version of the sentence and E contain passive constructions (*deceit should not **be used***); B and D contain comma splices.

12. D: Relative pronoun

Which rather than *what* should be used to set off a relative clause.

13. A: Who vs. which

Johannes Kepler was a person and should thus be referred to as *who* rather than *which*.

14. B: Subject-verb agreement

Feudalism, the subject of the sentence, is singular and therefore requires a singular verb (*specifies* rather than *specify*).

15. C: Verb tense/consistency

The sentence clearly describes a movement that took place in the past (*Harlem Renaissance*) and that should thus be discussed in the simple past (*represented* rather than *has represented*). In addition, the tense should remain consistent throughout the sentence: the underlined verb in C must be parallel to the non-underlined verb *took*.

16. B: Subject-verb agreement (subject – prepositional phrase – verb)

Success, the subject of the sentence, is singular and must take a singular verb (*is* rather than *are*). The plural noun *plays*, which immediately precedes the verb, belongs to the prepositional phrase beginning with *of*.

17. D: Parallel structure/logic

The items in the list name the things that Frederick Law Olmsted worked *as*. While he could clearly work as a clerk and a sailor, he could not work *as* numerous other fields.

18. C: Subject-verb agreement

Condition is singular and therefore requires singular verb (*inhibits* rather than *inhibit*).

19. E: No error

The trick answer is A, *in which*, because test-takers often believe that the construction *preposition* + *which* sounds odd. In reality, it is virtually always correct.

20. B: Adjective vs. adverb

An adverb (*mistakenly* rather than an adjective (*mistaken*) is required to modify the verb *believed*.

21. E: No error; verb tense

The primary concept that the sentence is testing is the use of the past perfect (*had been*). Since the sentence makes clear that the action described with the past perfect (Stanton was an active member of the abolitionist movement) occurred *before* the second action (narrowing her focus to women's rights), there is no tense error.

22. C: Preposition/idiom

The correct idiomatic phrase is *skepticism about*, not *skepticism with*.

23. B: Subject-verb agreement (subject – prepositional phrase – verb)

Development, the subject, is singular and thus requires a singular verb (*has* rather than *have*).

24. B: Idiom/gerund vs. infinitive

The correct idiomatic phrase is *regarded as* (or *regarded as being*), not *regarded to be*.

25. C: Pronoun case

Since you would not say, *The guide asked **I** to lower my voice*, you would not say, *The guide asked **Corey and I** to lower our voices* either.

26. E: No error

All of the underlined words and phrases in this sentence point to specific error categories, but no error actually appears. In A, *has argued* refers to a singular subject and is in the correct tense. In B, the preposition *toward* is correctly paired with *a trend*; in C, *they* correctly refers to a plural noun (*machines*) and is in the correct tense; and in D, there is no conclusive reason to switch *better* with *best*.

27. D: Pronoun-antecedent

The plural pronoun *their* is incorrectly used to refer to the singular noun *cheetah*. A singular pronoun (*its*) should be used instead.

28. D: Word pair

Between should always be paired with *and*, not *or*.

29. C: Redundancy

Since *simultaneously* and *at once* mean the same thing, *at once* should thus be eliminated from the sentence.

30. E: Modification; non-essential clause

E creates a non-essential clause that correctly describes penicillin, the noun that immediately precedes it. B does not make logical sense when the non-essential clause is removed (*The discovery of penicillin…was the first antibiotic*); C fails to follow the non-essential clause with a verb; and D incorrectly places a comma rather than a semicolon before *moreover*.

31. C: Dangling modifier

Who was not the neatest worker? *He* (Fleming), not a stack of cultures. So *he*, the subject, must appear immediately after the comma. Only C contains that construction.

32. B: Transition

Sentence 6 suggests that the fungus was capable of killing harmful bacteria (an *exciting development*), but sentence 7 tells us that Fleming didn't think to test it out. The contrast between those two ideas makes *Despite* an appropriate transition to place between the two sentences.

33. C: Transition

Sentence 9 describes Price's knowledge of the fact that Fleming had made accidental discoveries, and the action he took as a *result* of that knowledge (urging Fleming to experiment). A, B, and C contain transitions that indicate a result. In A, however, *therefore* is incorrectly preceded by a comma rather than a semicolon; and B requires a verb (*urged*) rather than a gerund (*urging*). C correctly uses a comma before the FANBOYS conjunction *so*.

34. D: Comma splice; pronoun-antecedent

Both A and C contain two independent clauses separated by a comma; B incorrectly uses the infinitive *to destroy* rather than the gerund *of destroying* after *capable*; and the use of *however* in E is illogical because the two clauses do not contradict one another. C correctly uses the pronoun *which* to modify the noun (*fungus*) that appears immediately before it.

35. A: Paragraph organization

The sentence belongs where it is because it contains information that must follow the information in sentence 11 (it would not make sense to discuss the production of large quantities of the fungus before saying that it could destroy disease-causing bacteria) and precede the information in sentence 13 (*Almost fifteen years later* must come after *At that time*).

Test 7, Section 2

1. D: Improper use of gerund

The original version of the sentence along with C and D all improperly use gerunds (*having, discovering*) in place of main verbs, and B lacks a verb entirely. Only D correctly provides a main verb (*have discovered*).

2. C: Passive required

This is one of the rare instances when a passive construction is absolutely required in order for a sentence to make sense. Desserts ***are known*** for their sweetness.

3. D: Gerund required

The conjunction *and*, while not grammatically incorrect, does not provide the correct logical relationship. The second clause indicates an explanation for *why* leisure gardens became popular refuges – the phrase *by providing* indicates this relationship.

4. E: Parallel structure

Both of the non-underlined items in the list begin with a gerund (*perching, climbing*), so the third item must also begin with a gerund (*foraging*).

5. D: Dangling modifier

Whose original auditorium was destroyed in 1951? The Abbey Theatre. So *the Abbey Theatre*, the subject, must appear immediately after the comma. Only D and E contain that construction, and D contains a pronoun-antecedent mismatch (*theatre…their*) and an unnecessary tense switch.

6. A: Word pair; parallel structure

The original version of the sentence correctly uses the word pair *not only…but also* and is otherwise the clearest, most concise choice.

7. B: Where vs. when

Where is for times, *when* is for places. An era refers to time, so *when* should be used. *In which* is also acceptable, but D contains an unnecessary gerund (*including*) and E incorrectly uses the singular pronoun *its* to refer to the plural noun *works*.

8. D: Preposition

The idiomatic phrase is *commitment to* not commitment *for*, so the preposition *for* after the word *passion* cannot also apply to *commitment*. Instead, *to* must be inserted after *commitment*.

9. E: Parallel structure

Only E creates a parallel construction by placing a noun on either side of the conjunction (*movement, intensity*) while including a correctly phrased comparison: *better…than*.

10. C: Dangling modifier

The dangling modification in this sentence can be very difficult to spot because a non-essential clause modifying *sport* has been placed between the introductory clause (*Often thought of as a modern sport*) and the subject (*surfing*). If the non-essential clause is removed, the problem becomes clearer: *Often thought of as a modern sport, but surfing was an important sport… Surfing*, the subject, must follow the comma in order for the sentence to make sense.

11. D: Dangling modifier

Who was renowned by his contemporaries for his virtuosic skill as a performer? Liszt. So *Liszt*, the subject, must immediately follow the comma. Both D and E contain this construction; however, D fails to provide a passive construction (*was said*) where one is necessary.

12. B: Faulty comparison

The original version of the sentence compares academic credentials (things) to Melanie Klein (a person). In order for the sentence to be correct, *credentials* must be compared to *credentials* – B and E do so, replacing the word *credentials* with the pronoun *those*. E creates a comma splice however, leaving B. Although the construction *those had by her male colleagues* may sound strange, it is in fact grammatically acceptable.

13. A: No error; parallel structure

The original version of the sentence contains the basic structure *noun + of + noun* on either side of the conjunction *and* (*rate of unemployment = inclination of shoppers*).

14. B: Idiom; pronoun-antecedent

Although the phrase *much like a human being…* may sound odd, it is correctly used to modify the previous clause and is the most concise option available. B rather than A is correct because the noun *a human being* is singular and must be referred to with a singular pronoun (*his or her*).

Test 8

Section 1

1. Ⓐ Ⓑ Ⓒ Ⓓ Ⓔ
2. Ⓐ Ⓑ Ⓒ Ⓓ Ⓔ
3. Ⓐ Ⓑ Ⓒ Ⓓ Ⓔ
4. Ⓐ Ⓑ Ⓒ Ⓓ Ⓔ
5. Ⓐ Ⓑ Ⓒ Ⓓ Ⓔ
6. Ⓐ Ⓑ Ⓒ Ⓓ Ⓔ
7. Ⓐ Ⓑ Ⓒ Ⓓ Ⓔ
8. Ⓐ Ⓑ Ⓒ Ⓓ Ⓔ
9. Ⓐ Ⓑ Ⓒ Ⓓ Ⓔ
10. Ⓐ Ⓑ Ⓒ Ⓓ Ⓔ
11. Ⓐ Ⓑ Ⓒ Ⓓ Ⓔ
12. Ⓐ Ⓑ Ⓒ Ⓓ Ⓔ
13. Ⓐ Ⓑ Ⓒ Ⓓ Ⓔ
14. Ⓐ Ⓑ Ⓒ Ⓓ Ⓔ
15. Ⓐ Ⓑ Ⓒ Ⓓ Ⓔ
16. Ⓐ Ⓑ Ⓒ Ⓓ Ⓔ
17. Ⓐ Ⓑ Ⓒ Ⓓ Ⓔ
18. Ⓐ Ⓑ Ⓒ Ⓓ Ⓔ
19. Ⓐ Ⓑ Ⓒ Ⓓ Ⓔ
20. Ⓐ Ⓑ Ⓒ Ⓓ Ⓔ
21. Ⓐ Ⓑ Ⓒ Ⓓ Ⓔ
22. Ⓐ Ⓑ Ⓒ Ⓓ Ⓔ
23. Ⓐ Ⓑ Ⓒ Ⓓ Ⓔ
24. Ⓐ Ⓑ Ⓒ Ⓓ Ⓔ
25. Ⓐ Ⓑ Ⓒ Ⓓ Ⓔ
26. Ⓐ Ⓑ Ⓒ Ⓓ Ⓔ
27. Ⓐ Ⓑ Ⓒ Ⓓ Ⓔ
28. Ⓐ Ⓑ Ⓒ Ⓓ Ⓔ
29. Ⓐ Ⓑ Ⓒ Ⓓ Ⓔ
30. Ⓐ Ⓑ Ⓒ Ⓓ Ⓔ
31. Ⓐ Ⓑ Ⓒ Ⓓ Ⓔ
32. Ⓐ Ⓑ Ⓒ Ⓓ Ⓔ
33. Ⓐ Ⓑ Ⓒ Ⓓ Ⓔ
34. Ⓐ Ⓑ Ⓒ Ⓓ Ⓔ
35. Ⓐ Ⓑ Ⓒ Ⓓ Ⓔ

Section 2

1. Ⓐ Ⓑ Ⓒ Ⓓ Ⓔ
2. Ⓐ Ⓑ Ⓒ Ⓓ Ⓔ
3. Ⓐ Ⓑ Ⓒ Ⓓ Ⓔ
4. Ⓐ Ⓑ Ⓒ Ⓓ Ⓔ
5. Ⓐ Ⓑ Ⓒ Ⓓ Ⓔ
6. Ⓐ Ⓑ Ⓒ Ⓓ Ⓔ
7. Ⓐ Ⓑ Ⓒ Ⓓ Ⓔ
8. Ⓐ Ⓑ Ⓒ Ⓓ Ⓔ
9. Ⓐ Ⓑ Ⓒ Ⓓ Ⓔ
10. Ⓐ Ⓑ Ⓒ Ⓓ Ⓔ
11. Ⓐ Ⓑ Ⓒ Ⓓ Ⓔ
12. Ⓐ Ⓑ Ⓒ Ⓓ Ⓔ
13. Ⓐ Ⓑ Ⓒ Ⓓ Ⓔ
14. Ⓐ Ⓑ Ⓒ Ⓓ Ⓔ

SECTION 1

Time – 25 Minutes
35 Questions

Directions: For each question in this section, select the best answer from among the choices given and fill in the corresponding circle on the answer sheet.

The following sentences test correctness and effectiveness of expression. Part of each sentence or the entire sentence is underlined; beneath each sentence are five ways of phrasing the underlined material. Choice A repeats the original phrasing; the other four choices are different. If you think the original phrasing produces a better sentence than any of the alternatives, select choice A; if not, select one of the other choices.

In making your selection, follow the requirements of standard written English; that is, pay attention to grammar, choice of words, sentence construction, and punctuation. Your selection should result in the most effective sentence—clear and precise, without awkwardness or ambiguity.

EXAMPLE:

○●○○○

Anna Robertson Moses completed her first painting and she was seventy-six years old then.

(A) and she was seventy-six years old then
(B) when she was seventy-six years old
(C) at age seventy-six years old
(D) upon arriving at the age of seventy-six
(E) at the time when she was seventy-six years old

1. The fig tree plays an important role in rainforest ecosystems, and their fruit provides food for animals as well as cloth for local inhabitants.

    (A) ecosystems, and their fruit provides
    (B) ecosystems, their fruit provides
    (C) ecosystems, and its fruit providing
    (D) ecosystems, and their fruit providing
    (E) ecosystems because its fruit provides

2. James Charles Rodgers was a country singer in the early twentieth century that was famous for rhythmic yodeling.

    (A) James Charles Rodgers was a country singer in the early twentieth century that
    (B) James Charles Rodgers, a country singer in the early twentieth century,
    (C) James Charles Rogers was a country singer in the early twentieth century, he
    (D) James Charles Rogers being a country singer in the early twentieth century,
    (E) James Charles Rogers, who had been a country singer in the early twentieth century, and

3. A lifelong naturalist, sweeping hypotheses about butterfly migration patterns were developed by Vladimir Nabokov that DNA analysis has now shown to be accurate.

    (A) sweeping hypotheses about butterfly migration patterns were developed by Vladimir Nabokov
    (B) sweeping hypotheses about butterfly migration patterns being developed by Vladimir Nabokov
    (C) Vladimir Nabokov developed sweeping hypotheses about butterfly migration patterns
    (D) the development of sweeping hypotheses about butterfly migration patterns by Vladimir Nabokov
    (E) butterfly migration patterns had sweeping hypotheses developed about them by Vladimir Nabokov

4. Orville and Wilbur Wright gained the skills <u>to become a successful airplane mechanic by working</u> for years in a shop with printing presses, motors, and many other kinds of machinery.

   (A) to become a successful airplane mechanic by working
   (B) to become successful airplane mechanics by working
   (C) to become a successful airplane mechanic in that they worked
   (D) for becoming successful airplanes mechanics, and they worked
   (E) for becoming a successful airplane mechanic because of their working

5. Over the past forty years, dolphin-protection advocates have run numerous educational campaigns, <u>distributing thousands of informational pamphlets, and protested</u> harmful fishing practices.

   (A) distributing thousands of informational pamphlets, and protested
   (B) distributing thousands of informational pamphlets, and to protest
   (C) distributed thousands of informational pamphlets, and protesting
   (D) distributed thousands of informational pamphlets, and would protest
   (E) distributing thousands of informational pamphlets and protesting

6. Although Shakespeare's portrayal of Richard III is often criticized as unnecessarily harsh, <u>but it was also politically wise</u>; Shakespeare's patrons, the Tudors, had seized the throne from Richard.

   (A) but it was also politically wise
   (B) it was also politically wise
   (C) and it was also politically wise
   (D) however it was politically wise also
   (E) whereas it was also politically wise

7. Tony Kushner's plays and screenplays often experiment with narrative form, <u>many of them depart</u> from conventional storytelling by using shorter episodes.

   (A) many of them depart
   (B) which many of them depart
   (C) with many of them departing
   (D) and many of them departing
   (E) however many of them depart

8. Because Atsuko often had trouble falling asleep at night, the doctor recommended <u>that she spend</u> half an hour relaxing and listening to music before going to bed.

   (A) that she spend
   (B) her spending
   (C) her to spend
   (D) she spends
   (E) she would spend

9. The poor taste and lack of sugar in the modern garden tomato <u>has resulted from</u> the breeding of plants that become uniformly red when they ripen.

   (A) has resulted from
   (B) have resulted from
   (C) has resulted through
   (D) having resulted through
   (E) is a result of

10. Recent studies have shown that by consuming a small amount of dark chocolate daily, <u>overall health can be improved</u>.

    (A) overall health can be improved
    (B) one can improve their overall health
    (C) people can improve his or her overall health
    (D) one's overall health can be improved
    (E) you can improve your overall health

11. <u>She left her native Dominican Republic for the United States in 1939,</u> Rhina Espaillat wrote many works in both English and Spanish and became the most prominent translator of Robert Frost's poetry.

    (A) She left her native Dominican Republic for the United States in 1939,
    (B) She had left her native Dominican Republic for the United States in 1939,
    (C) Having left her native Dominican Republic for the United States in 1939,
    (D) Because she left her native Dominican Republic for the United States in 1939,
    (E) She left her native Dominican Republic for the United States in 1939, and

The following sentences test your ability to recognize grammar and usage errors. Each sentence contains either a single error or none at all. No sentence contains more than one error. The error, if there is one, is underlined and lettered. If the sentence contains an error, select the one underlined part that must be changed in order to make the sentence correct. If the sentence is correct, select choice E. In choosing answers, follow the requirements of standard written English.

EXAMPLE:

Science fiction writer H.G. Wells, <u>the author of</u>
                                      A
more than 100 books, accurately <u>predicted</u> the
                                     B
the <u>invention</u> of television, the rise of the Internet,
      C
and <u>creating</u> the hydrogen bomb. <u>No error</u>
      D   E

○○○●○

12. Benjamin Banneker's first almanac, <u>published</u> in
                                          A
    1791, <u>included</u> times for the rising and setting of the
           B
    sun, <u>forecasts for</u> the weather, and dates for <u>yearly</u>
          C   D
    feasts. <u>No error</u>
            E

13. <u>While</u> a student, Cassini was as <u>interested in</u> the study
    A   B
    of astrology <u>than</u> he was in the study of mathematics
                  C
    <u>and</u> astronomy. <u>No error</u>
    D   E

14. <u>Although</u> more than 6,000 languages <u>are now spoke</u>
    A   B
    around the world, nearly half of <u>them</u> may be extinct
                                       C
    by the <u>end of</u> the twenty-first century. <u>No error</u>
            D   E

15. Faced with <u>increasing</u> stiff competition from virtual
                A
    booksellers, owners of local bookstores <u>must often</u>
                                              B
    find <u>novel</u> ways to appeal <u>to</u> longtime customers.
          C   D
    <u>No error</u>
    E

16. Margaret Cho is a comedian <u>which</u> often uses her
                                 A
    stand-up routines <u>as a means</u> of <u>critiquing</u>
                       B   C
    controversial social <u>and</u> political problems. <u>No error</u>
                          D   E

17. In 1793, the Louvre, <u>now</u> the most visited art museum
                          A
    in the world, <u>has opened</u> with an exhibition <u>of</u> more
                   B   C
    <u>than</u> five hundred paintings. <u>No error</u>
    D   E

18. <u>Invented</u> in the eighteenth century, the oboe d'amore
    A
    fell into <u>relative</u> obscurity <u>for nearly</u> a hundred years
               B   C
    before <u>being</u> re-discovered by composers such as
            D
    Ravel and Strauss. <u>No error</u>
                        E

19. <u>Asked</u> to choose between the gorilla and the
    A
    chimpanzee, experienced primate researchers
    <u>generally</u> do not hesitate <u>to declare</u> the chimpanzee
     B   C
    the <u>smartest</u> animal. <u>No error</u>
         D   E

20. The lands of the ancient Near East did not <u>develop as</u>
                                                A
    a single entity because they were <u>divided into</u>
                                        B
    individual states, each with <u>their</u> own distinct identity
                                   C
    <u>and</u> culture. <u>No error</u>
    D   E

288

21. Reading foreign books and watching international
    A
    television are recommended as a way for people to
                                  B
    improve their knowledge of world affairs, but neither
           C
    is a substitute for spending time in a different country.
    D
    No error
    E

22. Since Benjamin's Franklin's invention of the lightning
                                A
    rod in the mid-eighteenth century, the weather resisted
                                                   B
    numerous efforts at manipulation by meteorologists,
                      C
    physicists, and amateur scientists alike. No error
                                       D   E

    Althof

23. When they do not consume prey as fast as their
    A   B
    competitors do, jellyfish can efficiently transform
                                   C
    the energy that they obtain from food into body
                     D
    growth. No error
            E

24. One of the most widely recognized jazz musicians
              A
    of the 1950s were Miles Davis, who was recognized
                B
    as an outspoken social critic as well as an arbiter of
    C   D
    style. No error
          E

25. Ergonomic experts predict that as workers
                                 A
    communicate on more electronic devices in a wider
                B
    variety of situations, he or she will face a greater
                           C   D
    risk of injury. No error
                   E

26. Self-portraits have been made by artists since the
                    A
    earliest times, but not until the Renaissance
    B
    did painters begin to depict themselves frequently
    C
    in their work. No error
            D   E

27. Although the novels of Jhumpa Lahiri are fictional
    A   B
    creations, they frequently draw upon their author's
                               C
    own experiences as well as her parents, friends, and
                               D
    acquaintances within the Bengali-American
    community. No error
              E

28. Louise Glück's seemingly straightforward language
                   A
    and unadorned style gives her poems an air of
    B   C
    accessibility that masks the intensity of their content.
                     D
    No error
    E

29. Whether bees are truly capable of experiencing
    A   B
    emotions such as agitation and annoyance is a subject
                                             C
    of much speculation among naturalists. No error
    D   E

Directions: The following passage is an early draft of an essay. Some parts of the passage need to be rewritten.

Read the passage and select the best answer for the questions that follow. Some questions are about particular sentences or parts of sentences and ask you to improve sentence structure or word choice. Other questions ask you to consider organization and development. In choosing you answer, follow the requirements of standard written English.

Questions 30-35 are based on the following passage.

(1) In July of 1848, a group of men and women gathered in Seneca Fall, New York for the first women's rights convention held in the United States. (2) Some of the most important figures of the day attended, including Elizabeth Cady Stanton, Lucretia Mott, and Frederick Douglass. (3) Douglass had been born a slave in Maryland in 1818 but won his freedom at the age of twenty. (4) Many controversial issues were discussed. (5) For example, rights involving property, employment, children, and divorce. (6) During the convention, the problem of women's suffrage began to dominate.

(7) Earlier in the nineteenth century, the last of the property restrictions that prevented white males from voting had been abolished, but the question of voting rights for other groups – particularly women and former slaves – was still very controversial. (8) Even at the convention, there was bitter disagreement. (9) Elizabeth Cady Stanton and a group of women from the town of Seneca Falls that had helped organize the convention had prepared a document called The Declaration of Sentiments. (10) It was based on the Declaration of Independence and included demands for many basic rights, including the right to vote. (11) Lucretia Mott believed that it was far too radical and only relented after Frederick Douglass persuaded her.

(12) Today, some historians view the Seneca Falls Convention as part of a movement for women's rights which was popular in the mid-nineteenth century; others see it as the true beginning of the women's suffrage movement.

30. What is the best way to improve the focus of the first paragraph?

(A) Add a sentence after sentence 2 providing biographical information about Elizabeth Cady Stanton.
(B) Add a sentence after sentence 6 explaining the issues that had been discussed earlier at the convention.
(C) Delete sentence 2
(D) Delete sentence 3
(E) Delete sentence 6

31. What is the best way to revise and combine the underlined portion of sentences 4 and 5 (reproduced below)?

Many controversial issues <u>were discussed. For example, rights involving</u> property, employment, children, and divorce.

(A) were discussed, some of these being
(B) were discussed, they included
(C) were discussed, including
(D) were discussed, some examples were
(E) were discussed; and they included

32. In context, which is the best revision of the underlined portion of sentence 6 (reproduced below)?

<u>*During the convention,*</u> *the problem of women's suffrage began to dominate.*

(A) Over the course of convention, however,
(B) Likewise, during the convention,
(C) Indeed, throughout the convention,
(D) For instance, while the convention was happening,
(E) During the convention in particular,

33. In context, which of the following is the best version of sentence 9 (reproduced below)?

Elizabeth Cady Stanton and a group of women from the town of Seneca Falls that had helped organize the convention had prepared a document called The Declaration of Sentiments.

(A) Elizabeth Cady Stanton and a group of women from the town of Seneca Falls helping organize the convention and preparing a document called *The Declaration of Sentiments.*

(B) Elizabeth Cady Stanton and a group of women from the town of Seneca Falls who helped organize the convention and prepare a document called *The Declaration of Sentiments.*

(C) Elizabeth Cady Stanton, along with a group of women from the town of Seneca Falls, helped organize the convention and prepare a document called *The Declaration of Sentiments.*

(D) Elizabeth Cady Stanton and a group of women from the town of Seneca Falls, which helped organize the convention and prepare a document called *The Declaration of Sentiments.*

(E) Elizabeth Cady Stanton and a group of women from the town of Seneca Falls helped organize the convention and have prepared a document called *The Declaration of Sentiments.*

34. In context, which of the following is best to insert between sentence 10 and sentence 11?

(A) Although only 32 of the men signed it, 68 of the women did.

(B) A local newspaper article called the document shocking and unnatural.

(C) It was read in front of the Convention by E.C. Stanton.

(D) Not all of the women were eager to sign it, though.

(E) After it was read, a number of changes and suggestions were made.

35. Which of the following additions would most improve the last paragraph?

(A) Names of specific historians who have argued about the effects of the Seneca Falls Convention on the women's movement.

(B) A description of the relationship between Lucretia Mott and Frederick Douglass after the Seneca Fall Convention.

(C) An explanation of the historical significance of terms used in *The Declaration of Sentiments.*

(D) A comparison between the Seneca Falls Convention and similar gatherings in other countries.

(E) Information about the role that *The Declaration of Sentiments* played in helping women obtain the vote.

SECTION 2
Time – 10 Minutes
14 Questions

Directions: For each question in this section, select the best answer from among the choices given and fill in the corresponding circle on the answer sheet.

The following sentences test correctness and effectiveness of expression. Part of each sentence or the entire sentence is underlined; beneath each sentence are five ways of phrasing the underlined material. Choice A repeats the original phrasing; the other four choices are different. If you think the original phrasing produces a better sentence than any of the alternatives, select choice A; if not, select one of the other choices.

In making your selection, follow the requirements of standard written English; that is, pay attention to grammar, choice of words, sentence construction, and punctuation. Your selection should result in the most effective sentence—clear and precise, without awkwardness or ambiguity.

EXAMPLE:

○●○○○

Anna Robertson Moses completed her first painting <u>and she was seventy-six years old then</u>.

(A) and she was seventy-six years old then
(B) when she was seventy-six years old
(C) at age seventy-six years old
(D) upon arriving at the age of seventy-six
(E) at the time when she was seventy-six years old

---

1. Molecular biologist Anita <u>Roberts, who is known</u> for her pioneering observations of a protein that helps heal superficial wounds as well as bone fractures.

(A) Roberts, who is known
(B) Roberts being known
(C) Roberts is known
(D) Roberts, who has been known
(E) Roberts, and she is known

2. Diego Rivera's murals, <u>which were painted</u> only as frescoes after 1922, depict various aspects of Mexican society after the Revolution of 1910.

(A) which were painted
(B) they were painted
(C) when they were painted
(D) these being painted
(E) while having been painted

3. If you spend time in a room with people who are yawning, <u>it is almost certain as to whether you will begin to yawn as well</u>.

(A) it is almost certain as to whether you will begin to yawn as well
(B) your beginning to yawn is almost certain as well
(C) whether or not you will begin to yawn is almost certain as well
(D) yawning by you is almost certain to occur as well
(E) you will almost certainly begin to yawn as well

4. A group of stone slabs inscribed with commemorative <u>texts constituting one of the most comprehensive sources</u> of information about ancient Egypt.

(A) texts constituting one of the most comprehensive sources
(B) texts, which constitute one of the most comprehensive sources
(C) texts and constitutes one of the most comprehensive sources
(D) texts constitutes one of the most comprehensive sources
(E) texts, they constitute one of the most comprehensive sources

5. Although the selection of winning lottery numbers is typically considered to occur randomly, in reality it is governed by complex algorithms that may contain hidden patterns.

   (A) Although the selection of winning lottery numbers is typically considered to occur randomly,
   (B) The selection of winning lottery numbers, typically considered to occur randomly, but
   (C) The selection of winning lottery numbers, which is typically considered to be randomly occurring,
   (D) The selection of winning lottery numbers is typically considered to occur randomly,
   (E) The selection of winning lottery number typically being considered to occur randomly,

6. In the 1970s, feminist art critic Linda Nochlin became known for her pioneering investigation of the relationship between gender and how art is created.

   (A) and how art is created
   (B) or how they create art
   (C) and art being created
   (D) with creating art
   (E) and the creation of art

7. If Sarah would have arrived at the theater half an hour earlier, we would not have missed the beginning of the movie while we waited for her to appear.

   (A) If Sarah would have arrived
   (B) Had Sarah arrived
   (C) If Sarah would arrive
   (D) Whether Sarah had arrived
   (E) If Sarah's arrival

8. The word "volcano" comes from Vulcano, an Italian island the derivation of whose name from Vulcan, the god of fire in Roman mythology.

   (A) an Italian island the derivation of whose name from Vulcan
   (B) an Italian island whose name they derived from Vulcan
   (C) an Italian island, its name was derived from Vulcan
   (D) an Italian island whose name was derived from Vulcan
   (E) an Italian island and whose name was the derivation of Vulcan

9. While science can offer a biological explanation for the development of painting and storytelling, it can never provide the intense emotional experience those art forms provide.

   (A) While science can offer a biological explanation for the development of painting and storytelling,
   (B) Despite science being able to offer a biological explanation for why painting and storytelling developed,
   (C) Because science can offer a biological explanation for the development of painting and storytelling,
   (D) With science offering a biological explanation for the development of painting and storytelling
   (E) Science can offer an biological explanation for painting and storytelling's development; therefore,

10. Most medications should not be stored at high temperatures, since this can cause their active ingredients to lose their potency.

    (A) temperatures, since this can cause their active ingredients to lose their potency
    (B) temperature, this often causes their active ingredients to lose their potency
    (C) temperature, because these can cause their active ingredients to lose their potency
    (D) temperature, since the heat can cause a loss of potency by the active ingredients
    (E) temperatures; as a result of the heat, the ingredients may lose their potency

11. The difficulty of observing ambrosia beetles in their natural surroundings <u>have been offset by the invention of glass tubes, whereby their environment can be reproduced.</u>

    (A) have been offset by the invention of glass tubes, whereby their environment can be reproduced
    (B) have been offset by the invention of glass tubes, which can reproduce their environment
    (C) has been offset by the invention of glass tubes, these can reproduce the beetles' environment
    (D) has been offset by the invention of glass tubes that can reproduce the beetles' environment
    (E) have been offset by the invention of glass tubes, this reproducing the beetles' environment

12. On July 4th 1880, Frederic Auguste Bartholdi, the designer of the Statue of Liberty, presented his creation to the American minister in <u>Paris, the occasion was marked with a great banquet</u>.

    (A) Paris, the occasion was marked with a great banquet
    (B) Paris; the occasion was marked with a great banquet
    (C) Paris, and the occasion had been marked with a great banquet
    (D) Paris, which was marked with a great banquet
    (E) Paris, but they marked the occasion with a great banquet

13. In ancient Greece, the importation of edible <u>goods were crucial to</u> the economy because of the relative poverty of Greek soil.

    (A) goods were crucial to
    (B) goods were crucial for
    (C) goods was crucial as to
    (D) goods was crucial to
    (E) goods was crucial in

14. Drawn in black and white, <u>Marjane Satrapi's graphic novel *Persepolis*, a combination of comic-strip form and astute political commentary, depicts its author's</u> childhood and adolescence in Tehran and Vienna.

    (A) Marjane Satrapi's graphic novel *Persepolis*, a combination of comic-strip form and astute political commentary, depicts its author's
    (B) Marjane Satrapi combined comic-strip form with astute political commentary in her graphic novel *Persepolis*, depicting her
    (C) Marjane Satrapi combined comic-strip form and astute political commentary in her graphic novel *Persepolis*, which depicts her
    (D) Marjane Satrapi's graphic novel *Persepolis* combines comic-strip form with astute political commentary, it depicts her
    (E) comic-strip form and astute political commentary were combined by Marjane Satrapi in her graphic novel *Persepolis*, which depicts her

Answers: Test 8, Section 1

1. E: Pronoun-antecedent; conjunction

In A, B, and D, the plural pronoun *they* is incorrectly used to refer to the singular noun *tree*. C contains a gerund (*providing*) rather than a main verb in the second clause, creating a fragment; and E provides both a conjugated verb (*provides*) and a conjunction (*because*) that correctly indicates an explanation.

2. B: Misplaced modifier; non-essential clause

The original version of the sentence contains a misplaced modifier – it sounds as if the *twentieth century* rather than James Charles Rodgers was known for rhythmic yodeling. B corrects this error by creating non-essential clause that makes clear that Rodgers was the yodeler. B contains a comma splice; C contains a gerund (*being*) instead of a main verb; and D fails to put a verb immediately after the non-essential clause.

3. C: Dangling modifier

Who was a lifelong naturalist? Vladimir Nabokov. So *Vladimir Nabokov*, the subject, must come immediately after the comma. Only C contains this construction.

4: B: Noun agreement

Since Orville and Wilbur Wright were two people, they were *mechanics* rather than *a mechanic*. That eliminates A, C, and E. D is incorrect because the phrase *gained the skills* should be followed by the infinitive *to become* rather than the gerund *becoming*, and because the conjunction *and* does not provide the correct logical relationship.

5: E: Parallel structure; participle required

Although this appears to be a straightforward "list" parallel structure question, the correct phrase *distributing thousands of information pamphlets and protesting harmful fishing practices...* modifies the first clause and does not create a list at all. Still the shortcut is to recognize that that E is the only answer that contains two parallel items (*distributing...protesting*). 6. B: Double conjunction

6. B: Double conjunction

For any two clauses, only one conjunction is necessary: either *though* or *but*. It is both redundant and grammatically incorrect to use both.

7. C: Gerund required

The original version of the sentence contains a comma splice; B creates a nonsensical construction when plugged back into the sentence; D contains a fragment rather than an independent clause after *comma + FANBOYS* conjunction (*and*); and E contains an incorrect logical relationship (there is no contrast between the clauses, as *however* would indicate) and incorrectly places a comma rather than a semicolon before *however*. C correctly uses the gerund phrase *with some of them departing* to modify the first clause.

8. A: No error; subjunctive

The subjunctive is used with commands, suggestions, and recommendations, and is characterized by the omission of the *–s* at the end of third person singular verb. Here, the phrase, *the doctor recommended* indicates that the verb should be *spend* rather than *spends*. When the subjunctive is tested, it will often be used correctly in the original version of the sentence, in which case you will simply be responsible for recognizing that it is *not* incorrect.

9. B: Subject-verb agreement (compound subject)

The sentence contains a compound subject (*the poor taste* **and** *lack of sugar*), which is plural and requires a plural verb. A, C, and E can be eliminated because *has* and *is* are singular. Choice D contains the gerund *having*, which creates a fragment, as well as the incorrect preposition *through* and can be eliminated as well. B correctly provides a plural verb (*have*) as well as the correct preposition (*from*).

10. E: Dangling modifier; pronoun-antecedent

Who could consume a small amount of dark chocolate daily? Not *overall health*, as the original version of the sentence implies. The answer choices tell us that the subject, which must follow the comma, could be *one*, *you*, or *they* – E is correct because *you* remains consistent throughout the sentence.

11. C: Comma splice; participle required; conjunction

Both the original version of the sentence and B contain two independent clauses separated by a comma; D and E use conjunctions that create illogical relationships between the clauses. C creates a participial phrase (*Having left*) that modifies the first clause clearly and concisely.

12. E: No error; parallel structure; verb tense

The sentence contains a list that is already parallel in structure. In addition, it includes a date (1791), suggesting a tense error; however, the underlined verb (*published*) is correctly given in the simple past.

13. C: Word pair

As must be paired with *as*.

14. B: Verb form

The past participle (*spoken*) rather than the simple past (*spoke*) form of the verb *speak* should be used after any form of *to be* when forming the passive voice.

15. A: Adjective vs. adverb

An adverb (*increasingly*) rather than an adjective (*increasing*) must be used to modify the adjective *stiff*.

16. A: Who vs. which

Since Margaret Cho is a person, she should be referred to by the relative pronoun *who* rather than *which*.

17. B: Verb tense

The date *1793* indicates that the sentence is testing verb tense. In this case, a finished action in the past is being described (the Louvre only opened once), and so the simple past (*opened*) rather than the present perfect (*has opened*) should be used.

18. E: No error

Among the underlined words, B, C, and D point to commonly tested categories (B to adjective vs. adverb; C to adjective vs. adverb and preposition; and D to gerund vs. infinitive). Since both *relatively* and *nearly* should be used rather than *relative* and *near*, and since there is nothing wrong with the preposition *for*, both B and C are correct. Likewise, *being* (gerund) should not be replaced with *to be* (infinitive).

19. D: More vs. most

Since only two things are being compared (gorillas and chimpanzees), *more* rather than *most* should be used.

20. C: Pronoun-antecedent

Since *each* is singular, it should be referred to by a plural pronoun (*its* rather than *their*).

21. B: Noun agreement

Since reading foreign books and watching international television are two things, they are *ways* rather than a single *way* for people to improve their knowledge of world affairs.

22. B: Verb tense

The word *since* indicates that the present perfect (*has resisted*) rather than the simple past (*resisted*) should be used because an action beginning in the past and continuing into the present is being described.

23. A: Conjunction

The conjunction *when* is used to express relationships of time; however, the relationship indicated by the sentence is one of contrast, and so a conjunction such as *although* is required here.

24. B: Subject-verb agreement

One, the subject, is singular and thus requires a singular verb (*was* rather than *were*). The plural noun *1950s* belongs to the prepositional phrase *of the most widely recognized musicians of the 1950s* and does not affect the verb.

25. C: Pronoun-antecedent

Since *workers* is plural, it requires a plural pronoun (*they* rather than *he or she*).

26. E: No error

C is the answer that most test-takers are likely to pick, but although the syntax of the sentence may seem odd, the construction *not until...did* is perfectly acceptable. In A, the present perfect (*have made*) is correct because artists are still making self-portraits; in B, there is no reason that *earlier* rather than *earliest* should be used; and in D, *work* is understood to refer to a body of work – although the plural *works* could be used, the singular is correct as well.

27. D: Faulty comparison

The sentence compares *experiences* (things) to *parents, friends, and acquaintances* (people). In order for the sentence to be correct, experiences must be compared to experiences: *…they frequently draw upon their author's own* **experiences** *as well as* **the experiences of/those of** *her parents, friends, and acquaintances.*

28. C: Subject-verb agreement

The sentence contains a compound subject (*straightforward language* **and** *unadorned style*), which is plural and thus requires a plural verb (*give* rather than *gives*).

29. E: No error

A, C, and D could all be considered trick answers: A because many test-takers may not realize that it is acceptable to use *whether* as a subject; C because *is* could be mistakenly thought to be the verb of *agitation and annoyance* (plural) rather than *whether* (singular); and D because the phrase *of much* may strike some test-takers as odd. All, however, all correct.

30. D: Paragraph organization

The primary focus of the first paragraph is on explaining what the Seneca Falls Convention was; Frederick Douglass' biographical information is irrelevant to this topic.

31. C: Participle required; comma splice

C is the clearest, most concise option. A is wordy and contains an unnecessary gerund (*being*); B and D contain comma splices; and E incorrectly places a semicolon rather than a comma before the coordinating conjunction *and*.

32. A: Transition

The function of sentence 6 is to move the passage in a new direction: we shift from an overview of the topics discussed at the convention to a description of the most important topic (women's suffrage). Since there is a contrast with the previous sentence, *however* is the most appropriate transition word.

33. C: Misplaced modifier

The original version of the sentence implies that the town of Seneca Falls was responsible for organizing the convention and preparing *The Declaration of Sentiments*. C corrects this error by creating a non-essential clause that

makes clear that these activities were clearly the work of Elizabeth Cady Stanton and the group of women. B and D both contain fragments, and E contains an unnecessary tense switch.

34. D: Paragraph organization

Sentence 10 describes *The Declaration of Sentiments*, and sentence 11 states that Lucretia Mott did not initially want to sign it. D most effectively bridges these two thoughts by introducing the fact that some women were initially resistant to the Declaration.

35. E: Paragraph organization

The last paragraph states that historians now debate the importance of the role that the Convention played in the overall suffrage movement, but it does not include any factual information about the Convention's legacy that would provide context for sentence 12.

Test 8, Section 2

1. C: Fragment

The original version is a fragment because it lacks a main verb: *is* belongs to the clause beginning with *who* rather than to the subject, *Anita Roberts*. C resolves this issue by making *is* correspond to the subject.

2. A: No error; non-essential clause

The original version of the sentence contains a properly used non-essential clause, a construction that virtually always indicates a correct answer.

3. E: Parallel structure

The second clause should begin with *you*, the subject, in order to remain parallel to the first clause. That eliminates every option except E, which is also the clearest, most concise, and idiomatically correct (*it is almost certain* should be followed by *that*, not *as to*).

4. D: Gerund; sentence vs. fragment

The original version is a fragment because it includes only a gerund (*constituting*) rather than a conjugated verb (*constitutes*). D corrects this error by providing the conjugated verb.

5. A: No error

The original version of the sentence correctly uses a comma to separate a dependent clause from an independent clause. B, C, and E create nonsensical fragments when plugged back into the sentence, and D creates a comma splice.

6. E: Parallel structure; word pair

Between must go with *and*, eliminating B and D. Among the remaining choices, E is correct because the constructions on both sides of the conjunction *and* must match (*gender* and *creation* are both nouns).

7. B: Verb tense

A clause that begins with *if* should never include the construction *would have* + *past participle* (*would have arrived*); the correct construction is *had* + *noun* + *past participle* (*Had Sarah arrived*). The other possible correction, not listed here, would be *if* + *noun* + *had* + *past participle* (*If Sarah had arrived*).

8. D: Awkward construction

The original version is wordy, awkward, and un-grammatical; D is the clearest, most concise option.

9. A: No error; conjunction

The two clauses present contrasting ideas and thus require a conjunction that expresses that contrast. Only *while* in the original version and *despite* in B express this relationship, and B is wordy and contains the gerund *being*.

10. E: Antecedent-pronoun; comma

Neither *because* nor *since* should be preceded by a comma, eliminating A, C, and D; B contains a comma splice. The pronoun *this* also has no antecedent in A and B. E correctly uses a semicolon to separate two independent clauses.

11. D: subject-verb agreement

The subject of the sentence, *difficulty*, is singular and thus requires a singular verb (*has*), eliminating A, B, and E. C contains a comma splice, leaving D.

12. B: Comma splice; semicolon; antecedent-pronoun

The original version of the sentence uses a comma to separate two complete sentences. In B, the pronoun *which* is missing an antecedent (it refers to the *presentation* of the Statue of Liberty, but that noun does not appear in the sentence); C contains an unnecessary and illogical tense switch (the banquet did not occur before Bartholdi presented his creation, as the past perfect *had been marked* would imply); and in E, *but* is incorrect because the clauses do not provide contrasting information. D is correct because it uses a semicolon to separate the two original sentences.

13. D: Subject-verb agreement; preposition/idiom

Importation, the subject of the sentence, is singular and thus requires a singular verb (*was*), eliminating A and B. D is correct because *crucial* should be followed by the preposition *to*.

14. A: No error; dangling modifier

What was drawn in black and white? Marjane Satrapi's graphic novel *Persepolis*, not Marjane Satrapi. So *Marjane Satrapi's novel Persepolis*, the subject, must appear immediately after the comma. Only A and D place the subject after the comma, and D creates a comma splice by beginning a new independent clause with the pronoun *it*. The original version of the sentence also contains a correctly used non-essential clause (*a combination of comic-strip form and astute political commentary*), and sentences containing that construction are virtually always correct.

Raw Score	Scaled Score*
49	80
48	78-80
47	75-77
46	72-75
45	70-73
44	69-71
43	67-69
42	65-68
41	64-66
40	63-65
39	62-64
38	61-63
37	60-62
36	59-61
35	58-60
34	57-59
33	56-58
32	55-57
31	54-56
30	53-55
29	52-54
28	52-54
27	51-53
26	50-52
25	49-51
24	48-50
23	47-49
22	46-48

21	45-47
20	44-46
19	43-45
18	43-45
17	42-44
16	41-43
15	40-42
14	39-41
13	38-40
12	37-39
11	36-38
10	35-37
9	34-36
8	33-35
7	32-34
6	31-33
5	30-32
4	29-31
3	27-29
2	25-27
1	23-25
0	21-23
-1	20
-2	20
-3	20

*Because the tests here are based on multiple College Board exams and do not correspond to exact tests, I have provided a range of scores that can correspond to each raw score. For scaled scores with essay, see the Official Guide.

ABOUT THE AUTHOR

A graduate of Wellesley College, Erica Meltzer is based in New York City. She has tutored the SAT since 2004, helping numerous students raise both their Critical Reading and Writing scores by 200 points or more. From 2006 to 2010, she also wrote SAT, ACT, and GMAT Verbal exams for a variety of test-prep companies.

Made in the USA
San Bernardino, CA
04 December 2013